**Prescription
For Justice**

The Theory and Practice of
Sentencing Guidelines

Prescription For Justice

The Theory and Practice of Sentencing Guidelines

Jack M. Kress
Graduate School of Criminal Justice
State University of New York at Albany

Ballinger Publishing Company • Cambridge, Mass.
A Subsidiary of Harper & Row, Publishers, Inc.

International Standard Book Number: 0-88410-792-2

Library of Congress Catalog Card Number: 79-2141

Printed in the United States of America

Library of Congress Cataloging in Publication Data
Kress, Jack M.
Prescription for justice.

83-281

Bibliography: p.
Includes index.
1. Sentences (Criminal procedure)—United States.
KF9685.W54   345'.73'077   79-2141
ISBN 0-88410-792-2

Dedication

To Susan

Contents

List of Figures

List of Tables

Preface

When I began teaching law, I heard an apocryphal tale of an American Association of Law Schools meeting where the content of the law school curriculum was being debated. The issue was whether a course in criminal law should be taught as a prerequisite to one in criminal procedure or vice versa. One faction argued that substantive criminal law had to be taught first in order to provide that philosophical foundation so necessary to any explanation of the procedures used to implement the penal code. The other faction insisted, however, that the study of the criminal law was a sterile exercise without a prior comprehension of the practical realities of arrest, bail, prosecution, adjudication, and correctional practice. Finally, the giant of the field rose to speak, and all voices were stilled as the assembled educators awaited the now certain resolution of their difficulty: "I, for one," he intoned, "have never permitted any student to take either course until he or she has first had a thorough grounding in the other!"

You see my difficulty. Can one appreciate the theory of sentencing guidelines without a concrete understanding of its practice? On the other hand, can the practice be understood without a clear comprehension of the philosophy behind the guidelines approach? As a compromise, I offer in the first chapter a brief explanation of how sentencing guidelines systems operate, and then devote the remainder of the first part of this book to elaborating upon the theoretical base of sentencing guidelines systems; this suggests a conceptual and constitutional framework against which the need for such systems may be better understood. The second part of the book describes the action research approach, and the empirical effort, that led to the promulgation of sentencing guidelines in the counties of Denver (Colorado), Essex (Newark, New Jersey), Cook (Chicago, Illinois), Maricopa (Phoenix, Arizona), and Philadelphia (Pennsylvania). The appendixes are integral with Part Two, illustrative as they are of the varied products of sentencing guidelines research—there is one instructional booklet each for the calculation of guideline sentences, exemplifying the national project's general modeling approach (Denver) and the national project's generic approach (Maricopa); a separately funded and conducted effort (Philadelphia); and one that was both statewide and applicable to a less serious range of offenses than involved elsewhere (Washington). Finally, I offer the reader an implementation design for an operational sentencing guidelines system that should ensure that the twin goals of sentencing justice—equity and propriety—will be achieved in the courts.

This book is addressed to those directly affected by and interested in the improvement of the criminal justice system—primarily judges, legislators, and criminal justice agency personnel—as well as academics, students, and researchers who want to go beyond purely descriptive data analysis. Indeed, although statistical analysis is used in the development of the initial guidelines models, no statistical background on the part of the reader is either assumed or required; the educated layperson has been my perceived audience.

Those of us who thrive in the world of ideas like to regard our thoughts as original, but so many of them grow from the seeds planted by our teachers and I thank all of mine. As a student in Columbia Law School, I was particularly fortunate to take courses from such legendary figures as Walter Gellhorn, Monrad Paulsen, Sir Leon Radzinowicz, Telford Taylor, and Herbert Wechsler, and they stimulated my lifelong interest in criminal law reform. Moreover, Jack Weinstein, through his evidence course, taught me how that interest could be valuably combined with my love of science. Later, while Assistant District Attorney to Frank S. Hogan in Manhattan, I corresponded with now Judge Weinstein who was looking for ways in which to improve the court system through the use of computers; inspired by his research, I developed and sent on to him a list of decisionmaking factors that I, as a prosecutor, employed in plea negotiation.

When I joined the faculty of the Graduate School of Criminal Justice at SUNY Albany, I showed this list and described my interests to Leslie T. Wilkins, who had himself—from a statistician's point of view—been engaged in the similar endeavor of isolating factors used by parole board members in their own decisionmaking processes. Leslie and I found an immediate marriage of interests, personalities, and skills that has matured into one of the deepest friendships of my

life. I owe Leslie—my research mentor and an authentic genius—
more than I can ever repay.

The research project described in Part Two of this book involved
the collaborative efforts of dozens of researchers and judges, and it
would be impossible to thank them all, but I must designate three of
the research team as deserving my most special thanks. First, I
thank Don M. Gottfredson, dean of the Rutgers University School of
Criminal Justice—and co-director of the feasibility research with
Leslie and me—for all his guidance and his many contributions. Second, Arthur M. Gelman, now at INSLAW, who coordinated all of the
federal research and who co-directed the Washington State research
with me, cannot receive enough of my praise or appreciation; in his
quietly self-effacing way, Art achieved more and deserves more credit for the success of sentencing guidelines than anyone else. Finally,
if Art was my "right-hand man," then Joseph Calpin, now of MITRE,
made me ambidextrous; Joe's methodological talents and skillful guidance of the research analysis were simply invaluable.

Judge Anthony M. Critelli deserves my gratitude and respect for
the leadership he displayed on our Steering and Policy Committee. I
also want to credit the individual site leadership shown by Judges
Edward J. Bradley, Robert Broomfield, Warren Chan, Richard Fitzgerald, James C. Flanigan, Stanley Z. Goodfarb, Benjamin Mackoff,
John A. Marzulli, the late Russell Morss, Leonard Plank, Lewis
Springer, Jr., Roger Strand, and Leo Yanoff. I worked closely with all
of these judges, and I have learned to admire and respect each of
them, but I must also thank the hundreds of other judges across the
country who willingly gave me their time and advice at so many conferences where the views expressed in these pages were shaped.

The federal project that started the sentencing guidelines movement was monitored by Cheryl Martorana for the National Institute
of Law Enforcement and Criminal Justice of the Law Enforcement
Assistance Administration, United States Department of Justice.
Cheryl's vision kept this research alive, and the generous support of
her agency is gratefully acknowledged.

The separately funded efforts in Philadelphia and the state of
Washington were especially important in demonstrating that the
guidelines concept was generally applicable. I thank Philadelphia's
Saundra Di Ilio and David N. Savitt and Washington's James R. Lar-
sen for the encouragement they provided.

Many colleagues have read portions of the manuscript, and given
much useful advice. The insightful critiques of Graeme R. Newman
and Irvin Waller deserve special praise.

Having the opportunity to repay so many intellectual debts here is
a boon to the conscience and a marvelous fringe benefit of author-
ship, but the price paid is the nagging feeling that too many others

deserving thanks have been unjustly ignored. Those others, however, are at least spared any guilt by association with the views expressed in this book. Those views are entirely my own and should not be ascribed to any person or agency mentioned above.

My personal thanks are due to Harriet Spector and Joanne DeSilva, whose secretarial assistance should serve also to qualify them as translators of hieroglyphics. Finally, my deepest thanks of all go to Susan and Emma, both of whom helped so much and put up with more than they ever should have.

Foreword

One of the most glaring flaws in our current system of criminal justice can be traced to the arbitrariness of criminal sentencing procedures. During the past decade study after study has demonstrated that unfettered sentencing discretion results in increasing unfairness and uncertainty. The impact of such unfairness is devastating. Sentencing disparity and uncertainty affect society, the victims and the offenders themselves. The inescapable conclusion remains—public respect for our criminal justice system requires a complete overhaul of the way we go about sentencing the convicted offender.

In the past few years the sentencing debate has intensified in the Congress, in state legislatures, and among correctional experts and academicians. The battle lines have generally been drawn between those who advocate retention of the present sentencing system— with its emphasis on judicial discretion and the division of sentencing authority among judges and parole boards—and those who favor modifying the current system through the consolidation of sentencing authority and the imposition of limitations on sentencing discretion.

My views on the subject are well known. Retention of the current system or, indeed, piecemeal sentencing reform will not cure current ills. What is needed is a radical departure from current law. The basis for effective sentencing reform lies in the elimination of the indeterminate sentence, the abolition of the parole release function, the development of presumptive sentencing guidelines, and the creation, for the first time in our nation's history, of an appellate procedure to review sentences actually imposed.

The broad discretion conferred on our judges has historically been provided for in the name of benevolence. The argument offered in support of the current system is that it best takes into account the individual needs of the offender and the specific characteristics of the offense. Defenders of the current system consider criminal sentencing a very personal, deliberate undertaking. They are wary of current sentencing reform efforts aimed at standardizing sentencing practices. Reform opponents acknowledge the existence of sentencing disparity but claim that such disparity reflects the myriad differences among defenders and offenses. In addition, they argue that such disparity can also be traced to the absence of sufficient information in presentence reports concerning the background and history of the offender.

I acknowledge these arguments but do not agree. Of course, sentencing disparity is not per se unreasonable. Different offender and offense charcteristics can and should result in different sentences. But it is too late in the day to ignore growing evidence of unjustified sentencing disparity. It is time to recognize the flaws inherent in our system of criminal sentencing, flaws that permit a state judge in Illinois to sentence a convicted murderer to a maximum of twenty-six hundred years in prison with the knowledge that the offender will be eligible for parole in little more than a decade.

Current sentencing policy nurtures public cynicism on the part of the offender and society alike. It feeds the suspicion that sentences do not mean what they say, that parole boards are always available to release the offender if the offender knows how to perform when being interviewed by parole officials.

Although various states have undertaken sentencing reform, it is at the federal level that the most comprehensive, innovative departure from current law can be found. The Federal Criminal Code Reform Act of 1979 (successor to S. 1437) would make long overdue reforms in the federal criminal justice process. The bill articulates for the first time the philosophical purposes to be served by a sentence—deterrence, incapacitation, punishment, and to a very limited extent, rehabilitation—and sets out the factors that a court should consider in exercising its discretion. The bill creates a United States Sentencing Commission to develop a system of presumptive guidelines and policy statements designed to reduce sentencing disparity and make punishment more certain; Minnesota and Pennsylvania have already established such commissions at the state level. Necessary flexibility would be retained, moreover, by permitting a sentence to be imposed outside of the guidelines in an appropriate case. The bill would, however, encourage adherence to the guidelines by requiring that all sentences imposed be accompanied by a statement of reasons specifically justifying such sentence. In addition, sentences would be subject to appellate review, providing a further check against unreasonable punishment.

Most importantly, the parole release function would be abolished and all sentencing authority consolidated with the sentencing judge. Judges would sentence defendants to terms that represent their best estimate, in light of the applicable guidelines, as to how long the offender should actually spend in prison. The bill would eliminate the common judicial practice of imposing inordinately long sentences designed to ensure that a defendant remain incarcerated for at least one third of the sentence, as required by current federal law.

The federal legislation, therefore, preserves flexibility in sentencing while simultaneously promoting a procedure for the reduction of disparity and uncertainty through the development of presumptive guidelines. The offender, the victim, and society alike will all know *at the time of the initial sentencing decision* what the sentence will be and, if a prison term is imposed, the appropriate prison release date. We can reasonably hope that this increased fairness, and perhaps as importantly, the appearance of fairness, will reduce the widespread cynicism and mistrust that pervades the criminal justice system at the present time.

Despite the fact that criminal sentencing reform has become a frontline topic of debate during the past decade, little attention has been paid to the method of determining what the new sentencing guidelines should look like and how they will be implemented. The inherent difficulties in developing workable guidelines models have been ignored in the rush to debate the merits of determinate sentencing, abolition of parole, and the future of rehabilitation. How the guidelines will be structured and how one should go about developing a data base for their promulgation are among the significant issues which have, for the most part, been ignored in the current debate.

Jack Kress meets this problem head on in *Prescription for Justice*. Kress not only reviews the arguments for and against sentencing reform but then parts company with most of the leading treatises on the subject by proposing practical solutions—in the form of various models for the development and promulgation of sentencing guidelines. *Prescription for Justice* is the culmination of a four year research effort and offers the reader a first-hand, do-it-yourself account of how to develop and implement a sentencing guidelines system. Kress is a researcher, but also a lawyer, with a lawyer's intuition. He spent four years in Denver, Newark, Chicago, and Phoenix compiling the facts and witnessing the strengths and weaknesses of present sentencing procedures. The value of this book, therefore, lies primarily in Kress's eagerness to go one step beyond the already classic reform proposals of Marvin Frankel, Norval Morris, and others to develop a specific plan for the creation of the guidelines themselves based on current sentencing practices.

Nor does Kress stop with the development of several guidelines alternatives. He proposes a concrete and adaptable methodology for the implementation of the guidelines. In developing his guidelines models, Kress discusses the difficulties that are not often confronted by proponents of sentencing reform. Can a nationwide guidelines system be developed or do regional differences in sentencing make comprehensive reform unlikely? What are the advantages and disavantages associated with the creation of a sentencing commission? What factors should enter into the decision to adopt one guidelines approach as opposed to another? And, finally, what factors should be allowed to enter into the guidelines decision—should the prosecutor's charge be a part of the offender's prior record, or should the latter be limited to past convictions? What about the problem of how to treat juvenile records? To what extent should a prior record include convictions obtained years before? And what about the relevance of socioeconomic variables? All of these issues are discussed and debated by Kress.

Prescription for Justice is also important because it recognizes one of the underlying premises of sentencing reform—that a sentencing guidelines system initially directed at the sentencing judge holds future promise in regulating the charging and plea bargaining practices of the prosecutor. Kress makes clear what Marvin Frankel and others have long maintained—that sentencing guidelines aimed at the judge can ultimately have a much more pervasive impact on the entire criminal justice system.

Prescription for Justice is, therefore, a valuable addition to the current literature on sentencing reform. It should be read by those interested not only in the debate over whether or not sentencing reform should occur but how the theory of sentencing reform can be translated into practice. It is a sobering account of the unfinished work yet to be done before sentencing reform can become a reality; but, simultaneously, it is a study that demonstrates the plausibility of developing a just, effective, workable, and fair system of criminal sanctions. It is an answer to those who maintain that sentencing guidelines cannot be developed, that sentencing reform is by definition too complex a task, and that the current system—with all its flaws and unfairness—should be preferred over the risks and pitfalls of reform. Jack Kress lays these arguments to rest and offers all those interested in the subject a proposed prescription for sentencing reform, a prescription grounded in notions of justice and fair play.

Senator Edward M. Kennedy
January 1980

Part One
The Need For Sentencing Guidelines

Reason and Reform

If we would guide by the light of reason, we must let our minds be bold.
—Louis D. Brandeis[1]

THE NEXUS BETWEEN LAW REFORM AND SENTENCING REFORM

Why has the issue of sentencing reform so captured the imagination of law reformers these past few years?[2] Harvard's James Q. Wilson has declared: "The changes now under way in the laws governing the sentencing of criminals are perhaps the most important development in American criminal justice in the past half century."[3] In the 1960s the influence of the American Law Institute's Model Penal Code[4] was pervasive: reformers primarily concerned themselves with codification and reclassification of the substantive criminal law. While that reform effort continues, it has seemed lately that the procedural end of the trial court system—sentencing—has dominated the substantive body of that system—criminal law. Is this a case of the tail wagging the dog, or is sentencing really that important?

The answer lies in the usually unstated, often ignored, but always important interrelationship between the underlying law and the sentence imposed. Indeed, perhaps the most exciting aspect of the sentencing reform movement has been the recognition of systemic interrelationships, as well as a thrust towards comprehensiveness, usually only hinted at, but everpresent. The 1970s witnessed a startling reversal in fundamental philosophical perceptions, with the dominant philosophy of punishment becoming punishment—openly acknowledged[5] and replacing the rehabilitative ideal with incredible swiftness. Even apart from this, however, we have grown to recognize the existence of an interdependent criminal justice system.[6] When our attention was focused on the end points of the system— with police or correctional reform—we could almost ignore this fact

3

and suggest our improvements in splendid isolation from consequence. Now we face the mind-boggling task of evaluating in advance the interim effect of a reform of system component A upon system component B, which in turn affects component C, which has a feedback-change effect on A, which in turn affects B again, and so on and so on.[7]

Unfortunately, too many have failed to see the urgent link between sentencing reform and criminal law reform. Many, for example, have suggested that Congress break up S.1437 (the Federal Criminal Code Reform Act of 1978) into its various subdivisions, arguing that too much is being changed too soon. The problem is, however, that criminal law reform is meaningless without sentencing reform, and that sentencing reform necessitates concomitant reform in the criminal law.

In hindsight, 1972 may be seen as a watershed year. Many observers then read the United States Supreme Court's 1972 decision in *Furman v. Georgia*[8] as virtually abolishing capital punishment in the United States, capping the movement that had prevented an American from being executed for the previous five years. In another and deeper sense, however, this decision seemed to herald the utter triumph of the rehabilitative ideal and the indeterminate sentence; the very symbol of the retributive philosophy seemed finally to have been abandoned, and mandatory, determinate sentencing appeared to be a relic of the past. But the apparent triumph of indeterminacy meant much more. As it turned out, it was actually the criminal law itself that had been declared trivial.

Think of how surreal and impractical an endeavor it must have been to study the criminal law in 1972. Why should one belabor the felony-murder doctrine or concern oneself with the distinction between murder and manslaughter or between larceny by trick and larceny by false pretenses? If, as a practical matter, the *actual* time incarcerated would not vary for defendants convicted of first degree or second degree robbery, then why debate those differences seriously? Statutory distinctions hardly mattered. In the real world, a defendant convicted of any of these offenses was, after plea negotiations, given a reduced charge that often bore only the vaguest resemblance to the crime committed; such defendants were sentenced to indeterminate terms of imprisonment which bore no necessary proportionality to the offense that they were arrested for, charged with, or convicted of; and finally, they were released by a paroling authority that established their effective sentence on the basis of no stated policy whatsoever.

Penalty was all that mattered; time inside, all that counted. The concepts of guilt and innocence certainly still had meaning, but in a

practical sense, and upon an honest functional analysis, that meaning must bluntly be confessed to have become a distinction without a
real difference to the actual administration of criminal justice. The
hallowed concept of presumed innocence, for example, pragmatically
relates only to that small percentage of cases that result in a jury
trial. Otherwise, system agents—from arresting officers to plea bargaining prosecutors—typically presume the criminal defendant's
guilt.[9] Then we come to that portion of the criminal justice process
that directly concerns us—sentencing. It would be appropriate here
to introduce a caveat: when I just declared that penalty was all that
mattered, that was not equivalent to a statement that sentencing
was all that mattered. Important as it was and is, sentencing can
only account for one portion of the totality of punishment that a defendant will suffer in our justice system. Sentencing rarely relates to
predispositional incarceration occasioned by insufficient bail funds;[10]
nor can it affect the quality of any term of probation or imprisonment
imposed;[11] nor, usually (and until recently), would it more than indirectly affect the discretion of prison and parole authorities to grant
earlier release.[12] Still, the sentencing decision is and was a most important one in terms of both bound setting and the official public
sanctioning of the state's punishment process.

In 1772, even gross penal distinctions were of little consequence
under English law, since the death penalty applied to so many
crimes—hence the saying, "might as well be hung for a thief as a
beggar."[13] Law reformers of that period understood that criminal law
reform, of necessity, meant sentencing reform; further refinements of
degrees of homicide or theft made no practical difference. In 1972,
two centuries later, in a quite different context—but little realized—
the same situation obtained. With the advent and seemingly unchal-
lenged triumph of indeterminate sentencing, the enormous labors of
the American Law Institute in establishing the Model Penal Code
had gone for naught; for it was not only effective sentencing authority that had left the courtroom—it was law. The power of the sanction
is the power of the law; yet very little of that power remained with
the one visible agent of the criminal justice system assumed by the
general public to exercise all of that power—the local trial court
judge.[14]

Then, from 1972 on, a strange and sudden shift in opinion took
place. Some unconscious realization of what had been happening set
in. The results of decades of indeterminate sentencing were examined and found wanting; a consistant diagnosis of failure has been
directed against the rehabilitative promises of the indeterminate sentencing system.[15] Moreover, the attack has been conceptual as well
as pragmatic. Just about the time of *Furman*, the impact of *Struggle*

for Justice began to be felt; that book signaled a reversal in "liberal" thought concerning the merits of rehabilitation as a goal of punishment.[16] Soon a veritable flood of philosophical treatises began to inundate us with opposition to the rehabilitative rationale[17]—the ideological base of the indeterminate sentence. Opposition came from the right and from the left, from those whose primary concerns were persons suffering criminal victimization to those whose primary concerns were persons suffering unjustified incarceration.

The most important book in this debate was written by then United States District Court Judge Marvin E. Frankel; published contemporaneously with the *Furman* decision, *Criminal Sentences: Law Without Order* was the seminal work of the era. It synthesized the frustration of those who recognized the practical and philosophical inefficacy of the indeterminate sentence, but it has also been read as designating the principal villain as unfettered judicial discretion.[18] No matter that, in the age of the indeterminate sentence, the trial court judge lacked significant power, judicial sentencing disparity became the perceived and designated vice. The solution then became simple: eradicate judicial sentencing disparity by eliminating judicial sentencing discretion! Mandatory sentencing bills proliferated in virtually every legislature in America, and variants passed in some states.

Soon, however, questions began to be asked as to whether the cure was perhaps worse than the disease. Are not state legislators, after all, capable of institutionalizing disparity? This was, indeed, seen as a major difficulty with each of the variants of legislative sentencing—mandatory minimum, flat time, and presumptive sentences. Moreover, they each offered limited solutions to the disparity problem.

The *mandatory minimum* sentencing proposals, for example, put forth a sharply circumscribed approach, concerning themselves with only a narrow range of offenders committing limited sets of offenses.[19] Thus, the overwhelming percentage of convicted offenders were completely unaffected by these proposals. Furthermore, little if any guidance was offered regarding the length of any sentence actually imposed. The only active constraint upon judicial discretion was one sided—the offender must be incarcerated. The actual sentence, however, could usually be set anywhere within a broad range bounded by the mandatory minimum term on one end and the statutorily permitted maximum on the other. There would also be numerous offenders who would be unfairly punished—whose justifiably distinctive characteristics would be ignored—as a result of a mandatory sentencing provision. These mandatory proposals simply cannot take sufficient account of the myriad forms that criminal offenses can take. Greater disparity may indeed result if we treat unlike offenses similarly than if we treat like offenses dissimilarly! Aristotle had in fact long ago declared: "There can be no greater injustice than to treat unequal things equally."[20] Worse, this is a hidden disparity far less amenable to correction.[21]

The thrust of the *flat time* proposals would likewise appear to have little impact on reducing unjustified variation in sentencing. In these, a judge is still given complete discretion in deciding whether or not to incarcerate an offender, and although a definite period must be set for incarcerative sentences, the range within which that term is to be set is often quite wide.[22]

Perhaps the most serious flaw with *presumptive sentences* is that the legislature uses a priori reasoning to establish sentence lengths, with absolutely no factual support upon which to base the numbers chosen.[23] A legislature would rely only on its collective intuition. Yet legislative bodies are not constructed so as to facilitate reference to current judicial sentencing practices even as a minimal starting point upon which to build any set of presumptive sentences. Without such an empirically derived base, how can the legislature—far removed in thought and distance from the actual crime and criminal in question—intuitively predetermine the "best" sentence for a particular offender and offense years before the crime is committed? In such a system, insufficient regard is given both to the human element and to the collective expertise possessed by experienced sentencing judges.[24]

Furthermore, history demonstrates that, once a legislature has acted and any of these sentencing "reforms" have been enacted, then the sentences will remain fixed for many years; unfortunately, when change does come, it often takes the form of overreaction.[25] A dynamic criminal justice system instead requires a sentencing agency to possess the flexibility to accommodate to changed circumstances. Adaptability to variations in population concentrations, societal attitudes to given offenses, prison conditions and the like is the hallmark of informed, on the spot, timely, judicial sentencing and not that of a distant legislature. With the assistance of sentencing guidelines promulgated by an independent sentencing commission, that task may be even better performed by the local judiciary.

Finally, even though an individual judge would still retain final, though limited, sentencing authority under a legislatively imposed presumptive sentencing system, the total effect would be unfairly to force a policy on a judiciary that has had little input into the formulation of that policy. Instead of opening up the sentencing system and making it a more visible process, as the guidelines approach proposes, what is likely to develop under presumptive sentencing is an implicit policy that, because of its secretiveness, has the potential to result in even more "judge-shopping" and disparity than we see today. Local trial court judges, on the other hand, are on the firing line daily and therefore have the experience that, properly structured and directed, should result in both humane and just sentencing decisions. They see defendants as flesh and blood creatures rather than as statistical artifacts. Yet they are close enough to the victim (and to the police and prosecutor) to be able to account for the societal implications of the specific crime that has in fact occurred.

The solution is not to eviscerate or eradicate judicial sentencing, but rather to restructure it so as to control potential discretionary abuses and to provide articulated guidelines as to the judicial reasoning employed in a given case. The sentencing guidelines system seeks to correct the flaws of indeterminate sentencing but not at the cost of the inhumanity of fixed sentencing. The necessity for appropriately applied judicial discretion is recognized, and indeed strengthened, while its use is structured to check potential abuse. With sentencing guidelines, sentencing will give not *new* meaning to the criminal laws, but—finally—meaning. Under the sentencing guidelines system here described, distinctions in the criminal law will begin to make a real and effective difference in terms of the outcomes accorded individual criminal defendants. Now that equitable sentencing has become achievable, it has become a moral imperative.

THE APPEARANCE OF JUSTICE

Lest my central purpose in writing this book be lost during my descriptive analysis of prior research, let me make it clear at the outset: It is to open up a system too long shielded from public scrutiny. Sentencing guidelines research has demonstrated that society in general, and the courts in particular, have much to gain from such enhanced access to the sentencing decisionmaking process. While local trial court judges have been the primary direct beneficiaries of the systems that I and my collegues have developed, everyone involved in or concerned with criminal justice reform should find value in understanding these systems. Since perceived sentencing disparity has been the cutting edge applied by court critics, the ability of a sentencing guidelines system to help reduce such disparity, and thereby increase equity for criminal defendants, has usually been viewed as its principal asset. Such a reduction of disparity is achievable and desirable, but—at least to this writer—it is a derivative accomplishment of the system described in this book. It is my view that far more effective disparity reduction will occur as a result of increasing public awareness of what courts accomplish and what they actually

do than from any application of even the most sophisticated statistical techniques. The courts have nothing to fear from public scrutiny and much to gain.

Sentencing judges want to reach just determinations—that is, to sentence each defendant fairly and properly. To do this, they seek to individualize each sentencing decision, assuring that the punishment fits the criminal as well as the crime.[26] But there is also an overall equity dimension to sentencing, a desire to seek equal justice under law.[27] These goals of equity and individualization are each primary, yet they conflict in theory; whole justice may only be achieved by a finely formed synthesis of these concepts. Sentencing guidelines provide for such a synthesis as no totally determinate or indeterminate sentencing system can. The development and application of sentencing guidelines systems is therefore completely compatible with the channeling of judicial discretion so as to ensure a useful consistency in overall policy, without simultaneously upsetting the essentially necessary inconsistency that is inherent in the humane treatment of individual cases.

Sentencing guidelines systems are voluntary aids that enable individual judges better to structure and articulate their own judicial discretion. Under present sentencing systems, each court operates as an autonomous unit, essentially unaccountable to other courts or to any meaningful set of standards in determining what disposition to render convicted persons. When questioned on this issue, judges are generally desirous of having for their use the sentencing norms of their colleagues, so as either to conform to them or to differ from them with reason and knowledge. They wish this information in order to improve their own skills in sentencing. Yet this information is presently unavailable. The sentencing guidelines system seeks to furnish this information, initially by extracting the underlying criteria of present sentencing practices and then by reformulating them so as to create standards for judicial education and court improvement. Later, these standards are in turn reviewed and revised on a regular basis, to assure that they accurately reflect desired court policy.

By these means, sentencing guidelines systems help trial court judges to secure equity in sentencing practices—by achieving conscious and conscientious consistency over time and over an entire court system—and also to secure propriety in sentencing practices—by subjecting both case-by-case and policy decisions to constructive and informed internal and external review. Individual sentencing guidelines thus supply nonmandatory guidance and direction to judges—a starting point, as it were, for informed sentencing.

As vitally important as this improvement in justice is, Charles Silberman recently reminded us that the appearance of justice is perhaps also as important. He points out that the courts today "convey an aura of injustice that undermines respect for the law and belief in its legitimacy."[28] The guidelines should therefore be made known not only to a judge's own colleagues, but also to defendants and to the public, so that the reality and the perception of justice may coincide.

The sentencing guidelines concept is an idea whose time has undeniably arrived. Only a few short years ago, neither the scientific wherewithall for its creation, nor the perception of its need, nor the political climate for its acceptance were available. In the past decade, however, a dramatic turnabout has occurred in all three areas. The analytical basis for an empirically informed sentencing guidelines system has been established and has proven to be neither excessively complicated, time-consuming, nor costly;[29] recent studies by the score have denounced perceived sentencing disparities,[30] while many learned treatises have called into question the very legitimacy of present sentencing philosophies;[31] and simultaneously, a wave of mandatory sentencing proposals has inundated state legislatures, although the results of the congressional debates concerning S.1437[32] have raised hopes that the new sentencing commission/judicial sentencing guidelines approach to the problems of sentencing will prevail. In reviewing the alternatives, a consensus is beginning to emerge that totally unfettered judicial discretion and/or completely indeterminate sentencing necessarily lead to inequities; and further, that attempting to completely eliminate judicial discretion would lead to ridigity and/or circumvention of the law. Finally, it does not appear that any other presently available alternative would be as just, as practical, or as efficacious. Moreover, conscientious judges across the country appear quite ready, willing, and even anxious to adopt a guidelines approach to the problems of sentencing.

It is incredible to recall that only a few short years ago sentencing guidelines did not exist, either in fact or in theory. Work on the federally funded research project began as recently as 1974, and America's first sentencing guidelines were implemented in the Denver County District Court only in November 1976; the first statewide guidelines took effect in New Jersey in October 1978. At this writing, sentencing guidelines systems have been officially adopted for six county and three state judiciaries; full-scale implementation programs are underway in an additional ten states. Moreover, major studies recommending and/or aimed at establishing sentencing guidelines systems have either been concluded or are in process in a further ten states as well as in the federal system;[33] a recent British government body recommended the guidelines approach;[34] and finally, agencies of the Canadian and Australian governments are also actively considering guidelines. The urgency of the full explanation offered here is thus evident.

WHAT IS A SENTENCING GUIDELINES SYSTEM?

The ways in which a system of whole justice may actually be achieved will be better understood if I introduce the reader here directly to the sentencing guidelines approach. These points will, of course, be developed in later chapters, but I have always found an early expression of the special products of action research to be useful in comprehending its whys and wherefores. Under the sentencing guidelines approach, researchers, in full collaboration with the local judiciary:

1. Analyze present sentencing practices;
2. Identify the significant factors that judges do appear actually to consider in sentencing offenders;
3. Put these factors together into a graphic representation of overall court policy;
4. Apply this policy uniquely to each individual case;
5. Restate that policy to account for observed and desired policy changes; and
6. Continually revise and update the policy statement and simultaneously provide assistance to judges deciding individual cases

The technique employed is the practical and acceptable one of local action research. The methodology entails constant judicial consultation and involvement and the use of a series of mathematical and statistical techniques that serve as filters to develop pools of variables out of which local sentencing authorities select those best representing their actual and intended policy. Frequent review and continual feedback mechanisms are employed; there is thus a constant synergy of policy and practice.

This all sounds complicated, but in actual use the guidelines are simple to apply. In brief, in most cases, the "bottom line" for the sentencing judge is one additional item of information attached to the presentence investigative report now normally prepared. That item is a suggested guideline sentence, individually prepared and suited to the facts and circumstances of the crime and the criminal under consideration, yet also representing the overall policy views of the sentencing authorities in the particular jurisdiction. Other, more colloquial, ways of looking at the guideline sentence would be as an "average" of, or "benchmark" for, what that judge—and all of that judge's colleagues—would give as a sentence in a given case, in order to be "consistent" with the jurisdiction's sentencing policy.

It is important to understand, however, that the guideline sentence is in no sense intended to refer to a mandatory directive. Sentencing guidelines represent, and are useful as, an information device to assist judges in making their own sentencing decisions; not as a strait jacket forcing them to make someone else's "guideline" decision.[35]

Deviations from the suggested guideline sentences are expected and even encouraged, but accompanied always by specific reasons and subject to a now informed right of appeal. Sentencing guidelines thus tap the experience and expertise of veteran sentencing judges to supply each sentencing judge with a "going rate" or "tariff"—individually established for each case—that the judge may use as a starting point for reform: it is not intended to glorify the status quo, but to allow judges accurately to understand present policy, to articulate it, and therefore to be able to depart from it knowledgeably when they feel that it is in the interests of justice to do so.

Expressed in a form simple to apply, the guideline sentence is in turn simple to compute from graphic policy statements. Figures 1–1 and 1–2 are illustrative.

Figure 1–1 is a hypothetical guideline worksheet. Assume that, in a case before the judge, a defendant committed an armed robbery, a typical street "mugging," using a gun, but that no injury was caused to the victim. The defendant's crime score would be 2. Assume further that the defendant was a parolee whose criminal record, however, was limited to only one prior adult felony conviction that resulted in a prison sentence. The offender score would be 4. Now, turn to Figure 1–2, a hypothetical sentencing grid (which, for the sake of simplicity, is placed in determinate form). The intersection of the crime score of 2 and the offender score of 4 in this example is a cell that contains a range of three to five years. Effectively, this means that the suggested guideline sentence is four years, but the judge is given flexibility to sentence the offender to three years, five years, or anywhere in between to account for expected individual variations of a minor nature. Some judges using guidelines prefer to receive only the guideline sentence, but most prefer to receive the entire series of worksheets and grids; with only a little practice, they find that this computation takes less than a minute for each case.

I caution the reader that this example has only been intended as a relatively simple illustration. Part Two and the Appendixes to this book provide some sense of the detail and breadth that may be achieved by operational sentencing guidelines systems. Moreover, integral to the purpose of such systems are a host of regenerative feed-

Offender _____ Docket Number _____

Judge _____ Date _____

Offense(s) Convicted Of: _____

_____

_____

Crime Score
  A. Injury
     0 = No injury
     1 = Injury
     2 = Death   _____ +

  B. Weapon
     0 = No weapon
     1 = Weapon possessed
     2 = Weapon present and used   _____ +

  C. Drugs
     0 = No sale of drugs
     1 = Sale of drugs   _____ = [_____]

                                                          Crime
                                                          Score
Offender Score

  A. Current Legal Status
     0 = Not on probation/parole, escape
     1 = On probation/parole, escape   _____ +

  B. Prior Adult Misdemeanor Convictions
     0 = No convictions
     1 = One conviction
     2 = Two or more convictions   _____ +

  C. Prior Adult Felony Convictions
     0 = No convictions
     2 = One conviction
     4 = Two or more convictions   _____ +

  D. Prior Adult Probation/Parole Revocations
     0 = None
     1 = One or more revocations   _____ +

  E. Prior Adult Incarcerations (Over 60 Days)
     0 = None
     1 = One incarceration   [_____]
     2 = Two or more incarcerations   _____ =

                                                          Offender
                                                          Score
Guideline Sentence _____

Actual Sentence _____

Reasons (if actual sentence does not fall within guideline range):

Figure 1–1. Guideline Worksheet.

Crime Score				
4–5	4–6 Years	5–7 Years	6–8 Years	8–10 Years
3	3–5 Years	4–6 Years	6–8 Years	6–8 Years
2	2–4 Years	3–5 Years	3–5 Years	4–6 Years
1	Probation	Probation	2–4 Years	3–5 Years
0	Probation	Probation	Probation	2–4 Years
	0–1	2–4	5–7	8–10

Offender Score

Figure 1–2. Felony Sentencing Grid.

---

back and review procedures that constantly update policy provide and case-by-case assistance to the individual local trial court judge; these will be elaborated upon in the next chapter.[36]

SOME SPECIFIC GOALS

Aiding the Courts

In 1973, when the creators of empirically informed guidelines requested funds to test the applicability of that approach to sentencing, their statement of purpose read as follows:

> "All of the aims and objectives of the proposed project may be summed into a single phrase, 'to improve the performance of the courts in relation to their sentencing decisions.' "[37]

Thus, from the outset, the goal was to help the courts, not merely to study the courts.

Opening the System. Why the courts? And why sentencing? My own focus in guidelines research has consistently been on structuring judicial discretion at the point of sentencing. Other researchers have concentrated on parole or on prosecutorial decisionmaking with significant impact, but sentencing was, is, and will continue to be the decision point in the criminal justice system of most persistent concern to the public. As I will detail in the next chapter, the judicial sentencing decision is one that is actually shared with other participants in the criminal justice process; nevertheless, the public perception is clearly that sentencing is the most important discretionary decision for crime control purposes and that the trial court judge is the most significant sentencing authority. Opening up this decision point to public scrutiny will therefore most sharply affect public fears and concerns regarding criminal justice. This is presently the most visible and accountable point in the process; making it the most responsible point as well will ensure that this accountability will have meaning. It is for this reason that I espouse an unfashionable point of view, at variance with both the indeterminate sentencing systems generally in existence and the mandatory sentencing schemes now so frequently advanced. I propose *more* judicial sentencing discretion, not less, but *only* when coupled with the structuring device of sentencing guidelines that simultaneously assist judges exercising that discretion and the public in assessing the responsibility of their decisions.

An operational sentencing guidelines system will create an important communication device enabling judges to explain their policies in the aggregate, as well as in particular cases, far better than has hitherto been possible. The near-term goal of the sentencing guidelines approach is therefore to encourage and assist local trial court judges to communicate with each other in a clear and useful manner. Previously, they have not been able to do so effectively because of their heavy workloads and because of the physical distances separating some of them; it is logical to assume that judges concerned with equity will make use of this now available information base and thereby greatly reduce unwarranted variation. Next, that communication is expanded to the other actors in the criminal justice system and, finally, to society at large. The ultimate goal of the sentencing guidelines approach may then be seen as helping to achieve whole justice by thus opening up the criminal justice system to sufficient scrutiny as to ensure and enhance equity in sentencing, as well as to an improved policymaking process leading to propriety in individual cases.

As I have emphasized, this process helps establish both the "is" and the "ought" of the system. The development of an explicit and clearly articulated sentencing policy, empirically informed, is a valuable step, not only in and of itself, but also as a condition precedent to answering the "ought" question. The moral issues then may be debated further; the effectiveness issues can be more rigorously tested. The system can be revised and improved by the judges themselves, aided by the now enlightened views of others.

The "In/Out" Decision. The sentencing decision is really a two stage process. First, the judge considers whether or not the defendant should be incarcerated, or as many judges put it: Can the defendant be trusted on the streets? Having made this "in/out" decision (whether consciously or unconsciously), the judge asks a different question. If the defendant is to be imprisoned, the judge decides for how long; here the judge may consider available jail or prison resources as well as known paroling practices. If the defendant is to be placed in the community, the judge more usually focuses on the type of alternative sanction; the imposition of a fine or of various probationary conditions may require information concerning the offender's employment, educational, or family situation. Each stage of the decisionmaking process thus employs different information in reaching each decision.

The first decision—whether or not to incarcerate an offender—is, morally, the most important decision and has proven the most agonizing for sentencing judges. Others do not agree with this assessment, however. The flat time proposal, for example, provides no guidance to judges on the in/out decision, but focuses on eliminating incarcerative disparities only; the genesis of this approach lies in a recognition that those disparities have been causes of prison unrest. Frankly, however, I grow impatient with those whose exclusive orientation is the prison system. To them, length of time disparities are of paramount importance. This is perhaps understandable as a concern for prison administrators, but it is an extremely narrow viewpoint when one proposes reform for the entire justice system. One does not have to read Einstein to understand that time is relative. Five years may represent a given absolute amount of time, but both objectively and subjectively it varies in significance: the difference between zero imprisonment and five years imprisonment is not the same difference as between five and ten years. The choice of no imprisonment whatsoever, as opposed to some, has got to be recognized as the most important decision. This is obviously not to ignore the great significance of the length of time decision, but to understand its proper place in overall sentencing reform.[38]

The Utility of Sentencing Guidelines for Judges:

As a Benchmark. The sentencing guidelines system provides the individual trial court judge with standards, a baseline of data—a benchmark, if you will—against which a judge may measure his or her own sentencing decision in each and every case. Some judges have thought of guidelines as providing them with a handy consultation panel or, as Iowa District Court Judge Anthony M. Critelli put it:

> I think of these guidelines as the average of what I and all of my colleagues *would have done* in the case at hand if they had the same basic information as I had. Now, I may have *more* information than they do and therefore may still sentence differently, but the availability of guidelines means that I can sentence with the collected wisdom of all my veteran colleagues at my fingertips.
>
> Sometimes there are no colleagues around and you really would like to discuss a case, or other times you're simply too embarrassed to admit that you don't know what to do. In either event, guidelines provide the missing link.[39]

For Training and Education. The sentencing guidelines system may fairly be seen as a means of judicial education providing judges with the educated hindsight that they have never had before. There is simply no law school training for sentencing, and sentencing guidelines systems help to provide that training.[40] Continued reliance upon current "trial and error" methods of learning sentencing policies and practices is clearly unfair to both offenders and judges alike.

Frankly, this educational aspect of guidelines is neither so necessary nor so valuable for the older and more experienced judges. They, after all, are the local sentencing experts; it is their knowledge and experience that guidelines seek to tap and provide to new judges. "New" judges, I should add, are not as infrequent as either the election or appointment process might indicate, since a prevalent practice in American courts is that of judicial rotation. As the court unification movement has proceeded apace in America, more and more trial courts of general jurisdiction have been given both civil and criminal authority. Trial court judges are therefore more and more seen as generalists rather than specialists in criminal practice. "And, where do these generalist judges come from? They are selected from the ever more specialized practicing bar."[41] Moreover, judges are rotated on and off the criminal bench with what, to the research team, often seemed like alarming frequency. Further, judges take vacations or become ill and hence frequently have substitute judges assigned to take their places. Moreover, in many states, such as Connecticut and Massachusetts, judges ride circuit around the state and thus periodically completely change their sentencing environment, including both support staff and available community resources.

Finally, there is an element of psychological assurance that guidelines provide sentencing judges. As Arizona's Superior Court Judge Stanley Z. Goodfarb remarked:

> Within a growing community like Phoenix, and with a merit election process, there are inevitably new lawyers and new judges that enter the criminal justice system and they all receive much more *confidence* in what they are doing, by knowing what has gone before. We also have an increased degree of confidence that we are not all over the ballpark, and we can speak with some more certainty to the outside world as to what our policy actually is, on a joint basis.[42]

As a Means of Communication.   I have here stressed the capability of guidelines to help judges communicate with each other, but even more important in the long run is the ability of judicial sentencing authorities—including also a sentencing commission—to communicate sentencing policies and practices to others through the guidelines medium.

One policy decision made by the Essex County judiciary should be universally emulated. There, copies of the sentencing guidelines were made available to all of the actors in the criminal justice system. For sentencing guidelines to fulfill their role of supplying information and making this a far more open and effective system of criminal justice, it is important that the systemwide effects of sentencing guidelines be widely felt in a desirable, knowledgeable and conscious fashion. The appropriate roles of the district attorney, the defense attorney, the victim, the defendant, the probation officer, and all of the other actors in the criminal justice system can only be enhanced by a knowledge of what they are doing and, more particularly, of what the crucial sentencing decision is all about.

Aiding Probation Departments

Guidelines research to date has usually been conducted in close conjunction with local probation department investigators as our goals have been completely congruent. They, as we, have sought to help judges in making their sentencing decisions. In preparing presentence investigation reports, they seek to supply judges with the essential information that judges want and need concerning the case in point.

Sentencing guidelines offer useful direction to these investigators, ensuring that the information they collect will be relevant. As Professor Robert O. Dawson recently noted, there has been a marked "decline of the theory that the sentencing judge can never be provided with too much information."[43] Excessively long probation reports actually constitute "information overload" and impair the decision-making process![44] The quality of the information supplied is what counts, not its quantity; information must be limited and ordered to be useful, carefully structured and relevant to be comprehensible. Sentencing guidelines can help achieve these goals by highlighting the most significant information to be sought in each case.

Probation officers might thus better allocate their time in relation to the importance of the information they are collecting. While less time should be spent collecting excess data, at least some extra effort should be made to ensure the accuracy of those items contained in the core, and perhaps a summary of those items should be provided to the judge on the first page of any report, along with the suggested guideline sentence. This slight modification would better organize the judge's information needs, would constructively structure the judge's thought and decisionmaking processes, and should lead to more just and equitable sentences.

Unfortunately, conscientious probation investigators have often been hampered in the past by archaic statutes or rules requiring that they, frankly, waste their time collecting all sorts of irrelevant material. Probation officers writing reports for judges should no longer be required to seek out the educational history of a forty year old recidivist burglar since the judge will make no use whatsoever of that information; yet it takes many valuable hours of a probation officer's time to track that information down. By improving this process, therefore, sentencing guidelines may not only improve sentencing decisionmaking, but may also save time and money for probation departments, as well as cutting away, to some small extent, on the case backlog problem.

Curbing Disparity

Unfortunately, many judicial critics have failed to define clearly the meaning of the word "disparity." Consequently, the word connotes different things to different people. What is appropriate variation to one observer may be seen as disparity by another. The very word "disparity" has thus become pejorative, and the concept of "sentencing disparity" now carries with it the connotation of malicious practices on the part of judges. Much otherwise valid criticism has failed to make this separation of justified variation from the unjustified variation that is truly disparity. Not all sentencing variation should be considered unwarranted or disparate; much of it properly reflects varying degrees of seriousness in the offense and/or varying characteristics of the offender. In fact, I would contend that dispositional variation based upon permissible, rationally relevant and understandably distinctive characteristics of the offender and/or of the offense is wholly justified, beneficial, proper—and even necessary—so long as the variable qualities are carefully monitored for consistency and desirability over time. Disparity, or unjustified variation, should therefore always be clearly distinguished from warranted, or justified, variation, which is indeed essential for an individualized, yet equitable, sentencing system.

Justice demands, however, that two individuals convicted of the same offense, with similar backgrounds and criminal histories, should receive sentences that are roughly the same. Nevertheless, extreme disparities (unjustified variations) in sentencing do at least appear to be commonplace and thus lead the public to lose confidence in the fair and impartial administration of the criminal justice system. A great deal of criticism has been leveled against the judiciary for such disparate sentencing practices. Some of the sharpest criticism has actually come from within the judiciary itself; for example, Judge Frankel pronounced ours an unregulated and unjust sentencing system: "[T]he point is made in all its stark horror by the compelling evidence that widely unequal sentences are imposed every day in great numbers for crimes and criminals not essentially distinguishable from each other."[45] The general consensus was summed up by Professor James Q. Wilson: "That judges differ in sentences imposed on cases presenting similar facts is beyond dispute."[46]

The sentencing guidelines system offers judges a tool with which they may themselves cope with this disparity problem. Disparity is not a conscious goal of the judiciary; it is bred out of ignorance, ignorance as to what benchmark does or should exist for a given case.

For this reason, the sentencing guidelines system does not attempt to abolish judicial discretion as a simplistic "solution" to disparity, as mandatory sentencing proposals do. Rather, it recognizes the need for systemic discretion to account for human variation, provides that benchmark, and structures judicial discretion so as to make it open, visible, and accountable. The "hidden" disparity of the mandatory sentence is thus avoided—that far more dangerous disparity that results from not taking valid and justified variations in cases into account.

Disparity is thus not a disease of the courts; it is a symptom, resulting largely from a closed sanctioning process. While one of the stated goals of guidelines research has been the diminution of the disparity problem, I have aimed at achieving this goal indirectly, by prescribing a more open system, thereby enhancing sentencing equity as a necessary, and desired, derivative by-product. By opening up communication between judges, we may reasonably expect a decrease in unwarranted and unintended variation.

Judges have been frequently and harshly attacked for alleged abuses of their discretionary sentencing powers. It is probable that most of this criticism has been misdirected, but in any event, judges cannot and need not defend a closed, secret system that allows for no structure or review. They may choose instead a self-monitored, but open and reviewable, policy of articulated reasoning and structured discretion, a sentencing framework that ensures that any individual judge's separate decision will accurately reflect as well the local judiciary's collective wisdom and sense of justice. But judicial critics must realize too the necessity for judges to retain that quantum of discretion so urgently required in order that each individual sentence may remain simultaneously just and humane.

NOTES

1. New State Ice Company v. Ernest A. Liebmann, 285 U.S. 262, 311, 52 S. Ct. 371, 76 L. Ed. 747 (1932) (dissent).

2. See, for example, American Friends Service Committee, *Struggle for Justice* (New York: Hill and Wang, 1971); M.E. Frankel, *Criminal Sentences: Law Without Order* (New York: Hill and Wang, 1973); N. Morris, *The Future of Imprisonment* (Chicago: University of Chicago Press, 1974); J.Q. Wilson, *Thinking About Crime* (New York: Basic Books, 1975); E. van den Haag, *Punishing Criminals* (New York: Basic Books, 1975); D. Fogel, *"We Are the Living Proof":* *The Justice Model for Corrections* (Cincinnati: W.H. Anderson Co., 1975); Twentieth Century Fund Task Force on Criminal Sentencing, *Fair and Certain Punishment* (New York: McGraw Hill, 1976); A. Neier, *Criminal Punishment: A Radical Solution* (New York: Stein and Day, 1976); A. von Hirsch, *Doing Justice: The Choice of Punishments* (New York: Hill and Wang, 1976); S.R. Brody, *The Effectiveness of Sentencing—A Review of the Literature* (London: HMSO, 1976); F. Zimring,"Making the Punishment Fit the Crime: A Consumer's Guide to Sentencing Reform," 6 *Hastings Center Report* 1 (1976); E.M. Kennedy, "Criminal Sentencing: A Game of Chance," 60 *Judicature* 208 (December 1976); P. O'Donnell, M.J. Churgin, and D.E. Curtis, *Toward a Just and Effective Sentencing System: Agenda for Legislative Reform* (New York: Praeger, 1977); G.O.W. Mueller, *Sentencing—Process and Purpose* (Springfield, Ill.: Charles C. Thomas, 1977); A. Alschuler, "Sentencing Reform and Prosecutorial Power: A Critique of Recent Proposals for 'Fixed' and 'Presumptive' Sentencing," 126 *University of Pennsylvania Law Review* 550 (1978); G.R. Newman, *The Punishment Response* (Philadelphia: J.B. Lippincott, 1978); Executive Advisory Committee on Sentencing, *Crime and Punishment in New York: An Inquiry into Sentencing and the Crimi-*

nal Justice System (New York: Executive Advisory Committee on Sentencing, 1979); and B. Grosman, ed., *New Directions in Sentencing* (Toronto: Butterworths, 1979).

3. J.Q. Wilson, "Changing Criminal Sentences," *Harpers* 16 (November 1977).

4. American Law Institute, *Model Penal Code* (Proposed Official Draft, 1962). Columbia's Herbert Wechsler, Director of the Institute, is the "father" of that code and the guiding force behind much of the penal reform of the past two decades. See H. Wechsler, "Sentencing, Correction and the Model Penal Code," 109 *University of Pennsylvania Law Review* (1961); and H. Wechsler, "The Model Penal Code and the Codification of American Criminal Law," in R. Hood, ed., *Crime, Criminology and Public Policy: Essays in Honor of Sir Leon Radzinowicz* 419 (New York: Free Press, 1975). National Advisory Commission on Criminal Justice Standards and Goals, *A National Strategy To Reduce Crime* (Washington, D.C.: USGPO, 1973): "States whose criminal codes have not been revised in the last decade should initiate revisions; these revisions should be complete and thorough, not partial, and the revision should include where necessary a revamped penalty structure" (at 137).

5. California's revised sentencing provisions were among the first in the current wave. Section 1170 (a) (1): "The Legislature finds and declares that the purpose of imprisonment for crime is punishment" (West 1977). Most of its modern advocates, however, prefer to eschew the term "punishment," or the biblical *Lex Talionis* "vengeance" principle of an "eye for an eye" embodied in *Leviticus* (25: 17–22). They also avoid the traditional philosophical term "retribution," preferring instead to speak of giving offenders their "just deserts." See especially von Hirsch, *supra* note 2; see also M. Zalman, "The Rise and Fall of the Indeterminate Sentence," 24 *Wayne Law Review* 45 (November 1977).

6. See, for example, National Advisory Commission on Criminal Justice Standards and Goals, *Criminal Justice System* (Washington, D.C.: USGPO, 1973); H.L. Packer, *The Limits of the Criminal Sanction* (Palo Alto: Stanford University Press, 1968); and D.J. Newman, *Introduction to Criminal Justice,* 2nd ed. (Philadelphia: J.B. Lippincott, 1978).

7. See K.C. Davis, *Discretionary Justice: A Preliminary Inquiry* (Baton Rouge: Louisiana State University Press, 1969); D.J. Newman, *supra* note 6; and *infra* Chapter 2.

8. Furman v. Georgia, 408 U.S. 238, 92 S.C. 2726, 33 L.Ed. 2d 346 (1972). No matter that this reading eventually turned out to be incorrect; the perception is what counted. See also the discussion *infra* Chapter 3.

9. D.J. Newman, *supra* note 6 at 40–41; and Packer, *supra* Note 6 at 160–61.

10. See R.L. Goldfarb, *Ransom: A Critique of the American Bail System* (New York: Harper and Row, 1965); and C.B. Foote, "The Coming Constitutional Crisis in Bail," 113 *University of Pennsylvania Law Review* 1125 (1965). Guidelines research does indicate an indirect impact, however, at least in terms of the sentence of "time served."

11. While the brutality of a jail or prison guard is as unrelated to the use of discretion as the corruption of a judge (see *infra* Chapter 2), I at least mention here a point that so many critics have attacked; see, e.g., American Friends Service Committee, *supra* note 2. Again, however, guidelines research does indicate an indirect impact, at least in those jurisdictions like Essex County that leave the choice of institution to the sentencing judge.

12. Although formerly earned, "good time" is usually granted automatically today; the withdrawal of good time, however, survives as an internal disciplinary measure in most prisons. See generally, National Advisory Commission on Criminal Justice Standards and Goals, *Report on Corrections* (Washington, D.C.: USGPO, 1973). The role of parole will be discussed separately, *infra* Chapter 2 and Chapter 9.

13. See generally L. Radzinowicz, *A History of English Criminal Law* (London: Stevens and Co., 1948); and G.R. Newman, *supra* note 2.

14. This point will be developed further, *infra* Chapter 2.

15. R. Martinson, "What Works?—Questions and Answers About Prison Reform," 35 *The Public Interest* 22 (Spring 1974); J.O. Robison and G. Smith, "The Effectiveness of Correctional Programs," *17 Crime and Delinquency* 67 (1971). and D. Lipton, R. Martinson and J. Wilks, *The Effectiveness of Correctional Treatment: A Survey of Treatment Evaluation Studies* (New York: Praeger, 1975). See also L.T. Wilkins, *Evaluation of Penal Measures* (New York: Random House, 1969); W.C. Bailey, "Correctional Outcome: An Evaluation of 100 Reports," 57 *Journal of Criminal Law, Criminology and Police Science* 153 (1966); and S.R. Brody, *supra* note 2.

16. American Friends Service Committee, *supra* note 2. *Who* attacked rehabilitation was as important as what was said, for it was the Quakers who had helped devise the very concept of prison as a rehabilitative tool. See also D.J. Rothman, *The Discovery of the Asylum,: Social Order and Disorder in the New Republic* (Boston: Little, Brown, 1971); and M. Zalman, *supra* note 5.

17. *Supra,* note 2.

18. Frankel, *supra* note 2.

19. See, for example, "President's Message to Congress on Crime," 17 *Criminal Law Reporter* 3089 (June 25, 1975). Perhaps the most famous mandatory sentencing laws of this period were the "Rockefeller drug laws" (recently repealed) and the "Massachusetts gun law."

20. Quoted in National Probation and Parole Association, *Guides for Sentencing* (New York: Carnegie Press, 1957) at 4.

21. See particularly the hidden disparity involved in the "false positive" problem, *infra* Chapter 9 at note 42.

22. See D. Fogel, *supra* note 2; and P.D. McAnany, F.S. Merritt and E. Tromanhauser, "Illinois Reconsiders 'Flat-Time': An Analysis of the Impact of the Justice Model," 52 *Chicago-Kent Law Review* 621 (1976).

23. Twentieth Century Fund, *supra* note 2.

24. See J. M. Kress, L. T. Wilkins and D. M. Gottfredson, "Is the End of Judicial Sentencing in Sight?" 60 *Judicature* 216 (December 1976).

25. See the views to this effect by Senator Kennedy, *supra* note 2 at 213.

26. "This book holds that sentencing functions best when the judge demonstrates an understanding of *individualized treatment,* which must take into account the offender's needs." National Probation and Parole Association, *supra* note 20 (emphasis in original). The aim is clearly to *avoid* the Mikado's goal:

> My object all sublime
> I shall achieve in time—
> To let the punishment fit the crime,
> The punishment fit the crime.

W.S. Gilbert and A.S. Sullivan, *The Mikado,* Act I, Mikado's song.

27. "The rule of law also implies the precept that similar cases be treated similarly. Men could not regulate their actions by means of rules if this precept were not followed." J. Rawls, *A Theory of Justice* 237 (Cambridge, Mass.: Harvard University Press, 1971); see also the discussion, *infra* Chapter 3. J. J. Kilpatrick, "Study Fixes Guidelines Equal Justice" (syndicated column), *Washington Star,* February 12, 1977:

"The guidelines will not produce absolute uniformity. Such uniformity is neither achievable nor desirable. Too many human variations enter in. But the guidelines will provide a useful tool for the conscientious judge who strives for justice at once individualized and equal."

28. C. E. Silberman, *Criminal Violence, Criminal Justice* (New York: Random House, 1978) at 255.

29. See L. T. Wilkins, J. M. Kress, D. M. Gottfredson, J. C. Calpin, and A. M. Gelman, *Sentencing Guidelines: Structuring Judicial Discretion—Report on the Feasibility Study* (Washington, D.C.: USGPO, 1978); and especially, A. M. Gelman, J. M. Kress, and J. C. Calpin, *Establishing a Sentencing Guidelines System: A Methods Manual* (Washington, D.C.: University Research Corporation, 1978). See also J. C. Calpin, J. M. Kress, and A. M. Gelman, *The Analytical Basis for the Formulation of Sentencing Policy* (Washington, D.C.: USGPO, 1980).

30. See the discussion and sources cited *infra* Chapter 3, particularly at note 13.

31. See the references *supra* note 2, especially the works by American Friends Service Committee; Morris; Fogel; van den Haag; Twentieth Century Fund Task Force; von Hirsch; O'Donnell, Churgin, and Curtis; and G. R. Newman.

32. See S. 1437, *The Federal Criminal Code Reform Act of 1978,* 95th Cong., 2d sess. (1978); and *Reform of the Federal Criminal Laws, Hearings on S. 1437 Before the Subcommittee on Criminal Laws and Procedure of the Committee on the Judiciary,* United States Senate, 91st Cong.–95th Cong. (Parts I–XIII) (1971–1978).

33. See *infra* Chapter 4; see also National Conference of Commissioners on Uniform State Laws, *Uniform Corrections Act* 3–112 (1978 draft), which recommends a sentencing commission using the judicial sentencing guidelines approach for every state. See also the two actual presently existing examples in Minnesota (1978 Minn. Laws ch. 723) and Pennsylvania (Pa. Act 319, Nov. 1978); and R. G. Strand, "Sentencing Disparity: How One Jurisdiction Reduced It," 17 *The Judges' Journal* 33 (Spring 1978).

34. Advisory Council on the Penal System, *Sentences of Imprisonment–A Review of Maximum Penalties* (London: HMSO, 1978).

35. As one federal court said, in supporting the use, by the United States Board of Parole, of its analogous guidelines system: "It should be emphasized that these guidelines were promulgated as just that—merely *guidelines*—and that the Board is free to render a decision either above or below the guideline range where in the opinion of the Board circumstances warrant." Wiley v. United States Board of Parole, 380 F. Supp. 1194, 1197 (M.D. Pa. 1974). In practice, I expect reasoned deviation from the guideline sentence in approximately 15–25% of cases coming before individual sentencing judges.

36. *Infra* Chapter 2.

37. The "creators" referred to are Leslie T. Wilkins and Don M. Gottfredson. The application was to the Law Enforcement Assistance Administration. The initial research was co-directed by this author,

together with Professor Wilkins and Dean Gottfredson; the project that actually developed operational sentencing guidelines systems was, however, directed by this author alone. See the references cited *supra* note 29.

38. This understanding indeed provides one of the reasons why I favor abolishing parole release decisionmaking as a function separate and apart from sentencing. See *infra* Chapter 9. With regard to the real importance of this length of time disparity, however, see Fogel, *supra* note 2; R. B. McKay, "It's Time to Rehabilitate the Sentencing Process," 60 *Judicature* 223 (December 1976); President's Commission on Law Enforcement and Administration of Justice, *Task Force Report: The Courts* 14–26 (Washington, D.C.: U.S.G.P.O., 1967); and New York State Special Commission on Attica, *Attica: The Official Report of the New York State Special Commission on Attica* (New York: Bantam, 1972). See especially the conclusion of the Executive Advisory Committee on Sentencing, *supra* note 2: "As a result, disparity has been seen to cause prison unrest and further embitter inmates" (at 57, n. 3).

39. A. M. Critelli, *Preface* to Wilkins, et al., *supra* note 29 at xi (emphasis in original).

40. This is thus fully in line with all recent standards and suggestions for increased judicial education. See, for example, S. B. Nedilley, "How Can a New Judge Know What to Do?" 18 *The Judges' Journal* 34 (Summer 1979); American Bar Association Commission on Standards of Judicial Administration, *Standards Relating to Court Organization,* Standard 1.25 (New York: ABA, 1973); W. E. Burger, "School for Judges," 33 F.R.D. 139 (1969); E. O'Connell, "Continuing Legal Education for the Judiciary," 16 *Journal of Legal Education* 405 (1964). I and my staff have, moreover, practiced what we preached by participating in a host of statewide sentencing institutes, as well as the programs of both the National Judicial College and the American Academy of Judicial Education.

41. Nedilsky, *supra* note 40 at 37.

42. S. Z. Goodfarb in a speech to a Minnesota Sentencing Institute held in Minneapolis on May 18, 1978.

43. "Traditionally, the presentence report contained a great deal of information on the defendant's personal and family background. For example, in Administrative Office of the United States Courts, *The Presentence Investigation Report* No. 103 (1965), a standard work on the presentence report, the following categories are suggested in addition to the circumstances of the offense, the defendant's version of the offense, and his prior criminal and juvenile record: family history, marital history, home and neighborhood, education, religion, interests and leisure time activities, health, employment, military

service and financial condition. *Id* at 7–20. In recent years the need for such detailed "social history" information has been reevaluated in view of the heavy caseloads of probation officers, the time consumed in investigating and writing reports and the suspicion that judges and correctional decisionmakers do not read or pay attention to such data. In 1974, therefore, the Administrative Office recommended a shorter format for reports in routine cases. Administrative Office of the United States Courts, *The Selective Presentence Investigation Report* No. 104 (1974). Finally, in 1978, the Administrative Office formulated a "core concept" notion, that varied the amount of information presented with the needs of particular consumers of the report. Administrative Office of the United States Courts, *The Presentence Investigative Report* No. 105 (1978). This tendency toward shorter presentence reports marks the decline of the theory that the sentencing judge can never be provided with too much information." R.O. Dawson, "Sentencing Reform: The Current Round," 88 *Yale Law Journal*, 440, 445, n. 10 (December 1978).

44. See particularly, L. T. Wilkins, "Information Overload: War or Peace with the Computer" (Davis, Calif.: National Council on Crime and Delinquency, 1973); and the discussion *infra* Chapter 8.

45. M. E. Frankel, *supra* note 2 at 8. See also the judgment of Chief Justice Burger and the discussion *infra* Chapter 3.

46. J. Q. Wilson, *supra* note 3 at 17. See also W. Gaylin, *Partial Justice: A Study of Bias in Sentencing* (New York: A. Knopf, 1974). This general consensus is not a *universal* one, however. See C. E. Silberman, *National Law Journal*, February 12, 1979, at 19: "[I]t is *not* true that disparate sentencing practices undermine the deterrent power of the criminal law. The reason, quite simply, is that there is considerably less disparity than critics . . . have assumed" (emphasis in original).

The Problem of Discretion

Discretion in sentencing has been a double-edged sword. It permits the judge to accommodate unusual circumstances relative to each defendant. But this sometimes results in the defendants who ought to be similarly treated receiving substantially disparate sentences.[1]—Warren E. Burger

In order to comprehend properly the significance of the research outlined in later chapters, the reader should first be introduced to the theoretical underpinnings of the sentencing guidelines concept. The national research project was itself subtitled "Structuring Judicial Discretion," and this had been in conscious acknowledgement of the work of Kenneth Culp Davis, whose seminal book, *Discretionary Justice,* provided a number of insights concerning the existence and utility of discretion in the criminal justice system.[2] In this chapter, sentencing guidelines will be discussed in the context of this discretionary focus; initially, the need for discretion in the system will be described, then its uses, and finally, the control of its abuses.

ACKNOWLEDGING THE NEED FOR DISCRETION

"Discretion," it should first be noted, is a word that requires precise definition. I do not mean it to be synonymous with "corruption," which can take place no matter how structured or relatively "perfect" a system comprised of imperfect human beings may be; for corrupt activities, judges may, of course, be prosecuted. Nor do I mean it to apply to errors of judgment that may be involved in the assessment of relatively subjective matters of concern; such errors will again occur in any system run by human beings. For present purposes, it is useful to recall Professor Davis's own definition: "A public officer has discretion whenever the effective limits on his power leave him free to make a choice among possible courses of action or inaction."[3] This discretionary authority either to act, not to act, or to choose among alternatives is a necessary concomitant of decisionmaking power, and it is possessed in some degree by all actors in the criminal justice system. There is a view that strict rules can totally abolish discretion; New York State's respected former Chief Judge, Charles D. Breitel, has spoken of the naïveté of that position:

> If every policeman, every prosecutor, every court, and every post-sentence agency performed his or its responsibility in strict accordance with rules of law, precisely and narrowly laid down, the criminal law would be ordered but intolerable. Living would be a sterile compliance with soul-killing rules and taboos. By comparison, a primitive tribal society would seem free, indeed.[4]

For these reasons, the exercise of some discretion is both necessary and desirable in all criminal justice functions, but particularly at the stage of sentencing. Discretion is, indeed, pervasively exercised throughout the criminal justice system. From the outset, crime victims may exercise their discretion not to report crimes, thus enhancing the "dark" figure of unknown crime.[5] Police discretionarily decide what complaints to follow up, with what resources and with what diligence. The means employed for investigation—wiretaps, searches, surveillance, undercover operatives, uniformed squads and so on—are all relatively free choices of law enforcement officials.[6] The prosecutor has great latitude in preferring initial charges and in later reducing them through plea negotiations.[7] A magistrate is usually free to set bail in varying amounts; also, pretrial hearings may be conducted with judges affording defendants varying degrees of discovery.[8] Yet, it is at sentencing that the awesome discretionary power of the state over the individual is most evident: in many states, a judge is free to levy sentences ranging from imprisonment for decades down to a term of minimally supervised probation for almost all serious crimes.

From the beginning, the sentencing guidelines research team assumed not only the existence of sentencing discretion and variation, but also its desirability to meet one of the two primary sentencing goals, that of individualized justice.[9] We therefore found ourselves set in opposition to legislatively mandated sentences as being unrealistically rigid and mechanical, unworkable in practice, and philosophically objectionable. This had been the view, indeed, of the late nineteenth and early twentieth century reformers who repealed the mandatory sentencing laws of that period and ushered in the era of indeterminate sentencing that exists in most states today. The early 1900s, for example, had seen a series of prison riots across America. Many viewed the long, fixed sentences meted out then as a contributing factor; it was said that they left prisoners without hope. Thus, "hope" was instilled through the medium of the indeterminate sentence, which made early release a possibility.[10] These early reformers accurately recognized the need for discretion—but they were unconscionably excessive in their grant.

They gave vast amounts of discretionary power to judges and parole boards. Indeterminate sentencing was said to offer "the best of both worlds—long protection for the public yet a fully flexible opportunity for the convict's rehabilitation."[11] The judge could render a probationary sentence when the "expert" presentence investigation report showed that to be in the best interests of both the defendant and the public. The indeterminacy of any prison sentence handed down would leave the eventual release of the imprisoned defendant to other "experts"—correctional and paroling authorities who could diagnose the offender's problems, treat them, and best decide when (and under what circumstances) the offender should be released. The 1931 Wickersham Commission expressed the "medical model" then current:

> Physicians, upon discovering disease, cannot name the day upon which the patient will be healed. No more can judges intelligently set the day of release from prison at the time of trial. Boards of parole [on the other hand] can study the prisoner during his confinement . . . . Within their discretion they can grant a comparatively early release to youths, to first offenders, to particularly worthy cases who give high promise of leading a new life . . . and keep vicious criminals in confinement as long as the law allows.[12]

We must recognize, however, the flaws with the indeterminate sentencing movement, the tremendous quantities of unreviewable discretion now existing, and the problems this has wrought. The offender orientation of indeterminacy has simply gone too far in ignoring the facts of the crime. Moreover, the very hope of the indeterminate sentence has now been recognized as perpetuating a cruel uncertainty; there is a real psychological and material unfairness to prisoners who have no idea of their release dates, which dates seem often determined by a chance lottery.[13] This Kafkaesque situation has, moreover, undoubtedly contributed to many recent prison revolts.[14] Nevertheless, we must avoid the tendency to overreact and to throw out the proverbial baby with the bathwater: the solution to the prison riots of the 1970s is not to reintroduce the cause of the prison riots of the early 1900s.[15] We must avoid the extremes of either system and seek to integrate the valuable components of each.

STRUCTURING THE USE OF DISCRETION

Justice and Sentencing

While clearly recognizing the necessity for discretion, Professor Davis was concerned with controlling the potential abuses of unfettered discretionary power, and in aiding the informed use of discretion. These purposes are achieved primarily through the evolution of channeling, guidance, and performance devices. In the realm of judicial sentencing, sentencing guidelines may therefore be thought of as a means to structure judicial discretion so as to aid it in the performance of its proper functions while simultaneously serving as a check to control its abusive potential. I wrote earlier of the necessary balance, or synthesis, required between "individualized" justice and "equal" justice.[16] It is for this reason that I have so strongly opposed the extremes of both totally indeterminate and totally determinate sentencing. The development and application of sentencing guidelines systems is completely compatible with the channeling of discretion so as to assure a useful consistency in overall policy without simultaneously upsetting the necessary inconsistency that is inherent in the humanized treatment of individual cases.

Sentencing Agents

To place the uses of sentencing discretion in context, however, it will prove worthwhile to ascertain the locus of sentencing authority. Nowhere in America today is the judge the sole determinant of sanction; rather there is an unarticulated sharing of the sentencing function. Everywhere in America practices vary tremendously, so that generalization is extremely difficult. Nevertheless, we may profitably examine one at a time those who share responsibility with the judge. Let us consider the "alternatives" to judicial sentencing.

Juries The Supreme Court has much changed the practice of lay jury imposition of the death penalty in capital cases, but still permits it.[17] Moreover, a number of states today provide for jury sentencing in non-capital cases: primary sentencing authority for all serious crimes rests with the lay jury in eight of these states; four states restrict the jury's sentencing powers only to certain offenses; and Texas follows the unique procedure of offering the choice of judge or jury sentencing to most offenders.[18] The principal argument in favor of jury sentencing is one of introducing citizen input into an otherwise bureaucratic and overly professionalized system that insufficiently accounts for community standards and mores. Thus, the argument may be phrased in terms of either desirable jury leniency (as with, perhaps, a marijuana possession case where a younger jury might impose a sentence lower than that expected from a sitting judge) or severity (as with, for example, a child molestation case where, in certain communities, the reverse might arguably be true).

This reasoning is interesting but ultimately unconvincing. The National Advisory Commission on Criminal Justice Standards and Goals urged the abolition of jury sentencing as "non-professional and ... more likely than judge sentencing to be arbitrary and based on emotions rather than the needs of the offender or society."[19] Unguided lay jurors simply cannot reach equitable decisions when they have no baseline information to compare with the individual case before them. Furthermore, even the strongest advocates of offense-oriented "just deserts" sentencing would still wish to take the defendant's prior criminal record into account at sentencing,[20] and that information is, of course, not trial-admissible; thus, more informed jury sentencing might necessitate an extremely time-consuming, bifurcated procedure as well.[21] This process is patently costly and readily circumvented through plea bargaining practices.

Finally, jury sentencing will wreak havoc with any attempt to establish an overall, consistent sentencing policy. The concurring words of Supreme Court Justice Byron White, in declaring capital punishment to be cruel and unusual, in *Furman* v. *Georgia,* are apposite here:

> In this respect, I add only that past and present legislative judgment with respect to the death penalty loses much of its force when viewed in light of the recurring practice of delegating sentencing authority to the jury and the fact that a jury, in its own discretion and without violating its trust or any statutory policy, may refuse to impose the death penalty no matter what the circumstances of the crime. Legislative "policy" is thus necessarily defined not by what is legislatively authorized but by what juries and judges do in exercising the discretion so regularly conferred upon them. In my judgment what was done in these cases violated the Eighth Amendment.[22]

Sentencing Councils or Panels. These innovations involve either (in theory) a complete sharing of the sentencing decision between three judges or (as actually practiced) the placing of two of those judges in the position of advisors or consultants to the third judge, who still retains individual responsibility for the sentencing decision. It is seen as a means of reducing sentencing disparities between judges of the same court.

Sentencing panels have not been much commented upon in practice, although earlier, favorable reviews have been supplemented with more critical studies suggesting a second, closer, look at this "reform."[23] Moreover, it should be obvious that in a time of serious economic concern, one of the lowest priorities that any budgeting authority will have is using three judges to carry out the duties that only one judge is now discharging. Nevertheless, we need not be opposed to all uses of panels, only to their indiscriminate use for all cases. Indeed, once the more routine cases have been disposed of by means of the sentencing guidelines here advocated, then panels might well be employed to deal with that minority of cases that remain outside of the suggested sentencing guidelines ranges.

Probation Officers. There is no state that places the probation officer in a position of legal responsibility for sentencing, but it would be naïve not to acknowledge the power of the office. The probation officer (or a social worker of similar function attached to the trial court) usually prepares a postconviction presentence investigative report on each offender brought before the sentencing judge. Not only can the content, and even the phrasing, of this report be very persuasive, but many judges ask their probation officers to make specific recommendations, which these judges often follow.[24]

Prosecutors. As is the case with probation officers, no prosecutor in the United States is statutorily given any sentencing power. However, the prevalence of plea bargaining in this country—upwards of 90 percent in many jurisdictions—confers such practical powers upon many district attorneys. This is particularly true in those jurisdictions where negotiations involve specific sentence promises as opposed to discussions concerning only multiple counts or lesser charges—that is, sentence bargaining as opposed to merely charge bargaining.[25]

The extralegal sentencing authority of both the probation officer and the prosecutor may be dealt with summarily. The most basic administrative rule must be that responsibility and accountability go together as taxation with representation; no controls on potential abuses of discretionary power are at all possible when the powers are unauthorized in the first place.[26] This is not necessarily a critique either of probation office reports or of plea bargaining, but rather a suggestion as to their appropriate limits.[27]

The Parole Board. The heyday of parole has come and gone, but some years ago, the completely indeterminate sentence was a popular reform proposal.[28] Under such a system, neither the legislature nor the judge set the amount of time a convicted criminal actually served. That decision instead rested with the state parole board. The argument was that of the medical analogy: sentencing decisions were best left to correctional and/or paroling authorities who could carefully diagnose and treat the offender's needs and, therefore, best decide when and under what conditions the offender could or should be released from custody. Except for California and Washington, the states shied away from a totally indeterminate sentencing system. One major exception, however, has been for a few specially designated offenders, whose terms of custody—if they are diagnosed as "sex deviants," "psychopaths," or in some states, "narcotic addicts"—have rested largely within the discretion of state correctional authorities.[29]

Almost no one today makes the case for a totally indeterminate sentence. The California Adult Authority, for example, reversed itself even before the recent California sentencing revisions came into effect and made it official policy to announce firm inmate release dates within a short time after initial incarceration. Both prisoners' rights groups and law and order advocates have denounced the concept, the former contending that the indeterminate sentence was wholly unfair to the defendant in both a material and a psychological sense and the latter arguing that such an offender-oriented system ignored the cruel facts of the actual crime committed by the offender. Additionally—and probably more importantly—our faith in criminal justice system "expertise" has been badly shaken by years of abuse and failure.[30] Moreover, one now listens to a veritable chorus of voices attacking the very philosophy of rehabilitation that underlies the indeterminate sentence; not the softest voice in this chorus is heard in the revised California sentencing code, which went into effect on July 1, 1977, and which pronounces the death of the rehabilitative ideal: "The Legislature finds and declares that the purpose of imprisonment for crime is punishment."[31] Period.

The Legislature. This is the final—and clearly the most important—presently existing "alternative" agency: it obviously has immense significance in several respects and performs its "sentencing" tasks in coordination (one hopes) with the judiciary. The various calls heard today (for mandatory minimum, flat time, or presumptive sentencing) are really calls for legislative dominance over—or perhaps substitution for—the judiciary with regard to the sentencing decision. Mandatory sentencing takes many forms, reserving lesser or greater degrees of discretion to the various nonlegislative criminal justice agencies. Some suggested penal codes stipulate minimum (and sometimes maximum) sentences that must be imposed upon conviction of certain offenses, thus curbing the discretion of both the sentencing judge and the paroling authority. Some codes declare certain offenses to be nonprobational, thus forcing a period of incarceration, but leaving the judge to set its length. Still others curb only sentence length, by allowing the judge the choice of sentencing the offender to either probation or incarceration, but statutorily fixing the length of whichever is chosen.[32]

Politically, many claims are made for such statutorily prescribed sentences. They are urged as a means of controlling the discretion of overly lenient or overly harsh (the epithet usually depending upon one's own biases) trial court judges. Proponents decry judicial sentencing disparity and contend that only a system of punishment exclusively commensurate with perceived offense seriousness can provide equality and evenhandedness of treatment. They argue that equality is impossible to achieve when one pursues individualization—that noble attempt to tailor fit the sentence to the personal and social characteristics of the particular offender.

Confessedly, the concept of a legislatively fixed sentence almost seems natural in a society where our knee-jerk response to a problem appears to be "there oughta be a law." Furthermore, mandatory sentencing is a very difficult concept to attack—but only because it seems to mean so many different things to so many different people and because, upon close examination, some proposals are not really mandatory after all![33]

The sentencing guidelines system does not prohibit legislatures from prescribing the range of permissible judicial sentencing—that is, the outer limits (or bounds) of probation or maximum terms of imprisonment. Opposition is here expressed only to those provisions that deny the trial judge an essential flexibility in accommodating to the realities of the case before the bench—that is, those wherein terms of probation and/or incarceration are precisely fixed by statutory law with regard to the offense of conviction only. Such a system is unrealistic, impractical, and philosophically undesirable as it is too far removed from the person who is being sentenced.

The primary problem with legislatively fixed sentences is that they are pre-fixed. There is a priori establishment of the "right" sentence with little or no empirical research to support any sentence set forth. Years before the crime in question occurs, the legislature sets the precise duration of imprisonment for a general class of crime with virtually no consideration given to either extenuating or exacerbating factors surrounding the specific case that will actually come before the judge. In fact, if the legislature makes its decision only on the basis of theoretical argument and the skimpy factual information it now possesses, it will inevitably draw unrealistic conclusions that will ensure the wholesale discretionary avoidance of the legislative mandate by police, prosecutors, and judges which has rendered so many prior reform efforts nugatory.[34]

Instead, primary sentencing responsibility must continue to reside with the trial judge, who is more than an automaton, and reform should be based upon a careful review of actual sentencing practices. This explains both the research methods of sentencing guidelines analysis and why I and my colleagues have worked cooperatively to aid local trial court sentencing judges.

CONTROLLING THE ABUSE OF DISCRETION

Articulation of Policy: Reasons and Reform

One reason for the growth of the above discussed alternatives to judicial sentencing has been a general perception, often accurate, of the flaws in the present methodology employed by judges in reaching their conclusions as to the appropriate sentence to place upon a given offender. Harshness, leniency, disparity, inequity, inappropriateness, inhumanity, and so forth have all been epithets applied at various times to present sentencing practices.[35] There can be little dispute, at the present time, with Judge Frankel's contention that the result "is a wild array of sentencing judgments"[36] or with Chief Justice Warren Burger's assessment that some defendants do receive "substantially disparate sentencing."[37]

The cause of this disparity, however, cannot be said to be conscious judicial malevolence. It seems clear that the judiciary is entitled to a presumption of innocence. It is logical to infer, and it would be fair of us to assume, that sentencing disparities are not due to design on the part of judges, but rather to their inability to see the full picture. In responding to the critics of judicial sentencing disparities, Iowa District Court Judge Anthony M. Critelli conceded:

> Some of the criticism may be correct for sometimes the criminal behavior and the criminal's background may be sufficiently similar to warrant similar treatment. But no judge at present can rightly be blamed for treating these similarly situated individuals differently for there is no way today for either of us to know what the other is doing. We *are* sentencing differently, not out of malice, but out of sheer *ignorance,* or to put it another way, without guidelines—without the tool that tells each of us what the other is doing.[38]

Now that sentencing guidelines can provide the courts with a tool to curb disparity from within, judges should be offered this opportunity for self-improvement before legislators attempt to impose mandatory solutions upon an independent branch of government.

Recognition of the evidence regarding disparity does not require acceptance of the facile view that all variation is "disparity." There is scope for legitimate and necessary moral variations in sentencing practice. The goal is individual propriety as well as overall equity in sentencing practices. The use of discretion is a necessary means to achieving these ends. Its uses must be assisted while its abuses are retarded; this has been the aim of sentencing guidelines. Informed analysis, however, has generally floundered in the past because of the overambition of would-be reformers. So much has seemed wrong that too much has usually been attempted too soon, thus aggravating rather than alleviating the problem. Moreover, there has been a confusion of terminology, with value-loaded words and phrases being bandied about as if they possessed statistical objectivity; equity, fairness, and propriety are simply not terms that should be employed interchangeably in this area. The solution is not to eradicate judicial sentencing, but rather to restructure it so as to control potential discretionary abuses and provide articulated guidelines as to the judicial reasoning employed in a given case.

The very first step in the elimination of discretionary abuses is the frank recognition of their existence both on a field and on a "command" level.[39] Professor Davis then recommends creating structuring devices by openly articulating policy guidelines and by establishing defined review mechanisms for both individual and policy decisions. Sentencing guidelines research has tried to recognize this distinction between case-by-case and policy decisions and has also tried to establish a veritable network of review procedures. Understanding this network involves first understanding the difference between a singular sentencing guideline and the entire sentencing guidelines *system*; there are some who have assumed that the latter is merely a collection of the former. This is not so; it is much more.

The individual guideline sentence is the culmination in many ways of a methodological approach that incorporates offense and offender factors and their weights.[40] It is that one additional information item provided to sentencing judges that tells them what their colleagues would likely do in a similar case and that sets the benchmark for their own sentencing. Nevertheless, to see it as the totality of the system would be simply to see guidelines as a statistical glorification of the status quo. The sentencing guidelines system is, instead, a fluid, dynamic, and synergistic response to the problems of sentencing.

One, but only one, aspect of the individual guideline sentence is that it is that open articulation of policy—individualized to each particular case as required—that Professor Davis sees as an essential discretionary control. It is also the beginning of a guidelines review network upon which I should now elaborate.

Review and Regeneration Mechanisms

The Sentencing Judge. Rather than see the individual sentencing guideline as an end product, it will be helpful in this section to treat it as a starting point. In each jurisdiction in which we have worked, judges receive the guideline sentence at some point in advance of the formal imposition of sentence. The most common method of receipt is attachment to the front of the presentence investigation report, when that is prepared, so that the guideline sentence effectively becomes one more information item in that report.

At this point, the use to which the information will be put is entirely up to the judge. While I here state my own preferences, I do not share the ultimate responsibility of sentencing human beings, and hence I could never (even had I wished to do so) force my wishes upon the judiciary. Theoretically, judges may completely ignore guideline sentence recommendations or assiduously follow them; the only formal requirement in a guidelines jurisdiction has been that, when and if the actual sentence differs from the guideline sentence, the judge must offer a specific, written reason for that difference. We have previously employed the phrase "going outside the guidelines" to explain this process. However, as is made clear later in this chapter, sentences both "inside" and "outside" the suggested guideline sentence range are still a part of—or "inside"—the sentencing guidelines *system*.

In actual practice, judges make different uses of the guidelines. One judge, for example, told me that he makes a tentative sentencing decision and then looks at the guideline sentence. When the two coincide, he says that he feels more secure in the appropriateness of his decision; when they differ, however, he reconsiders his tentative decision. In this way, he says, the guideline provides "a check to my conscience," forcing him to give the case a "hard second look" so as to ensure that no unconscious bias or emotion led him to the tentative decision.[41] In that small percentage of cases where the two still differ, he states that the exercise of forcing him to articulate his reasons in writing has proved very helpful to him personally.

While other judges tend to agree with him as to the written reasons requirement, most incorporate the guideline sentence, together with the other material in the presentence investigative report, rather than make a tentative sentencing decision first. Most judges use the guideline sentence—and the items of information that go along with it—as a sort of benchmark, or check, against which to measure the sentence that the judge expects to impose. If that sentence is within the range provided for by the guidelines, judges do not generally state any reasons for imposing the particular sanction, since the guidelines themselves (i.e., the information decision base that makes up the guidelines) provide the reasons. Many judges have, moreover, indicated to me that they too feel more confident—and frankly more morally comfortable—in handing down that specific sentence. I should emphasize here that the guidelines do not suggest an exact sentence, but instead offer a small range so that the judge may distinguish between offenses and/or offenders that are grouped into somewhat broad categories. For example, the guidelines may consider only the offender's total number of prior felony convictions, but by providing a range, the guidelines permit the judge more heavily to weigh past robbery convictions than those for grand larceny, without having to go "outside" the guidelines.

If, however, the judge wishes to impose a sentence outside the guidelines, then the judge of course has absolute freedom to do so. Nevertheless, written reasons must be given for such a departure. This much, at least, is due the defendant, society, and the judge's colleagues. It is imperative that the reasons not simply be an expression of something already contained in the guidelines or some phrase made meaningless through rote repetition (which I believe would occur frequently were written reasons required for *all* sentences), but that they instead be a thoughtful and "reasoned" justification as to why the guideline sentence is inappropriate for the case at hand. A judge may still refer to an item in the guidelines, but rather than merely state the obvious—that the particular item was considered—the judge should explain why a different weighting was given to the item.

Some judges I have met oppose the giving of reasons at sentence. They argue the ineffable nature of the sentencing decision and want instead to employ their own "sense" of what is right, a sense that cannot be put into words. I understand their position; as a prosecutor, I too objected to giving reasons for accepting pleas, beyond my own gut sense of doing the right thing. Over time, however, I have become convinced that we must declare this "sense" to be nonsense. If the courts of this nation can and do force high-school-educated police officers clearly and specifically to articulate their reasons for making the split-second decision to stop a car, search a suspect, and/or question a witness, then it seems the grossest of law enforcement double standards not to require law-trained jurists, under relatively little or no time pressure, to articulate their reasons for making decisions that will have at least as great an impact on the lives of criminal defendants.[42]

To the individual judge, the articulation of these reasons is useful as a personal thought- and decision-structuring tool. It will act as a spur to thoughtful reasoning with regard to this very important decision. For similar reasons, and entirely apart from the other review considerations to be discussed shortly, many states have begun to require such statements by sentencing judges.

For example, the Pennsylvania Supreme Court, on August 17, 1977, dramatically reversed past practice and mandated judicial explanations on the record for all sentences, declaring that "reasoned sentencing decisions may encourage the development of sentencing criteria and reduce disparities in sentences—decreasing the number of unusually lenient as well as unusually harsh sentences."[43] In testimony before the Pennsylvania House of Representatives only a month later, the Honorable David N. Savitt, Philadelphia Court of Common Pleas Court Administrator, urged the adoption of sentencing guidelines on a statewide basis as a continuation of the reform suggested by that Pennsylvania Supreme Court opinion. Indeed, in order to decrease the burden upon appellate courts, he urged "that the trial court not be required to explain the particular reasons behind every sentence. Failure to explain a sentence should be grounds for remand only when the sentence imposed falls outside of the established guidelines."[44] As he noted, this is because the sentencing guidelines system itself supplies the reasons underlying most sentencing decisions.

Sentencing Panels. The use of panels for every case would (as would a universal use of written reasons for sentencing) trivialize a procedure that, if used properly, could be a helpful tool to aid the judge in reaching sentencing decisions.[45] A better procedure would be to use panels in conjunction with guidelines. The panel would operate in a strictly advisory capacity to the judge who wished to impose a sentence outside the guidelines. No sentencing guidelines jurisdiction has adopted this procedure, and this notion is therefore offered only as a speculative possibility. (Such a panel might perhaps be employed as an intermediate level appellate review body.) This procedure could act as a protection against the potential abuse of a guidelines system, and it would only be employed for those cases in which the judge wished to depart from the guidelines. The final decision, as always, would rest with the original judge; but in that small percentage of out of the ordinary and more difficult cases, the opinions of one's judicial colleagues would likely be welcomed.[46] In any event, this is an idea that should be explored by jurisdictions considering the future implementation of sentencing guidelines systems.

Peer Review. Another review mechanism designed to combat potential abuses, as well as the sloth that the use of any device even partly based on past practice can engender, is a regular collegial review process. This mechanism is not speculative and has been adopted in every guidelines jurisdiction; it establishes a cybernetic feedback system that is vital to systemic adaptability and flexibility as well as being a safeguard against systemic stagnation. In a fully operational sentencing guidelines system, every four to six months, all of the judges in the jurisdiction (or a representative group) meet as a collective body and monitor the previous period's use of the guidelines. This peer group commonly reviews the effectiveness of the guidelines in accurately reflecting the overall policy of the court. Decisions that have fallen outside the guidelines are also reviewed in order to see if such departures represent desirable policy revisions that should be reflected in a reconstructed guidelines model or whether they simply represent the presence of extremely unusual circumstances that justified a guideline override. In practice, individual departures from the guidelines recommendations and revised policy directives from the collective body of judges involved have been fed back into the data base used in constructing each jurisdiction's sentencing guidelines system, thereby injecting a continuous element of regeneration and self-improvement into the guidelines.

Sentencing Commission Review. This again is a speculative suggestion, but such a review appears to be an intended feature of those sentencing commissions which have been proposed.[47] The commission would act much as would the panel and peer review processes just discussed. However, in addition to reviewing those decisions falling outside the guidelines, the commission would also continually reevaluate the guidelines themselves, ensuring that they comported with evolving sentencing policy in the state. Commissions would also serve other desirable research functions for the courts—for example, the collection, analysis, and dissemination of data concerning the deterrent effectiveness of various sentencing alternatives.

Appellate Review: The Evolution of a Common Law of Sentencing. The articulated reasons required for departure from the suggested guideline sentences are not only intrinsically and intuitively valuable, they also provide the focal point for a major legal protection against abuse of the system—appellate review. At present, meaningful appellate review of criminal sentences is almost nonexistent in America.[48] In those rare instances where it does occur, cases are decided individually, generalized reasons for review are not supplied, and no precedent is established.

Judge Frankel finds this situation "horrendous": "Consider that a civil judgment for $2,000 is reviewable in every state at least once, possibly on two appellate levels. Then consider the unreviewability of a sentence of twenty years in prison and a fine of $10,000."[49] In reference to the unreviewability of a trial judge's sentencing discretion, even the American Bar Association has noted "that in no other area of our law does one man exercise such unrestricted power. No other country in the free world permits this condition to exist."[50]

Indeed, England, Australia, and other common law countries with whom we share our legal heritage have a long history of appellate review of sentences.[51] This means of curbing sentencing disparity may be referred to as the evolution of a common law of sentencing— that is, a system that structures judicial discretion by a set of principles, evolved through the case law of the appellate courts over a period of time, that provides guidance to lower court judges, yet leaves them sufficient scope for judgment in individual cases.[52]

Cambridge University Lecturer in Criminology David A. Thomas sees three major reasons for the failure of appellate review to affect sentencing procedures in America as it has in England. "The first is the indeterminacy of so many sentences";[53] this is because the effective length of time decision lies with the parole board.[54] Thomas notes the pervasiveness of plea bargaining in America as a second reason; the appellate review that does take place can, after all, only affect the relatively small proportion of contested cases.[55] The third reason is the historical reluctance of the appellate courts to assume the task:

> The American judiciary, which has identified questions of law in many areas which in other jurisdictions are considered beyond the reach of litigation, has shown an amazing reluctance to apply to its own exercise of power the same scrutiny that it has applied so effectively to the exercise of power by other branches of government.[56]

While I eagerly anticipate appellate review of sentencing guidelines,[57] I must point out that in its present state, appellate review is unlikely to result in more than a decision to approve sentencing guidelines in principle, whereas I look forward here to its use in the development of specifically approved criteria for sentencing. One aspect of appellate review that has been overlooked in most of the literature on the subject is the uneven nature of review. Not only are appeals taken without regard for their precedential value, but they are one sided. If a common law of sentencing is to develop rationally, and if appellate review is to be applied impartially, then review should be equally available to both defense and prosecution, and sentences must be subject to being increased as well as decreased by the higher court. That, of course, is not presently the case, although it was one of the controversial reforms initially proposed in S. 1437.[58]

Moreover, appellate review, without an attached and explicit statement of court policy, is likely merely to substitute the judgment of an appellate court as to the "correct" sentence in a given case for that of the lower court. While the presence of accompanying opinions would indeed aid in the evolution of a common law of sentencing, these opinions are not always forthcoming, as appellate courts tend to reach decisions on an ad hoc basis without always considering whether or not there should be a considered overreaching policy behind them. There is no reason now to believe that present appellate review is anywhere in America any better than that in Connecticut, where a study of the practice concluded: "The (Sentence Review) Division's failure, in most of its opinions, to articulate (the reason for its decisions) creates a major limitation on its value as a forum for the development of uniform sentencing principles."[59] Additionally, under present conditions, the appellate review process is quite time-consuming, and a common law of sentencing may well take several decades to develop.

It is important to bear in mind that these views expressed concerning the limitations of appellate review of sentencing are not criticisms of appellate review per se, but only of review absent the sort of articulated criteria that sentencing guidelines provide. Under a guidelines system, appellate review can be used far more effectively than ever before in deciding policy issues, a function more in line with that which is its best purpose. First, the guidelines system itself may undergo review,[60] and then each of the factors included as components within each jurisdiction's sentencing guidelines system—as well as their respective weights—may become subject to meaningful review upon appeal. Furthermore, the reasons supplied for going outside of the specified guideline sentence recommendation will furnish a record upon which an appeal may be based, but review will now be based more cogently on the judicially articulated reasons for departure. Therefore, it is in conjunction with guidelines that appellate courts will best be able to perform at their peak by focusing on the salient issues in deciding the propriety of a sentence.

"Outside" Review: Guidelines as Communication. The final measure of review is definitionally beyond my ken. It will be supplied by those commentators in the learned journals, the press, the public, the bar, and elsewhere who see flaws and benefits in a sentencing guidelines system and in its individual components. In the long run, I have no doubt that the single greatest benefit of a sentencing guidelines system will be in the way that it opens up the sentencing function to outside scrutiny and attention. Sentencing has for too long been a closed process; sentencing guidelines will disclose it to a wider audience, permitting far more critical appraisal of it than has hitherto seemed possible. This criticism may rankle at first, but improvements of which the judiciary will be justly proud are bound to result. No agent in the criminal justice system operates in a vacuum, least of all judges, and they will take account of the currents around them and benefit from the insights offered.

While I have just spoken of the potential criticism from others, I should note that the guidelines may in turn be used to communicate concerns to others outside the judiciary. In a very real sense, sentencing judges may use guidelines to communicate, both among themselves and to others. Owing to their tenure, typical judicial selection processes, and the Canons of Judicial Ethics,[61] judges have often failed to make their positions known either to the general public[62] or to other participants in the criminal justice process. A guidelines system is a statement of court policy to the public, the crime victim, the defendant, the police, the defense attorney, and the public prosecutor. This review section has perhaps focused overly much on how others will review the work of the sentencing judges; if only briefly here, let me sketch the means by which sentencing guidelines will enable the judiciary to review the work of others and to communicate with them. Three examples should make the point:

Probation Department Investigators. In most jurisdictions, probation officers prepare the reports upon which sentencing decisions are based. Almost always, there is a cooperative relationship between the investigative probation officer and the judge. Yet neither fully understands the constraints of the other. Too often, for example, judges have criticized probation officers for not giving them "enough" information, when what they really meant was "better" information.[63] The signal advantage of a sentencing guidelines model is that it highlights those variables that are most relevant to local judges and thus, in turn, to probation officers preparing reports for them. In a fully operational guidelines system, judges would insist upon the accuracy and completeness of those variables making up the guidelines. A guidelines system would thus provide judicial direction and focus to the investigative staffs of local probation departments.

For these departments, therefore, guidelines may prove a useful reformist device—suggesting the abolition, for example, of outdated statutes that mandate the collection of useless and time-consuming information in all cases. By applying the decisionmaking analysis offered by a guidelines system, a probation officer may see, for instance, that the local judges are not concerned with the high school record of anyone over thirty, but that they want a fuller assessment of every property offender's prior performance on probation. Eventually, this system would save time and money for probation departments by usefully redirecting the allocation of their scarce resources and suggesting the deletion from reports of items with a record of irrelevance to the sentencing decision.[64]

Corrections. This is meant to include the other side of probation—supervision—in addition to other correctional agents. As statewide and federal sentencing guidelines systems come into operation, it will become more important than it has been for judges to engage in a dialogue (at least through the guidelines device) with correctional system workers. One basic question that must be explored, for example, is how differently the availability of varied correctional facilities and diversionary alternatives affect the sentencing process. One Massachusetts judge who rides circuit throughout the state has stated to me that he would never consider probation in some counties because of the poor quality of their probation services, whereas he would consider it the preferable alternative for almost all crimes in one county where he has a very high regard for the probation facilities. What about the availability of drug rehabilitation program? Work projects? Farm labor alternatives? Half-way houses? Local jail versus state Penitentiary? So far, these questions have not had to be explored at length, owing to the general homogeneity of alternatives within each of the countywide jurisdictions within which empirically informed systems have to date been established. But as statewide sentencing guidelines systems become more commonplace, such regional differences will have to be accommodated.

The Parole Board. I have grown convinced that much of what is labeled "disparity" is the result of imperfect or missing information. A sentencing guidelines system may help to provide a communication bridge over this information gap. I have identified one significant communication failure that necessarily causes disparity, and I further believe that it can be overcome. This failure is a perceptual one and lies at the interface between sentencing judges and paroling authorities and the concept of "real time."

Until recently, neither the judge nor the parole board had more than the vaguest notion of what the other did and certainly not how or why they did it. The parole board member would see a judge's sentence as one small bit of information in a huge file. True, it usually set the outer bounds on a possible release date and, occasionally, even fixed a minimum term before release could be considered. Almost never, however, were reasons for sentencing passed along by the judge.

Judges, however, were even worse off, for they acted first, in almost total ignorance of what the parole board might do. Unfortunately, I say "almost" for it was worse than total ignorance—the judges may have made some tacit assumptions that were downright wrong! They may have heard rumors of paroling policy or generalized inappropriately from one fortuitous instance that came to their attention. The worst example is what Federal District Court Judge Jon O. Newman has aptly called the "Slovik Syndrome":

> On November 11, 1944, a general court-martial of nine members imposed a sentence of death upon Private Eddie Slovik, the only American serviceman executed for desertion since 1864. That fateful judgment was reviewed by numerous levels of military command that were authorized to exercise clemency. None did. Long after Private Slovik's death, the presiding officer of the original court-martial was asked about the sentencing decision. His reply captured a horrifying aspect that pervades sentencing in America: no member of the court-martial believed the sentence would be carried out.[65]

The projective analysis suggested by Judge Newman requires us to ascertain what assumptions about corrections underlie judicial sentencing patterns. Two major assumptions must be tested. The first, as far as I know, has not even been seriously raised before, despite its obvious researchability as a testable assumption: to what conditions does a judge believe he or she is subjecting a sentenced offender? Clearly, this must have some impact on sentencing. At one extreme, Judge X might read glowing accounts of color television, group counseling, and frequent furlough programs. At another extreme, Judge Y might envision a vile, Dantesque pit where homosexual rape is common and where thorazine and electroconvulsive shocks are regularly employed as internal disciplinary devices. Certainly, Judge Y could more readily be expected to administer any prison sentence only most reluctantly as a last resort. Bear in mind that I am not here talking about different philosophies of sentencing, but rather of different mythic *perceptions* of the prison. Notwithstanding its significance, it is the rarest of judges who tests out his or her own mythic perception by even a cursory prison inspection visit.[66]

The second major assumption to be tested, and once again it is verifiable, is the length of actual incarceration envisioned when a judge imposes a sentence. Assume that Judge R believes that parole authorities will release an offender after one-third of the maximum time imposed; further, assume that Judge S (in the same jurisdiction) believes that a similarly situated defendant will be released after one-half of the maximum sentence imposed. If Judge *R* sentences the defendant to fifteen years and Judge *S* sentences the defendant to ten years, there is real disparity, but no conceptual disparity, as both judges intended an effective "real time" sentence of five years in prison. The problem is one simply of lack of communication. The sentencing judge today rarely passes along reasons for a given sentence to a parole board, and the parole agency never submits its policy decisions to even after the fact review by the sentencing judge. The second communications failure (i.e., from paroling agency to judge) is one that a paroling guidelines system seeks to stem;[67] the first communications breakdown (i.e., from judge to parole board) is the one that an operational sentencing guidelines system attempts to alleviate.

STRUCTURING JUDICIAL DISCRETION

In this chapter, I have tried to provide a conceptual framework for the sentencing guidelines approach. This approach recognizes the necessity for the employment of sentencing discretion on the part of local trial court judges, while recognizing also that limits need to be placed on this discretion. These limits to an unfettered exercise of judicial power are partly negative—that is, partly designed to ward off potential abuse. Discretion is power, and unchecked discretion is virtually absolute power. Lord Acton's dictum must be recalled: "power tends to corrupt; absolute power corrupts absolutely." Judicial sentencing discretion involves the exercise of an awesome power over years of human beings' lives; some checks upon that discretion are essential in a system premised upon law.

Nevertheless, the limits placed on judicial discretion need not be thought of as wholly negative. They can become positive, purposeful, guidance mechanisms that assist sentencing judges in achieving justice in sentencing. They can help local trial court judges ensure the constitutional guarantees of due process and equal protection of the laws. This has been the aim of sentencing guidelines research.

NOTES

1. W. E. Burger, quoted in *New York Times*, January 2, 1977.

2. K. C. Davis, *Discretionary Justice: A Preliminary Inquiry* (Baton Rouge: Louisiana State University Press, 1969); see also D. J. Newman, *Introduction to Criminal Justice,* 2nd ed. (Philadelphia: J. B. Lippincott Co., 1978).

3. Davis, *supra* note 2 at 4.

4. C. D. Breitel, "Controls in Law Enforcement," 27 *University of Chicago Law Review* 427 (1960). See also J. M. Kress, "Progress and Prosecution," 423 *The Annals of the American Academy of Political and Social Science* 99 (January 1976); B. Atkins and M. Pogrebin, eds, *The Invisible Justice System: Discretion and the Law* (Cincinnati: Anderson Publishing Co., 1978); and M. Evans, ed., *Discretion and Control* (Beverly Hills: Sage Publications, 1978).

5. R. Hood and R. Sparks, *Key Issues in Criminology* 6–79 (New York: World University Library, 1970).

6. See K. C. Davis, *Police Discretion* (St. Paul: West Publishing Co., 1975); J. Q. Wilson, *Varieties of Police Behavior* (Cambridge, Mass.: Harvard University Press, 1968); W. LaFave, *Arrest: The Decision to Take a Suspect Into Custody* (Boston: Little, Brown, 1965); and S. Kadish, "Legal Norm and Discretion in the Police and Sentencing Process," 75 *Harvard Law Review* 904 (1962).

7. See D. J. Newman, *Conviction: The Determination of Guilt or Innocence Without Trial* (Boston: Little, Brown, 1966); Kress, *supra* note 4; Davis, *supra* note 2; John Kaplan, "The Prosecutorial Discretion—A Comment," 60 *N. W. U. Law Review* 174 (1965); B. A. Grosman, *The Prosecutor: An Inquiry Into the Exercise of Discretion* (Toronto: University of Toronto Press, 1969); A. Rosett and D. R. Cressey, *Justice by Consent* (Philadelphia: J. B. Lippincott, 1976); A. Alschuler, "The Trial Judge's Role in Plea Bargaining, Part I," 76 *Colum. L. Rev.* 1059 (1976); J. E. Bond, *Plea Bargaining and Guilty Pleas* (New York: Clark Boardman, 1975); and Georgetown University Law Center, *Plea Bargaining in the United States–Phase I Report* (Washington, D.C.: Georgetown University Law Center, 1977).

8. See H. Sturz, "Experiments in the Criminal Justice System," 25 *Legal Aid Briefcase* 111 (1967); P. Wald, "Pretrial Detention and Ultimate Freedom: A Statistical Study," 39 *N.Y.U. Law Review* 631 (1964); A. Rankin, "The Effect of Pretrial Detention," 39 *N.Y.U. Law Review* 641 (1964); M. Zander, "A Study of Bail/Custody Decisions in London Magistrates' Courts," 1971 *Crim. L. R.* 196; and R. L. Goldfarb, *Ransom: A Critique of the American Bail System* (New York: Harper and Row, 1965).

9. The other goal is equal justice; see Chapter 1 at note 27 and also the discussion below.

10. See especially C. R. Henderson, ed., *Prison Reform* (New York: Charities Publication Committee of the Russell Sage Foundation, 1910); B. McKelvey, *American Prisons* (Montclair, N.J.: Patterson Smith, 1972); and American Friends Service Committee, *Struggle for Justice* (New York: Hill and Wane, 1971). As McKelvey notes, prison unrest had served as an inpetus for reform one century earlier, in 1816 when "A population of 225 convicts together with numerous de-

tention cases had crowded all semblance of discipline from [Philadelphia's Walnut Street jail], and a series of riots compelled the authorities to consider measures of reform" (at 6–7).

11. R. Clark, *Crime in America* (New York: Simon and Schuster, 1970) at 204 ; see also J. M. Kress, L. T. Wilkins, and D. M. Gottfredson, "Is the End of Judicial Sentencing in Sight?" 60 *Judicature* 216 (December 1976).

12. National Commission on Law Observance and Enforcement (Wickersham Commission), *Report on Penal Institutions, Probation and Parole* 142–43 (Washington, D.C.: USGPO, 1931).

13. E. M. Kennedy, "Criminal Sentencing: A Game of Chance," 60 *Judicature* 208 (December 1976). It is interesting to note that this cruel uncertainty was once considered a major advance in penology: "The very uncertainty and indefiniteness of the term enhances its moral weight upon the convict and intensifies its effect both as a punitive and reformative agency." A. H. Hall, "Indeterminate Sentence and Release on Parole," 2 *J. Crim. Law, Criminology & Police Science* 832, 838 (1912).

14. See New York State Special Commission on Attica, *Attica: The Official Report of the New York State Special Commission on Attica* (New York: Bantam Books, Inc., 1972); and R. McKay, "It's Time to Rehabilitate the Sentencing Process," 60 *Judicature* 223 (December 1976). See also the attack on indeterminate sentencing by the American Friends Service Committee, *supra* note 10; and *D. Fogel, "We are the Living Proof": The Justice Model for Corrections* (Cincinnati: W. H. Anderson Co., 1975).

15. In this regard, it is particularly instructive to review the history of New York's Baumes Law of 1926 (a severe habitual offender statute) and its aftermath, as assessed by the Lewisohn Commission. Commission to Investigate Prison Administration and Construction (Lewisohn Commission), *Prisoners: Their Crimes and Sentences* (New York, 1933), especially at 39–40. See also Executive Advisory Committee on Sentencing, *Crime and Punishment in New York: An Inquiry into Sentencing and the Criminal Justice System* 4–19, (New York, 1979); M. Zalman, "The Rise and Fall of the Indeterminate Sentence," 24 *Wayne Law Review* 45 (November 1977); D. J. Rothman, *Discovery of the Asylum: Social Order and Disorder in the New Republic* (Boston: Little, Brown, 1971); and H. Toch, *Living in Prison: The Ecology of Survival* (New York: Free Press, 1977).

16. See the text in Chapter 1 at notes 26 and 27.

17. Gregg v. Georgia, 428 U.S. 153 (1976); Proffitt v. Florida, 428 U.S. 242 (1976); Jurek v. Texas, 428 U.S. 262 (1976); Woodson v. North Carolina, 428 U.S. 280 (1976); Roberts v. Louisiana, 428 U.S.

325 (1976); Furman v. Georgia, 408 U.S. 238 (1972); Gardner v. Florida, 430 U.S. 349 (1977).

18. See Newman, *supra* note 2 at 254; see also H. M. LaFont, "Assessment of Punishment—A Judge or Jury Function?" 38 *Texas Law Review* 835 (1960); Note, "Jury Sentencing in Virginia," 53 *Virginia Law Review* 968 (1967); and Texas Code of Criminal Procedure Act 37.07 (1966).

19. National Advisory Commission on Criminal Justice Standards and Goals, *Task Force Report on Courts,* Standard 5.1, commentary at 110 (Washington, D.C.: USGPO, 1973).

20. See A. von Hirsch, *Doing Justice: The Choice of Punishments* 84–88 (New York: Hill and Wang, 1967).

21. As it does, indeed, in the death penalty area; see the cases cited *supra* note 17.

22. Furman v. Georgia, 408 U.S. 238, 314 (1972).

23. See especially S. S. Diamond and H. Zeisel, "Sentencing Councils: A Study of Sentence Disparity and Its Reduction," 43 *University of Chicago Law Review* 108 (1976); and A. Partridge and W. B. Eldridge, *Second Circuit Sentencing Study* (Washington, D.C.: Federal Judicial Center, 1974); see also M. E. Frankel, *Criminal Sentences: Law Without Order* 69–74 (New York: Hill and Wang, 1972); T. Levin, "Toward a More Enlightened Sentencing Procedure," 45 *Nebraska Law Review* 505–508, 511–12 (1966); R. F. Doyle, "A Sentencing Council in Operation," *Federal Probation* 27–30 (September 1961); and W. Strauss and L. Bashir, "Controlling Discretion in Sentencing," 51 *Notre Dame Lawyer* 919 (July 1976).

24. Note, "The Presentence Report: An Empirical Study of Its Use in the Federal Criminal Process," 58 *Georgetown L. J.* 451 (1970); B. A. Shapiro and C. Clement, "Presentence Information in Felony Cases in the Massachusetts Superior Court," 10 *Suffolk U. L. Rev.* 27 (Fall 1973); R. A. Harkness, "Due Process in Sentencing: Right to Rebut the Presentence Report," 2 *Hastings Constitutional L. Q.* 1065 (Fall 1975); S. D. Raymond, "Standardized Presentence Report: One State's Response," 41 *Fed. Prob.* 40 (June 1977); and W. J. Genego, P. D. Goldberger, and V. C. Jackson, "Parole Release Decisionmaking and the Sentencing Process," 84 *Yale Law Journal* 810 (March 1975), particularly authorities collected at 878–79.

See also the argument that the judge is *not* following the recommendation of the probation officer; rather, the probation officer's "recommendation" is more truly a *forecast* of the judge's decision. A similar claim has been urged concerning the observed relationship between the decision to deny bail and findings of guilt. W. M. Landes, "Legality and Reality: Some Evidence on Criminal Procedure," 3 *J. Leg. Studies* 287 (1974); and N. Parisi, "The Effects of

Pretrial Status on Adjudication and Sentencing," *Proceedings of the 21st Annual Meeting of the Southern Conference on Corrections* 372–92 (Tallahassee: Florida State University, 1976).

25. See the authorities cited *supra* note 7. See also the interesting attempts to structure prosecutorial discretion made by United States Attorney General Levi and New York County District Attorney Kuh. E. H. Levi, "U.S. Department of Justice Materials Relating to Prosecutorial Discretion," 24 *Criminal Law Reporter* 3001 (November 22, 1978); R. H. Kuh, "Plea Bargaining Guidelines for the Manhattan District Attorney's Office," 11 *Criminal Law Bulletin* 48 (1975).

26. See Davis, *supra* note 4; see also W. Gellhorn and C. Byse, *Administrative Law,* 5th ed. (Mineola, New York: Foundation Press, 1970).

27. See especially the very perceptive analysis provided by Professor Albert Alschuler in a number of recent articles, most notably "Sentencing Reform and Prosecutorial Power: A Critique of Recent Proposals for 'Fixed' and 'Presumptive' Sentencing," 126 *University of Pennsylvania Law Review* 550 (1978).

28. See the authorities *supra* notes 10 through 15.

29. See F. R. Remington, D. J. Newman, E. L. Kimball, M. Melli, and H. Goldstein, *Criminal Justice Administration: Materials and Cases* (Indianapolis: Bobbs-Merrill, 1969), especially at 761–91. The best critiques of these "diagnoses" may be found in the writings of Thomas Szasz; see, for example, his *Law, Liberty and Psychiatry* (New York: Macmillan & Co., 1963); and his *Ideology and Insanity* (Garden City, N.Y.: Doubleday Anchor, 1970).

30. See the books by Szasz, *supra* note 29. See also W. C. Bailey, "Correctional Outcome: An Evaluation of 100 Reports," 57 *J. Crim. L. C. & P. S.* 153 (1966); J. Q. Wilson, *Thinking About Crime* (New York: Basic Books, 1975); R. Martinson, "What Works?—Questions and Answers About Prison Reform," 35 *Public Interest* 22 (Spring 1974); and G. F. Cole and S. Talarico, "Second Thoughts on Parole," 63 *A. B. A. J.* 972 (July 1977).

31. Section 1170(a)(1). See also, American Friends Service Committee, *supra* note 13; Wilson, *supra* note 28; N. Morris, *The Future of Imprisonment* (Chicago: University of Chicago Press, 1974); E. van den Haag, *Punishing Criminals* (New York: Basic Books, 1975); von Hirsch, *supra* note 20; Twentieth Century Fund Task Force on Criminal Sentencing, *Fair and Certain Punishment* (New York: McGraw-Hill, 1976); and G. R. Newman, *The Punishment Response* (Philadephia: J. B. Lippincott, 1978). The most frequently proposed alternative philosophy is "just deserts," which is retribution in present-day garb. Reluctantly supporting this philosophy, Leslie Wilkins argued: "It seems that we have rediscovered 'sin,' in the absence of a

better alternative" in Appendix to von Hirsch, *supra* note 20 at 178. Ou bien, comme diraient mes collegues distingués de la belle province de Quebec, "Plus ça change, plus ça reste la même."

32. For a more detailed discussion of sentencing structures, see J. M. Kress, "Reforming Sentencing Laws: The American Perspective," in B. Grosman, ed., *New Directions in Sentencing* (Toronto: Butterworths, 1979); D. J. Newman, *supra* note 2, ch. VII; R. C. Hand and R. G. Singer, *Sentencing Computation Laws and Practice* (Washington, D.C.: Correctional Law Center, 1974); G. O. W. Mueller, *Sentencing: Process and Purpose* (Springfield, Ill.: Charles C. Thomas, 1975); and American Bar Association, Project on Minimum Standards for Criminal Justice, *Standards Relating to Sentencing Alternatives and Procedures,* approved draft (New York, 1968).

33. See F. Hussey, J. Kramer, D. Katkin, and S. Lagoy, "The Anatomy of Law Reform: The Effect of Criminal Code Revision on Sentencing—The Maine Experience" (Paper presented to the American Society of Criminology, November 1976); and also the keen analysis of a similar measure enacted in Indiana, by T. Clear, J. D. Hewitt, and R. M. Regoli, "Discretion and the Determinate Sentence" (Paper presented to the American Society of Criminology, November 1977). The argument made on these pages was elaborated upon in Kress, Wilkins, and Gottfredson, *supra* note 11.

34. See N. Morris, "Conceptual Overview and Commentary on the Movement Toward Determinacy," in LEAA, *Determinate Sentencing: Reform or Regression?* 1–11 (Washington, D.C.: USGPO, March 1978); Joint Committee on New York Drug Law Evaluation, *The Nation's Toughest Drug Law: Evaluating the New York Experience* (Washington, D.C.: USGPO, 1978); and Executive Advisory Committee on Sentencing, *supra* note 15 at 212–21. A recent example may be found in the controversial four to three California Supreme Court decision that invalidated a 1975 statute mandating prison terms for persons convicted of using guns while committing certain crimes. California v. Tanner, 587 P. 2d 1112 (1978), *reversed* California v. Tanner, 596 P.2d 328 (1979). (Allegations concerning the announcement of the *Tanner* decision led to an official inquiry by the California Commission on Judicial Performance into possible judicial misconduct by the Chief Justice and others in that court.)

35. J. S. Mattina, "Sentencing: A Judge's Inherent Responsibility," 57 *Judicature* 105 (October 1973); see also L. Downie, Jr., *Justice Denied* (New York: Praeger Publishers, 1971); J. C. Goulden, *The Benchwarmers* (New York: Ballantine Books, 1976); W. Gaylin, *Partial Justice* (New York: Alfred A. Knopf, 1974); and S. Nagel, "Disparities in Criminal Procedure," 14 *U.C.L.A. Law Review* 1272 (1967).

36. Frankel, *supra* note 23 at 7.

37. Burger, *supra* note 1.

38. A. M. Critelli, Preface to L. T. Wilkins, J. M. Kress, D. M. Gottfredson, J. C. Calpin, and A. M. Gelman, *Sentencing Guidelines: Structuring Judicial Discretion—Report on the Feasibility Study* xi (Washington, D.C.: USGPO, 1978).

39. See the arguments of K. C. Davis, *supra* note 6. The discretionary analysis pursued in this chapter has had its most dramatic impact recently in the field of policing: in addition to the references *supra* note 6, see, for example, National Advisory Commission of Criminal Justice Standards and Goals, *Report on Police* (Washington, D.C.: USGPO, 1973) at Standard 1.3; J. Goldstein, "Police Discretion Not to Invoke the Criminal Process: Low Visibility Decisions in the Administration of Justice," 69 *Yale Law Journal* 143 (1960); and H. Goldstein, *Policing a Free Society* (Cambridge, Mass.: Ballinger Publishing Co., 1976).

40. See *infra*, especially Chapters 4–7. For a more technical discussion, see A. M. Gelman, J. M. Kress, and J. C. Calpin, *Establishing a Sentencing Guidelines System: A Methods Manual* (Washington, D.C.: University Research Corp., 1978); and J. C. Calpin, J. M. Kress, and A. M. Gelman, *The Analytical Basis for the Formulation of Sentencing Policy* (Washington, D.C.: USGPO, 1980).

41. The process of making a preliminary, tentative, or "paper" sentencing decision—prior to the actual imposition of sentence—is apparently common. See A. M. Gelman, "The Sentencing Hearing: Forgotten Phase of Sentencing Reform," in Evans, *supra* note 4 at 124–41.

42. One Florida judge with whom I recently spoke has also changed his views on this issue and declared to me, only half in jest: "It's all right for clever *me* to sentence without giving reasons, but what about that crazy guy they just elected in the next county? I sure want him to spell out *his* reasons." The underlying rationale for this requirement, of course, is the desire to improve the overall rationality of the sentencing process and to ensure against unconscious judicial bias or emotion having a substantial and unfair impact upon the defendant's sentence. ABA, Project on Minimum Standards for Criminal Justice, *Standards Relating to Appellate Review of Sentences,* approved draft (New York: American Bar Association, 1968).

43. Commonwealth v. Riggins, 377 A.2d 140, 147 (Pa. 1977). Moreover, ABA, Project on Minimum Standards for Criminal Justice, *supra* note 42, provides at Section 2.3(c): "The sentencing judge should be required in every case to state his reasons for selecting the particular sentence proposed." See also Davis, *supra* note 2; and Frankel, *supra* note 23.

44. Statement of Judge David N. Savitt, Court Administrator, Court of Common Pleas, Philadelphia County, to the Judiciary Committee of the Pennsylvania House of Representatives on September 20, 1977. The respected Director of Cambridge University's Institute of Criminology, Nigel Walker, took the point a step farther and argued that the norm—or guideline, if you will—was indeed the principal justification for the sentence: "It is only the departure from the norm that calls for and is capable of a justification which is based on consideration of the individual case." N. Walker, *Sentencing in a Rational Society* 194 (Middlesex: Penguin, 1969).

45. See also text accompanying note 23, *supra*.

46. This is a view expressed, for example, by U.S. District Court Judge James M. Burns in J. M. Burns and J. S. Mattina, eds., *Sentencing* 267–76 (Reno: National Judicial College, 1978).

47. See the discussion, *infra* Chapter 9.

48. H. Zeisel and S. S. Diamond, "Search for Sentencing Equity: Sentence Review in Massachusetts and Connecticut," 4 *American Bar Foundation Research Journal* 881 (1977); D. A. Thomas, "Equity in Sentencing" (Sixth Annual Pinkerton Lecture, presented at Albany State University, April 1977); and Frankel, *supra* note 23 at 75–85.

49. Frankel, *supra* note 23 at 76–77.

50. See ABA, *supra* note 42 at 1–2.

51. *Id.*, generally; see also sources cited *supra* note 47; D. A. Thomas, *Principles of Sentencing* (London: Heinemann, 1970); Morris, *supra* note 31; R. J. Kutak and J. M. Gottschalk, "In Search of a Rational Sentence: A Return to the Concept of Appellate Review," 53 *Nebraska Law Review* 463 (1974); M. F. Knowles, "Lawlessness in our Criminal Law: Criminal Sentences and the Need for Appellate Review," 35 *Alabama Lawyer* 450 (1974); J. D. Hopkins, "Reviewing Sentencing Discretion: A Method of Swift Appellate Action," 23 *U. C. L. A. L. Rev.* 491 (February 1976); and C. C. Blake, "Appellate Review of Criminal Sentencing in the Federal Courts," 24 *Kansas L. Rev.* 279 (Winter 1976).

52. Wilkins et al., *supra* note 34 at 2; see also Frankel, *supra* note 23 at 75–85; and Morris, *supra* note 31.

53. Thomas, *supra* note 47.

54. See the text *supra* at note 28. Thomas (*supra* note 47) observes, however, that as indeterminate sentencing declines in significance, so the importance of this reason diminishes; see also A. M. Dershowitz, "Criminal Sentencing in the United States: An Historical and Conceptual Overview," 423 *The Annals of the American Academy of Political and Social Science* 117 (January 1976).

55. See the discussion *infra* Chapter 8 and the authorities cited *supra* note 7.

56. Thomas, *supra* note 47.

57. As of this writing, there is one sentencing guidelines case that has been accepted for review on appeal, State v. Whitehead, 159 N.J. Super. 433 (1978).

58. Note, however, the provisions to the contrary contained in the revised version of S. 1437, 95th Cong., 2d sess. at 3725 (1978); see also J. C. Coffee, Jr., "The Repressed Issues of Sentencing: Accountability, Predictability, and Equality in the Era of the Sentencing Commission," 66 *Georgetown L. J.* 975 (1978); and Walker, *supra* note 43.

59. Note, "Appellate Review of Primary Sentencing Decisions: A Connecticut Case Study," 69 *Yale Law Journal* 1453, 1475 (1969); see also sources cited *supra* note 47.

60. As is presently taking place in New Jersey; see State v. Whitehead, 159 N.J. Super. 433 (1978).

61. See, for example, Canon 21: "In imposing sentence [a judge] should endeavor to conform to a reasonable standard of punishment and should not seek popularity or publicity either by exceptional severity or undue leniency." While this canon may obviously be read in support of our procedures, which aim at delineating the "reasonable standard of punishment" referred to, some may see them as a means of seeking publicity, which judges are generally loathe to do.

62. One interesting method of communication to the public, which should be considered by trial court judges, may be found in Burns and Mattina, *supra* note 45, at 210–213.

63. I will deal with this "more is better" fallacy later; *infra* Chapter 8.

64. In my research, I and my staff have reviewed thousands of presentence investigation reports in dozens of states and interviewed many probation officers. These officers are usually dedicated, sincere, intelligent, and hard-working; it is very disheartening to see their talents wasted. Yet, by custom or statute, they are often forced to collect and describe trivial and useless—and time-consuming—items for all cases, which at some time were felt possibly relevant to one particular case. I am talking about items I have seen, such as the age at which a defendant stopped bed-wetting or the complete psychological profile of the *siblings* of the defendant, with which siblings the defendant has not had any contact in years. Couldn't the trained and intelligent mind of the investigative probation officer be put to better use?

65. J. O. Newman, in Forward to Genego, Goldberger, and Jackson, *supra* note 24 at 811. For a further elaboration of the argument presented here, see J. M. Kress, "The Realities and Myths of Sen-

tencing and Parole in the Criminal Justice Non-System," *Proceedings of the 21st Annual Meeting of the Southern Conference on Corrections* 316 (Tallahassee: Florida State University, 1976); see also J. O. Newman, "A Better Way to Sentence Criminals," 63 *A.B.A.J.* 1562 (November 1977).

66. See Burns and Mattina, *supra* note 45 at 204.

67. And these *are* employed in this manner. See, e.g., the presentence reports currently available to federal judges, as seen in Burns and Mattina, *supra* note 45 at 270–76.

To Establish Justice: A Constitutional Rationale

We the People of the United States, in order to . . . establish justice . . . do ordain and establish this Constitution for the United States of America.—Preamble, Constitution of the United States

In the preceding chapter, I dealt with the sentencing guidelines approach from a discretionary perspective; that, in some ways, was a practical, systems analysis approach, although in other ways it was a conceptual and theoretical approach as well. As a former prosecutor in America's busiest sentencing-bargaining jurisdiction, I have a first-hand, working knowledge of the impact of that discretionary power that I personally exercised and observed daily. It is therefore perhaps to be expected that I would begin laying the foundation for sentencing guidelines with some analysis of this pragmatic reality.

As a lawyer, however, I am also keenly aware of the need to establish a firm legal and constitutional base of authority. Nevertheless, I can in no sense put forward, in this brief space, an exhaustive treatise on the constitutional case for a sentencing guidelines system. This chapter should not be read as such: literally hundreds of learned volumes have been written on each of the constitutional elements discussed here. All that can be offered is an outline of the major principles that lend support to the sentencing guidelines concept—principles that Americans speak of as constitutional, but that are in fact universally respected precepts of fundamental fairness. In practice, sentencing guidelines systems should greatly assist local trial courts in assuring the compliance of their individual sentencing decisions with the mandates of the Constitution. Although the rationale for sentencing guidelines rests on a number of interlocking constitutional grounds, it will prove helpful, for analytical purposes, to separately explain the equal protection, substantive due process, procedural due process, and cruel and unusual punishment bases for such systems.

EQUAL PROTECTION: THE ALLEVIATION OF DISPARITY

The Fourteenth Amendment declares that "No State shall ... deny any person within its jurisdiction the equal protection of the law." The Thirteenth, Fourteenth, and Fifteenth Amendments were ratified following America's Civil War and were primarily designed to end the institution of slavery and to secure for black citizens the same rights and privileges enjoyed by all other United States citizens. As with other constitutional phrases, however, broader implications have been read into the phrase "equal protection" over the years. Early Supreme Court interpretation did specifically read the clause as "clearly a provision for [the Negro] race,"[1] but other racial groups,[2] and even corporations,[3] soon came under the ambit of the clause. The kinds of protections not to be denied similarly expanded from racial to economic,[4] and, by the 1930s, to the protection of most personal rights as well.[5] By now, a vast body of constitutional caselaw has also applied the clause to various criminal matters.[6]

More pertinently, in a host of cases, the proposition has been forcefully advanced that disparate sentencing denies to the criminal defendant the equal protection of the laws.[7] While several courts have rejected this specific contention, it does appear to be universally recognized that the equal protection clause is a major safeguard for the individual against arbitrary or capricious governmental action. This is so at all other stages of the criminal justice process and must be so at sentencing. As Mr. Justice Stewart cogently observed:

> It is an anomaly that a judicial system which has developed so scrupulous a concern for the protection of a criminal defendant throughout every other stage of the proceedings against him should have so neglected this most important dimension of fundamental justice.[8]

Indeed, of all the constitutional underpinnings for sentencing guidelines, the equal protection clause is perhaps the most obvious, as it so directly relates to the concern of disparity. In *Criminal Sentences,* Judge Frankel expressed his view that existing sentence disparities may offend the equal protection clause of the Constitution:

> The crazy guilt of disparities—the wide differences in treatment of defendants whose situations and crimes look similar and whose divergent sentences are unaccounted for—stirs doubts as to whether the guarantee of the "equal protection of the laws" is being fulfilled.[9]

Chief Justice Warren E. Burger further pointed to this most pressing judicial concern in his 1977 Annual Report on the State of the Judiciary, in the passage that introduced the preceding chapter.[10] He then went on to urge the creation of some procedure to solve this problem. The position taken here is that the tool provided by sentencing guidelines is just that procedure called for by the Chief Justice of the United States.

Chief Justice Burger's remarks reflect the common claim of disparity that I addressed earlier.[11] Whether or not the claim is true, the widespread belief in it stimulates a universal feeling of injustice, thereby undermining the confidence of the general public in the judicial system, as well as causing hostility among prison inmates, which in turn can lead to violent, counterproductive and/or antirehabilitative behavior. The sentencing guidelines research team, however, did not seek to partake in yet another disparity study, but sought instead to establish a more positive result.

Numerous studies have examined various factors that were of current popular interest and have related these to the sentence of the courts.[12] Dispositions have been looked at to determine whether there was any bias apparent against minority group defendants,[13] whether the type of defense counsel employed had any effect upon sentences,[14] or whether the method of conviction caused sentence variation.[15] A major weakness of these prior studies has been the apparent academic expectation on the part of the researchers concerned that the findings were adequate in and of themselves. No previous study has gone on to provide any concrete tools that could help minimize perceived deficiencies in the sentencing process; they have presented only the clear showing that a serious problem does exist. It is important to grasp that judges need some assistance in making a sentencing decision, not simply further criticism that is unrelated to a solution of a more practical form. A sentencing guidelines system provides that practical solution.

Another weakness of these prior studies has been a failure to recognize the necessity for properly exercised sentencing discretion in the first place. Much otherwise valid criticism has, therefore, failed to adequately distinguish justified variation from the unjustified variation referred to as disparity; as I pointed out, not all sentencing variation should be considered unwarranted or disparate. Much of it properly reflects varying degrees of seriousness in the offense and/or varying characteristics of the offender. Moreover, since no two offenses or offenders are identical, the labeling of variation as disparity perforce involves a value judgment—what is disparity to one person may simply be justified variation to another. It is only when such variation takes the form of differing sentences for similar offenders committing similar offenses that it can be considered disparate.

As related in the preceding chapter, one often hears lawyers argue for the "reform" of requiring the judge to provide written reasons for the sentence imposed. Those reasons are, in one sense, the criteria we sought to discover through statistical analysis. But perhaps more fundamentally, it is the relative *weight* accorded these criteria that is important. Indeed, to a lawyer such as myself, it is the certainty that these weights will not vary from defendant to defendant that provides concrete meaning to the otherwise abstract concepts of equity, evenhandedness of treatment, and equal justice under law.

The concept of sentencing disparity as "unequal" treatment is one that fairly shouts out the need for statistical analysis. It is thus appropriate to note that the statistical arguments on disparity, and the constitutional concerns of equal protection, reached their point of highest conjunction at the time of the *Furman* decision.[16] In that case, the United States Supreme Court reviewed the statistical evidence as to how the death penalty had been applied in America. Each of the nine justices wrote a separate opinion, with five concurring in a finding that, as actually applied, the death sentence had been imposed in an arbitrary and capricious manner and was thus in violation of the Constitution. (Several justices found grounds for disapproval of the death penalty as violative of the cruel and unusual punishment, the due process, *and* the equal protection clauses of the Constitution, but here we are concerned only with the equal protection argument.) Mr. Justice Douglas, for example, favorably quoted the earlier work of the President's Commission on Law Enforcement and Administration of Justice to the effect that the "death sentence is disproportionately imposed and carried out on the poor, the Negro, and the members of unpopular groups."[17] Mr. Justice Brennan reviewed the data and declared that "the conclusion is virtually inescapable, that it is being inflicted arbitrarily. Indeed, it smacks of little more than a lottery system."[18] In terms remarkably relevant to our purpose here, he further declared that present sanctioners "make the decision whether to impose the death sentence wholly unguided by standards governing that decision."[19]

Among the five *Furman* justices arguing the unconstitutionality of the death penalty, Mr. Justice Stewart has been the most widely quoted, and he most heavily relied upon the equal protection clause in his conclusion that we "cannot tolerate the infliction of a sentence of death under legal systems that permit this unique penalty to be so wantonly and so freakishly imposed."[20] Indeed, in retrospect, in light of the 1976 decisions of the United States Supreme Court upholding the death penalty,[21] it now appears clear that it was the arbitrary and unequal nature of the application of the death penalty that was the most significant aspect of those statutes that the *Furman* Court held unconstitutional.

The justices of the Supreme Court have specifically and repeatedly declared the death penalty to be unique.[22] Therefore, it may be contended that the constitutional standards and concerns established in the death penalty cases are neither applicable nor capable of extrapolation to other sentencing decisions. Nevertheless, legal history records that many of the procedural rights now guaranteed to all criminal defendants were first won by those facing capital sentencing. Therefore, I not only see clear analogies between the arguments concerning the imposition of the death penalty and the arguments concerning the selection of other sentencing alternatives open to the judiciary, but also feel certain that, in the not too distant future, each of three salient criteria required by the Supreme Court's 1976 death penalty decisions will be made applicable to the consideration of *all* serious sentencing options: (1) a finding of guilt separated from the sentencing decision; (2) consideration by the sentencing authority of both aggravating and mitigating circumstances, with a finding as to which predominates; and (3) appellate review. The first criterion is unlikely to prove important outside of jury sentencing jurisdictions, and the case for the third was argued in the preceding chapter, but the second criterion is the one that sentencing guidelines are designed to provide—accurately and usefully—for all sentencing decisions.

Owing to the great interest in capital cases, a relatively large body of data has accumulated concerning both the application of the penalty and its purported deterrent impact.[23] While some statistical relationships do appear to exist, causal connections are impossible to impute, and the results may be fairly summarized as ambiguous; with regard to noncapital sentencing, the data are even less susceptible to precise analysis.[24] The point is, given present-day knowledge, we simply cannot really say whether any judge has been sentencing arbitrarily or unequally, since the "going rate" or "tariff" is an uncertain thing at best.[25]

SUBSTANTIVE DUE PROCESS: THE GOALS OF PUNISHMENT

The Fifth Amendment asserts that, in federal cases, "No person shall be . . . deprived of life, liberty, or property, without due process of law . . . ." The Fourteenth Amendment provides the same protection against improper state action: "No State shall . . . deprive any person of life, liberty, or property, without due process of law. . . ." As with each of the constitutional phrases here described, due process is a term that has undergone frequent refinement and reinterpretation through countless appellate court opinions; volumes have been written in attempts to define the term precisely and to explain the meaning of each case more thoroughly. It is an alternative expression of the jurisprudential concept of fundamental fairness and is often subdivided, for analytical purposes, into the areas of substantive due process and procedural due process.

Substantive due process refers to the constitutional safeguard that any enacted legislation must be rationally related to the furtherance of a legitimate governmental purpose or objective.[26] The reviewing court must thus ascertain the legislative purpose and determine whether that end is permissible or prohibited by the Constitution; then, the court must decide whether the state's means of achieving that end bears a constitutionally permissible relationship to that end.

Furthermore, the method by which that governmental purpose is to be achieved should be the least burdensome of other rights; the courts have sometimes declared that the "least restrictive alternative" must be employed.[27] Substantive due process analysis may thus be seen as readily applying to criminal sentencing, implying that a probationary sentence, for example, must be meted out to a defendant in preference to an incarcerative one, assuming that the objectives of the sentence may be achieved as well by either sentencing alternative. Moreover, this means of analysis is used by the courts to define the primary aims or objectives of sentencing itself!

Sentencing serves many, often conflicting, purposes. The principal theories of punishment have often been enunciated as guides for the sentencing judge, but no one of them has ever seemed to be sufficiently encompassing to include the wide scope of criminal activity within its coverage. Retribution, deterrence, incapacitation, rehabilitation, and so forth operate differentially in practice as well as in theory. Even the strict retributionist jurist is usually willing to "take a chance" on the reform of a young first offender, whereas the most liberal rehabilitationist will cry out "enough is enough" in the case of a violent recidivist. Sometimes these theories have taken on a faddish nature, and sometimes judges have rattled them off in rote fashion as if they were independent reasons for a given sentence—yet that cannot be the case. While a vast body of literature exists with regard to these theories, it is a curious fact that no previous study has related them in a way that would be useful to the sentencing judge—namely, a systematic categorization of the criteria (and their weights) that each theory implies and that should therefore be considered by the judge at the time of sentencing. Later in this book, I will briefly discuss these theories in the context of a full-scale sentencing guidelines system, proposing that just such a systematic categorization be undertaken.[28]

Many theories of punishment have been advanced, and there has been little consensus achieved among either philosophers or practitioners on the relative desirability or efficacy of any of them. Indeed, the various distinct purposes have each often been urged as the basis for a system of sanction, but rarely has the individual relevance of each been considered. Sometimes, one has been said to be more significant than others, but most often some vague "combination" of them has been proposed for judicial consideration.[29] Of necessity, therefore, very little real guidance has been provided to trial court judges. As New Jersey's Chief Justice Weintraub put it in 1960:

> No single aim or thesis can claim scientific verity or universal support. Agreement can hardly be expected until much more is known about human behavior. Until then, the sentencing judge must deal with the complex of purposes, determining in each situation how the public interest will best be served.[30]

Unfortunately, at present, sentencing judges have no aids to guide them in reaching those determinations.

PROCEDURAL DUE PROCESS I: RATIONALITY V. CAPRICIOUSNESS

While substantive due process analysis has been enjoying renewed interest of late, it is procedural due process that has dominated the criminal law debates of the past two decades. Rather than focusing on the overall aims of the criminal law, procedural due process analysis employs a means-ends test to determine whether any specific case falls within the legislature's purpose. "The more fundamental the individual interest involved in a case, the closer the relationship between means and ends required and hence the greater degree of procedural due process required."[31] The protection involved relates to the administrative procedures of the courts of justice, assuring the competency of the court rendering the judgment and the procedures afforded to the defendant prior to any deprivation of life or liberty. Essentially, the due process protection means that a state may not arbitrarily or capriciously interfere with the lives or liberties of its citizens, even when that citizen has been properly convicted of a crime.

Much of the criticism against present sentencing practices has been directed against the apparently emotional, arbitrary and capricious nature of them. Senator Edward M. Kennedy has referred to our present criminal sentencing procedures as "a game of chance."[32] Judge Frankel has also explicitly addressed this issue:

> The arbitrary cruelties perpetrated daily under our existing sentencing practices are not easy to reconcile with the cardinal principles of our Constitution. The largely unbridled powers of judges and prison officials stir questions under the clauses promising that life and liberty will not be denied except by "due process of law."[33]

The most appalling aspect of this arbitrariness is that it is likely not due to any emotional or malevolent bias, but rather to an unconscious ignorance of the meaning of the particular sentencing decision. Perhaps the worst example of this is the "Slovik Syndrome," to which I referred in the preceding chapter; the reader will recall that this involved a sentence of death that the sentencing authority did not believe would be carried out.[34] It might similarly be argued that during the ten year American hiatus in executions, which ended with the almost self-inflicted execution of Gary Gilmore on January 17, 1977,[35] hundreds of Americans were sentenced to death by judges and juries who never believed that the state would actually execute the defendant. Thus, the ignorance pervading sentencing may not simply be of what one's colleagues would have given, but of the very life or death meaning of sentencing itself!

In recent years, the most direct analysis of the principles of sentencing provided by the United States Supreme Court has come in the various death penalty cases.[36] Although there is now majority approval for the application of capital punishment, an issue that both sides have had to address was the empirical question of whether or not this particular sentencing sanction had been applied "arbitrarily," "capriciously," "discriminatorily," or in a "wanton" or "freakish" manner. As noted earlier, this is an equal protection argument in large measure, but it also responds to procedural due process analysis and to all cases: "[T]he central point about whimsical and unequal sentencing is in principle germane in non-capital cases."[37] Thus, the procedural due process issue in capital cases is as applicable to all judicial sentencing.

In the 1976 death penalty cases, inter alia, the Supreme Court made clear that a significant factor in the approved statutes was the clear articulation of criteria for the imposition of the death penalty. Extrapolated to other forms of sentencing as well, that aspect of the Court's view had been presaged by the American Bar Association in its suggested standards for appellate review of sentences, where it argued that a primary objective of sentence review was "to promote the development and application of criteria for sentencing which are both rational and just."[38]

Now there are two major ways in which such criteria might evolve. One is to have them thrust upon the trial judge by a legislature in the form of a mandatory sentence or perhaps, in time, by an appellate court. The second is to analyze how experienced, local trial court judges are actually sentencing offenders, with a view toward frankly and openly articulating the criteria that they are presently using—this is, of course, the sentencing guidelines approach. While such an articulation cannot guarantee rationality or justice in and of itself, it is a realistic and important first step in that direction. Moreover, this approach does not unfairly assume irrationality on the part of the local trial court judiciary.

PROCEDURAL DUE PROCESS II: NOTICE

The requirement that notice be provided beforehand as to both the kind of crime liable to sanction and the kind and degree of sanction to be imposed is generally seen as a fundamental element of procedural due process. In *Screws v. United States,* the Supreme Court wrote about the requirement of specificity in criminal statutes, and this five to four opinion is frequently cited to explain the "void for vagueness" doctrine. A phrase used in dissent by Justice Roberts points the issue nicely, noting that a statute must "satisfy the due process requirement of giving decent advance notice of what it is which, if happening, will be visited with punishment. . . ."[39] The Supreme Court majority in *Winters v. New York* similarly used the term as a component of due process in striking down an obscenity statute: "A failure of a statute . . . to give fair notice of what acts will be punished . . . violates an accused's rights under procedural due process. . . ."[40]

Some would maintain that the requirement of notice is so fundamental as to predate the Constitution.[41] It is argued that this is clear from the principle of legality upon which our entire criminal law is based: *Nullum Crimen, Nulla Poena, Sine Lege.* Lord Denning has referred to this as the civil law's "great charter of liberty,"[42] and it is as important in common law countries. Others would see the notice requirement as deriving from the Sixth Amendment.[43] In any event, it is clear today that criminal defendants are entitled to notice (no matter the derivation of the requirement) both as to the kind of act prohibited and the kind of punishment visited upon a violation of that prohibition.

The notice issue also relates to the disparity problem; it is a statement by the courts, *before* the fact of sentencing, that sentencing will be rational and not arbitrary and that there will be reasoned grounds for the sentencing decision. Yet in most states today, as I noted earlier, there is no requirement that judges give reasons for the sentences they hand down—even after the sentencing. In the few states that do require reasons, anecdotal evidence suggests that they become rote catechisms (e.g., "In the interests of justice"; "Owing to the serious nature of your offense"; "Because of your criminal record").[44] As Judge Frankel puts it:

> Since, as I have said, judges usually say little or nothing to explain their sentences, the possibility that they were moved by absurd or vicious considerations is not usually open to inquiry. And the circle proceeds to be closed. The judges, if they are merely human rather than depraved, do not enjoy being caught in error. They know that an unexplained decision does not flaunt its possible fallacies. When they are not required to explain, many at least find this conclusive grounds for not explaining. There is no way of knowing, then, how many sentences, for how many thousands of years, have rested upon hidden premises that could not have survived scrutiny.[45]

Judge Frankel refers to this lack of explanation as the "Walls of Silence"[46] that judges put up. A sentencing guidelines system razes those walls and provides reasons, first, in the body of the guidelines for the vast majority of cases and, second, in the sharply particularized reasons for going outside the guidelines.

Much has been written about the principle of legality and the constitutional prohibition against statutory enactments of crimes that are so vague and indefinite in meaning as to be stricken down as void. Little, however, has been written concerning that same advance notice requirement with regard to the type and severity of punishment. One flaw of indeterminate sentencing systems has to be their denial of notice to criminal defendants. Too much is uncertain—or at least not made public. To some extent, mandatory sentencing laws are premised upon the notice requirement, arguing that judicial discretion must be decreased in order to give more informed notice to criminal defendants. But the solution is not a 180 degree turn to fixed sentencing. That is too rigid. A sentencing guidelines system, put into effect and given wide dissemination, will provide criminal defendants with far more adequate notice than they have ever had before of a court's sentencing policies. The solution lies in the provision of a basic tariff accounting for attributes of the crime and the criminal, published in advance, but possessing the flexibility to accommodate to the unique circumstances of human behavior. In short, the solution to the need for advance notice of sanction lies in sentencing guidelines.[47]

CRUEL AND UNUSUAL PUNISHMENT: PROPORTIONALITY

The Eighth Amendment declares that "cruel and unusual punishments" may not be inflicted upon criminal defendants.[48] This doctrine once appeared to apply only to examples of torture or "cruelty inherent in the method of punishment";[49] it has recently been voiced as an argument against the death penalty, although a majority of the Supreme Court rejects that view.[50]

More pertinent to our concerns, however, is that courts have been coming around to the view that the clause establishes a principle of proportionality of punishment. This principle is only now being developed, but there is a growing body of supportive case law at both the state[51] and the federal[52] levels. Indeed, several U.S. Supreme Court cases are supportive of this proportionality principle. As early as 1910, in *Weems v. United States,* the Court noted the applicability of the Eighth Amendment prohibition specifically to a custodial sentence that was unusually and disproportionately long.[53] In 1958, in *Trop v. Dulles,* a plurality of the U.S. Supreme Court further recognized that a penalty could not be "excessive in relation to the gravity of the crime."[54] That is, a penalty far in excess of that normally imposed for like crimes renders the punishment cruel and unusual and, hence, prohibited. The *Trop* plurality declared that the Eighth Amendment "must draw its meaning from the evolving standards of decency that mark the progress of a maturing society."[55] Finally, as recently as 1977, in *Coker v. Georgia,* the Supreme Court showed renewed interest in the concept when it declared invalid, as disproportionate to the offense, the death penalty when applied to a convicted rapist; a four justice plurality declared death "an excessive penalty for the rapist who, as such, does not take human life."[56] Thus, while a majority of the Court upholds capital punishment in cases of aggravated homicide, death is not seen as an appropriately proportionate penalty for the crime of rape.[57]

Assuming that a ruling precept of proportionality does emerge from this constitutional analysis, that precept would have firm philosophical support in the works of Jeremy Bentham [58] and H. L. A. Hart. Hart argued: "The guiding principle is that of a proportion within a system of penalties between those imposed for different offences where these have a distinct place in a commonsense scale of gravity."[59]

Elsewhere, Hart indeed pressed the proportionality notion one logical step further and provided a direct link to the benefits of a sentencing guidelines system:

> [P]rinciples of justice or fairness between different offenders require morally distinguishable offences to be treated differently and morally similar offences to be treated alike ... [W]hen the question of punishment for such conduct is raised, we should defer to principles which make relative moral wickedness of different offenders a partial determinant of the severity of punishment.[60]

Relative measures of wickedness are the appropriate province of the legislature; assessing and applying those measures in the particular case is the job of the sentencing judge. The value of sentencing guidelines is that they provide an experiential measure of proportionality that is applicable, for review purposes, in the aggregate as well as to each individual situation.

THE CONSTITUTIONAL CASE

In one sense, making the argument for a particular social science innovation is a simple exercise; normally, if it is within the rational powers of an agency to adopt a rule, then the courts will not upset that rule—barring a clear showing of unconstitutionality. Over the years, the dissenting 1932 voice of Mr. Justice Brandeis has taken on persuasive authority:

> To stay experimentation in things social and economic is a grave responsibility. Denial of the right to experiment may be fraught with serious consequences to the Nation. It is one of the happy incidents of the federal system that a single courageous State may, if its citizens choose, serve as a laboratory; and try novel social and economic experiments without risk to the rest of the country. This Court has the power to prevent an experiment. We may strike down the statute which embodies it on the ground that in our opinion, the measure is arbitrary, capricious or unreasonable. We have power to do this, because the due process clause has been held by the Court applicable to matters of substantive laws as well as to matters of procedure. But in the exercise of this high power, we must be ever on our guard, lest we erect our prejudices into legal principles.[61]

Thus it is very unlikely that the courageous counties and states that first tested and developed sentencing guidelines systems will have their experiments stayed or that constitutional impediments will arise for those courts and sentencing commissions that develop such systems in the future.

Yet, it is more than this negative, permissive authority that has been argued in this chapter. There is a strong, affirmative case to be made. While this chapter could in no sense exhaustively review all of the relevant constitutional principles and cases, I trust that it will have become clear that an operational sentencing guidelines system provides benefits by augmenting the constitutional protections guaranteed to us all. Disparity will be relieved and equal protection enhanced; proportionality of punishment will be pragmatically established; and, substantively and procedurally, due process protections will be advanced for each citizen. The implementation of a sentencing guidelines system is no panacea for the problems of the courts, but it is a practical procedural device that will provide local trial courts with a constitutional means of improving upon present sentencing practices.

NOTES

1. The Slaughter House Cases, 83 U.S. (16 Wall.) 36, 81 (1873).

2. Yick Wo v. Hopkins, 118 U.S. 356 (1886).

3. Santa Clara County v. Southern Pacific Railroad, 118 U.S. 394 (1886).

4. See the analysis offered by Professor R. J. Harris in *The Quest for Equality* (Baton Rouge: Louisiana State University Press, 1960).

5. *Id.* See also N. T. Dowling and G. Gunther, *Cases and Materials on Constitutional Law,* 8th ed. (Mineola: Foundation Press, 1970); and J. Tussman and J. Tenbroek "The Equal Protection of the Laws," 37 *California Law Review* 341 (1949).

6. See, for example, Norris v. Alabama, 294 U.S. 587 (1935) (jury service); Griffin v. Illinois, 351 U.S. 12 (1956) (right to a criminal appeal); and Douglas v. California, 372 U.S. 353 (1963) (counsel on criminal appeal).

7. Some examples: State *ex rel.* Johnson v. Mayo, 69 So. 2d 307 (Florida), *cert. denied,* 347 U.S. 992 (1956); Florida *ex rel.* Thomas v. Culver, 253 F. 2d 507 (5th Cir.), *cert denied,* 358 U.S. 822 (1958); Meyer v. United States, 446 F. 2d 37 (2nd Cir., 1971); United States v. McCord, 466 F. 2d 17 (2d Cir., 1972); and Simon v. Woodson, 454 F. 2d 161 (5th Cir., 1972).

8. Shepard v. United States, 257 F. 2d 293 (6th Cir., 1958).

9. M. E. Frankel, *Criminal Sentences: Law Without Order* 103 (New York: Hill and Wang, 1972).

10. Warren E. Burger, quoted in *New York Times,* January 2, 1977 *supra* Chapter 2, headnote.

11. See, for example, the view of Senator Edward M. Kennedy that "sentencing disparity is a national scandal," in E. M. Kennedy, "Criminal Sentencing: A Game of Chance," 60 *Judicature* 208, 210 (December 1976); see also "Equal Justice?" (editorial), *New York Times,* June 18, 1976; and J. J. Kilpatrick, "Study Fixes Guidelines for Equal Justice"(syndicated column), *Washington Star,* February 12, 1977.

12. The list is almost endless; some of the better known statistical studies are cited here: G. Antunes and A. L. Hunt, "The Deterrent Impact of Criminal Sanctions: Some Implications for Criminal Justice Policy," 51 *J. of Urban Law* 145 (1973); H. A. Bedau, "Capital Punishment in Oregon, 1903–64," 45 *Oregon Law Review* 1 (1965); S. F. Browne, J. D. Carr, G. Cooper and T. A. Giancinti, *Adult Recidivism: Characteristics and Recidivism of Adult Felony Offenders in Denver* (Denver: High Impact Anti-Crime Program, 1974); H. Bullock, "Significance of the Racial Factor in the Length of Prison Sentences," 52 *Journal of Criminal Law, Criminology and Police Science* 411 (November-December 1961); T. G. Chiricos and G. P. Waldo, "Punishment and Crime: An Examination of Some Empirical Evidence," 18 *Social Problems* 200 (Fall 1970); Comment, "Texas Sentencing Practices: A Statistical Study," 45 *Texas Law Review* 471 (1967); D. R. Cressey, "The Nature and Effectiveness of Correctional Techniques," 23 *Law and Contemporary Problems* 754 (August 1958); I. Ehrlich, "The Deterrent Effect of Capital Punishment: A Question of Life and Death," 65 *American Economic Review* 397 (1975); E. Green, "Inter- and Intra-Racial Crime Relative to Sentencing," 54 *Journal of Criminal Law, Criminology, and Police Science* 348 (1964); J. Hogarth, *Sentencing As A Human Process* (Toronto: University of Toronto Press, 1971); R. Hood, "Research on the Effectiveness of Punishments and Treatments," in Council of Europe, *Collected Studies in Criminological Research* 74 (Strasbourg, 1967); B. L. Johnston, N. P. Miller, R. Schoenberg, and L. R. Weatherly, "Discretion in Felony Sentencing —A Study of Influencing Factors," 48 *Washington Law Review* 857 (August 1973); C. J. Judson, J. P. Pandell, J. B. Owens, J. L. McIntosh, and D. S. Matschullat, "A Study of the California Penalty Jury in First Degree Murder Cases," 21 *Stanford Law Review* 1297 (1969); S. Nagel, *The Legal Process From a Behavioral Perspective* (Homewood, Ill.: The Dorsey Press, 1969); A. Partridge and W. Eldridge, *Second Circuit Sentencing Study* (Washington, D.C.: Federal Judicial Center, 1974); J. Petersilia and P. W. Greenwood, "Mandatory Prison Sentences: Their Projected Effects on Crime and Prison Populations," An Abstract (Santa Monica, Calif.: RAND, 1977); L. P. Tiffany, Y. Avichai, and G. W. Peters, "A Statistical Analysis of Sentencing in Federal Courts: De-

fendants Convicted After Trial, 1967–1968," 4 *Journal of Legal Studies* 369 (1975); C. Tittle, "Crime Rates and Legal Sanctions," 16 *Social Problems* 409 (1969); M. E. Wolfgang and M. Riedel, "Race, Judicial Discretion, and the Death Penalty," 407 *The Annals of the American Academy of Political and Social Science* 119 (May 1973).

13. Bullock, *supra* note 12; Green, *supra* note 12; Johnston, et al., *supra* note 12; and Wolfgang and Riedel, *supra* note 12.

14. Browne et al., *supra* note 12; and Comment, *supra* note 12.

15. Tiffany, Avichai, and Peters, *supra* note 12.

16. Furman v. Georgia, 408 U.S. 238, 92 S. C. 2726, 33 L. Ed. 2d 346 (1972). See also S. Wheeler, "Towards A Theory of Limited Punishment II: The Eighth Amendment After *Furman v. Georgia*," 25 *Stanford Law Review* 62 (1972).

17. Furman v. Georgia, 408 U.S. 238, 249–50. The President's Commission citation was to, *The Challenge of A Crime in a Free Society* at 143 (Washington, D.C.: USGPO, 1967). Other statistical studies cited favorably in this opinion were Koeninger, "Capital Punishment in Texas, 1924–1968," 15 *Crime and Delinquency* 132, 141 (1969); and H. Bedau, *The Death Penalty in America*, 469, 474 (Chicago: Aldine, 1967 rev. ed.).

18. Furman v. Georgia, 408 U.S. 238, 293.

19. *Id.* at 295.

20. *Id.* at 310.

21. Gregg v. Georgia, 428 U.S. 153 (1976); Proffitt v. Florida, 428 U.S. 242 (1976); Jurek v. Texas, 428 U.S. 262 (1976); Woodson v. North Carolina, 428 U.S. 280 (1976); Roberts v. Louisiana, 428 U.S. 325 (1976).

22. Gregg v. Georgia, 428 U.S. 153, 188–95. In his plurality opinion in Gardner v. Florida, 430 U.S. 349, 358 (1977), Mr. Justice Stewart related one unique aspect of capital punishment when he declared that the "extinction of all possibility of rehabilitation is one of the aspects of the death sentence that makes it different in kind from any other sentence a state may legitimately impose."

23. Wolfgang and Riedel, *supra* note 12; Ehrlich, *supra* note 12; Bedau, *supra* note12; Judson et al., *supra* note 12; see also C. L. Black, Jr., *Capital Punishment: The Inevitability of Caprice and Mistake* (New York: W. W. Norton, 1974); E. van den Haag, *Punishing Criminals* (New York: Basic Books, 1975); and G. R. Newman, *The Punishment Response* (Philadelphia: J. B. Lippincott,1978).

24. This was the conclusion offered after one recent study conducted for the National Academy of Sciences, A. Blumstein, ed., *Deterrence and Incapacitation: Estimating the Effects of Criminal Sanctions on Crime Rates* (Washington, D.C.: National Academy of Sciences, 1978). Criminologist Jack Gibbs argues: "Only an incorrigi-

ble ideologist would regard such evidence as conclusive one way or another," quoted in C. Silberman, *Criminal Violence, Criminal Justice* (New York: Random House, 1978) at 195.

25. See also the statement of Iowa Judge Anthony M. Critelli, referred to *supra* Chapter 1 at note 33.

26. See especially the thorough and incisive analysis of substantive due process offered in M. Angel, "Substantive Due Process and the Criminal Law," 9 *Loyola University of Chicago Law Journal* 61 (1977); see also H. Packer, "The Aims of the Criminal Law Revisited: A Plea for a New Look at 'Substantive Due Process,'" 44 *Southern California Law Review* 490 (1971); and R. M. Bastress, Jr., "The Less Restrictive Alternative in Constitutional Adjudication: An Analysis, A Justification, and Some Criteria," 27 *Vanderbilt Law Review* 971 (1974).

27. See the analysis by L. Tribe, "Foreword: Toward A Model of Roles in the Due Process of Life and Law," 97 *Harv. L. Rev.* 1 (1973); and Bastress, *supra* note 26.

28. See *infra* Chapter 9; see also P. O'Donnell, M. J. Churgin, and D. E. Curtis, *Toward a Just and Effective Sentencing System: Agenda for Legislative Reform* (New York: Praeger, 1977).

29. New York State's Penal Code is typical in its setting out of a number of purposes to be served without describing when, or under what circumstances, any one of these purposes should predominate. Penal Code §1.05 (1967):

The general purposes of the provisions of this Chapter are:

1. To proscribe conduct which unjustifiably and inexcusably abuses or threatens substantial harm to individual or public interests;

2. To give fair warning of the nature of the conduct proscribed and of the sentences authorized upon conviction;

3. To define the act or omission and the accompanying mental state which constitute each offense;

4. To differentiate on reasonable grounds between serious and minor offenses and to prescribe proportionate penalties therefor; and

5. To insure the public safety by preventing the commission of offenses through the deterrent influence of the sentences authorized, the rehabilitation of those convicted, and their confinement when required in the interests of public protection.

30. State v. Ivan, 33 N.J. 147, 201 (1960).

31. Angel, *supra* note 26 at 65; see also Pennoyer v. Neff, 95 U.S. 733 (1881).

32. Kennedy, *supra* note 11.

33. Frankel, *supra* note 9 at 103.

34. See *supra* Chapter 2 at note 65 and accompanying text.

35. See J. M. Kress, "Special Report: Capital Punishment," *Americana Annual* 235 (1978).

36. See cases cited *supra* notes 16, 21, and 22.

37. Frankel, *supra* note 9 at 104. "Due process" as applied to statutes requires "only that a law shall not be unreasonable, arbitrary or capricious, and that the means selected shall bear a rational relation to the legislative object sought to be obtained." Robson v. Rodriguez, 26 N.J. 517, 522 (1958). "A fortiori, where the issue is whether a judge may use certain material to influence his mental processes, it is reasonable to conclude that the same principle applies." State v. Whitehead, 388 A.2d 280, 292, 159 N.J. Super. 433 (1978). The author is indebted to New Jersey Superior Court Justice Leo Yanoff for this argument.

38. American Bar Association, Project on Minimum Standards for Criminal Justice, *Standards Relating to Appellate Review of Sentences,* Standard 1.2(iv) (New York, 1968 app. draft). See generally J. M. Kress, "Sentencing: The Search for Rational Criteria" (Paper presented at the Annual Meeting of the American Society of Criminology; Toronto, Canada, 1975).

39. Screws v. United States, 325 U.S. 91, 153 (1945).

40. Winters v. New York, 333 U.S. 507, 509 (1948).

41. See the argument by Professor Donald R. Cressey that the concept of "advance notice" provides the basic meaning of "justice" in criminal cases. D. R. Cressey, "The Function and Structure of Criminal Syndicates," in President's Commission on Law Enforcement and the Administration of Justice, *Task Force Report: Organized Crime* 46 (Washington, D.C.: USGPO, 1967). See also L. Fuller, *The Morality of Law*, ch. II (Cambridge, Mass.: Harvard University Press, 1964).

42. R. Denning, *Freedom Under the Law* 40 (London: Stevens and Sons, 1949). The phrase is freely translated to mean that neither crime nor punishment will be permitted, save on the basis of preexisting law.

43. "In all criminal prosecutions, the accused shall . . . be informed of the nature and cause of the accusations; . . ."

44. Decisions involving federal parole hearings may shed light on the problem. While grant of parole is an act of legislative grace, some recent cases have declared that a prospective parolee is entitled to a modicum of due process protection. Garcia v. U.S. Board of Parole, 409 F. Supp. 1230 (N.D. Ill. 1976), *aff'd* 557 F.2d 100 (7th

Cir. 1977). *Cf.* Morrissey v. Brewer, 408 U.S. 471 (1972). One Circuit has concluded that a federal applicant for parole is entitled to a statement of reasons for refusal. Mower v. Britton, 504 F.2d 396 (10th Cir. 1974). Thus, "boiler plate" reasons, such as "Your release ... would depreciate the seriousness of the offense committed ... ," are deficient. Garcia v. U.S. Board of Parole, 409 F. Supp. 1230, 1238 (N.D. Ill. 1976); Lupo v. Norton, 371 F. Supp. 156 (D. Conn. 1974); Billiteri v. U.S. Board of Parole, 385 F. Supp. 1217 (N.D. N.Y. 1974).

45. Frankel, *supra* note 9 at 42.

46. *Id.*, ch. 4.

47. Although this section deals primarily with constitutional issues, it is worth noting an important corollary to the notice issue— that is, the broad movement today toward increased disclosure of materials, often including presentence reports, to criminal defendants. Certainly, as this movement gains momentum, the increased awareness that guidelines bring to all participants in the criminal justice process, as to the actual historical practice of the courts, can only be considered beneficial for all. See, for example, American Bar Association, Project on Minimum Standards for Criminal Justice, *Standards Relating to Discovery and Procedure Before Trial* (New York, 1970 app. draft).

48. The Eighth Amendment's prohibition against federal infliction of such punishments was applied against the states through the due process clause of the Fourteenth Amendment, in Robinson v. California, 370 U.S. 660 (1962).

49. Louisiana *ex. rel.* Francis v. Resweber, 329 U.S. 459 (1947).

50. See cases *supra* note 21.

51. *In re* Lynch, 503 P.2d 921 (Cal. 1972); *In re* Rodriquez, 537 P.2d 384 (1975).

52. Hart v. Coiner, 483 F.2d 136 (4th Cir., 1973).

53. Weems v. United States, 217 U.S. 349 (1910).

54. Trop v. Dulles, 356 U.S. 86, 99 (1958).

55. *Id.* at 101

56. Coker v. Georgia, 433 U.S. 584, 598 (1977).

57. I should note that, in *Coker*, Justice Powell did, however, express the view that the death penalty might be appropriate in "the case of an outrageous rape resulting in serious, lasting harm to the victim." *Id.* at 604.

58. J. Bentham, *An Introduction to the Principles of Morals and Legislation*, in *Collected Works*, ed. J. H. Burns and H. L. A. Hart (London: Athcone Press, 1970). See also G. Newman, *supra* note 33; and L. Radzinowicz, *A History of English Criminal Law and Its Administration from 1750* (London: Stevens, 1948).

59. H. L. A. Hart, *Punishment and Responsibility* 25 (New York: Oxford University Press, 1968); see also H. M. Hart, "The Aims of the Criminal Law," 23 *Law and Contemporary Problems* 401 (1958); J. Feinberg, *Doing and Deserving* (Princeton, N.J.: Princeton University Press, 1970); and A. von Hirsch, *Doing Justice: The Choice of Punishments* (New York: Hill and Wang, 1976).

60. H. L. A. Hart, *Law, Liberty and Morality* 36–37 (Oxford: Oxford University Press, 1963). See also G. Newman, *supra* note 23; and E. van den Haag, *supra* note 23.

61. New State Ice Company v. Ernest A. Liebmann, 285 U.S. 262, 311, 52 S. Ct. 371, 76 L. Ed. 747 (1932). See also the dissenting argument of Chief Justice Warren Burger in Bivens v. Six Unknown Named Agents, 403 U.S. 388, 424 (1971).

Part Two
The Research Effort

4

Action Research in the Courts

The great end of life is not knowledge but action.—Thomas Henry Huxley[1]

In the preceding chapters, I attempted to establish the desirability of a sentencing guidelines system on a principled basis. For various legal and ethical reasons, and also as a solution to the problem of unchecked discretion, it is essential that the structuring mechanism of sentencing guidelines be established and implemented in American courts. But how were such systems first developed, and how should they be developed in the future? In the next few chapters, I discuss the research that resulted in operational sentencing guidelines systems in both their general and their specific aspects. Later, I suggest a strategy for improvements in the sentencing process that goes far beyond the establishment of an historical data base.

In this chapter, I will explore and explain the concept of action research as it was actually employed in the original sentencing guidelines project. First, the premises of action research are elaborated upon, and the antecedent federal parole study is reviewed. I then explain the collaborative nature of the relationship between the research staff and the judicial members of the team, while describing the procedures employed in developing and implementing an action research methodology.

THE PREMISES OF ACTION RESEARCH

"Pure," or basic, scientific research is essential to the improvement of society; so too is applied research, aimed at the alleviation of specifically designated social ills. Sentencing guidelines research has been both basic and applied: the early phases of the research involved the basic investigation of an uncertain methodology, while the latter phases investigated extended applications of a now tested technology.

Always, however, the goals of the research team were action oriented. We sought to achieve results that would make a concrete difference to sentencing, to the courts, to deffendants, and to the law itself.

One of the principal aims of action research is that some effect
actually be accomplished in the system where the research has been
carried out. Much research has been maligned in the past because
researchers came in, disrupted the system, gathered their data, made
their observations, wrote a paper—usually unconstructively critical—and then disappeared. From its inception, the goal of the sentencing guidelines research project was to leave the study courts with
a new tool to aid them in their sentencing duties and thereby assist
judges in their own efforts to control discretion and to structure policy in the administration of criminal sanctions within each jurisdiction. If this tool is to have true utility and worth, it has to be
something that not only has value to the researchers but also to the
judges and, further still, to the management staff of the local criminal justice system as it is presently constituted.

Scientific curiosity alone would have been insufficient justification
for the action research team to begin its work; nor would our delight
in discovery have been sufficient reward. Similarly, we did not set
out to satisfy an academic audience by writing lengthy reports intended to be seen only by a very few colleagues. Our work would
have meant little to us if we did not see it as being put into effect.
Thus it was that we did not conduct a study of judicial behavior;
rather, we sought to conduct research *with* the judges.

From the outset, our major premise was an intent to assist local
trial court judges rather than to analyze them.[2] We hoped to provide
courts with a workable sentencing information system, to upgrade
the quality of probation reports, and to help judges in their most difficult task. In short, we consciously decided to work together with the
judiciary in a fully collaborative venture (not merely a cooperative
one) and not on, around, or against judges. This was our primary
goal from the first, and it provided strengths as well as limitations.

The major limitations revealed themselves after the fact. We are
often asked now what we "found": How much disparity was there?
What are the judges like? How are defendants treated? Do the judges
favor rehabilitation over retribution or deterrence? What is the recidivism rate? These are all valid and valuable questions: they are not
the questions we asked, however, and therefore our answers to them
are no more than educated guesses or perhaps "feelings" derived
from closely working with people.

We instead asked, How can we help? When judges recognized that
this was indeed our desire,[3] our major premise of assistance became a
tremendous asset; once judges realized our intent to provide them

with a useful working tool, they extended to us the fullest cooperation possible, and this made our goals achievable.

BACKGROUND: THE FEDERAL PAROLE ANALOGY

It will prove worthwhile to attend to the predecessor guidelines study
before I explain further the evolution and implementation of an action research methodology in the courts. The sentencing guidelines
research project itself grew out of the successful completion of a
study that developed operating guidelines for the United States
Board of Parole (now called the Parole Commission). The Parole
Decisionmaking Study, co-directed by Don M. Gottfredson, dean of
the Rutgers University School of Criminal Justice, and Leslie T. Wilkins, professor of criminal justice at Albany State University, represented the first successful application of guidelines in the criminal
justice system. That three year study resulted in the official administrative promulgation of paroling guidelines in 1972. They have been
revised and publically disseminated every year since.[4]

While the sentencing guidelines research discussed here diverged
in many ways from the parole guidelines approach taken then, it is
important to examine the roots of the sentencing guidelines project
in some detail. Since the parole study provided the initial conceptual
and methodological analogies for the sentencing research project—
and since Professor Wilkins and Dean Gottfredson co-directed early
sentencing guidelines research, together with the author—a brief review of the Parole Decisionmaking Study will provide a useful frame
of reference for understanding research on sentencing guidelines.

Wilkins and Gottfredson have viewed guidelines, in a policy sense,
as referring to a system of data functioning as a tool in assisting
decisionmakers in arriving at individual and policy determinations.
The federal parole guidelines system accomplishes this purpose by
using an equation to summarize the link among the main concerns,
or focal dimensions, of decisionmakers and their decisions. (A similar
approach was taken in early sentencing guidelines research.)

The research task was one of "predicting" the Parole Commission's
decisions on the basis of case information. If such predictions could
be made with some degree of accuracy, then that would suggest the
existence of at least an implicit policy present regarding the decision
to grant parole. Interestingly, the parole commissioners, much as the
sentencing judges with whom we later spoke, at first denied making
that decision on the basis of any overall policy; rather, they declared
that each case was decided on its intrinsic individual merits. Therefore, the original research hypothesis was formulated in terms of a

yes-no dichotomy—the researchers taking the view that parole board members (or hearing examiners) did indeed review each case individually, deciding in each whether or not to release the given applicant on the date in question.

The research staff soon realized, however, that what was involved was not simply a "yes-no" decision, but rather a question of length of time—that is, a question as to when to release the applicant. (This is so because virtually all federal prisoners are eventually released on parole, owing to "good time" and other statutory provisions, no matter what information appears in their records.) At this point, the researchers' working assumption became that when minimum sentences were short or indeterminate, the parole decision was, in effect, what they thought of as a deferred sentencing decision.[5]

The initial research demonstrated that the decisions of the Parole Commission could be adequately predicted from a knowledge of the Commission's estimates of three dimensions, or focal concerns: (1) the seriousness of the criminal behavior involved in the offense, as gauged by a multistep, quasi-statutory ranking performed by the Parole Commission; (2) the "salient factor score," or offender characteristics deemed to indicate the prognosis for success upon release of the prospective parolee; and (3) the institutional behavior and program performance of the individual. The research staff worked at identifying the particular items of information comprising these dimensions, as well as the specific weights, or significance, attached to those items. (In the event, as the third dimension appeared to carry much less weight in the Commission's decision when compared to the other two dimensions, it was later deleted from consideration in the construction of the parole guidelines.) The next step was to transform the subjective estimates of these dimensions into measures that were as apparently objective as possible.

The United States Parole Commission's decisionmaking guidelines are characterized by a two dimensional model that links the intersection of the dimension of offense seriousness and the dimension of parole prognosis with a time (in months) to be served prior to release on parole. The dimension of offense seriousness is measured by a six category Offense Severity Classification System. This classification system was developed, as a policy decision, by the United States Parole Commission regarding its own subjective evaluation of the seriousness of the criminal behavior involved in an offense. It should be noted that (1) this system of classification is not based on the length of sentence imposed, and (2) the cases involved are drawn only from that subgroup of offenders who were incarcerated in federal prisons upon conviction. The parole prognosis dimension is measured by an eleven point Salient Factor Score. The terms "parole prognosis" and

"Salient Factor Score," it should be understood, do not refer to any empirical or objective evaluation of the actual probability of an offender's recidivism, but rather to the subjective assessment by members of the Parole Commission as to the relative importance of nine weighted offender characteristics. It is interesting to observe that the members tend to give somewhat more weight to the dimension of seriousness than they do to that of "parole prognosis."[6]

In actual use, a parole hearing examiner scores an individual case in terms of both offense seriousness and parole prognosis and then locates the cell of intersection; this provides an expected range of months to be served by the offender. A range in time is provided even within cells so as to allow for some variation in the broad categories of risk and severity, but hearing examiners must usually set the exact length of incarceration within that range. If the examiner decides to depart from the range called for in a particular case, written reasons must be provided for doing so. These are later reviewed, first by a panel of three decisionmakers and then by the full commission.

DEVELOPING AN ACTION RESEARCH METHODOLOGY

Selecting Judges as Participant Researchers

It appeared to the directors of the federal parole study that there was value in the guidelines concept that could be adapted to many other decisionmaking problems, particularly to sentencing, and that state court judges might find their use beneficial. Therefore, we queried trial court judges in several American jurisdictions as to their willingness to engage in collaborative research and action along the lines of the methodology that had proven its value in the analogous area of parole decisionmaking. Four different judicial jurisdictions were selected to take part in our basic research study—two as active participants and two as "observers" who were to be involved in all possible ways, except that data would not actually be collected in those jurisdictions.

The Denver District Court (Denver County, Colorado) and the District Courts of the State of Vermont were designated as "participants" —that is, jurisdictions in which the project conducted on-site research. The Essex County and Superior Courts (Essex County, Newark, New Jersey) and the Polk County Court (Polk County, Des Moines, Iowa) were designated our observer courts. We felt this use of four sites to be optimal during our early research; this represented the minimum number of courts required to provide an indication of the usefulness of sentencing guidelines, as well as the possibility of replicating them elsewhere. We were engaged in an extensive basic research enterprise that would have been prohibitively expensive had we increased the number of participant courts. Moreover, we were then interested only in validating the feasibility of the guidelines concept as applied to sentencing; establishing and operating additional participant sites would have delayed this effort. Data collection, analysis and reporting in any research project, particularly one focusing on such a complex decisionmaking process as sentencing, is time consuming and expensive. This is especially true if the research effort is an innovative, collaborative one, such as it was in this project.

The involvement of the two "observer" courts, in Essex and Polk counties, was therefore integral to our efforts in many ways, providing us with an invaluable resource of field experience at little additional cost. Indeed, these "observer" courts participated in every aspect of the project, excepting only that the research staff did not collect or analyze data from them. The inclusion of observer courts increased judicial advice to the research effort—advice that the judges from Denver and Vermont often recognized as critical. Thus it was that each judge involved in the project became a "researcher" as well.

The observer court judges were, in some respects, actually improved participants owing to the absence of researchers in their own courts. They could be candid and indeed blunt in suggesting new leads for researchers and new approaches to their colleagues from the participant courts. It was thought also that the judges from these courts would be less likely to be affected by any possible effect linked to the direct involvement of being a participant jurisdiction—that is, they would not be influenced by what researchers refer to as the "Hawthorne effect."[7] We further believed that participant jurisdictions might be less stringent in their criticisms of the concept of sentencing guidelines simply because they were actively participating in the research. In addition, observer courts provided the opportunity to examine how dissemination of the concept and methodology might best be accomplished in jurisdictions other than the participant ones. In the event, of course, this latter feature paid off handsomely as the Essex County and Superior Courts moved rapidly into the implementation phase of our work with almost no discrete preparation required.

There were three major criteria employed in the selection of both the participant and the observer courts involved during the initial basic research. First, we wanted to involve both urban and rural jurisdictions and large and small population concentrations to test the potential for nationwide applicability of guidelines. Second, we wished to work in jurisdictions in which the number of judges was small enough to facilitate direct communication between the judges and a research staff member based in each participating site. Our third major criterion was that we wanted to work in courts in which the judge actually sentenced—that is, although we expected to find that variant of plea bargaining referred to as charge bargaining, we wanted courts in which there was no sentence bargaining.[8] This latter practice involves a "bargained" sanction or penalty determined by negotiations between the prosecution and defense. In such instances, it seemed to us that the judge might be more the ratifier of the decisions of others than the primary decisionmaker. Our initial research focused on the concept of guidelines as related to decision processes and not to compromises, negotiations, or ratifications. The main problem is that as soon as more than one decisionmaker enters the process, the variations increase exponentially. Thus, we simplified our research design by avoiding sentence bargaining and were able to assume with increased confidence that the responsibility and action of sentencing were accountable to the same individual—the sentencing judge with whom we worked.[9]

Formalizing Judicial Involvement With A View To Maximizing Research Impact

It was our belief that the success of the project and the eventual acceptance of sentencing guidelines would in large measure depend upon the extent to which the judiciary made this project their own. Thus, it was our intention from the start to involve the judiciary thoroughly in all stages of the project. This was an essential component of our action research philosophy. Therefore, immediately subsequent to site selection, we established a Steering and Policy Committee that met frequently and regularly. At least one judge from each jurisdiction attended each meeting of this committee. This Steering and Policy Committee was the principal mechanism, during all phases of our work, by which we established that desired communication between observer and participant courts and between all the judges and the research staff. Committee meetings were, moreover, rotated between various of the jurisdictions involved, so that all of us could receive additional input from other judges at each of the locations.

By June of 1976, our basic research goals had been accomplished; the Law Enforcement Assistance Administration evaluated our efforts, concluded that we had indeed proven the feasibility of establishing a sentencing guidelines system, and funded us to continue research. Our efforts now were to be geared toward actually implementing sentencing guidelines systems and expanding the number of jurisdictions with which we were to be involved. In establishing the criteria for site involvement at this point, we were fortunate enough to be able to work in conjunction with our partners in research, the judicial members of the Steering and Policy Committee.

The Role of the Research Staff: Partners in Research

It would be appropriate now to step back for a moment to examine the role that the research staff played. While we were partners in research with the judges, our degree of partnership varied, and we became more and more junior the closer any particular court came to implementing its own sentencing guidelines system. This had to be so as we could not assume the responsibility for actual sentencing that local judges shouldered daily. Our role was to highlight the significance of particular decisions, lay out the available options, and then construct sentencing guidelines according to the express—and now informed—desires of the local judiciary. Only in this way could the guidelines become the public policy statement of the judiciary that they were intended to be.

In many ways, therefore, we saw ourselves as performing a service function for the judiciary, supplying them with a necessary "product." At the outset, the research staff set out to learn as much as possible concerning the problems of sentencing, and here the judges taught the staff a great deal. The research staff in turn indicated to judges some of the available research methods that might be brought to bear on judicial problems. A large amount of our early research involved such a mutual learning situation, and it is in this sense that our work was truly collaborative and in which we view ourselves as partners in research. The inclusion of the judges from the "observer" courts, as described above, proved particularly valuable in this regard. As equal members of our Steering and Policy Committee, yet representing nonparticipant courts, the observer court judges greatly helped us break down any "them" and "us" division that might otherwise have bedeviled us.[10]

IMPLEMENTING ACTION RESEARCH: SELECTING THE FIRST SENTENCING GUIDELINES JURISDICTIONS IN AMERICA

Denver

As we now wished to move broadly in implementing a concept the feasibility of which was no longer in doubt, we doubled the number of participant courts. We first chose to continue working with the Denver District Court, as our work there was far advanced—so advanced, indeed, that we were able to achieve guidelines inplementation in

November 1976, only five months after our implementation research began. Denver had been chosen as a basic research site largely because of the expressed willingness of its judiciary to engage in a highly speculative research enterprise. The relatively accessible data base in Denver, the logistical compactness of the jurisdiction (thus necessitating less travel), the manageable size of the caseload, the absence of sentence bargaining, and the geographical diversity that the court offered were all further reasons for the selection of Denver as both a basic and an applied implementation site.

Newark

For the second sentencing guidelines jurisdiction in America, we chose the Essex County and Superior Courts in Newark, New Jersey. Essex County was not only a major, urban, Eastern county offering a contrast to Denver, but it had also been an "observer" court during our basic research. The choice of Essex County thus enabled us to measure whether knowledge of our procedures (gained by observer status) hastened the implementation process, thus affording us the opportunity to speed up the otherwise time-consuming preliminary explanation so necessary to securing the full cooperation of the judiciary. Indeed, a paramount reason for choosing Essex County was that the judges there were exceptionally ready and eager for the assistance we offered. Judges Leo Yanoff and John Marzulli had served as representatives of this observer court, on the Steering and Policy Committee, all through the basic research phase of sentencing guidelines research. Their enthusiasm had been communicated to their colleagues, as evidenced by the fact that the research staff required virtually no advance preparation there; our site staff began work in Essex County during the very first week of implementation research, and guidelines were developed relatively quickly for judicial use.

Furthermore, the judges of Essex County required no demonstration of a need for guidelines; other researchers had already documented what the Administrative Director of the New Jersey Courts referred to as "alarming . . . wide and undue disparity."[11] Thus, the judges of the state had been very much aware of the issues. Moreover, they were particularly receptive to those aspects of our approach that coincided with a recently enumerated policy decision of the New Jersey Supreme Court that had directed all criminal judges to set forth the reasons for their sentences.[12] Hence, we experienced little difficulty in convincing the local judiciary to give specific and detailed reasons for going outside of the guidelines: this amounted only to an application of one aspect of their current practice.

Chicago

The third and fourth participant sites were to be chosen from among the largest of America's urban courts. In choosing such sites, we were consciously testing the possibility of shortening even further the otherwise time-consuming explanation of procedures that we felt to be so essential during the feasibility phase of our study. We realized many of the difficulties we would encounter by such an approach. This was clearly not the path of least resistance to the adoption and utilization of guidelines models. Not only would available explanation time be decreased, but it was further expected that judges from major urban centers would argue that the sheer volume of the cases they must dispose of and the serious types of crimes and criminals they encountered would prohibit the use of guidelines in their jurisdictions. Rather than share in this pessimism, however, we accepted it as a challenge. Therefore, our implementation research effort was designed to add two additional court systems as participants, each selected from an urban center having at least ten criminal trial court judges. The two additional participant courts we eventually selected were the Cook County Circuit Court (Chicago, Illinois) and the Maricopa County Superior Court (Phoenix, Arizona).

The selection of the Cook County Circuit Court as a participant site was both easy and difficult. It was easy in the sense that it readily met all of our criteria; it was difficult in that, in many ways, it met them too well! While we wanted a large urban court, we were frankly apprehensive about working with the very largest court of unlimited original jurisdiction in America.[13] We wanted to work in a more complex environment with less judicial communication, but one that eventually entailed four different branches seemed dangerously beyond our physical capabilities. We wanted to include a sentence bargaining jurisdiction, but the pervasiveness of the practice here was intimidating. We also wanted to work with a different sort of data base, but not one as difficult as the one we encountered here. Finally, we wanted the challenge of aiding a group of judges who had previously—loudly and frequently—rejected federal research assistance because of their fear that what one judge called "the screaming federal eagle" would impose onerous conditions upon them.[14]

In sum, therefore, Cook County presented a major test for the applicability of the sentencing guidelines concept; the complexity of this urban court system, coupled with the volume and seriousness of the cases processed through it each year, provided a rigorous proving ground for our research. Moreover, as opposed to practice in the other project sites, Cook County practice much more often revealed that variant of plea bargaining referred to as sentence bargaining. While many jurisdictions have both forms of plea bargaining, it is most common to find that the prosecutor and the defense attorney bargain only over the appropriate criminal charge, rather than the type of disposition (i.e., the sentence). However, following our successful feasibility work in charge bargaining jurisdictions, we wanted very much to test out the guidelines concept in a sentence bargaining site. Although it is more difficult to develop guidelines for this variation of plea negotiation, there are a number of benefits that we felt would accrue from its implementation.[15]

Other reasons for choosing the Cook County Circuit Court included the willingness of the judiciary to collaborate fully in this research[16] and the very nature of the select class of cases that we eventually decided would be studied in depth—primarily, already incarcerated offenders—which factor later confounded analytical comparisons between Cook County and the other sites.[17] This "biased" sample, however, did allow us to study the more serious cases in far greater detail.

Phoenix

Our search for a fourth participant site ended in December 1976, when the Maricopa County Superior Court (Phoenix, Arizona) joined our collaborative effort. The recent population (and caseload) boom there made Phoenix a fascinating study site. The availability of extremely well-qualified coders from the student body of the Criminal Justice Center at Arizona State University was also a positive factor. A primary reason for selecting Maricopa County, however, was the cooperation of the probation and court administration staff, who serve the judiciary well, combined with the ready access that they afforded us to a modern, sophisticated, well-developed, and comprehensive data base.

The Observer Courts

Once again, we looked forward to the involvement of observer courts; they were again to be involved in all possible ways, except that the project did not include the financing of the actual carrying out of research in their area. The number of courts involved was thereby multiplied through this process with very little increase in cost. It was again hoped that by the special "observer" status, we would build an extended reservoir of good will and that, during the guidelines information dissemination process, other courts would take greater note of the views expressed by observers than they would of participants, who might be seen as biased because of their direct involvement. This procedure worked very well during the basic research study, and we indeed experienced even greater success with it during our guidelines implementation work.

Since our second phase (implementation) research involved four participant courts, we sought to enlist four observer courts as well, so as to balance the discussion at our Steering and Policy Committee meetings. Each of the two other courts with which we had worked during our feasibility research agreed to continue collaborating with us during our pilot implementation work. The willingness of the District Courts of the State of Vermont to move from a participant to an observer status was particularly helpful; since we were constantly concerned with the generalizability of the guidelines concept, their statewide focus, as well as their more rural orientation, provided especially useful contributions at the quarterly meetings of the Steering and Policy Committee. As the Honorable Anthony Critelli, of Iowa's Polk County Court, had been the extremely effective chair of our Steering and Policy Committee during the feasibility study, the continued involvement of that court during the second phase provided us with both strong leadership and continuity of direction.

Once again, we hoped that the two additional observer courts that we wanted to include would possess the same criteria that we looked for in our participant courts. We were fortunate enough to enlist the support of the Philadelphia (Pennsylvania) Court of Common Pleas and the King County (Seattle, Washington) Superior Court.

RESEARCH AS ACTION

It has been particularly rewarding for those of us engaged in action research to see the recognition that sentencing guidelines have received. Initial judicial skepticism was replaced by fervent support as our goal of assisting trial court judges was realized in one jurisdiction after another. Judges actively joined hands with academics in a collaborative effort at achieving reforms in the sentencing process: the action research methodology employed by the sentencing guidelines research team has had concrete and positive results.

Each of the first four sentencing guidelines jurisdictions has maintained the program even after federal support was discontinued. The Denver program was independently replicated and adapted for use in the courts of neighboring Boulder, Colorado. The Newark program served as a working model for an independently developed statewide sentencing guidelines system—the first in the nation—in New Jersey.[18] The Chicago program, initially employed in only two of the four court branches, has successfully been expanded to the other two branches and continues in force. After the development of the Phoenix guidelines, a complete penal code revision took place in Arizona, and the guidelines are proving their flexibility as they are being adapted for use with the new code.

The two latest observer courts—the Philadelphia Court of Common Pleas and the King County Superior Court—had posed a dilemma for us. They both very much wanted to be involved as participant courts; yet while we would very much have desired this, our funding and other constraints simply made this impossible. Nevertheless, both courts proved so enthusiastic concerning the sentencing guidelines concept that each eventually adopted sentencing guidelines systems, although in different ways.

As I will explain in Chapter 6, the Philadelphia Court of Common Pleas, unable to be a part of the federally funded guidelines implementation project I directed, found its own source of funding and developed guidelines. While we provided as much advice and technical assistance as we could, it was a locally based research team, headed by Saundra Dillio, that developed an operational sentencing guidelines system in collaboration with the Philadelphia judiciary, headed by President Judge Edward J. Bradley and Court Administrator David N. Savitt. That system was in turn replicated in Polk County, Pennsylvania, and finally, statewide, as Pennsylvania became the second state to establish a Sentencing Commission incorporating the sentencing guidelines methodology.[19]

While the King County Superior Court wanted to develop guidelines as well, funding constraints made that impossible during the life of the federal effort reported here. Nevertheless, primarily due to the efforts of the Honorable Warren Chan, who served as King County's representative on our Steering and Policy Committee, the Superior Court judges of the state of Washington decided to advance toward a statewide sentencing guidelines system through funds provided by their own State Court Administrator's Office and through research conducted by Justice Analysis Center of Schenectady, New York. By early 1979, separate sentencing guidelines systems had been developed for the courts of general jurisdiction and the courts of limited jurisdiction in the state of Washington.[20]

Other countywide guidelines systems are presently being developed in Florida, Georgia, Louisiana, Maryland, and Montana. Other statewide systems have been or are being developed in Alaska, Connecticut, Massachusetts, Michigan, Minnesota, North Dakota, Oregon, Rhode Island, Utah, and Wisconsin.[21] Legislation and research are also pending in the federal system, in New York, and elsewhere.

Such solid results are tremendously gratifying to me personally and, I know, to my colleagues as well. Action research has established the credibility and viability of a major sentencing alternative that did not exist only a few short years ago. It remains now to detail the general research design that our team employed and the specific applications of the sentencing guidelines approach brought to fruition through the action research methodology.

NOTES

1. T. H. Huxley, "Technical Education," in T. H. Huxley, *Science and Education: Essays* (New York: D. Appleton and Company, 1898) at 422. "Even in the learned professions, knowledge alone is of less consequence than people are apt to suppose" (at 414).

2. See the reference *supra* Chapter 1 at note 37. Our singular goal was "to improve the performance of the courts in relation to their sentencing decisions." That was the aim then and is the aim now. While it is for others to say whether or not guidelines have succeeded, the intent has always been clear. We did not set out to "study" the courts; we set out to help the courts.

3. And initially they did *not* recognize this. After the fact of our successful effort, there has been a tendency to downplay the early difficulties that we had to overcome. Listening to critics of our early research, one would think that judges welcomed us with open arms and docket books. This, unfortunately, was not the case at all. Indeed, our very sincerity was constantly challenged; virtually every judge with whom we worked was initially suspicious of our motives. For example, Cook County's Presiding Judge Richard J. Fitzgerald recalls: "Frankly, at first I was skeptical. I thought that the project might simply be making work for psychologists, researchers and grantsmen." (These remarks were made in an address to the chief judges of Illinois on November 18, 1977.) I should note also that skepticism was not the province alone of the judiciary. Not only did we have to convince judges, but in three of the four jurisdictions in which we first implemented guidelines, we had to further enlist the cooperation of a suspicious probation department. They feared, initially, that our intent was to render them superfluous—substituting mechanical guidelines for documented presentence investigation reports. We thus had to overcome this early distrust, as well as a perhaps more significant suspicion that we were out to attack their sentencing recommendation function. In the end, of course, we demonstrated our constructive intent to both judges and probation personnel.

4. 28 C.F.R. §2.20 (revised 1979); see also 18 U.S.C. §4206.

5. D. M. Gottfredson, P. B. Hoffman, M. H. Sigler, and L. T. Wilkins, "Making Paroling Policy Explicit," 21 *Crime and Delinquency* 34 (January 1975); see also W. J. Genego, P. D. Goldberger, and V. C. Jackson, "Parole Release Decisionmaking and the Sentencing Pro-

cess," 84 *Yale Law Journal* 810 (March 1975); D. M. Gottfredson, L. T. Wilkins and P. B. Hoffman, *Guidelines for Parole and Sentencing* (Lexington, Mass.: Lexington Books, 1978). Curiously, taking into account what we have learned of the bifurcated nature of the sentencing decision, it seems that the initial research hypotheses of both the parole and the sentencing guidelines studies have had to be reversed! See L. T. Wilkins, J. M. Kress, D. M. Gottfredson, J. C. Calpin, and A. M. Gelman, *Sentencing Guidelines: Structuring Judicial Discretion–Report on the Feasibility Study* 1–2 (Washington, D.C.: USGPO, 1978).

6. Wilkins, et al., *supra* note 5 at 4–6, 33–37.

7. J. Ross and P. Smith, "Orthodox Experimental Designs," in H. M. Blalock, Jr., and A. B. Blalock, *Methodology in Social Research* (New York: McGraw-Hill, 1968) at 340, referring to F. J. Roethlisberger and W. J. Dickson, *Management and the Worker* (Cambridge, Mass.: Harvard University Press, 1939).

8. See D. J. Newman, *Conviction: The Determination of Guilt or Innocence Without Trial* (Boston: Little, Brown, 1966); J. Bond, *Plea-Bargaining and Guilty Pleas* (New York: Clark Boardman, 1975); Georgetown University Law Center, *Plea Bargaining in the United States–Phase I Report* (Washington, D. C.: Georgetown University Law Center, 1978); and A. Rosett and D. R. Cressey, *Justice by Consent* (Philadelphia: J. B. Lippincott, 1976).

9. I should note here that our later work demonstrated that our early fears were unfounded. The sentencing guidelines concept is applicable to large, as well as to small, jurisdictions and also to those where sentence bargaining predominates. See the section on Implementing Action Research, *infra*. The implementation phase of guidelines research was directed solely by the author.

10. For an elaboration of this procedure, see L. T. Wilkins, J. M. Kress, and D. M. Gottfredson, "Guidelines for Sentencers: Strategy of the Research and Management of the Feasibility Study" (unpublished working paper, 1977).

11. See the remarks of the Honorable Arthur J. Simpson, Jr., at the September 3, 1974, Judicial Conference of New Jersey; see also "Sentence Disparity Among Prison Commitments," a report put out on May 6, 1974, by the Division of Correction and Parole, Department of Institutions and Agencies, State of New Jersey.

12. Revised New Jersey Supreme Court Rule 3.21 (1974).

13. J. S. Boyle, "Making a Big Court Better," 60 *Judicature* 233 (December 1976).

14. With regard to these two latter points, I wish to acknowledge with gratitude the "*Miranda* warnings" received from Professor Franklin Zimring of the University of Chicago School of Law. His

advice, coupled with that of his law school colleague Hans Zeisel, was invaluable with regard to our successful research effort in Cook County.

15. See *infra* Chapter 8, as well as the references *supra* note 7.

16. Indeed, primary credit for the success of our Cook County research must be given to the inspired and unflagging leadership of Presiding Judge Richard J. Fitzgerald.

17. See *infra* Chapter 7; and J. M. Kress, *Sentencing in Four Courts* (Washington, D.C.: USGPO, 1980).

18. New Jersey's system was implemented through the medium of the Administrative Office of the Courts, headed by the Honorable Arthur J. Simpson, Jr.; the research itself was directed by Jack McCarthy and took effect in October 1978.

19. The first statewide Sentencing Commission was established in Minnesota and is chaired by Jan Smaby and directed by Dale G. Parent; the commission is due to submit sentencing guidelines in early 1980. The Pennsylvania Sentencing Commission began operating on April 1, 1979, chaired by the Honorable Richard P. Conaboy; it is due to submit guidelines on September 30, 1980.

20. The actual research involved was performed under the direction of Jack M. Kress and Arthur M. Gelman, who worked through the facilities of Justice Analysis Center, Inc., 301 Parkview Drive, Schenectady, New York 12303.

21. Criminal Courts Technical Assistance Project, "Overview of State and Local Sentencing Guidelines Activity" (Washington, D.C.: American University Law Institute monograph, April 1979).

5

The General Research Design

One aim of this book was to place the distrust of science on a scientific basis.—Samuel Butler[1]

While this book is primarily written for a lay audience—detailed explanations of the statistical methodology are available elsewhere[2]—some summary explanation of the analytical research procedures employed by the research team is nevertheless in order. Our initial data collection methods and statistical techniques were derived from those applied in the federal parole decisionmaking study described in the preceding chapter. Nonetheless, the sentencing decision is very different from the paroling decision—it is far more complicated—and we therefore made many procedural alterations and accommodations in terms of systematic data collection, coding, analysis, and modeling. In this chapter, I will summarize the methods that we employed during both phases of our work, focusing more comprehensively on our later work. This overview of our research methodology should serve as a useful background in helping the reader to understand the specific site activity discussed in succeeding chapters. While significant adaptations were made to suit the requirements of each individual sentencing guidelines jurisdiction, the general research design remained the same.

DATA COLLECTION AND REFINEMENT

As discussed in the preceding chapter, our first research step was the selection of sites for activity and the establishment of our Steering and Policy Committee. Following that, we could begin to assess the feasibility of the sentencing guidelines concept. As a start, we amassed a list of all items of information thought to be relevant to reaching the sentencing decision, whether by authorities in the literature or by members of the Steering and Policy Committee. A list of some 205 information items was eventually drawn up.[3] These items were coded for, and we sought to collect each one, in hundreds of randomly selected sentencing decisions in each of the two participating courts. Our attempt was to have at our disposal all the information that was available to the judge for consideration in deciding upon an actual sentence.

In the event, nearly one-quarter of the 205 items turned out to be "missing" (or unavailable) in over 25 percent of the cases.[4] Much of this missing information concerned factors relating to the offender's social stability (e.g., school attendance, employment evaluation). Upon hearing these findings, members of the Steering and Policy Committee saw that they were not getting all the information that they at first thought they were taking into consideration in their sentencing decisions. Thus, the judges realized, for example, that they were more concerned with the dimension of social stability than with any specific item of information relating to that dimension. Hence, if one information item relating to social stability was missing, another piece of available data could conceivably be used as a substitute.

The available information was then analyzed for those offense/offender characteristics that statistically accounted for the largest percentage of variation in the sentencing decision. Our analyses indicated that the seriousness of the current offense and the extent of the offender's prior criminal record were the two most influential sets (or dimensions) of information items. The data thus furnished preliminary, descriptive conclusions as to what underlying factors influenced the sentencing decision as well as the weights accorded to each of those factors.

TESTING DIFFERENT SENTENCING GUIDELINES MODELS

Five preliminary guidelines models were then designed.[5] These models attempted to indicate what the average, or "modified" average, sentence of all judges in that particular jurisdiction would have been in a particular case. By tapping the same data base available to the judges in constructing our models, we made valuable use of the accumulated experiences of veteran sentencing judges. The models were based on empirical and/or theoretical evidence; such an approach permitted us to test whether guidelines models constructed on differing assumptions might not in fact achieve the same or a similar end result.

All of these models were presented to the Steering and Policy Committee, whose members were then able to see clearly the potential value of even this rough sort of tool as an aid in the making of the sentencing decision. The committee instructed the staff to test the models against a further sample of cases currently coming before the judiciary. This was completed against a small validation sample with the various models found to be correctly "predicting" between 73 and 84 percent of the "in" (the decision to incarcerate) or "out" (the decision to grant probation or otherwise not incarcerate) part of the sentencing decision.[6] We believed that many, although certainly not all, of the "misses" could be regarded as examples of warranted variation because of some unusual facts of circumstances, some of which we hoped to account for in more refined guidelines models.

The committee then asked the research staff to formulate one model, perhaps a synthesis of the five preliminary ones. As our data collection, refinement, and analysis work had proceeded more quickly in Denver than in Vermont, we prepared this synthesis, demonstration test model for use by the Denver judiciary. Because the model was still rough and because Colorado statutes already provided judges with a short period in which to reflect upon sentences handed down, the demonstration model's guideline sentences were delivered to sentencing judges after actual sentencing had taken place for their own consideration and review.

This somewhat cautious approach was also taken so as to allow us a little more time for "honing" the model. Owing to the relative infrequency of incarcerative sentences, it took a somewhat larger sample to collect an adequate number of "in" sentences from which to estimate accurately the "length" part of the sentencing decision. Moreover, it must be remembered that our primary concern during this first phase was only testing the feasibility of guidelines, not implementing them.

By the end of our basic research phase, therefore, all six criminal court judges in the Denver County District Court were receiving a guidelines sentence some two to three days after sentencing. They were in turn providing the research team with feedback as to why they thought the actual sentence different from the model sentence, in those cases in which such a result occurred.

ADAPTING THE GENERAL RESEARCH DESIGN
TO SPECIFIC CONDITIONS

Given the go-ahead to proceed in implementing sentencing guidelines, we selected the implementation sites as described in the preceding chapter. The research staff then began an examination of the procedural rules applicable in the local court systems, as well as of the caselaw and criminal code in each jurisdiction, so as to determine their effects on sentencing decisions. Judges, probation officers, prosecutors, public defenders, court personnel, and others familiar with the local criminal justice system were all interviewed to gain insight into the operations of the courts. Furthermore, court files were examined to determine the quantity, quality, and nature of the information available to the judges at sentencing. Finally, collateral sources of information, such as sentencing manuals and previous sentencing reports, were examined by the research team. As a result of these activities, the researchers acquired that working knowledge of the local jurisdictions that we found vital in adapting our basic research strategy to the needs of each specific court system.

This background information was critical in the development of a codification system to collect the data required for analysis.[7] A detailed coding manual was painstakingly and individually prepared for each jurisdiction so as to meet the legal and pragmatic requirements of that jurisdiction. Information items were included based on the staff's examination of criminal codes, caselaw, local sentencing practice, judicial advice and requests, and the staff's prior experience. To guide those who would actually collect the data, specific decision rules were developed that provided uniform standards for quantifying data as well as a consistent approach to the handling of missing, contradictory, or ambiguous information. The researchers closely reviewed the data collection sheets and coding manuals with the judges in each jurisdiction as one means of ensuring their adequacy. In addition, these instruments were pretested on a small sample of sentencing decisions so as to assess their reliability and validity.

This preliminary analysis of criminal codes and court practices was also useful in determining the timing of the data collection. The research staff established time frames for data collection so as to include the most recent sentencing decisions available. Whenever possible, the cases were sampled over a twelve month period in order to minimize the possible prejudicing influences of such sources of variation as season (e.g., Christmas leniency), court staff turnover, or vacations.

The confidence that can be placed in the results of statistical analysis and the interpretation of those results depends to no small extent on the accuracy with which the data is collected. The careful preparation of data collection instruments is one way of ensuring data reliability. But this is not enough, as coders must be well trained and their work continually monitored and tested. Consequently, training and review sessions were conducted for the coders employed in each jurisdiction. Throughout data collection their reliability was continually tested through the use of spot checks and other means.

When the data had been collected, additional reliability tests were introduced to assure the quality of the information base.[8]

STATISTICAL ANALYSIS

Once the research staff was certain that the input information items were as accurate as possible, a variety of statistical techniques were used as "mathematical filters" designed to identify those items of information that were most strongly related to sentencing decisions.

The first set of techniques used focused on what is referred to statistically as a bivariate analysis—that is, a measure of the relation between sentencing decisions and each individual information item contained in the case files. (The researchers in particular used such bivariate methods as contingency table analysis and Pearson's correlation coefficient at this stage of the analysis.) Based on the results obtained at this stage, factors were selected for multivariate analysis. Unlike bivariate analysis, multivariate statistical techniques examine the relation between sentencing decisions and sets of information items. (In particular, the research staff employed such multivariate techniques as multiple regression and discriminant function analysis.) These multivariate techniques served as a check on the results obtained from the application of bivariate methods and provided an additional indication of which information items in a body of data might be the most important.

As a result of the application of all these techniques, the researchers were able to establish a "pool," or set, of items of information significantly related to sentencing decisions.

Next, the research staff applied unit weighting scales to this data as the basis for their development of sentencing guidelines models. There are several reasons for using such unit weighting systems to analyze the data, predict sentencing decisions, and construct sentencing guidelines. First, when both unit weighting systems and differential weighting systems are used to predict the same set of outcomes the unit weighting systems are almost as accurate as the differential weighting system. But when both are applied to another (validation) set of cases, the unit weight system tends to perform at least as well as the differential weight system—and often even more accurately.[9] Moreover, the information that is available regarding sentencing decisions does not generally meet the standards required for the proper application of the more sophisticated analytic and predictive instruments. Additionally, the use of simple, equal weighting plans reduces the possibility of error from incorrect coding and/or incorrect mathematical computation. Finally, such systems minimize the amount of time needed to calculate the offense and offender scores. While this time saving is important in all courts, it is particularly important in those courts where the judges must calculate the scores themselves.

As the first step in the development of such unit point scales, the research staff used the earlier cross-tabular analyses to examine the relation between the decision whether or not to incarcerate (that is, the "in/out" decision) and items of information identified as describing sentencing decisions. Cross-tabulation is merely the joint frequency distribution of sentencing decisions according to the sentence imposed and some other factor—for example, the number of prior adult convictions. The nature of cross-tabular analysis and its role in the development of unit weighting systems can best be illustrated by example (see Table 5–1).

Table 5–1. Hypothetical Example of Cross-Tabular Analysis (percent).

Sentence		*Number of prior adult convictions*			
		0	*1*	*2*	*3+*
Nonprison	(62)	75	56	33	27
Prison	(38)	25	44	67	73

As shown by this hypothetical example, there appears to be a relation between the number of prior adult convictions in an offender's criminal history record and the probability of that particular offender being incarcerated. An examination of Table 5–1 indicates that as the number of convictions increases, the percentage of offenders who were incarcerated also tends to increase. The researchers would then examine such a table to determine the specific weights or points to be assigned to each of the categories of the independent variable, number of prior adult convictions. The goal is to establish categories for the independent variables (e.g., prior adult convictions: 0, 1, or 2) that have different rates of incarceration and that in turn differ from the overall rate of incarceration (which in this example is 38 percent). In practice, once the categorization of the independent variables was decided upon, the staff applied various unit weighting point systems to the categories of the independent variables. In our example, 0 points could be given to an offender who had no prior convictions and 1 point to every offender who had been previously convicted as an adult. Of course, there are a variety of approaches to unit weighting: for example, points could be assigned in terms of "rewarding" noncriminal behavior rather than "penalizing" criminal behavior—that is, 1 point might be assigned to each offender who had no prior adult convictions and 0 points to each offender who had such a prior record.

MODEL DEVELOPMENT

The next step in the development of preliminary models of sentencing guidelines was the construction of offender scales and offense (crime) scales. Different offender and offense scales were developed by varying the factors included in these scales as well as the weighting schemes accorded these factors. By varying these components (weights and factors) alone, the researchers were able to generate a large and diverse group of guidelines models in each jurisdiction. But there is another aspect to guidelines modeling that also increases the diversity of the models that can be developed and that is the type of model that can be designed.

During our research, two basic model types were developed and implemented—the "general" or "class" model (used in Denver and Cook counties) and the "generic" model (used in Essex and Maricopa counties). We have tested, but not employed so far, a third approach, referred to as the "crime-specific" model. We have furthermore explored alternate modeling schemes and combinations of these models are quite conceivable.

The "General" or "Class" Model

The term "general model" is used here to describe a sentencing guidelines system in which decisionmaking matrixes are developed parallel to and coordinate with the statutory classification system established by the state's criminal code. For example, both Illinois and Colorado use a Model Penal Code type of approach to the classification of offenses—that is, there is a graded system of felonies and misdemeanors structured in such a way that the higher classes are considered to contain more serious offenses, and thus greater potential penalties apply to offenders convicted of committing such a higher class of crime.

The significant point about this class structure is that many different types or kinds of crimes are to be found within each class rank. Thus, to use Colorado as an example: Murder in the First Degree and First Degree Kidnapping are each Felony 1 offenses with a possible death penalty; Murder in the Second Degree and Sexual Assault in the First Degree are each Felony 2 offenses with a possible maximum penalty of fifty years imprisonment attached; Manslaughter and Theft are Felony 4 Offenses with a possible maximum penalty of ten years imprisonment; while Soliciting for Prostitution and Criminal Possession of a Credit Device are each Misdemeanor 3 offenses for which an offender may not receive more than six months jail sentence. Matrixes constructed for any specific class rank must therefore, of necessity, relate to a broad or general range of offenses encompassing a wide range of criminal activity, less wide as to degree of criminality (at least as measured by the legislatively set equivalent penalty ranges), but quite wide as to differences in kind or type.

Constraints of both a philosophical nature and data base availability have affected both the choice and the design of the various guidelines models. Expressed fears of breaching the separation of powers between the legislative and judicial branches of government were one concern that led to the development of the general model. It was felt by some judges that the state legislature had supplied them with the leeway to differentially order and treat offenses within the same class, but had not given them similar authority to cross class rankings. Moreover, constructing a different grid for each class of offense effectively turned each two dimensional grid into a part of a very useful three dimensional system.

In the application of this approach, as it turned out, the same set of information items was used for all classes of offenses; indeed, this set of information items remained constant in factor content and weighting of factors across the various statutory classes of offense. However, there are probably jurisdictions where there will be shifts in factor content and/or weighting of factors. (Indeed, recent updating of the Denver system seems to bear this out.) A major advantage of the general model over any of the other models has so far been the simplicity of calculation it has afforded, particularly inasmuch as only the one set of information items has been used.

The "Generic" Model

The theoretical principle underlying the "generic" approach is perhaps best expressed in decisionmaking terms. We have seen the judge as a sentencing decisionmaker, carefully sifting, sorting, and ranking the various pieces of information available so as to process these items in a useful manner. It has seemed more logical that different items of information will make a differential impact upon the sentencing decisionmaker, more with regard to matters of kind than matters of degree or, to put it another way, that typological crime classifications would prove better information sorters than statutory class categories.

Some illustrations might prove helpful and, for the moment, let me consider examples we did not employ in practice, but which may possess theoretical force. Let us compare the generic groupings of (1) arsons without any apparent profit motive, and (2) fraud and forgery offenses. Think how differently the various information items available to the sentencing judge will influence that decisionmaker. In sentencing an arsonist, a judge may be very concerned to receive potentially aggravating information about the likelihood of occupancy (the nature of the building, the time of day) or whether any physical injury was suffered by tenants or firefighters; some judges would request a detailed evaluation concerning possible mitigating factors such as alleged victim precipitation of the event (e.g., the landlord having threatened eviction of the tenant defendant) or a recent change in the health status of the offender. With regard to the arsonist's prior record, a judge would likely be more concerned with the type of prior arrests or convictions than the number of them, being far more interested in seeing whether the offender had previously shown proclivities toward mental aberration than in how serious those charges had been—for example, a prior misdemeanor conviction for vandalism or criminal mischief might appear more significant to the sentencing judge than one for felony grand theft.

None of these things would be relevant, however, in the sentencing of, say, a forger or counterfeiter. The amount of monetary or property loss suffered by the victim might be significant in each case, but physical injury information is irrelevant in terms of providing depth or meaning to any harm-loss modifier of the instant offense. Steady employment as a printer, as another example, might actually tell against the counterfeiter. The prior record of concern in this case may not involve even serious assaults, but rather, violations of positions of trust and other offenses demonstrating dishonesty.

Some factors, such as whether the disposition was by plea or the number of charges, may actually be relevant in both situations, but a "generic" model focuses on the salient factors specifically related to the type of crime committed. The logic of this approach is that information is fitted ever more closely to information needs as measures of relevance are more sharply developed. Thus, in the "generic" approach to guidelines, an offense typology is developed that classifies offenses into broad categories based on similarities in the criminal *behavior* involved in the offenses. One generic category we did employ involved grouping together in one sentencing decisionmaking matrix all offenses involving violent behavior—for example, simple assaults and rapes fell into the same "violent" typology, even though they were in different statutory classifications, with different potential penalty structures. As it turned out, in our application of this approach, there was variation in the set of information items used for each typology; but there was no variation across the types of offenses in the weights assigned to the items of information. However, I am of the opinion that there are likely to be jurisdictions where, if the same information item is used for more than one typology, different weights will have to be assigned to that item depending on the type of offense in question. (It is also conceivable, albeit unlikely, that "generic" models may be developed in which both factors used, and their weights, remain constant over all the offenses in the guidelines system.)

In practice so far, the generic model has employed four typological offense classifications—violent, property, drugs, and miscellaneous. The procedure for ascertaining the appropriate guidelines sentence has been for the person performing the computation to turn to the information set appropriate to the type of offense in question, score the relevant offense and offender scores, and then locate their intersection on a matrix established for that offense typology, rather than the matrix for a particular statutory class, as in the general model.

The "Crime-specific" Model

A third type of guidelines model, the "crime-specific" approach, was considered. In many ways, this is a theoretically significant extrapolation of the logic of the generic model, although it has not yet been adopted for use in any sentencing guidelines jurisdiction. In the crime-specific model, both offense and offender information sets and the decisionmaking matrixes are uniquely designed for each individual offense of which the offender was convicted.

According to this concept, a decisionmaking matrix could be developed for every specific statutory offense at conviction. Thus, whatever offense factors might be used would vary from crime to crime, as might the offender factors. This model has the potential for obtaining the highest predictive power of all models since the guidelines are being devised to encompass sharply delineated fact situations. Yet, crime-specific models are extremely costly to develop and to implement both in terms of money and time. First of all, the necessary statistical analysis would not be valid unless a very large number of cases were sampled for each crime for which we are attempting to develop models. Moreover, the analyses must be performed separately for each discrete crime, thus multiplying computer costs. Finally, once crime-specific guidelines were developed, a separate calculation would be necessary to determine the guidelines sentence for each and every offense; therefore, the chances for computational error dramatically increase.

For all of these reasons, I feel that it is not presently practical to develop crime-specific guidelines except perhaps for the most commonly occurring offenses within a jurisdiction (robbery and burglary are likely candidates in felony courts); indeed, even then, some other type of model, either general or generic, would have to be used in conjunction with the crime-specific model in order to accommodate the entire range of criminal offenses. Nevertheless, a statewide or national sentencing commission, or any guidelines maintenance body, would be well advised to look into the possibility of incorporating a crime-specific model with regard to some offenses, particularly as case data (and experience with guidelines) increase over time.

Other Types of Models

There is a variant of each of the preceding three models that is based on the concept of the sentencing decision as a branching network; this would at least double the number of conceptual models. We are convinced, in fact, that this theoretical model would provide us with a more statistically elegant prediction device; this is the *bifurcated* model—that is, one that takes advantage of our finding that sentencing decisionmakers first make an "in/out" decision with regard to a given offender before moving on to the decisions concerning the type or length of any "in" or "out" sentence. According to this concept, a judge first makes the decision whether or not to incarcerate the offender. If the decision is to incarcerate, the judge must then decide the length of incarceration. If the decision is not to incarcerate, the judge must select some alternative to incarceration. Depending on the alternative chosen, the judge may be required to decide, for example, the length of probation, the amount of fine, or the components of a split sentence—assuming such a sentence is viewed as primarily nonincarcerative in the given jurisdiction. To develop and implement this approach, a distinct decisionmaking standard would have to be designed for each major decision point.

The primary theoretical justification for this model lies in the differential impact that various information items would logically make on each stage of the decision. One example might be weekly salary of the offender: this may add no information to the variable of employment status as the judge makes the "in" or" out" decision, but if the judge has decided upon an "out" sentence, then the salary amount might be very relevant in deciding whether to fine the offender or in what amount to fine the offender. This approach to guidelines modeling would be likely to be more accurate in describing sentencing decisions, as different information items and/or different weights would then be more closely related to the decisions at each major branch in the network of sentencing decisions. Nonetheless, the very complexity of this modeling process is its principal drawback; this has, indeed, been the major argument against its adoption in any jurisdiction to date.

Still another theoretical model, and one that we explored early in our work, involves incorporating a *scaling* system by looking at the maximum sentence set by the legislature and using factor weights to establish proportions or percentages of that maximum to be applied in a given case. Also, in states where paroling guidelines have been adopted, sentencing guidelines might be established inferentially, at least with regard to the more serious cases.

Finally, and significantly, various combinations of these models can and have been tested. In fact, in updating its early guidelines system, the Denver District Court has added "generic" components to what initially was a purely "general" model. None of this should be read, however, as a plea for more complicated statistical analysis. Put plainly, there is virtue in simplicity. Involved analytical constructs are elegant to behold, but they may obfuscate more than clarify. The purpose of these models is, after all, to facilitate judicial comprehension and control of all significant aspects of the sentencing decision.

JUDICIAL REVIEW

As a result of this interlocking complexity of weighting plans, sets of factors, and types of models, the research staff considered various combinations of all of these components in the design of sentencing guidelines models. The models that were developed varied from jurisdiction to jurisdiction. Their validity was tested primarily by determining the accuracy with which they described the decision whether or not to incarcerate. In each jurisdiction, the models that proved to be most accurate were selected for further testing. These interim results were discussed with the local judges in each case, in terms of their implications for the articulation of sentencing policy in each court. Unless the judges requested changes in the models presented to them or the development of new models, the researchers then proceeded to subject these models to a further test of their accuracy.

To accomplish this task, new samples of sentencing decisions were gathered with a meticulous striving for accuracy and reliability that paralleled that expended during the first data collection effort. The models were tested again—this time to determine their validity in predicting the length of incarceration decision as well. Those models that demonstrated the greatest validity were selected for still further testing. The judges were then presented with literal pictures of sentencing decisions—of both the "in/out" decision and the length of incarceration decision—as mapped by the specifics of each model. The researchers next assisted the judges in an analysis of the distribution of sentences within each cell of intersection and of the pattern of these cells within each matrix. The judges were consequently able clearly to assess the potential of each model as a graphic statement of local sentencing policy. Based on this assessment, the judges were able to choose a model, or modify one, and to make policy determinations regarding the categorization of cells in terms of the decision whether or not to incarcerate and also the decision as to length of incarceration, when that alternative was chosen.

Once a guidelines model had been agreed upon in each jurisdiction, a test implementation phase was initiated. During this period, we tested the mechanics of processing the data contained in case files into useful guidelines information (that is, offense and offender scores and the linking of those scores to guidelines sentences). In addition to the information usually received at sentencing, the judges in each jurisdiction now received what we termed a guideline worksheet, designed specifically to meet the individual requirements of each jurisdiction.[11] In addition to containing the calculation of the offense and offender scores, the worksheet presented a suggested sentence. When the judges felt that the recommended sentence was appropriate, they merely noted the specific sentence imposed. In those instances in which it was felt that the suggested sentence was inappropriate, the judges recorded the sentence imposed and the reasons for that sentence. The guideline worksheets were collected in each jurisdiction over a period of approximately four months and then analyzed. Of particular interest to the research staff were decisions that differed from the suggested sentence; such cases were analyzed in relation to the reasons given in order to determine whether they indicated a shift in sentencing policy or simply exceptional fact situations.

The researchers reviewed this analysis with the judges, who were then in a position to determine whether modifications should be made in the guidelines. These review sessions were held regularly as a means of maintaini g the guidelines and of keeping them up to date. Handbooks were then prepared so that local staff could take over and operate the local sentencing guidelines system after our research team departed.[12] It was in this way that we exercised our principles of action research, helped local judges to formulate their own explicit court policy, and ensured that that policy would be put into practice.

THE SCOPE OF THE GENERAL RESEARCH DESIGN

My purpose in this chapter has been to provide an overview of the research methodology employed in implementing sentencing guidelines over the course of a four year research project. This discussion has obviously not been detailed enough for researchers, but the information that they require has been made readily available elsewhere.[13] This overview has been intended to provide the reader with a sufficient background to make understandable the procedures undertaken in each of the sentencing guidelines jurisdictions described in the next chapter. The sentencing guidelines methodology has proven to be remarkably flexible and adaptable to local variations. As our four participating courts were chosen in large part because of their differences, it is perhaps not too surprising that the localities varied in many ways, as did the sentencing guidelines systems developed in each county. Perhaps more surprising, therefore, are the many similarities that we encountered and the very fact that the general research design could indeed be reshaped for use in each jurisdiction. We are now able to take a detailed look at the research process, and our findings, in each of America's first five sentencing guidelines jurisdictions.

NOTES

1. S. Butler, "Extracts from 'The Note-Books,' " in *The Essential Samuel Butler*, ed. by G.D.H. Cole (New York: E. P. Dutton & Company, 1950), at 520.

2. A. M. Gelman, J. M. Kress, and J. C. Calpin, *Establishing a Sentencing Guidelines System: A Methods Manual* (Washington, D.C.: University Research Corp., 1978); J. C. Calpin, J. M. Kress, and A. M. Gelman, *The Analytical Basis for the Formulation of Sentencing Policy* (Washington, D.C.: USGPO, 1980); and J. M. Kress and J. C. Calpin, "Research Problems Encountered in Moving Towards Equity in Judicial Decisionmaking," 4 *Justice System Journal* 71 (Fall 1978). For an explanation of the procedures employed in our earliest research, see L. T. Wilkins, J. M. Kress, D. M. Gottfredson, J. C. Calpin, and A. M. Gelman, *Sentencing Guidelines: Structuring Judicial Discretion–Report on the Feasibility Study* (Washington, D.C.: USGPO, 1978).

3. Wilkins, et. al., *supra* note 2 at 39–44.

4. *Id.* at 10–12; 45–50.

5. *Id.* at 12–19.

6. *Id.* at 19–22.

7. See J. M. Kress, *Sentencing in Four Courts* (Washington, D.C.: USGPO, 1980); and J. C. Calpin et al., *supra* note 2 for examples of the data collection instruments the research team actually employed in practice. For a more detailed explanation of how these instruments were employed, see A. M. Gelman, et al., *supra* note 2.

8. For further elaboration on these checks, see Calpin et. al., *supra* note 2.

9. See L. T. Wilkins, *The Problem of Overlap in Experience Table Construction*, Supplemental Report Three (Davis, Calif.: Parole Decision-Making Project, NCCD Research Center, June 1973); H. Mannheim and L. T. Wilkins, *Prediction Methods In Relation to Borstal Training* (London: HMSO, 1955); D. M. Gottfredson, "Assessment and Prediction Methods in Crime and Deliquency," in President's Commission on Law Enforcement and Criminal Justice, *Task Force Report: Juvenile Deliquency*, Appendix K at 176–77 (Washington, D.C.: USGPO, 1967); R. M. Dawes and B. Corrigan, "Linear Models in Decision-Making," 81 *Psychological Bulletin* 95 (1974); H. Wainer, "Estimating Coefficients in Linear Models: It Don't Make No Nevermind," 83 *Psychological Bulletin* 213, 215–16 (1976); and F. H. Simon, *Prediction Methods in Criminology* 111, 150–58 (London: HMSO, 1971).

10. Wilkins et al., *supra* note 2 at 1.

11. See the Appendixes of this book for examples of these worksheets; other examples may be found in the references cited *supra* note 7.

12. *Id.* Appendix A provides a relatively complete example.

13. See sources cited *supra* note 2.

Research in the Field

Knowledge must come through action;
thou canst have no test which is not
fanciful, save by trial. —Sophocles[1]

This chapter provides a demonstration of the applicability of the general sentencing guidelines research design. For each of the five jurisdictions involved, I will describe the structure of the court, including its caseload and crime classification system. Then I will explain the specific process by which the general design was adapted to the unique attributes of each local court system. Sentencing guidelines systems have successfully been established by my team in each of the first four courts discussed—those in Denver, Newark, Chicago, and Phoenix—and I feel that the usefulness of the sentencing guidelines concept has thereby been established, especially in light of all the differences encountered in these sites. Even more to the point, however, is the implementation process that took place in Philadelphia. My staff and I were only peripherally involved in the study there; this replication of the guidelines concept by others is thus demonstrative evidence of the generalizable nature of sentencing guidelines systems.

THE DENVER COUNTY DISTRICT COURT

Court Structure

Located in the City and County of Denver, the Denver County District Court constitutes the second judicial district of the Colorado Judicial Department.[2] The smallest of the five sentencing guidelines jurisdictions to be discussed here, Denver has a population of just over 500,000. The Criminal Division of the District Court has original jurisdiction over all violations of state laws at the felony level arising in the City and County of Denver. The District Court also maintains concurrent original jurisdiction with the County Court for misdemeanor infractions. The Criminal Division of the District Court is staffed by six full-time judges. Five of these judges maintain a normal calendar, while the sixth is utilized principally to hear lengthy trial matters.

The 1974 caseload for the Denver District Court shows 2,785 felony filings. These filings resulted in 881 dismissals, 1,656 guilty pleas accepted, and 248 cases proceeding to trial. Of the cases proceeding to trial, 162 were adjudicated by jury verdict, and the remaining 86 were tried before the court. Trials for 1974 resulted in 116 convictions, 57 acquittals, and 75 not guilty verdicts by reason of insanity. In sum, the caseload of the Denver District Court constitutes a total of 1,772 felony convictions in 1974. Sentencing data from the Denver District Court shows that 867 of those convictions resulted in sentences to probation, 638 in prison terms, 78 in jail terms, and 189 in a suspended sentence or some other form of sanction.

Criminal violations in Denver can be of three different types—general sessions misdemeanors, state misdemeanors, and state felonies. General sessions misdemeanors are offenses against city ordinances and are resolved in the City Court. State misdemeanors are resolved in either the County Court or the District Court; felonies are resolved in the District Court.

The state of Colorado has a Model Penal Code type of sentencing structure and stratifies the seriousness of offenses on the basis of minimum and maximum sentences. As Table 6–1 illustrates, Colorado felonies are separated into six levels of seriousness, and Colorado misdemeanors into three levels of seriousness.

Among the "sentencing" options available to the judge, we came across one that deserves separate explanation. This is the deferred prosecution, which had all the earmarks of a disposition, but which the judges saw primarily as a tentative "holding action" on a case. As originally designed, the deferred prosecution (the awarding of a term of one year of supervised probation with successful completion resulting in the dismissal of all charges) was intended solely for use with first offenders involved in drug infractions. Since 1970, however, the deferred prosecution mechanism has found its way into check and forgery cases and then into the mainstream of possible criminal adjudications. This "probationary probation" procedure is indeed now in use for the full gamut of criminal offenses in Denver County.

Such was the sentencing structure throughout the data collection effort during our earliest guidelines research. On May 27, 1976, however, House Bill 1111 became law and set forth specific provisions for mandatory sentences in the instances of violent offenders and habitual offenders. Under the provisions of that law, any person previously

Table 6-1.   Colorado Sentencing Structure.

Felonies	Minimum Sentence	Maximum Sentence
Class 1	Life	Death
Class 2	10 years	50 years
Class 3	5 years	40 years
Class 4	1 year and/or $2,000	10 years and/or $30,000
Class 5	1 year and/or $1,000	5 years and/or $15,000
Unclassified		

Misdemeanors	Minimum Sentence	Maximum Sentence
Class 1	6 months and/or $500	24 months and/or $5,000
Class 2	3 months and/or $250	12 months and/or $1,000
Class 3	$50	6 months and/or $750

convicted of a felony within the last five years shall not be eligible for an indeterminate sentence. That law specifies that the minimum sentence for such a person shall be not less than one year for a class 5 felony and not less than two years for a class 4 felony. The law further requires that any person convicted of a crime of violence, as defined, be sentenced without suspension to at least the minimum term of incarceration for such offense. (Some modification for extenuating circumstances is left to the court.) The section further provides that any person convicted of a crime of violence shall also not be eligible for an indeterminate sentence. Moreover, the habitual offender statute has been modified to provide that any person convicted of a felony for which the maximum penalty exceeds five years, who within ten years of such offense has been twice previously convicted of a felony, shall be punished by confinement in the state penitentiary for twenty-five to fifty years.

Preliminary Data Collection

After examining the Colorado statutes and discussing the project with the Denver District Court judiciary, our first direct research activity was a preliminary analysis of the data available in the court;

we wanted to determine the quality as well as the quantity of the information available to the Denver judges at sentencing. As the initial step in "predicting" or describing sentencing decisions, the research staff planned to gather a simple random sample of 200 individual Denver District Court sentencing decisions over a two year period.[3] We attempted to collect 205 different items of information for each of those cases, which were drawn from the court docket files. Usually, court docket files will contain the presentence investigation report and other supporting documents of only one defendant. In those instances in which there were co-defendants, however, the Denver court docket files contained the documents pertaining to all co-defendants. It was decided to randomly sample only one individual case from those court docket files that contained co-defendants in order to include only individual sentencing decisions.

The research staff also excluded judicial decisions that dealt solely with sanctions for probation revocation rather than with sentencing for the conviction of a new criminal offense. It was believed that decisions dealing with sanctions for probation revocations might involve different issues as well as different information and decisionmaking processes and might therefore only confound the initial analysis.

Based on our initial results, efforts to predict sentencing decisions continued; the staff decided to develop several different models, as the development of only one model at this early stage in the research was seen as potentially restricting rather than as facilitating the full expression of the variety of issues and concerns discussed and debated by the judges during meetings of the Steering and Policy Committee. As it turned out, three models, differing in several significant respects, were designed for testing in Denver.

Model Testing

We tested each of these three models in Denver, beginning in November 1975, when the probation officers began completing forms that we supplied for each case on which they prepared a presentence investigation report. The judges were then asked to review the form, which accompanied each case, and to indicate any additional items of information that they had taken into account in reaching their sentencing decisions in that particular case. This testing was performed on a 221 case sample of cases drawn as the cases were processed through the judicial system at sentencing. Again, probation revocation cases were excluded.

Measured against this sample, the models accurately predicted 79 percent, 80 percent, and 84 percent, respectively, of the "in/out" decisions. Thus, the models tested in Denver achieved approximately the same results in spite of differences in their design and construction.

In fact, they often "missed" the very same cases. The performance of the various Denver models and the assumptions on which they were based were then reviewed by the judges on the Steering and Policy Committee.

One interesting pattern revealed in our analysis of the models was that offender variables (e.g., prior criminal history records) appeared to have a greater influence on the sentencing decision than did offense seriousness variables. When the offense was one of a very grave nature, however (e.g., one involving major physical injury to the victim), the seriousness of offense variables seemed to have a greater impact on the sentencing decision than did the offender variables.

Action Research Feedback

In the discussion that followed the presentation of these alternative models, the judges on the Steering and Policy Committee did not seem to favor one model to the exclusion of the others. On the basis of judicial advice, therefore, the research staffers turned to the development of some type of "synthesis" model. We referred to this as the Denver Demonstration Model. This model was put forth solely to demonstrate the feasibility of a potential sentencing guidelines system and was thus designed for computational simplicity in charting what underlying factors may have influenced decisions in the past and in estimating what weights may have been accorded each of these factors.

It is important to understand here that the research feedback involved all the judges on the Steering and Policy Committee, not just those in Denver. This Denver Demonstration Model did not therefore have the stated approval of the local judiciary and was in that respect different from all later models that we developed in other jurisdictions. The first direct involvement of the Denver judiciary (outside of the one committee member) was in testing the Denver Demonstration Model. During testing, the model sentences were given to the Denver judges only after formal imposition of sentences; when the model sentences differed from the actual decision, the judges were asked to indicate why they thought the model decision did not correctly estimate their actual "in/out" decision.

On our second Denver sample of 221 cases, the Denver Demonstration Model performed at a 90 percent rate of accuracy in predicting the "in/out" decision. An additional 5 percent of the cases were considered to have fallen outside of the guidelines as a result of a sentence to a period of incarceration that varied from the range suggested by the guidelines by more than one year—a figure we chose in a conscious effort to be conservative with regard to any variation from a suggested guideline length of sentence. Thus, 85 percent of the sentences in the construction sample gathered in Denver from November 1975 to mid-January 1976 fell within the guidelines, both as to whether or not the offender was incarcerated and also—if the sentence was to a period of incarceration—as to the length of incarceration. The model was validated on another sample of 155 cases drawn in Denver from March to April 1976. In this sample, 12 percent of the cases fell outside of the guidelines on the basis of the "in/out" decision. An additional 8 percent of the cases were considered to have fallen outside of the guidelines as a result of an incarceration term that varied by more than one year from the range specified in the guidelines. Thus, 80 percent of the cases in the validation sample fell completely within the guidelines.

Implementation

As the Denver Demonstration Model had not been constructed exclusively on the advice of the Denver judiciary, our first step in implementing some variation of this model in Denver was to familiarize all the Denver judges with all aspects of our previous research. Over the summer of 1976, research staffers met with the Denver judges and reviewed our past efforts. Most importantly, we explained the purpose of the implementation process and further asked the judges as a collective body to resolve several important policy questions. The judges were then asked to design the actual guidelines that they would be using. Staff had worked out and tested various models utilizing slightly differing combinations of information. Alternative solutions to problems were laid open for consideration by the judges along with any options they might have suggested. As it happened, an entirely new model was developed and validated.

On November 15, 1976, the first set of sentencing guidelines ever employed began to be used by the Denver District Court judges.[4] In Denver, the Chief Investigative Probation Officer actually computes the guideline sentence on the worksheets we provided. Upon completion of the guideline worksheet and the generation of the guideline sentence, the presentence report and guideline worksheet are forwarded together to the appropriate district courtroom.

Before sentencing an offender, therefore, the judge has received (1) the complete presentence investigation report, together with the sentencing recommendations of the probation department; and (2) the guidelines model sentence. The judge then uses both of these information items, together with any other information known about the case,[5] and makes a sentencing decision. When the sentence is imposed, the judge indicates, in the space provided on the guideline worksheet, the actual sentence that is given in the case. If the judge has made a sentencing decision that departs from the guidelines model sentence indicated on the worksheet, he or she is asked to respond with reasons for this departure as well as the actual sentence rendered. The guideline worksheets are then picked up from the court clerks by research staff. A copy of each is left for the judges' files, and another copy is transmitted to the data center for inclusion in the expanding experience table.

The first judicial feedback and review session was held in April 1977 and reviewed District Court sentences handed out between November 15, 1976, and February 28, 1977. The "in/out" accuracy rate was 85.8 percent. The second report covered the period to September 29, 1977; the "in/out" accuracy rate reported then was 86.7 percent. In terms of offense frequency, a small number of offenses account for a large proportion of the caseload. Of the 318 cases coded from November 15, 1976, through February 28, 1977, for example, fourteen offenses accounted for 220 of the total. The first two feedback and review sessions were conducted with the assistance of the main project research staff; later coordination of the feedback and review sessions, as well as all other aspects of a working, operational sentencing guidelines system, were placed in local hands in the fall of 1977. We worked closely with the Denver staff, trained them in the use of all necessary materials, and thus feel that we achieved our action research goal. This federally funded research project concluded by leaving the Denver District Court with a simple to operate and highly reliable aid for decisionmaking in sentencing, as well as a clear and articulate statement of that court's criminal sentencing policy.

THE ESSEX COUNTY AND SUPERIOR COURTS

Court Structure

Essex County is a large, urban county in the Northeast with a substantial minority population accounting for almost one-third of its one million residents.[6] Seventeen trial court judges—either Superior Court or County Court judges—shared criminal jurisdiction during 1976, and they disposed of over 2,801 criminal cases during that period by way of a final disposition. There was a fairly even split between incarcerative sentences and nonincarcerative probationary sentences. During our sample period, approximately 30 percent of the most serious offenses at conviction were violent crimes against the person (mostly robbery), another 30 percent were drug offenses, 20 percent were property cases, and the other 20 percent fell into what we referred to as our miscellaneous category.

The offenses proscribed by New Jersey's criminal statutes are ordered in the following categories—disorderly persons offenses, misdemeanors, high misdemeanors, and the felony classification of murder. The penalties prescribed for these offenses are contained either in the substantive criminal statutes or in the general provisions. If the substantive statute does not contain a specified punishment provision, a disorderly persons offense may be punished by a fine of not more than $500 or by imprisonment for not more than six months, or both; a misdemeanor may be punished by a fine of not more than $1,000 or by imprisonment for not more than three years, or both; a high misdemeanor may be punished by a fine of not more than $2,000 or by imprisonment for not more than seven years, or both; manslaughter offenses may be punished by a fine of not more than $1,000 or by imprisonment for not more than ten years, or both; second degree murder offenses, by imprisonment for not more than thirty years; and first degree murder offenses, by life imprisonment.

Sentencing options include probation for not less than one nor more than five years, except in cases in which the jury has determined that the sentence shall be life imprisonment; that determination is then binding upon the judge. Common law authority and New Jersey statutes also permit the sentencing court to suspend the imposition of, or the execution of, sentence. If the court imposes a custodial sentence, but partially or totally suspends it, then the court may place the defendant on probation. Furthermore, it is the responsibility of the judge to determine whether the standard conditions, or any special conditions, of probation should be applied in a particular case.

In addition, there is special authority for more severe sentencing of persons who have been convicted of a misdemeanor or a high misdemeanor and who had been previously convicted of a high misdemeanor (or its equivalent if the conviction occurred in another jurisdiction), but this authorization is not mandatory. These "habitual offender" statutes permit the judge to enhance the maximum punishment if the conviction warrants that additional punishment.

More so than is the case with the judges in the other court systems here considered, the Essex County judiciary possesses the power to sentence offenders to specific institutions of incarceration. As they felt this to be a potential source of disparity and an area in which the practice of their colleagues would provide useful guidance, they urged us to focus on this decision as well in establishing sentencing guidelines. Terms of confinement imposed by sentencing judges in Essex County may be to the county jail (or county penitentiary), the Youth Correctional Institution Complex, the State Prison, or the Correctional Institution for Women. Sentences to the county jail are for a definite term without establishing a minimum or a maximum ranges.

Male offenders between the ages of fifteen and thirty years may be sentenced to the Youth Correctional Institution Complex at Yardville. The offender, however, must have been convicted of a crime punishable by imprisonment in the State Prison and must not have been sentenced at a prior time to a State Prison in New Jersey or any other state. Moreover, the judge's discretion in determining the length of Correctional Institution sentences is limited. The sentence is indeterminate—it will have no minimum—and the maximum terms are assumed ordinarily to be five years or the maximum for the crime involved, whichever is shorter. For cases in which the statutory maximum is more than five years, the judge may, for good cause, set the maximum term above five years, subject to the statutory limit. The indeterminacy of the prison sentence leaves the eventual release of the defendant to the correctional and paroling authorities. Recent state parole statistics reveal that the average time served on an indeterminate sentence is approximately 14 percent of the maximum (or about nine months on a five year term).

Any male over sixteen who has committed an offense that carries a term of incarceration for more than a year may be sentenced to the State Prison. State Prison sentences carry a minimum and maximum term to be served, except in the case of a sentence of life.

All custodial sentences of women over sixteen are to be served at the Correctional Institution for Women at Clinton. Women over thirty are sentenced to a minimum and maximum term, again except in the case of a life sentence. Women under thirty may be given a determinate sentence.

Model Development

One sample was drawn for the construction of guidelines models, consisting of 1,250 cases randomly drawn from the 2,800 cases assigned to the Probation Department for investigative preparation in the calendar year 1975.[7] The validation sample consisted of the first 500 cases sentenced during January, February, and March 1977. The judicial representatives of the Essex County and Superior Courts decided to exclude gambling and welfare cases, given unique circumstances surrounding imposition of sentence for each of these crimes.

Over a dozen different models were devised, tested, and presented to the Essex County judiciary; extensive discussion ensued, with a number of significant decisions resulting. Unlike the other sentencing guidelines jurisdictions, the Essex County judges opted to avoid any early "smoothing" of apparent inconsistencies. Instead, the judges decided to include early data results on the face of the grids enclosed with their coding packages during test implementation. The judges were further in agreement that the median sentence would serve as an adequate guide, together with the historical data, to help them decide on the length of sentence.

Both general and generic models were tested in Essex County. When presented with the results, the judges opted for implementation of the generic model, as developed, with four separate matrixes, one each for violent, property, drugs, and miscellaneous offenses.

Implementation

On June 29, 1977, the generic models adopted by the Essex County judiciary for implementation purposes were presented to all pertinent agencies of the criminal courts system. The model was described by the Honorable John Marzulli and the Honorable Leo Yanoff to all criminal court judges, as well as to representatives of the probation department, the public defender's office, the district attorney's office, and the Administrative Office of the Courts.[8] The Essex County judiciary considered it desirable to include all of those involved in the court process, as they felt that such a widespread awareness would be essential to the successful implementation of the guidelines system. By involving all actors in an open atmosphere, the research team was also able to gain additional information that led to valuable revisions in the guidelines models.

In Essex County, judges receive presentence investigation reports for most of the more serious offenses they sentence; because of this, it seemed useful for the probation officer to be the person doing the actual calculation of the individual guideline sentence. This is especially so in cases resulting in guilty pleas where there is no trial and where the judge is usually acquainted with the individual defendant primarily through the medium of the presentence investigation report. Thus the judge in Essex County now receives a total information packet, including the recommended guideline sentence along with the usual presentence investigation report.

The research staff met with the Chief Probation Officer and other top probation department staff to discuss coordination of implementation activities. A series of training sessions were held with the supervising probation officers who prepare presentence investigation reports. These sessions, with three groups of ten officers each, were designed to familiarize the probation officers with the coding manual's instructions and the sentencing sheet's calculations. Officers were given actual cases on which to practice calculating sentencing guidelines for each different generic grouping.

Feedback and Review

In addition to these meetings and training sessions with the probation department, the research staff conducted seminars with representatives of the judiciary, the prosecutor, and the public defender. These seminars demonstrated the sentencing sheet calculations and explained the theory, methodology, and planned operational aspects of a guidelines system. Along with these seminars, there were individual conferences with most sentencing judges to obtain feedback regarding their respective opinions about the planned implementation of a guidelines system.

The development of a series of instructional booklets for the calculation of guideline sentences was the primary product of this operational phase. These booklets contain the mechanics of coding a given guideline sentence. Since the judges selected a model based on generic groupings of criminal offenses (i.e., violent, drugs, property, and miscellaneous), a booklet had to be developed for each type. Essentially, each booklet has four parts: (1) decision rules, (2) coding procedures regarding scoring offense variables and offender variables, (3) the sentencing sheet, and, (4) the sentencing grids. The decision rules within each booklet (or manual, as we alternatively referred to them) are used to determine which offense and generic offense type will be used in calculating the guideline sentence. The sentencing sheet itself has five copies, so that a copy is distributed to, and filed with, the judge, the public defender's office, the district attorney's office, the probation office, and the research team.

The sentencing decisionmaking matrixes contain historical sentencing analyses of the Essex County and Superior Courts and form the sentence recommendation or guideline sentence. An explanation of an Essex County sentencing grid cell is provided in Table 6–2.

It was jointly decided by the researchers and the judiciary to use the median sentence as the best measure of central tendency in suggesting what length of incarceration should be imposed, as the mean can be so easily biased by extremes.

The Essex County and Superior Courts then initiated a testing phase for an operational sentencing guidelines system. From September 1977 on, sentencing sheets were calculated by the probation officer for each case to be sentenced on a given day. These worksheets were in turn forwarded to the judge and then to the research staff, which developed a separate coding manual for the information contained on the sentencing sheet. In March 1978, the first review session took place. At that time policy decisions regarding length consistency within the four sentencing grids were discussed along with possible changes in relative weights or ranking of offenses.

Table 6–2. Explanation of Essex County Grids.

			Number of Incarcerative				
		12	Sentences				
			Number of Nonincarcerative				
		3	Sentences				
Youth Corrections Institution Complex	(7)	52	.5	60	.0	67	.5
Essex County Corrections Center	(2)	10	.5	12	.0	13	.5
New Jersey State Prison	(3)	52	.5	60	.0	67	.5

Number of Offenders		Median Sentence (in months)	
	Lower Range	Upper Range	
	(−12.5% from median)	(+12.5% from median)	

Here too, we followed our action research plan by training local court officials to take over the system upon our departure and by preparing the instructional booklets so that they could be readily used without the need for us to explain procedures. As it turned out, the state of New Jersey developed a statewide sentencing guidelines system that eventually incorporated the Essex system we had implemented. Under the supervision of the Honorable Arthur J. Simpson, Administrator for the Courts, and under the direction of John Mc-Carthy, with only some limited assistance from our staff, New Jersey's research project in October 1978 implemented the nation's first statewide sentencing guidelines system.

THE COOK COUNTY CIRCUIT COURT

Court Structure

Serving a population of just under six million, and located in Chicago, the Circuit Court of Cook County is the nation's largest court of unlimited original jurisdiction.[9] As our study there began, there were

307 judges on the bench in Cook County and more than six million cases—civil and criminal, minor and serious—filed there each year.

The Criminal Division of the Circuit Court of Cook County operates from four major branches—the Criminal Court Building at 26th Street and California Avenue (adjacent to the Cook County Jail); the Richard J. Daley Center (formerly known as the Civic Center Branch); the Maybrook Courts Building, located in the suburb of Maywood; and the 1340 Michigan Avenue Courtroom located at 13th Street and Michigan Avenue (opened in January 1978). Cook County's Criminal Division has undergone a relatively recent expansion to cope with the large caseload on the criminal docket. In mid-1976, the suburban branch of the court was opened at Maybrook, and six new judges were assigned to the bench. During that year, with two criminal court branches then operating—joined by the third, newly opened Maybrook branch in August—approximately 6,500 criminal cases were disposed of by the forty judges then assigned to the Criminal Division of the Cook County Circuit Court. In early December 1977, four new criminal court judges were assigned to the bench, in anticipation of the expansion planned for the fourth criminal court site at 13th Street and Michigan Avenue; by April 1978, eleven additional judges were hearing and disposing of cases.

At the request of the Presiding Judge of the Criminal Division (the Honorable Richard Fitzgerald), guidelines model development and testing implementation began, in the fall of 1976, in only two of the then three courts—the Maybrook branch and the 26th Street and California branch. Not only was it deemed more prudent to begin initial work with only the two branches, but there was also a greater similarity in the types of crimes and criminals processed by the Maybrook and the 25th Street branches than with the other major felony court, the one at Daley Center.

Offenders dealt with at Daley Center are almost universally released on some form of bail or bond. The average defendant at the 26th Street and California Branch or at Maybrook, on the other hand, is incarcerated awaiting disposition. This is so because offenders at Daley Center tend to have committed less serious offenses and/or to have less serious prior criminal history records than those at the other court branches. In addition, Presiding Judge Fitzgerald noted that the judges in these two courts could more easily aid our work as they had regular and frequent contacts with each other through daily luncheon meetings; they could thus more easily discuss any pertinent matter that might arise during the course of the project.

Illinois, much as Colorado, employs a Model Penal Code type of statutory structure, with eight categories of offenses—Felony 1 through Felony 4, Misdemeanor A, B, and C, and Murder, which is a separate class of felony. Illinois criminal statutes also have provisions for Petty Offenses and Business Offenses, for which a fine or conditional discharge are the only dispositions available.

Data collection for guidelines model development occurred on two samples, with a total of 796 cases analyzed in model building.[10] The construction sample of 485 cases was collected during October through December 1976 from cases that were disposed of by the judiciary during that time period. The validation sample of 311 cases was collected during March and April 1977 from cases that had been disposed of during January through March 1977. Analysis of the offender-offense characteristics used in model development showed a high degree of similarity for the pre-December and the post-December data collection periods. The percentage of Felony 1, 2, and 3 offenses showed markedly high consistency, with Felony 2 offenses appearing most frequently in both samples.

Model Development

There are several unique characteristics of the Cook County data base that should be highlighted. First, at the other project sites, the primary source from which data has been drawn was the presentence investigation report prepared by the staff of the local probation departments. However, Cook County judges do not employ the presentence investigation report as their primary information source. While Illinois statutes mandate such reports for all felony offenses, this requirement can be, and often is, waived. Staff found that such reports existed in only 25 percent of even serious cases, the reports usually being waived at the time that defendants waived their right to trial. Therefore, the staff had to develop alternate data collection procedures to secure the information necessary for guidelines model construction. These alternate procedures turned out to be satisfactory, albeit time consuming. Moreover, some definite information inadequacies developed, most notably including social stability and juvenile criminal history variables. Despite data collection problems encountered with the construction sample, a data base that covered eighty-nine information items was secured for statistical analysis. For the validation sample, however, only fifty-nine information items were collected, primarily due to our analysis of the information inadequacies discussed above.

Statistical techniques were performed on the sample for guidelines model development primarily along statutory class lines—that is, for Felony 1, 2, and 3 offenses. Models were not developed for murders, a separate class of felony, owing to the extremely small sample size ($n=21$), which hampered meaningful statistical analysis. Similarly, grids were not developed for Felony 4 or misdemeanor offenses since they too were underrepresented in the construction sample. The models eventually adopted by the Cook County District Court were of the types we have referred to as "general." Nevertheless, we considered the feasibility of both generic and crime-specific models as well.

Investigation of the feasibility of using a crime-specific model revealed that while seven discrete crimes accounted for 74 percent of all the first charged offenses at conviction in the construction sample, the small number of cases for each crime limited the reliability of any analysis performed. Our analysis of generic models indicated that there was little difference in predictor variables that were used in the more general models developed along statutory class lines. Therefore, it was just as sound statistically, as well as simpler, to use the general model adopted for use in Cook County.

The various models tested proved very similar in the percentage of "in/out" decisions that they correctly predicted (all within 7 percent of each other). As to the length of time decision, we were far better able to predict the minimum term than the maximum. The judges informed us, however, that the minimum term set was far more important to them than the maximum term and hence more significant in any statement of court policy. The two models presented to the Chicago judiciary utilized the same offense score (judges' seriousness rankings, weapon, injury), but differed by the presence (or absence) of a weight for employment/education status in the offender score.

Presentation of these two models was made to the judiciary from the two participating branches in May 1977. At that time, the judiciary made a policy decision to use the model without a variable for employment or education. As a policy matter, the judiciary decided that they did not want to be constrained to consider employment and/or education in every case and that it would be more appropriate to use this as a reason for departure from the guidelines in those instances in which it was a strong mitigating factor.

Implementation

Implementation of the guidelines began in June 1977 at the Maybrook and the 26th Street courtrooms. In Denver and Essex (and later in Maricopa and Philadelphia), court personnel or probation staff prepared the guideline computations at the time that information on the offender was gathered; in Cook County, however, the judges computed the guideline sentence at the time of sentencing or plea negotiations. This was necessitated in part by the fact that so few presentence investigation reports are normally prepared prior to sentencing in the Cook County court system. It was also the judiciary's policy decision to personally handle the computational worksheet and not to have them completed by their court clerks.

In monitoring the progress of the implementation process, we found that the usual grid layout of the decisionmaking matrixes was not very functional for the judges to use in determining the guideline sentence. Thus, the grids were converted to a tabular format for ease and convenience in reading, as well as for computational speed on the bench (see Table 7–2 for an example). During the implementation process, completed guideline worksheets were collected weekly by the on-site court liaison and sent to the staff office, where they were reviewed for computational or other clerical errors. A guideline worksheet coding manual was prepared for coding the guideline worksheets on to coding sheets, in preparation for keypunching and transfer of this data to computer files for subsequent analysis of guidelines model utility.

Feedback and Review

The first review of the accuracy of the guidelines models was conducted in December 1977, approximately six months after guidelines model test implementation. At that time, by reviewing those instances in which members of the Cook County judiciary departed from the guidelines, the judges as a group, aided by project staff, were able to map the changes in court policy that appeared to have occurred since guidelines implementation began and to make policy decisions to adjust the guidelines models accordingly.

When implementation commenced at the Maybrook and the 26th Street court branches, data were also collected for the purpose of later expanding the guidelines into use at the Daley Center and Michigan Avenue facilities as well. A 796 case sample was collected at these two "new" branches. Analysis of these data, collected from the Daley Center and the Michigan Avenue branches, revealed that while there were differences in some specific information items that appeared to be the best predictors of type of sentence (e.g., Prior Adult Convictions for a Similar Offense instead of Prior Adult Felony Convictions Against the Person), the same dimensions appeared as the best predictors of the sentence. Given that the same dimensions were appearing as the best predictors of type of sentence and that our aim was not to compare differences among the four locations, but rather to develop a sentencing guidelines system useful in all four facilities, the data samples were merged and analysis reperformed. The same dimensions again appeared as the best predictors of sentences, although a few individual information items varied slightly.

At this point, it was our intention to test various models on the merged data set and to present our findings to the Cook County judiciary. However, this was not done, as the Illinois legislature had just passed a revised sentencing bill, to become effective February 1, 1978. The projected time for presentation and implementation of a new guidelines model, based on the merged samples from all of the three then operating branches, was mid-December 1977, while sentencing under the new act would commence just six weeks later. Due to this relatively short time period, and after consultation with the Cook County judiciary, we decided that it was more useful to expand use of the current guidelines model, if possible, to the Daley Center and Michigan Avenue branches and to then investigate how that model might be converted to the new sentencing scheme for use under the new statutes. Thus, the existing implementation guidelines model was tested upon the sample collected from the Daley Center and the Michigan Avenue facilities. It was found that this model predicted the in/out decision only 1 percent less accurately (original construction sample model—82.3 percent; model run on Daley Center and Michigan Avenue branches—81.3 percent) than in the original development of the model. Owing to the different offense-offender "mix" found in the two new branches, it had been expected, of course, that the length of time decision would be much more greatly affected than the in/out decisions and that revisions thus would more likely be required in individual cells of the decision-making matrix. These revisions in length of time were in fact made, specifically taking into account the very pertinent "feedback" received from judges using the guidelines since June.

We studied the provisions of the new sentencing bill and found that while the publically stated thrust of the bill had been to limit judicial discretion and to require judges to sentence certain offenders to a determinate or fixed term, there was still available to the judiciary a rather wide range of judicial discretion.[11] Thus, converting the length of sentences currently suggested by the guidelines to correspond with allowable sentences under the determinate sentencing bill would prove useful to the Cook County judiciary. In the conversion of sentences, the length of time to be served under a determinate sentence was made equivalent to the time currently being served under the indeterminate sentence system. Under the old sentencing structure (including statutory "good time" provisions), the implicit policy of the parole board was to grant parole to offenders with no prior incarcerations at the first parole hearing date (which took place at a date set approximately at six-tenths of the minimum term to which the prisoner was sentenced). If, on the other hand, the offender had been previously incarcerated, then release was generally granted at the second parole hearing—approximately one year later. (The actual time served by these repeat prisoners would therefore be "0.6" of the minimum term to which he or she was sentenced, plus one year.)

Under the new act, there would be no paroling authority to determine release dates for offenders sentenced after February 1, 1978. However, "good time" was to be earned at the rate of day for day, meaning that an offender would actually serve only one-half of the term to which he or she was sentenced. Therefore, in most cases, the determinate guideline sentence became the adjusted indeterminate guideline sentence ("0.6"; or "0.6" of the term to which an offender was sentenced, plus one year) doubled. All converted sentences were doubled because conversations with members of the Cook County judiciary had indicated that it would be most appropriate to assume, when determining the new guideline sentences, that offenders would receive all the good time to which they were entitled.

Guidelines models for use under the new determinate sentencing bill were developed and began to be used by the judiciary in February 1978. Guideline worksheets continued to be collected by project staff for approximately another month, at which time we prepared system handbooks and trained local personnel, once again according to our action research plan. Transfer of the sentencing guidelines model review technology was accomplished immediately thereafter as court staff from Cook County undertook the maintenance of the system.

THE MARICOPA COUNTY SUPERIOR COURT

Court Structure

The Maricopa County Superior Court is located in downtown Phoenix and serves the entire county, which in addition to Phoenix includes the affluent districts of Paradise Valley and Scottsdale, the university town of Tempe, and the poor Mexican-American town of Guadaloupe.[12] The present estimated county population of 1.3 million is over half that of the entire state of Arizona. The minority population in Maricopa County is primarily Mexican-American, with a small proportion of blacks and Indians. Criminal cases involving Indians, with few exceptions, are handled in the federal courts.

There are ten Superior Court judges assigned to criminal duties; they operate on a centralized calendar and rotate their assignments between the civil and criminal courts. Plea bargaining is as prevalent here as it is in other systems, although the process is somewhat more formalized. The defendant who pleads guilty or nolo contendere signs a plea agreement form, specifying the possible minimum and maximum penalty for the final charge. This form may also contain a specific condition that the state must satisfy, such as the waiver of an allegation of a prior conviction. The sentencing judge is informed of the plea agreement and also receives copies of the presentence report and the rap sheet for an offender. In cases where either the prosecutor or the defense attorney wishes to make the judge aware of information not provided by the presentence report, a separate mitigation-aggravation hearing may be held.

The Arizona Revised Statutes categorize the offenses defined therein into felonies, high misdemeanors, misdemeanors, and "open ended." The broad felony and misdemeanor classifications are not divided into classes to which a specific penalty is assigned, but rather assign an extensive array of penalties (over forty alternative incarcerative penalties), many of which grant the sentencing judge broad discretion as to the range of sentence. The "open ended" classification contains offenses upon conviction of which offenders may receive either a jail or a prison term—for example, the crime of "Resisting, Delaying, Coercing or Obstructing a Public Officer" is punishable by either a jail term or imprisonment in the state prison for up to five years. In addition, an "open ended" offense may be designated "open ended" at conviction, with the offense later subject to designation as either a felony or a misdemeanor, depending upon the offender's performance on probation. The Maricopa County Superior Court has original jurisdiction over all cases in which the offense at indictment or information is designated a felony, a high misdemeanor, or is open ended.

Model Development

Two samples of cases sentenced by the judges sitting in the Maricopa County Superior Court were collected.[13] A construction sample of 1,200 cases was randomly selected from among the 3,398 cases sentenced in 1976. The validation sample used to confirm the relationships observed in the construction sample was drawn from the 510 cases sentenced from April 1, 1977, to May 31, 1977.

None of the sentencing guidelines models that we developed here was comprised of more than ten variables, and in fact, six or seven variables generally accounted for most of the predictive power of the models. The models differed in content—the number and type of variables included and the weights assigned to them—but they shared the same basic structure as in the other guidelines jurisdictions. That structure was a two dimensional decisionmaking matrix reflecting the two focal concerns or dimensions informing the determination of sentence—perceived severity of the offense and characteristics of the offender. The offense severity dimension was represented by a seriousness index and various "real offense" seriousness modifiers such as injury to victim and type of drugs. The offender dimension was typified by social stability information and prior adult and juvenile criminal record.

As elsewhere, the Maricopa judiciary rejected the bifurcated model of sentencing decisionmaking as too complex. Instead, the judges in Maricopa expressed a preference for a one stage model to represent both stages of the sentencing decision in order to avoid the need for a double set of calculations to determine the guideline sentences. Thus, the decision was made to devise a model that had as its primary focus the prediction of the "in/out" decision; then, secondarily, the "appropriate" length of sentence would be established on the basis of the configuration of predicted "in" sentences.

The models were based on the most serious offense at conviction. The decision was made not to take additional charges into account because the charging decision was entirely within the discretionary control of the prosecutor. The most serious offense at conviction was determined during the coding process on the basis of a seriousness index that assigned a rank to each of forty penalties prescribed by the Arizona State Legislature. Offenses within the same rank were further distinguished by their violent-nonviolent designation.

Two different types of models were developed for testing in Maricopa—the general model and the generic model. As Maricopa was the last of the four sites implemented during the federal study, we had now had experience in employing both types of models and so wished further to test out the relative merits of each. In the event, the general model was characterized by six decisionmaking matrixes, each representing a class of offense and grouped according to the penalties prescribed for them by the legislature. The seriousness index for the general model, which we referred to as the intraclass ranking system, was created by having the judges rank the offenses within the six classifications. The general models invariably included some combination of these factors—prior adult and juvenile criminal history record, legal status of offender, drug use, addiction to opiates, employment status, victim classification, victim injury, and weapon use. The predictive ability of most of the general models tested was around 81 percent on the in/out decision.

The potential utility of generic models was suggested by the statistical analysis and the judges' rankings, which had clearly demonstrated to the research staff that distinctions were drawn by the judges between property crimes, drug offenses, and violent crimes. A separate model was constructed for each of these types of crimes in order to reflect the operation of varying factors and weights. The intraclass ranking system for the general model was not adaptable to the generic models because the judges had not ranked the offenses within crime subtypes. Thus, a seriousness index was created for each subtype, based on the maximum allowable penalty. A slightly different ranking system was devised for each crime type because the distribution of cases among the categories of possible maximum penalties varied according to crime type. Numerous generic models were developed, and their predictive efficiency (with respect to the "in/out" decision) was assessed by means of the same procedures employed for the general models. The drug models had the most predictive power, ranging from 86 to 87 percent. The violent models accurately predicted between 79 and 86 percent of the cases, and the property models, between 77 and 79 percent of the cases.

The generic models were eventually selected for implementation over the general model primarily because they provided better discrimination of the "in/out" decision. At a September 28, 1977, meeting, all the Maricopa County judges assigned to criminal duties voted and selected from among a variety of models that the research staff had developed; the judges made a number of policy decisions regarding the models for each crime type, and the staff reconstructed the models according to the instructions of the judiciary. These models were then applied to the validation sample to verify relationships seen in the construction sample. The drugs model experienced no change in predictive accuracy and the violent and property models suffered only slight shrinkage in their ability to predict subsequent sentencing decisions.

Implementation

Guideline sentences were then prepared for the implementation model. The guideline sentence for each "in" cell of the decisionmaking matrixes was determined by the median of the minimum sentence and the median of the maximum sentence within each cell; a sentencing range of 25 percent around the median (12.5 percent below and 12.5 percent above) was set to allow for some flexibility. In reviewing these matrixes, the guideline sentences did not always conform to the desirable pattern—that is, increase as offense and offender scores increase. The judges allotted the research team the task of initially "smoothing" the grids to rectify such apparent incongruities. The median sentences were thus primarily used by the research team as points of reference to discern the general pattern of sentences across each decisionmaking matrix. The guideline sentence for each cell was established by examining the range of sentences within the cell, as well as the median sentences for contiguous cells. Guideline sentences for cells possessing a relatively small number of cases were determined mainly by extrapolating from the configuration of sentences in surrounding cells. The judges *en banc* then examined the matrixes and the information on which they were based and then approved the decisions that we had made and decided upon the models to be employed in sentencing guidelines implementation.

A handbook was prepared for each generic crime typology, so as to supply instructions to the judges for the appropriate use of the guidelines. A series of instructions explained the manner of determining the most serious offense at conviction when the offender was convicted of two or more offenses; the variables included in the models were carefully defined, and the procedures for coding them were delineated. Detailed instructions were further given on how to compute the offense and offender scores and locate the applicable guideline sentence on the decisionmaking matrixes.

The judges used the guidelines on an experimental basis for over a month and approved the results. Sentencing guidelines implementation formally began in Maricopa County on March 1, 1978. Using the handbooks that we had prepared, and after some training sessions with our staff, personnel from the probation department then assumed the task of calculating the guideline sentences. Representatives of the court administrator's office agreed to be responsible for the compilation of the relevant statistics necessary for the periodic review of the operation of the guidelines system. As the sentencing guidelines system in Maricopa was the last implemented under the federally funded research project, however neither I nor my staff had a chance to directly supervise any subsequent feedback and review sessions.

A future difficulty to be dealt with, moreover, was a major change in the penal code structure that went into effect in Arizona on October 1, 1978. The revised code contains six felony and three misdemeanor classes, each of which is assigned a presumptive penalty. Provision is made for departures from the presumptive sentences within predetermined limits if the existence of one of the statutorily defined aggravating or mitigating factors or enhancements is established. The feasibility of inserting the guidelines, which are based on the old criminal code, into this more restrictive system will ultimately depend on how the code operates in practice. The guidelines are in the process of being adapted to the new code, but they will require substantial modification, because the definition and classification of offenses, as well as the sentencing structure, have undergone far-reaching revision. We anticipate that the guidelines can, at a minimum, be applied to an area the legislature has left untouched—the discretionary judicial determination of whether or not to incarcerate an offender. The structuring of this aspect of judicial discretion alone would be of considerable value because, for many offenders, it means the significant difference between no deprivation of liberty and years of confinement.

THE PHILADELPHIA COURT OF COMMON PLEAS

The Participant Observer: A Cooperative Venture

In Chapter 4, I described how the Philadelphia Court of Common Pleas was selected as an observer during the guidelines implementation study. President Judge Edward J. Bradley expressed the strong desire of his court to be involved as a participant, but the required additional federal funds were not available to us. Undaunted, Judge Bradley, together with Court Administrator David N. Savitt, decided to go ahead with the development of sentencing guidelines. Since the Philadelphia judiciary very quickly saw the potential advantages of such a guidelines system, they decided to establish one using their own funding sources.

What follows are the summary results of an interesting cooperative venture between the Philadelphia Court of Common Pleas and the research team of the sentencing guidelines project. This is not meant to overstate our contribution, for the research team led by Saundra Dillio deserves primary credit for constructing and implementing Philadelphia's sentencing guidelines system.[14] I report this replication effort here at length primarily to demonstrate how universally applicable the sentencing guidelines concept is. Because the Philadelphia system was discretely constructed, however, I will discuss the special elements of the Philadelphia system here only and not in the next chapter, where I make some systemic comparisons between the four courts involved in the federal study.

While the Philadelphia effort involves one specific sentencing reform procedure, the change mechanism employed may be adaptable to all types of judicial reform activities. If I might employ an architectural analogy, the New York staff provided rough blueprints to the Pennsylvania construction firm, which actually built the house to fit the contours of the land (i.e., the Philadelphia court system) as well as the wishes of the owners (i.e., the judges of the Court of Common Pleas) and adapted those plans accordingly—and often in a major way. The New York and Pennsylvania staffs were, however, in frequent communication as to the design. The singular advantage of this technique over a prefabricated model is that the house will better suit the needs and desires of the occupants, since they participate at each and every level of construction and also have the ultimate investment in it.

Court Structure

Philadelphia is the largest city in Pennsylvania and the fourth largest in America, with a population of just under two million. The city and county of Philadelphia are conterminous.

The Philadelphia judicial system is composed of two courts—Common Pleas Court, which has complete trial jurisdiction, and Municipal Court. The Philadelphia sentencing guidelines system was developed only for the Common Pleas Court. All criminal cases in which the maximum potential penalty does not exceed five years imprisonment are tried before a judge with or without a jury in the Municipal Court. The defendant, upon conviction in the Municipal Court, has an absolute right to appeal for a trial de novo before a judge and jury in the trial division of the Court of Common Pleas. Along with these trials de novo, which may be on a minor charge, the Court of Common Pleas has original jurisdiction over all cases for which the potential penalty may exceed five years. There are forty-five trial court judges in the Court of Common Pleas. Dispositions in 1975 (the year of the construction sample) totaled 9,464, of which 5,238 were convictions. Of those convictions, 64.4 percent were guilty pleas, 29.6 percent resulted from trials before a judge, and 5.9 percent were the outcome of jury trials.

Philadelphia researchers worked with ten judges who comprised a Judges' Advisory Committee, which was selected by the Criminal Justice Committee of the Board of Judges—a body elected by all of the judges of the Court of Common Pleas. The purpose of the advisory committee was to assist and advise the researchers as to problems involving policy and legal questions and to help explain the sentencing guidelines approach to the other thirty-five trial court judges in the court system. It was also the responsibility of this committee to select the model or models to be tested in the courtrooms.

Methodology

Learning from the experiences of the national study in other jurisdictions, the Philadelphia research team decided to collect ninety-three pieces of information initially thought to be possibly related to the sentencing decision. The information collected fell into three categories: (1) information concerning the instant offense, such as victim injury and weapon usage; (2) information concerning the offender's criminal record, such as prior arrests and convictions; and (3) information concerning the offender's background and social stability, such as marital status and employment history. One thousand cases disposed of in 1975 were randomly selected for the construction sample. The decision to code calendar year 1975 cases was made on the basis of file availability and information accessibility. Coder training and coding for the construction sample began in December 1976. The validation sample was made up of 250 randomly selected cases disposed of in the first six months of 1977.

It was necessary to search two locations in order to obtain all the information: (1) the court case files for information about the instant offense; and (2) Probation Department files for criminal record and social stability information contained in the presentence report. Coding of the construction sample, including the checking of most files, was completed in May 1977. Coding of the validation sample began in July 1977 and was completed by December 1977.

As a result of missing or incorrectly coded data, forty-five cases had to be dropped from the construction sample during the data collection and refinement period. Most analysis, then, was actually performed on a random sample of 955 cases. Analysis proceeded in several stages, the first of which was to select a large number of variables that the research staff felt might be important to the sentencing decision and to run cross-tabulations of each of these variables against the "in/out" decision. This technique was used merely as a preliminary measure as to whether the staff was using variables that were significantly related to the sentencing decision.

In terms of their data analysis, the Philadelphia researchers then applied bivariate and multivariate statistical techniques in a manner much as we did. In order to assess the relative importance of each variable, they employed stepwise regression analysis, incorporating the listwise deletion method of dealing with missing information.[15] Multiple regression equations using several dependent variables were run (1) on the "in/out" decision as a dichotomy; (2) on the minimum sentence, coding "0" for an "out" sentence, with the minimum years to be served as the minimum; (3) on the maximum years set to be served; and (4) on the length of probation (although the results with regard to this latter variable proved inconclusive).

Model Development

Upon receiving preliminary results derived from employing these statistical techniques, the Philadelphia research staff, in consultation with the Judges' Advisory Committee, decided to develop two models, one using rankings based on a statutory classification of crimes as to seriousness and a second based on seriousness rankings made by the trial division judges. Both models used a two dimension decisionmaking matrix, as well as a unit weighting scheme, in an attempt to make the models computationally simple and to assure knowing and understanding judicial implementation. The model using a statutory-based seriousness ranking is described below.

Several criteria were used to eliminate variables from the models. First, some variables, such as offenses for which the offender was arrested, were eliminated because they are excluded from judicial consideration by law if there was no subsequent conviction. Second, some variables were eliminated because the large amount of missing information concerning them would have produced too much "shrinkage" in the number of cases; drug and alcohol use information, for example, was missing 70 percent of the time. Finally, variables unrelated or only weakly related to the sentencing decision were also excluded. The resulting regression analysis revealed that there were about fifteen variables (excluding estimated seriousness of offense) that were significantly related to the sentencing decision. Of those variables, the Philadelphia research team chose twelve with which to experiment in designing sentence predictor equations; occasionally, other variables were included at the suggestion of members of the Judges' Advisory Committee.

The offense score was comprised of four variables, the first of which was the seriousness of the offense. Seriousness was determined by ranking the crimes within each statutory classification. Murder was given a rank of 8; a Felony 1 against the person (e.g., robbery) a 7; a Felony 1 not against the person (e.g., burglary) a 6; and so on until a Misdemeanor not against the person was given a rank of 1 (see Table 6–3). This seriousness score was then modified to reflect the actual behavior of the defendant during the commission of the offense. Table 6–4 illustrates how the overall offense score was computed.

Table 6–3. Philadelphia Court of Common Pleas Offense Seriousness Score—Offense Class.

Class	Seriousness Code
Murder	8
Felony 1, against person	7
Felony 1, not against person	6
Felony 2, against person	5
Felony 2, not against person	4
Felony 3 (all)	3
Misdemeanor, against person	2
Misdemeanor, not against person	1

The other major dimension summed on the decisionmaking matrix was an offender score comprising five variables (see Table 6–5). The

fifth of these items, employment history, was adopted at the suggestion of the Judges' Advisory Committee and was phrased in terms of
"rewarding" employment rather than "penalizing" unemployment—
that is, employed offenders had points subtracted from the sum of the
first four variables comprising the offender score.

Table 6–4. Philadelphia Court of Common Pleas Offense Seriousness Score

		Points
Item 1:	*SERIOUSNESS*	
	Offense class	1–8
Item 2:	*VICTIM INJURY*	
	Death	+2
	Injury	+1
	No injury	0
Item 3:	*WEAPON USAGE*	
	Yes	+1
	No	0
Item 4:	*VICTIM CLASSIFICATION*	
	Private citizen	+1
	Organization or institution	0

The highest number of points that may be assigned is 12, the
lowest 1. The higher the score, the "worse" the offense.

The two models were each tested on the validation sample; a further model was then approved for use by the Judges' Advisory Committee, and the full field testing of sentencing guidelines began in
late 1978. Final implementation of a revised set of sentencing guidelines for the use of the judges of the Philadelphia Court of Common
Pleas began on March 5, 1979. In the event, a generic model was
employed, with one matrix for crimes against the person and another
for crimes not against the person—the principal distinction being in
the victim variables. The latter matrix employed a victim classification variable as found in Table 6–4 and also substituted property loss
for victim injury. For crimes against the person, however, the
number of victims involved proved significant; moreover, the victim
injury variable added a fourth category by distinguishing two categories of "injury" on the basis of their permanence. The offender score

varied from that found in Table 6–5 primarily in that a high school education was included as a permissible substitute for employment.

It is generally believed that the work of the Philadelphia Court of Common Pleas in developing its own sentencing guidelines system was an important factor involved in defeating mandatory sentencing legislation, which had cleared one house of the Commonwealth of Pennsylvania's Legislature. In fact, a substitute measure was adopted and signed into law in early 1979, establishing a Commonwealth of Pennsylvania Sentencing Commission that was charged to develop a statewide sentencing guidelines system, and the commission is expected to employ the technology described in this report.[16]

Table 6–5. Philadelphia Court of Common Pleas Offender Score

Item 1:	*PRIOR ADULT INCARCERATIONS*	*POINTS*
	3 or more	+3
	2	+2
	1	+1
	0	0
Item 2:	*SYSTEM RELATIONSHIP*	
	Supervision by criminal justice agency	+1
	No supervision	0
Item 3:	*PRIOR ADULT CONVICTIONS*	
	3 or more	+3
	2	+2
	1	+1
	0	0
Item 4:	*PRIOR FELONY (AGAINST PERSON) CONVICTIONS*	
	3 or more	1
	0, 1, or 2	0
Item 5:	*EMPLOYMENT HISTORY*	
	Employed at arrest	–2
	Employed in past	–1
	Not employed	0

The highest number of points an offender may receive is "8," the lowest is "–2." The higher the score, the "worse" the offender.

ACTION RESEARCH IN THE FIELD

In this chapter, I have attempted to give the reader a feeling for the flexibility of the sentencing guidelines concept by discussing the various adaptations made in the general research design to suit the needs of local courts. In a sense, these last two chapters have taken the reader two steps back, for they have elaborated upon the process by which a sentencing guidelines system, itself a procedural device, became established in five different court systems. As may be seen, the procedures have been variations on a single theme, but the need to localize the system to fit the particularized needs of a specific community or state should never be ignored by those engaged in action research.

It is now appropriate to move one step ahead and to describe the different sentencing guidelines systems that were developed uniquely for each of the four jurisdictions involved in the federal study that I directed. These too will appear as variations on a theme, all designed with the single goal of helping trial court judges engaged in making that terribly difficult and significant sentencing decision.

NOTES

1. Sophocles, *Trachiniae*, tr. R. C. Jebb (Amsterdam: Adolf M. Hakkert, 1962), at 93:

> *Chorus*: Nay, if these measures give any ground of confidence, we think that thy design is not amiss.
>
> *Deianeira*: Well, the ground stands thus,—there is a fair promise; but I have not yet essayed the proof.
>
> *Chorus*: Nay, knowledge must come through action; thou canst have no test which is not fanciful, save by trial.

2. Further descriptive details than are offered here may be found in J. M. Kress, *Sentencing in Four Courts* (Washington, D.C.: USGPO, 1980). Unless otherwise noted, the descriptions of penal codes and individual court procedures refer only to the period of project data collection and analysis.

3. The data collection and analysis work performed during the preliminary, or feasibility, phase of sentencing guidelines research is explained in detail in L. T. Wilkins, J. M. Kress, D. M. Gottfredson, J. C. Calpin, and A. M. Gelman, *Sentencing Guidelines: Structuring Ju-*

dicial Discretion–Report on the Feasibility Study 10-25 (Washington, D.C.: USGPO, 1978).

4. A more recent and revised version of the Denver guidelines may be found as Appendix A, *infra*.

5. The significance of the sentencing hearing should be considered here. See A. M. Gelman, "The Sentencing Hearing: Forgotten Phase of Sentencing Reform," in M. Evans, ed., *Discretion and Control* (Beverly Hills: Sage Publication, 1978).

6. Further descriptive details concerning the Essex County and superior courts may be found in Kress, *supra* note 1.

7. The Essex County data collection and statistical analysis effort took place during the second (implementation) phase of the project and is explained in greater detail in J. C. Calpin, J. M. Kress, and A. M. Gelman, *The Analytical Basis for the Formulation of Sentencing Policy* (Washington, D.C.: USGPO, 1980). As the reader may observe, the data sample involved in establishing the Essex model was much larger than that employed in Denver; we also built upon the knowledge gained through our early Denver effort. Therefore, the research staff had a far greater statistical confidence in the guidelines developed in Essex County.

8. This involvement of other criminal justice agencies was unique among the early sentencing guidelines jurisdictions, but clearly in line with the sentencing guidelines philosophy I earlier enunciated, particularly *supra* Chapter 2.

9. J. S. Boyle, "Making A Big Court Better," 60 *Judicature* 233 (December 1976). Further descriptive details concerning Cook County may be found in Kress, *supra* note 1.

10. The Cook County data collection and statistical analysis effort is explained in greater detail in Calpin et al., *supra* note 7. As explained further in Kress, *supra* note 1, the skewed (and smaller) data sample collected in Cook County caused us to be more tentative concerning our initial findings there.

11. This was the highly publicized "Class X" legislation. The reader will note this as one example of the fact I noted *supra* Chapter 2, when I pointed out that certain so-called "mandatory" laws were not as determinate as they purported to be.

12. Further descriptive details concerning Maricopa County may be found in Kress, *supra* note 1.

13. The Maricopa County data collection and statistical analysis effort is explained in greater detail in Calpin et al., *supra* note 7. As in Essex County, we were able to collect a large data sample here; moreover, as this was the fourth site involved in the national project, we were able to build upon the knowledge gained in our work in all previous sites. Therefore, the research staff had the

highest degree of statistical confidence in the guidelines developed here.

14. Saundra Dillio is the Courts Programs Analyst for the Research and Planning Unit of the Probation Department of the Philadelphia Court of Common Pleas. The assistance of Michael Altier during the early stage of this effort is also gratefully acknowledged. See J. M. Kress and S. L. Dillio, "Sentencing Guidelines: Judicial Reform in the Philadelphia Court of Common Pleas," in M. Evans, ed., *Discretion and Control* (Beverly Hills: Sage Publication, 1978).

15. See H. M. Blalock, Jr., *Social Statistics,* 2nd ed., 429-50 (New York: McGraw-Hill, 1972); and N. R. Draper and H. Smith, *Applied Regression Analysis* (New York: John Wiley and Sons, 1966). The analytically inclined reader should note that all data were recoded so as to meet the assumptions of regression analysis; thus, noninterval data were recoded to dichotomies so as to be treated as interval data. A further description of such methodological procedures may be found in Calpin et al., *supra* note 6; and in A. M. Gelman, J. M. Kress, and J. C. Calpin, *Establishing A Sentencing Guidelines System: A Methods Manual* (Washington, D.C.: University Research Corporation, 1978).

16. The Pennsylvania Sentencing Commission is chaired by the Honorable Richard P. Conaboy and began operations on April 1, 1979; it is due to submit guidelines on September 30, 1980.

7

Four Sentencing Guidelines Systems: A Comparison

In England we have come to rely upon a comfortable time-lag of fifty years or a century intervening between the perception that something ought to be done and a serious attempt to do it.
—H. G. Wells[1]

As suggested in the first chapter, the problems of sentencing have been with us for some time, yet only in the past decade have concrete efforts been made to solve these problems. Nevertheless, once guidelines research began, the time between conceptualization and implementation has been remarkably swift. It is my purpose in this chapter to set forth the specific results of our research project—that is, the actual sentencing guidelines models developed for each of the four jurisdictions involved in the federal study. While I have emphasized in preceding chapters that the guidelines models must be viewed only as one part of an overall sentencing guidelines *system*, these models do fairly represent the heart of those systems devised for each court. In this chapter, I will describe in some detail the components of these models, including the offense or crime score dimension for each model (particularly stressing the offense rank-ordering procedural subsystems we devised, as well as the seriousness modifiers actually adopted in each site), the offender score dimension for each model (emphasizing the differential construction and weighting systems employed), and the various presentation formats of the decisionmaking matrixes, or grids, adopted in each jurisdiction.

THE LIMITS OF COMPARISON

Sampling periods and techniques varied among the four courts; the profiles of defendants and their offenses differed; charging and sentencing practices differed; and for many other reasons, direct comparisons between these courts, for the sake of those comparisons, would be difficult and undesirable. That, however, would miss the purpose of this chapter and, indeed, the purpose of selecting these sites for study. The sites were chosen not for their similarities, but for their differences. Our purpose was to test the generalizability of the sentencing guidelines concept and not to provide simple replications of our early work. The reader should understand, therefore, that our work was never contemplated as an interjurisdictional study. The guidelines models are rather presented for the interest of the reader who may find it instructive to have highlighted here the differences that exist in the sentencing guidelines systems that were developed for each of the first four courts ever to incorporate such systems within their structures.

The very localized orientation of our efforts, which is a major strength of the guidelines approach, at the same time creates the principal limitation of comparing our methods and our findings. Most of the data we collected in Denver, for example, was collected during our feasibility study. We were still groping to establish this new concept and were unsure as to whether the approach we took in the state of Vermont (our other participant court during the early feasibility research) might prove a more useful one. As we were more interested in concept testing and less in actual local guidelines construction, we took a much smaller construction sample in Denver than we did elsewhere. We also developed the initial Denver models on the basis of views expressed by the judicial members in our Steering and Policy Committee, only one of whom was from Denver. True, before implementation, we modified our designs to the explicitly stated specifications of the Denver judiciary, but the differences in our data base must be understood before comparing our Denver results to those in the other jurisdictions. (On the other hand, I should note that there are some apparent differences that are not differences in fact; for example, our Denver County construction sample did include homicide cases, although we eventually determined not to establish a grid for Felony 1 cases in Colorado.)

Our Chicago activities were similarly sui generis. We worked in only two of Cook County's four court locations for most of our implementation research—the branch at Maybrook and the one at 26th and California (adjacent to the Cook County Jail). These courts handle the "heavier" cases—that is, those where the defendants were detained prior to trial—and our data of necessity reflects the skewing or statistical "bias" attendant to these facts.

The data sets collected in Essex County (Newark, New Jersey) and Maricopa County (Phoenix, Arizona) were both much larger than those collected in the other two jurisdictions. Even here, however, the temptation to see interjurisdictionally comparative relationships arising from the data must be contained, as the demographic characteristics and other noncourt processing factors in these two jurisdictions are so diverse. Moreover, our sampling from Essex focused on 1975 cases while the Maricopa sample focused on 1976 cases. Thus, we should only charily attempt to provide more than "ball park" comparisons.[2]

THE OFFENSE DIMENSION

General Models

The reader is first reminded of the discussion in the preceding chapter concerning modeling typologies: the general model of sentencing guidelines has been adopted for use by the judges of Denver and Cook counties, whereas the generic model was adopted for use by the courts in Essex and Maricopa counties. Understanding the similarities and differences between these model types is essential to comprehending the significance of their component elements in each jurisdiction.

Each type of guidelines model has focused on each of the major sentencing dimensions—the seriousness of the offense and an assessment of the offender's prior history. In assessing the seriousness of the offense, the judges of the Cook County Circuit Court and the Denver County District Court both, as a matter of policy, rank ordered all possibly occurring offenses within each statutory class (in two, three, or four divisions) according to their perceived seriousness. Table 7-1 presents the "intraclass" ranks established by the Denver County District Court judiciary for offenses placed within the same statutory class (here, Class 4 felonies) by the Colorado State Legislature.

In Colorado, the legislated maximum possible sentence a judge may set for any of these Class 4 felonies is ten years, although a judge may set a maximum sentence well below ten years; the sentence is an indeterminate one, and the judge may not set a minimum term of confinement. The judge in Colorado is also authorized to establish a nonincarcerative sentence for the Felony 4 offender; probation is the principal "out" sentence handed down, although fines and deferred judgments are also allowed.

These intraclass ranking schemes take advantage of the experience and expertise of the local judiciary in that the judges were instructed to rank the most realistically occurring example, or "typical" offense of each type, in making the ranking comparisons within each class. This sharply diverges from the public perception of a given offense, which is usually of the most heinous illustration and which often affects the legislator's view as well. When a legislature declares that "heroin sale," for example, is equivalent to murder in terms of penalty, it is likely that the legislators have in mind some

TABLE 7–1. Denver County Intraclass Ranks for Felony 4 Offenses.

Intraclass Rank 1

18–4–401 (2)	Theft (if amount taken is $200 or more)
18–4–410 (2)	Theft by Receiving ($200 or more)
18–4–501	Criminal Mischief (if damage amounts to $100 or more)
18–5–103	Second Degree Forgery

Intraclass Rank 2

18–3–106	Vehicular Homicide
18–3–203	Assault in the Second Degree
18–4–103 (2)	Second Degree Arson (if damage amounts to $100 or more)
18–4–202	Conspiracy to Commit First Degree Burglary
18–4–203 (2)	Second Degree Burglary
18–4–203 (2)	Attempt to Commit Second Degree Burglary (if burglary is of a dwelling)

Intraclass Rank 3

18–3–403	Sexual Assault in the Second Degree
18–3–404	Sexual Assault in the Degree (use of force, intimidation, or threat)
18–4–301	Robbery
18–4–302	Attempt to Commit Aggravated Robbery
18–4–302	Conspiracy to Commit Aggravated Robbery
18–8–502	Perjury in the First Degree
18–12–109 (3)	Unlawful Possession or Use of Explosives or Incendiary Devices

Intraclass Rank 4

18–3–104	Manslaughter
18–3–405	Sexual Assault on a Child

---

incorrigible, unaddicted adult pushing in a schoolyard and preying on innocent children. Often, however, the reality turns out to be the youthful addict-pusher selling to support his or her own habit.

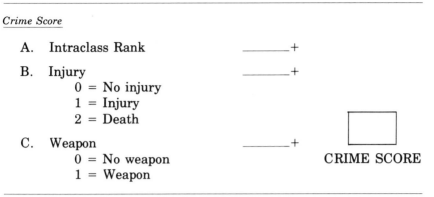

Figure 7-1. Cook County Crime Score.

The rankings made by the Cook County and Denver County judges thus usefully tempered legislative theory with courtroom reality.

The intraclass rank, as the ranking of a given offense became known, established the starting point for assessing offense seriousness within any given statutory class. A seriousness modifier was then developed, so that mitigating and aggravating aspects involved in the actual crime might be taken into account. The reader will recall that the offense score made up one of the two major dimensions we employed—the other being the offender score. Figure 7-1 reproduces the portion of the Cook County guideline worksheet devoted to the derivation of the offense score (or crime score as it was called in Cook County).

As it developed, the seriousness modifiers employed in Cook County were the quite simple ones of physical injury and weapon usage. Sufficient information was established by the simply coded injury trichotomy of no injury/injury/death. Weapon usage too was simply divided into no weapon/weapon, with the latter encompassing all examples of possession, display, threat or use.

Figure 7-2 sets out that portion of the actual Denver County guideline worksheet explaining the derivation of the offense score in that jurisdiction. While the intraclass rank again provides the starting point for computation, the reader can see at once that the seriousness modifiers were more complex in Denver County. In addition to the same injury and weapon breakdown as in Cook County, sale of drugs was added, as it appeared significant in our statistical analyses. However, it should be noted that the weighting system in Denver is also very different. These three items are not additive as the Cook County version is—only the highest score achieved individually (0, 1, or 2) is reported. We referred to the final seriousness modifier

OFFENSE SCORE

A. Intraclass Rank   _____+

□
Offense
class

B. Seriousness Modifier   _____+
    0 = No injury   0 = No weapon   0 = No sale of drugs
    1 = Injury   1 = Weapon   1 = Sale of drugs
    2 = Death

C. Victim Modifier (crime against person) _____=
     0 = Unknown victim
    −1 = Known victim

□
Offense
score

Figure 7–2.   Denver County Offense Score.

in Denver as a "victim modifier" because it is conceptually distinct. The first three serve in aggravation. In contrast, the nature of the offender-victim relationship is seen as a potentially mitigating factor. If the offender was previously acquainted with the victim, then the scored seriousness of the offense (when the offense is a crime against the person) is mitigated by subtracting a point from the offense score.

Generic Models

Using the "generic" modeling system of guidelines, the courts in Essex and Maricopa counties took a different approach. Once offenses had been categorized, an index of seriousness that we referred to as the interclass rank was devised based on the maximum sentence that could be imposed by law. (The reader is also referred back to Table 6–3, which presents an interesting variation devised for use in the Philadelphia Court of Common Pleas.) The Essex County guidelines consisted of four grids—one each for violent, property, drugs, and miscellaneous crimes. In Essex County, only the guidelines for property offenses incorporated a seriousness modifier. Figure 7–3 reproduces that portion of the actual Essex County guideline worksheet explaining the derivation of the offense score for property offenses in that jurisdiction. If an individual person was seen as the victim, then one point was added to the offense score; if the state of New Jersey or a business was the victim, then no points were added. (A similar item proved significant in Philadelphia; see Table 6–4.)

The other generic model developed was the one adopted by the Maricopa County Superior Court. The Maricopa County guidelines system utilized only three decisionmaking grids or matrixes—one each for violent, property, or drugs offenses. There again, the interclass rank of each offense provided the starting point for computation of the offense score. Figure 7-4 reproduces that portion of the Maricopa County guideline worksheet explaining the derivation of the offense score for violent offenses in that jurisdiction.[4]

Offense Type (Most serious offense):

> *PROPERTY*

> *OFFENSE TYPE*

Offense Score

   A.   Interclass Rank   ————+

   B.   Victim Classification   ————=
          0 = Business/state of
              New Jersey   **OFFENSE**
          1 = Citizen/officer   **SCORE**

Figure 7-3. Essex County Property Offense Score.

Offense Type (Most serious offense)

> *VIOLENT*

> *OFFENSE TYPE*

Offense Score

   A.   Interclass Rank   ————+

   B.   Number of Criminal   ————+
          Events
          0 = One
          1 = Two or more

   C.   Injury to Victim(s)   ————=
          0 = No injury or minor
          injury
          1 = Injury requiring
          hospitalization; death; rape;   **OFFENSE**
          sexual molestation of child   **SCORE**

Figure 7-4. Maricopa County Violent Offense Score.

As the reader can see, two factors turned up as offense seriousness modifiers to the interclass rank of the offense at conviction—number of criminal events and injury to victim(s). Criminal events were defined as distinct crimes separated either by time or distance and not merely multiple charges or counts in an indictment. The injury modifier may be seen to have a different definition and weighting from that employed in other jurisdictions. (Compare, for example, to Figures 7–1 or 7–2 or, indeed, to Table 6–4, outlining Philadelphia's comparable offense scoring system.)

Figure 7–5 reproduces that portion of the actual Maricopa County guideline worksheet explaining the derivation of the offense score for property offenses in that jurisdiction. The only offense seriousness modifier of significance here turned out to be the number of criminal events.

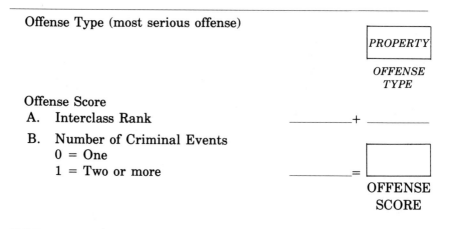

Figure 7–5. Maricopa County Property Offense Score

Figure 7–6 reproduces that portion of the actual Maricopa County guideline worksheet explaining the derivation of the offense score for drug offenses in that jurisdiction. Once again, the number of criminal events was revealed to be a significant seriousness modifier. (Future researchers might wish to explore whether the reason for this factor appearing to be so significant is due to prosecution charging or negotiation practice, to joinder of offense practices, or to some other constraint unique to Maricopa County.) The base interclass rank of a drug offense was also modified owing to the type of drug involved, and the modification was a major one. One point was added to the seriousness score if the drug involved was listed in the Uniform Narcotics Drug Act; one point was subtracted if the drug was cannabis or some other substance listed in the Dangerous Drug Act.

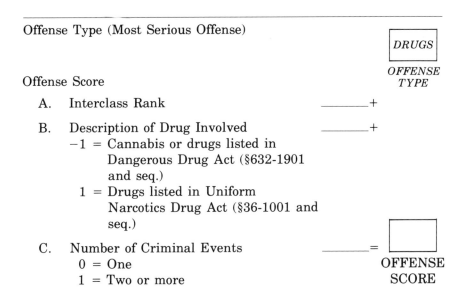

Figure 7–6. Maricopa County Drugs Offense Score.

THE OFFENDER DIMENSION

General Models

In addition to taking different approaches to the development of offense scores, each jurisdiction also differed in the construction of offender scores. As we have noted elsewhere,[5] offender variables tend to have a more significant impact upon the sentencing decision than offense variables, except where the offense is extremely serious. When we look at the various offender scores displayed in this section, the most striking feature is the number of variables that appear as significant. When we look at the various matrixes in the following section, we shall see that the axis displaying the offender score is lengthier and that relatively high offender scores may therefore occur.

Figure 7–7 reproduces that portion of the actual Cook County guideline worksheet explaining the derivation of the offender score, the second primary dimension in the calculation of guideline sentences. The salient factors in the Cook County offender score were liberty status at the time of the present offense, prior adult convictions, prior adult felony convictions against the person, prior adult incarcerations (over thirty days), and prior adult probation/parole revocations.

Offender Score

A. Legal Status at Time of the Offense   _____+
    0 = Not on probation/parole, no other
    charges pending, not an escapee
    1 = On probation/parole, other charges
    pending, escapee

B. Prior Adult Convictions   _____+ (maximum
    0 = No convictions   of 2)
    1 = 1 conviction
    2 = 2,3,4,5, or more convictions

C. Prior Adult Felony Convictions Against   _____+
    Person
    0 = No convictions
    1 = 1,2,3,4,5, or more convictions

D. Prior Adult Incarcerations (over 30 days) _____+
    0 = No incarcerations
    1 = 1,2,3,4,5, or more incarcerations

E. Prior Adult Probation/Parole Revocations _____= ┌────────┐
    0 = No revocations   │   │
    1 = 1,2,3,4,5, or more revocations   └────────┘
                                                      OFFENDER
                                                      SCORE

Figure 7-7. Cook County Offender Score.

The results obtained in Cook County are especially interesting when compared with the resulting offender score in the other court employing a general model—the Denver County District Court. Figure 7-8 reproduces that portion of the actual Denver County guideline worksheet explaining the derivation of the offender score in that jurisdiction.

The reader will see that the Denver County guidelines use six factors to provide a measure of the offender dimension—liberty status at time of present offense, prior juvenile convictions, prior adult misdemeanor convictions, prior adult felony convictions, prior adult probation-parole revocations, and prior adult incarcerations (over thirty days). The dissimilarities between the Cook County and the Denver County offender scores are apparent.

In Cook County, four prior criminal history variables enter the equation, whereas five are used in Denver. Denver employs a measure of the offender's juvenile record, whereas Cook County limits itself to consideration of the adult record of the offender. Both consider the liberty status of the offender, as well as the number of prior adult incarcerations (over thirty days) and the number of prior adult probation/parole revocations, although in the latter two cases, the weightings employed in each jurisdiction are quite different.

Offender Score

A. Current Legal Status   ____+
    0 = Not on probation/parole, escape
    1 = On probation/parole, escape

B. Prior Juvenile Convictions   ____+
    0 = No convictions
    1 = 1–3 convictions
    2 = 4 or more convictions

C. Prior Adult Misdemeanor Convictions   ____+
    0 = No convictions
    1 = 1–3 convictions
    2 = 4 or more convictions

D. Prior Adult Felony Convictions   ____+
    0 = No convictions
    1 = 1 conviction
    3 = 2 or more convictions

E. Prior Adult Probation/Parole Revocations ____+
    0 = None
    2 = One or more revocations

F. Prior Adult Incarcerations (over 30 days) ____=
    0 = None
    1 = 1 incarceration   Offender
    3 = 2 or more incarcerations   Score

Figure 7–8. Denver County Offender Score.

Generic Model: Essex County

Any analysis of the offender scores obtained in Essex and Maricopa counties becomes more complicated because the different types of crimes accounted for were separately established. As it turned out, Essex County employed four different sentencing grids, and each of them employed different factors and weighting systems. Figure 7–9 reproduces that portion of the actual Essex County guideline work-sheet explaining the derivation of the offender score for violent offenses in that jurisdiction.

Offender Score
A. Legal Status at Time of Offense   _____+
    0 = Free
    1 = Not free

B. Prior Juvenile Delinquency Petition(s)   _____+
    Sustained
    0 = None or one
    1 = Two or more

C. Prior Adult Incarcerations   _____+
    0 = None
    1 = One or more incarcerations

D. Drug Addiction   _____+
    0 = No use/not addicted
    1 = Addicted

E. Offender Status   _____=
    −1 = Part/full-time employment/school   OFFENDER
    0 = Unemployed/not in school   SCORE

Figure 7–9.   Essex County Violent Offender Score.

The violent offender score employed five factors in Essex County—the liberty status of the offender at the time of offense commission, prior juvenile delinquency petitions sustained, prior adult incarcerations, drug addiction, and the offender's employment-school status. This latter factor is relatively controversial[6] and did not enter the equation with regard to drug or miscellaneous offenses (see Figures 7–11 and 7–12), but did appear in all three Maricopa equations (see Figures 7–13 and 7–14) and appears to be a very influential factor in Philadelphia (see Table 6–4). These results are most interesting when compared to the other three offender scores derived for Essex County. Figure 7–10 reproduces that portion of the actual Essex County guideline worksheet explaining the derivation of the offender score for property offenses there.

As we can see, the only difference in offender scores between these two offense typologies is the introduction into the property offender score of one variable—prior adult convictions. There is a more significant difference observable when we compare these two crime typologies with the offender scores obtained for the next two typologies.

Figure 7–11 reproduces that portion of the actual Essex County guideline worksheet explaining the derivation of the offender score for the drug offenses typology in Essex County.

Offender Score

A. Legal Status at Time of Offense   ____+
    0 = Free
    1 = Not free

B. Prior Juvenile Delinquency Petition(s)   ____+
    Sustained
    0 = None
    1 = One or more

C. Prior Adult Convictions   ____+
    0 = None or one conviction
    1 = Two or more convictions

D. Prior Adult Incarcerations (over 30 days) ____+
    0 = None
    1 = One or more incarcerations

E. Drug Addiction   ____+
    0 = No use/not addicted
    1 = Addicted

F. Offender's Status   ____=
    −1 = Part/full-time employment/school   OFFENDER
    0 = Unemployed/not in school   SCORE

Figure 7–10. Essex County Property Offender Score.

With regard to the drug typology, only five factors affected the offender score—the liberty status of the offender, prior juvenile incarcerations, prior adult convictions, prior adult incarcerations (over thirty days), and drug addiction. In only this one offense typology (since in this respect, the miscellaneous offender score was more like that for violent and property offenses), the juvenile history variable that appeared significant was prior juvenile incarcerations rather than prior juvenile delinquency petition (s) sustained. Like the property offender score, but unlike the violent offender score, prior adult convictions entered the guidelines equation. Perhaps surprisingly, while drug addiction was significant across all four Essex County offender scores, it had no different weighting in the drug offense category.

Figure 7–12 reproduces that portion of the actual Essex County guideline worksheet explaining the derivation of the offender score for miscellaneous offenses in that jurisdiction. As we can see, the miscellaneous offender score was composed of the same five factors as the drug offenses grid, except that prior sustained juvenile delinquency petitions was substituted for prior juvenile incarcerations.

Offender Score

    A.   Legal Status at Time of Offense   _____+
         0 = Free
         1 = Not free

    B.   Prior Juvenile Incarcerations   _____+
         0 = No incarcerations
         1 = One or more incarcerations

    C.   Prior Adult Convictions   _____+
         0 = No convictions
         1 = One or more convictions

    D.   Prior Adult Incarcerations (over 30 days) _____+
         0 = No incarcerations
         1 = One or more incarcerations

    E.   Drug Addiction   _____= **OFFENDER**
         0 = No use/not addicted   **SCORE**
         1 = Addicted

Figure 7–11. Essex County Drugs Offender Score.

Generic Model: Maricopa County

Maricopa County employed three different offense typologies, but with regard to the offender variables that here concern us, the violent offender score and the drug offender score each employed the same seven factors—liberty status, prior juvenile convictions, prior juvenile incarcerations, prior adult convictions, prior adult convictions for crimes against the person, prior adult incarcerations, and school-employment status. Figure 7–13 reproduces that portion of the actual Maricopa County guideline worksheet explaining the derivation of the offender score for violent offenses in that jurisdiction.

Figure 7–14 presents the final offender score to be discussed here; it reproduces that portion of the actual Maricopa County guideline worksheet explaining the derivation of the offender score for property offenses in that jurisdiction. As may be seen, the same seven factors were also included in the Maricopa County offender score for property offenses, except that prior adult convictions for crimes not against the person replaced prior adult convictions. Thus, with respect to the offender score variables in Maricopa County, the differences within the typological classifications were not as significant as they were in Essex County.

Offender Score
    A.   Legal Status at Time of Offense   ____+
          0 = Free
          1 = Not free

    B.   Prior Juvenile Delinquency Petition(s)   ____+
          Sustained
          0 = None
          1 = One or more

    C.   Prior Adult Convictions   ____+
          0 = No convictions
          1 = One or more convictions

    D.   Prior Adult Incarcerations (over 30 days) ____+
          0 = None
          1 = One or more incarcerations

    E.   Drug Addiction   ____= OFFENDER
          0 = No use/not addicted   SCORE
          1 = Addicted

Figure 7–12. Essex County Miscellaneous Offender Score.

DECISIONMAKING MATRIXES

Rationale

Sentencing guidelines models have been expressed in a three dimensional format—that is, a series of two dimensional grids or matrixes, each of which array an offense dimension against an offender dimension. The preceding two sections have described the factors that went into each of these two latter dimensions. The third dimension lies in the series itself, and its measurement lies in the modeling typology employed. In the general models adopted in Cook and Denver counties, the derivation is legislative; the dimension is formed from the various classes of crimes and punishments established by the jurisdiction's penal code. For the generic models employed in Essex and Maricopa counties, however, the third dimension is categorical; its derivation comes primarily from the action research collaborative logic employed by the research team working together with the judges of each jurisdiction.

Offender Score
  A. Legal Status at Time of Offense   _____+
      0 = Not under state control
      1 = Under state control
  B. Prior Juvenile Convictions   _____+
      0 = None
      1 = One or more
  C. Prior Juvenile Incarcerations (over 30   _____+
      days)
      0 = None
      1 = One or more
  D. Prior Adult Convictions   _____=
      0 = None
      1 = One or more
  E. Prior Adult Convictions Against the   _____+
      Person
      0 = None
      1 = One or more
  F. Prior Adult Incarcerations (over 30 days) _____+
      0 = None
      1 = One or more
  G. Employment Status   _____=
      −1 = Part/full-time employment   OFFENDER
      0 = Unemployed   SCORE

Figure 7–13. Maricopa County Violent Offender Score.

We have elsewhere[7] described in some detail the theory behind the decisionmaking matrix approach, but some summary is here in order. The vertical axis is divided into levels of seriousness of the offense, or crime, and those levels are determined as explained earlier in this chapter. The horizontal axis is divided into offender scores, which are determined as explained in the preceding section. The interior of the grid consists of cells, each of which contains a suggested sentence or sentence range. One ascertains this "guideline" sentence by first determining the offense score, then the offender score, and then plotting the intersection of these scores, finding the appropriate cell much as one plots the location of a city on a map by noting the intersection of two known coordinates.

The value of this scheme is both theoretical and practical. On a theoretical level, it accounts for the interactive effects of the two

Offender Score

A. Legal Status at Time of Offense ____+
    0 = Not under state control
    1 = Under state control

B. Prior Juvenile Convictions ____+
    0 = None
    1 = One or more

C. Prior Juvenile Incarcerations (over 30 ____+
    days)
    0 = None
    1 = One or more

D. Prior Adult Convictions not Against the ____+
    Person
    0 = None
    1 = One or more

E. Prior Adult Convictions Against the ____+
    Person
    0 = None
    1 = One or more

F. Prior Adult Incarcerations (over 30 days) ____+
    0 = None
    1 = One or more

G. Employment Status ____=
    −1 = Part-time or full-time employment   OFFENDER
    0 = Unemployed   SCORE

Figure 7–14. Maricopa County Property Offender Score.

dimensions and creates a large number of information categories from a relatively limited information base. Pragmatically, its very simplicity facilitates comprehension of its purpose as well as speed of calculation with a minimum amount of error. The grid system has been employed since the sentencing guidelines concept was first implemented in November 1976, and even now, thousands of decisions later, each sentencing guidelines jurisdiction still finds it useful, even though rankings, factors, and weightings have since changed. (These changes, of course, were part of the planned, dynamic, self-improvement mechanism we have always incorporated in guidelines systems.) In all four of the jurisdictions studied here, the concept of a decisionmaking grid was positively employed to great profit, although the grids, and the associated guidelines systems, are often sharply dissimilar from one another. Finally, the sentencing guidelines research team has found the concept of a decisionmaking grid to have consistent value as a visible and usable representation of court policy. As proven over time, it offers a policymaking device that is adaptable to change and that accommodates well to judicial purpose.

Denver County

In each of the counties, a primary constraint upon the sentencing ranges to be found within the matrixes is any legislatively fixed lower or upper limit or a mandated minimum or maximum sentence. This was especially pertinent in jurisdictions employing a general model, as the potential sentencing range established the third dimension of the matrix system—that is, the felony or misdemeanor class of the offense at conviction.

Because of the special nature of the crimes and penalties found in Colorado's Felony 1 and Felony 2 classes of offenses, as well as the relative infrequency of Denver convictions in these classes, the research team did not establish grids for these classes. We did, however, establish eight different matrixes, ranging in seriousness from Class 3 felonies down to Class 3 misdemeanors. Moreover, owing to the distinctive sentencing patterns involving drug offenses in Denver County, we later established two separate grids for each of Denver's Class 4 and Class 5 felony categories—one for drug offenses in that category and one for other offenses. (In one sense, therefore, the Denver County guidelines scheme may presently be fairly described as a "mixed" general and generic model.)

The decisionmaking matrix for Misdemeanor 1 offenses in Denver County is reproduced in Figure 7–15. On this grid, the offense score may range from 1–5 and the offender score from 0–13. Stretched out, this would imply a grid consisting of 5 x 14 (or 70) cells. However, since our analysis showed that the distinctions made were not that fine, we collapsed a number of rows and columns resulting in a 24 (4 x 6) cell table or matrix.

The general trend of this matrix follows the theoretical assumptions of a working guidelines model—that is, as the offense and offender scores increase (or move from lower left to upper right on the matrix) there is a general increase in the severity of the sanction applied. The maximum penalty possible is a flat two year (twenty-four month) sentence. The sentencing judge has a number of nonincarcerative alternatives, all here referred to as "OUT." One of the cells has a note (a) indicating that an offender whose case profile fits this one would be likely to be a candidate for one of two particular work release programs that are operational in Denver County—the

Offense Score	0-1	2-3	4-5	6-7	8-11	12-13
4-5	20-24 month	20-24 month	20-24 month	20-24 month	20-24 month	20-24 month
3	OUT[a]	9-12 month	14-18 month	20-24 month	20-24 month	20-24 month
2	OUT	OUT	14-18 month	14-18 month	14-18 month	20-24 month
1	OUT	OUT	OUT	9-12 month	14-18 month	14-18 month

[a]Work project or community correction center.

Figure 7-15. Denver County Decisionmaking Matrix: Misdemeanor 1.

Rocky Mountain Work Project or the Denver Community Corrections Center.

I have set out this grid, and described it at some length, so that I may now briefly describe the range of matrixes existing in the Denver County District Court sentencing guidelines system and be better able to compare them with the other sets of decisionmaking grids.[8]

There are eight such matrixes in Denver County, five felony and three misdemeanor. The offense score is most limited with regard to Felony 5 drug offenses, with a possible range of 1–3, establishing only two rows of useful information. The offense score is least limited with respect to Felony 4 offenses, with a possible range of 1–6, establishing four rows of useful information. The offender score is most limited with respect to Misdemeanor 3 offenses, with a possible range of 0–13, establishing only five columns of useful information. The offender score is least limited with respect to Felony 4 offenses, with a possible range of 0–13, establishing eight columns of useful information. The number of matrix cells ranges from a low of twelve, with respect to Felony 5 drug offenses, to a high of thirty-two, with respect to Felony 4 offenses.

Cook County

In Cook County, we initially formulated the guidelines in the same grid or matrix manner that had first been adopted during our feasibility research. While the principle and the theory were the same, there were elements in Cook County practice that caused us to consider a variation in the method of display or presentation. I have elsewhere discussed at length several of the unique attributes of the Cook County Circuit Court.[9] Among these was the fact that there was a good deal of sentence bargaining, which took place before judges received a presentence investigation report and which was often hurriedly engaged in at the bench. If sentencing guidelines were to prove truly useful to Cook County judges, then speed of use was an absolute necessity.

After some experimentation, we developed the grid alternate form of guidelines presentation. This contained the exact same information as the matrix, but the Cook County judiciary found it far more convenient to work with. In "cleaning" the data,[10] we noticed that far fewer errors occurred after its introduction, and the judges reported greater satisfaction with it. Table 7–2 reproduces the Cook County decisionmaking matrix for felony offenses in the grid alternate form.

Unlike the situation in Denver County, we had a sufficient Cook County data base from which to establish guidelines for the most serious statutory classes. Our limitation here was with the less serious offenses. Earlier, I referred to the skewed data base in Cook County, and this was one effect that held. Cook County matrixes were developed only for Felony 1, Felony 2, and Felony 3 offenses.

Table 7–2. Cook County Decisionmaking Matrix: Grid Alternate Form—Felony Two Offenses.

GUIDELINE SENTENCE–FELONY TWO OFFENSES

Crime Score	Offender Score	Guideline Sentence Minimum	Maximum
1	0	Probation	
	1	Probation*	
	2–3	1 year	1–3 years
	4–6	1–2 years	3–6 years
2	0	Probation	
	1	1 year*	1–3 years
	2	1 year	1–3 years
	3	1–2 years	1–6 years
	4	1–2 years	3–6 years
	5–6	1–3 years	3–9 years
3	0	1–2 years*	3–6 years
	1–4	1–2 years	3–6 years
	5–6	1–3 years	3–9 years
4	0	1–2 years	3–6 years
	1	1–3 years	6–9 years
	2–6	2–3 years	6–9 years
5	0–2	2–5 years	6–15 years
	3–6	4–6 years	12–18 years

*Or an alternative sentence such as periodic imprisonment, drug program, or a split sentence with or without credit for time served.

The crime score for these three matrixes is most limited with regard to Felony 1 offenses, with a possible range of 1–4, establishing only two rows of useful information. The crime score is least limited with respect to Felony 3 offenses, with a possible range of 1–6, establishing six rows of useful information. The offender score, on the other hand, is most limited with respect to Felony 3 offenses, with a possible range of 0–6, establishing only four columns of useful information. Translated to the usual matrix format, the number of guideline cells ranges from a low of twenty, with respect to Felony 1 offenses, to a high of thirty, with respect to Felony 2 offenses.

Essex County

The judiciary in Essex County requested yet another variation in sentencing. The Essex County and Superior Court judges were quite willing to acknowledge openly the existence of present disparity and thus to attack it conspicuously. To this end, they determined that the data be presented to them in a relatively raw form; they did not want the decisionmaking matrixes "smoothed" to conform to the theoretical assumption that sentences should increase concomitanty with increases in the offense and offender scores.[11]

There were four Essex County decisionmaking matrixes, one for each of the typologies developed—violent, property, drugs, miscellaneous. Figure 7–16 reproduces here the grid for drugs. The reader's attention is called to the grid found at the intersection of offense score 4 and offender score 4. The results of this grid conform to our early construction sample's descriptive findings, but not to the prescriptive requirements of the Essex County judiciary, for the results are out of kilter with the remainder of the grid: the median is much too high. Yet the judges wanted it left this way. They felt that corrective action could best be made consciously and individually if they were made aware of the problem in this very direct way. Whereas the judiciary in the other three courts sought to combine the normative and descriptive elements of guidelines construction as a matter of overall policy, the Essex County judiciary decided, initially, to tackle the problem by this ad hoc procedure. While such a system demands more statistical sophistication on the part of the judiciary, it does have the advantage of making strikingly clear the individual sentencing policy decisions involved in particular cases.

The reader will note another unique attribute of the guidelines system developed for Essex County. The judges of Essex County have the power to choose the institution of incarceration and wanted guidance on this matter. Rather than have the guidelines actually recommend one or another institution, however, the judges wished to utilize the grids as a base of experience in this area also. Therefore, each grid relates two items to the significant sentencing decision (i.e., to the maximum sentence meted out in Essex County)—time and institution. Time is expressed in columnar categorization of lower, median, and upper ranges of the maximum sentence imposed. The rows provide a history of institutional choice ranging from the Yardville Reformatory to the Essex County Correctional Center to the New Jersey State Prison in Trenton.

As further employed in use, each of the four grids included an experience tabulation of all incarcerative and nonincarcerative

Figure 7-16. Essex County Decisionmanking Matrix: Drugs.

construction

Offense Score	0	1	2	3	4	5
4	2 / 6 / OUT	2 / 5 / OUT	7 / 7 / (1) 52.5 60.0 67.5 / (3) 10.5 12.0 13.5 / (3) 52.5 60.0 67.5	10 / 9 / (1) 52.5 60.0 67.5 / (6) 11.8 13.5 15.2 / (3) 52.5 60.0 67.5	18 / 7 / (1) 252.0 288.0 324.0 / (6) 15.7 18.0 20.2 / (11) 52.5 60.0 67.5	7 / 2 / (2)52.5 60.0 67.5 / (2) 10.5 12.0 13.5 / (3) 31.5 36.0 40.5
3	6 / 51 / OUT	6 / 55 / OUT	8 / 26 / OUT	15 / 28 / OUT	21 / 12 / (1) 52.5 60.0 67.5 / (15) 10.7 18.0 20.2 / (5) 31.5 36.0 40.5	12 / 2 / (3) 52.5 60.0 67.5 / (6) 10.8 12.0 13.5 / (3) 31.5 36.0 40.5
2	1 / 1 / OUT	0 / 1 / OUT	0 / 1 / OUT	0 / 1 / OUT	0 / 0 / OUT	0 / 0 / OUT
1	0 / 2 / OUT	0 / 0 / OUT	1 / 0 / OUT	0 / 0 / OUT	0 / 1 / OUT	0 / 0 / OUT
	0	1	2	3	4	5

Offender Score

Rows represent:
1st line = Yardville sentence
2nd line = Essex County Correctional Center
3rd line = New Jersey State Prison/Trenton

Columns represent:
1st column = Lower range of maximum
2nd column = Median range of maximum
3rd column = Upper range of maximum

sentences given in each of the cells, as well as the ranges discussed above.

Maricopa County

There were three Maricopa County decisionmaking matrixes—violent, property and drugs. Figure 7–17 reproduces the property matrix.

Here the format is the more traditional one and looks more like the matrix found in Denver County than either of the matrixes employed in Cook or Essex counties, even though this Maricopa matrix is a generic model, while Denver utilized a general model. It thus becomes apparent that the method of presentation of information can significantly affect the sentencing guidelines modeling system employed.

As it worked out, the Maricopa County offense score has its greatest range here at 1–6, establishing six rows of useful information (as it does in its drugs grid, too). Its most limited use comes in the violent grid, with a possible range of 1–5, providing only five rows of useful information. The offender score is most limited with respect to the property grids, with a possible range of −1–+6, establishig only six columns of useful information (which is all the drugs grid establishes). The offense score is least limited with respect to the violent grid, also with a possible range of −1–+6, but establishing, however, eight columns of useful information. The number of guideline cells ranges from a low of thirty, with respect to the drug and property grids, to a high of forty, with respect to the violent grid.

THE GENERAL APPLICABILITY OF SENTENCING GUIDELINES

Courts considering the implementation of sentencing guidelines will be interested in the apparently broad applicability of the concept. The courts discussed here are remarkably diverse. Demographic characteristics of the jurisdictions, sentencing options available to the judges, plea bargaining practices, political attitudes of the judiciaries, defendant profiles, and so forth, have all differed sharply. Nevertheless, the sentencing guidelines concept has proven durable and flexible enough to accommodate all of these variations.

The reason for this is simple. While the sentencing guidelines concept is general, the actual development of operational sentencing guidelines systems has been local and specific. While we have always built upon our past experience in constructing a given guidelines system, we on the research team have nevertheless custom-fit the guidelines to the contours of each jurisdiction, always taking unique

Offender Score

Offense Score	-1	0	1	2	3	4	5	6
6	OUT	OUT	4-6	30-36 48-60	30-36 48-60	30-36 48-60	42-54 60-72	42-54 60-72
5	OUT	OUT	OUT	24 30-36	24 30-36	30-36 48-60	30-36 48-60	30-36 48-60
4	OUT	OUT	OUT	12-15 24-36	12-15 24-36	30-36 48-60	30-36 48-60	30-36 48-60
3	OUT	OUT	OUT	4-6	8-10	12 24	12-15 36-48	12-15 36-48
2	OUT	OUT	OUT	OUT	4-6	10-12	10-12	10-12
1	OUT	OUT	OUT	OUT	4-6	10-12	10-12	10-12

Figure 7-17.   Maricopa County Decisionmaking Matrix: Property.

characteristics carefully into account. Our goal has been the concrete one of providing a working tool that would actually help the local judiciary in its difficult sentencing tasks.

Consequently, however, there are a number of caveats that apply to any attempt to analyze or compare the results across the four jurisdictions. The different sampling frames and sampling techniques and the size of two of the data bases certainly restrain one's conclusions. Furthermore, the influence of the demographic variables and different penal codes, as well as the varied systemic pressures and sentencing alternatives available to the judge, cannot be ignored. These differences indeed mean that no cross-comparison can hope to "explain" how and why the sentencing practices in each jurisdiction differ or how and why their guidelines systems differ. But that has not been my purpose; nor has my purpose been to perform an evaluation either of these courts or of our own research.

Accepting the limitations of comparisons, I sought to present some of the findings that later researchers, analysts, reviewers, and evaluators may require. Our site selection criterion was difference, not similarity. Sentencing guidelines are developed locally, yet we wished to demonstrate through our work the generalizability of the guidelines concept. I hope that I have indeed demonstrated that sentencing guidelines systems can be developed in different courts, operating under different constraints, and further, that they can be developed on different premises. Four specific courts were chosen for study on the basis of their unique characteristics, and the guidelines examples for each of them have been worked out in considerable detail. As the sentencing guidelines concept is, presently, generally accepted across the nation,it may appear strange to prove what is by now obvious, but these four examples—and also the Philadelphia one addressed in the preceding chapter[12]—should lay to rest any claims that sentencing guidelines cannot be developed for courts with different characteristics. As other courts consider the guidelines concept as a means of structuring judicial discretion in a useful fashion, they should therefore find this a useful reference document.

Analysis of the data across all four jurisdictions indicates that there are generally two major areas of judicial concern that appear to affect the sentencing decision. First in priority, judges seem concerned about how serious the instant offense is. Offenders commiting extremely serious crimes (e.g., crimes of violence involving great bodily injury) are generally sentenced to prison. Second, the decision of whether or not to incarcerate an individual who has committed a less serious offense seems to turn on the nature of the individual's prior criminal history. Other factors that some have seen as linked to the probability of recidivism may be present—employment or school data appears to be an example. However, many well-regarded studies have indicated that the elements comprising prior criminal history data are continually the "best" predictors of the probability of recidivism.[13]

These results are not particularly surprising, especially to the audience of practicing sentencing judges to whom much of this book is addressed. Indeed, in many ways it only confirms what many knowledgeable people already knew or assumed. It is nonetheless valuable as confirmation by specific field demonstrations of perhaps widely accepted hypotheses. It is of course also much more than that, for the sentencing guidelines system provides a useful method that individual trial court judges may employ to tap both the generality and the specificity of these acknowledged concerns; they offer a means by which the locally accepted tariffs for offense-offender characteristics may be viewed and reviewed, structured and restructured, according to the conscious and explicit policy concerns of the local judiciary.

Thus, despite the severe limitations that must be applied to any comparative analyses, the results reported here may be seen as significant. At a minimum, the findings, extrapolations, hypotheses, and suggestions for further inquiry should be of value to persons with any interest in any of the four study jurisdictions. This not only includes those presently working in the four courts—judges, prosecutors, defense attorneys, probation officers—but people who later enter these courts and require background information, as well as those persons across each of the four states who can best understand the uses and limits of extrapolation from the study counties.

Each system was uniquely derived, but the similarities as well as the differences may be seen. With all the caveats registered here, we may still profit from an interjurisdictional comparison. The sentencing guidelines concept has proved adaptable, and operational sentencing guidelines systems may be devised for different court systems, receive judicial approval, and prove useful to local judiciaries everywhere. Planners (and evaluators) should review this work with an eye toward highlighting localized differences that they should take into account in constructing their own sentencing guidelines systems.

Indeed, the very act of making a close analysis of sentencing procedures and practices in each of the study jurisdictions should itself stimulate those who work in those courts, and/or those affected by that work, to examine ever more closely their own premises concerning the sentencing of criminal defendants. This, in turn, I hope and expect, will stimulate the search for improvements in the presently existing and all-important sentencing process. It is in this sense that I believe that the findings described here will prove helpful to those in the jurisdictions, to those interested in sentencing guidelines, and to those interested in sentencing itself.

NOTES

1. H. G. Wells, *The Work, Wealth and Happiness of Mankind* (Garden City, N.Y.; Doubleday, Doran and Company, 1931) at 616. "Even in America they have time to think things over if they want to " (at 616). These views are found in his famous chapter on the role of women.

2. A futher elaboration on the unique characteristics of each of these courts may be found in J. M. Kress, *Sentencing in Four Courts* (Washington, D.C.: USGPO, 1980).

3. For illustrative purposes, sample Instructional Booklets for the Calculation of Guideline Sentences are set forth as Appendixes to this book.

4. The coding instructions for such terms as the "Number of Criminal Events" and the "Injury to Victim(s)" offense seriousness modifiers may be found in the Appendixes to this book.

5. L. T. Wilkins, J. M. Kress, D. M. Gottfredson, J. C. Calpin, and A. M. Gelman, *Sentencing Guidelines: Structuring Judicial Discretion–Report on the Feasibility Study* xvii, 25–27 (Washington, D.C.: USGPO, 1978).

6. Some of the controversial aspects concerning the consideration of this—and others of the factors discussed in this chapter—will be dealt with *infra* Chapter 8.

7. See J. C. Calpin, J. M. Kress, and A. M. Gelman, *The Analytical Basis for the Formulation of Sentencing Policy* (Washington, D.C.: USGPO, 1980); and A. M. Gelman, J. M. Kress, and J. C. Calpin, *Establishing a Sentencing Guidelines System: A Methods Manual* (Washington, D.C.: University Research Corporation, 1978).

8. The ensuing discussion of the matrixes, and the score ranges encompassed by them, may better be understood if the reader also refers to the matrixes contained in the Appendixes to this book.

9. Kress, *supra* note 2; see also Calpin et al., *supra* note 7.

10. For an explanation of this data-cleaning process, see the works referred to *supra* note. 7.

11. Since the Essex County system was incorporated into the New Jersey statewide system before the planned eventual "smoothing" could take place, this does mean that, in one narrowly defined sense, the Essex approach did not amount to a totally developed sentencing guidelines system, although it was clearly viewed as such by the local judiciary.

12. See *supra* Chapter 6, as well as the Philadelphia booklet found as an Appendix to this book.

13. L. T. Wilkins, *Evaluation of Penal Measures* (New York: Random House, 1969); S. R. Brody, *The Effectiveness of Sentencing* (London: H.M.S.O., 1976).

Part Three
The Future of Sentencing Reform

Methods and Morals

Finally, there are those precepts defining the notion of natural justice. These are guidelines intended to preserve the integrity of the judicial process. If laws are directives addressed to rational persons for their guidance, courts must be concerned to apply and to enforce these rules in an appropriate way. A conscientious effort must be made to determine whether an infraction has taken place and to impose the correct penalty.—John Rawls[1]

In Part Two of this book, I summarized the products of a four year research effort that established and implemented the first sentencing guidelines systems. Sentencing guidelines research would not presently be ongoing in literally dozens of jurisdictions if the purposes and advantages of our previous work had not become manifest. Nevertheless, it is important to reiterate that sentencing guidelines systems are not simple historical statements of past court practices; instead, they are realistic, generally applicable, and flexibly adaptive reformist devices capable of locally conscious policy control.

In this section, I address the many judges, legislators, and others interested in improving the sentencing process who have queried me for information as to how they might actually begin to enact an integrated system of pragmatic and normative sentencing reform within their own jurisdictions. In this chapter, I will suggest some cautions, laying out in detail some of the significant policy alternatives that will have to be considered by future reformers. Although "technical" manuals are by now widely available,[2] they are not as important to this audience as a "policy" manual—that is, a strategic plan that will provide direction to the techicians, thus assuring that the ethical issues of sentencing reform have been addressed as well. The final chapter of this book consists of such a plan.

ACTION RESEARCH AND ETHICS

In the physical and biological sciences, we are beginning to realize that moral concerns (or "political" ones, in the Aristotelian sense) significantly affect our procedures and our results. America's nuclear physicists, for example, must resolve environmental and ecological doubts as well as the technical questions of their colleagues; Soviet biologists were retarded for decades by an ideological commitment to Lysenko; today's geneticists must quiet worldwide fears raised regarding the ethics and potential of cloning. Even more so in the social sciences have we come to understand that virtually every methodological approach rests upon a moral premise with which one may express lesser or greater agreement.

This places a great burden upon the ethically aware researcher. It is insufficient to spew forth computer printouts or to declare that the equations say it must be so; it is inappropriate to arrogate to one's self the underlying data and processes and only release the results. With respect to our narrower concerns here, it is an absolute moral imperative that the court researcher thoroughly explain *all* aspects of sentencing guidelines research to the judges, probation officers, and others who will be making use of it in the real world of flesh and blood criminal defendants. Concomitantly, the judge should not accept "The computer says so" for an answer until fully satisfied as to why the computer says so, what data was fed into it, what premises underlay the analytical techniques, and what interpretations were employed.[3] The computer is a tool, analytical statistics are tools, and indeed, the sentencing guidelines device is only a tool—all tools that should never supplant the human decisionmaker in the courtroom.

When I wrote in Chapter 4 of our collaboration with the judiciary in developing sentencing guidelines, I stressed the methodological advantages of that procedure. Here, I wish to emphasize the ethical advantages of that same procedure. Within the Steering and Policy Committee, the issues discussed in this chapter were thrashed out at great length. In each and every participating sentencing guidelines jurisdiction, there was a full-time, on-site court liaison present whose primary function was to explain every aspect of continuing sentencing guidelines research to the local judiciary.

Frankly, I did not personally agree with every policy decision made by the judges and often voiced my dissenting views to them privately, but that is beside the point. The job of the researcher in such a situation, is not to decide, but to set forth the significant policy options for the local, judicial decisionmakers. The judges would, after all, be held accountable for the results of their decisions and it was therefore fair and appropriate that they make them—but always fully aware of the alternatives available, as well as the full import of their conclusions. My principal satisfaction came in knowing that previously unconscious reasons would now become explicit, that information could replace speculation in the minds of both sentencing judges and sentenced defendants; defendants might still disagree with the propriety of considering certain factors, but they would now at least know that those factors had indeed been considered and would even know the degree of significance that the judge attached to them.

The reader will recall that the research staff saw themselves as collaborative partners with the judges, with each jurisdiction's judiciary making the principal operational decisions. Race and sex were excluded by all, juvenile record included by some, some prior adult record variable by all, and so on. The point is that we, as nonjudicial researchers, did not make any of these decisions. Rather, we highlighted the significance of those decisions, laid out the options, and then constructed sentencing guidelines according to the express—and now informed—desires of the local judiciary. Only in this way could guidelines by the policy statement of the judiciary that they were intended to be.

As to the guidelines and the factors that go into their makeup, they are, in one sense, an information-restructuring device. Those who have criticized specific guidelines models for including a juvenile record (and thus arguably holding a youthful mistake against an adult) or for including employment information (and thus arguably using information that masks race and is therefore an improper consideration) have mistaken their target. They are attacking the old sentencing system, not the new. Sentencing guidelines are now being used only as a supplement to presently received information, usually provided in a presentence investigative report (PSI). The juvenile record and employment information that the critics wish deleted from sentencing guidelines are still available in the PSI, only a few pages further along for the judge to see.

Other critics have questioned the propriety of looking at the "real offense" (an issue to be explored later in this chapter). That too is presently provided judges, either in an "official version of the offense" section of the PSI or via a copy of the police arrest report. Moreover, just as with the other controversial items discussed later, I remind the reader that the inclusion of some sort of harm-loss modifier, to account for the real offense, was made as a policy decision by the local judiciary, and in any event, it consists only of items available to sentencing judges in the material already supplied to them at or before sentencing. Also again, however, a signal advantage of a sentencing guidelines system will be the systemic honesty it will fos-

ter. The implementation of guidelines will necessitate that "real offense" sentencing be made far more explicit than it has been in the
past.

What the critics fail to understand is that a sentencing guidelines
system now makes these problems clearly visible and thus susceptible to correction. Under the old system, if a defendant attacked a PSI
for including such information, an appellate court might conceivably
say: (1) sentence overturned—that information should not have been
included in the PSI; (2) sentence upheld—that information may or
may not have been improper to consider, but it was only one item,
and the judge considered it among many others; or (3) sentence upheld—the information was properly included *and* considered. In the
past, appellate courts have usually chosen option (3),[4] but in terms of
future reform, the critics have ignored option (2), perhaps the most
likely of all. Option (2) is a variant of the jury being instructed to
disregard an improper statement, of the judge who says I looked at
that bit of improper information but paid no attention to it at the
time of sentencing, of the whole legal doctrine of "harmless error." It
is not dishonest to assume that the defendant was not prejudiced by
the error; it is not even naïve, for often it is true. But it is also often
wrong—a wrong built on ignorance.

With a sentencing guidelines system, that ignorance disappears.
The effect of that error—if error there be—is now not only ascertain-
able, but potentially quantifiable as well. The court adopting sentencing guidelines has published a policy statement that it must be
prepared to defend. The issue is now real, not hypothetical, and informed review of the sentencing decision may now take place; a common law of sentencing may develop.[5]

DECISIONMAKING: Check Your Premises

In many ways, I have perhaps made the process of constructing and
establishing sentencing guidelines systems look easy. It has not been
so. Some who have attempted early replication of our results have
encountered a number of problems. Part of this is attributable to an
overconcentration on the statistical aspects of guidelines construction, some, on the contrary, to an underemphasis on the methodological problems likely to be encountered. Apparently, the former
problem predominates, since there seems to be an irresistible temptation to attempt quantification of such elusive ethical concepts as justice and fairness.[6] Harvard Law Professor Laurence Tribe presciently
warned against this Gresham's Law of social science research when
he declared that a concentration on "hard" data tends to "dwarf" recognition of "soft" data.[7] In an action research project of this sort, a

balance of practice and policy is required, and we must be ever mindful of these dangers.

The concept of action research implies both an action goal and a methodological research premise. Our goal was judicial assistance; the research premises of sentencing guidelines lay in a background of decisionmaking research that had preceded us. Four tenets of decisionmaking theory should be set forth here: (1) most decisions are made on the basis of a limited number of information items; (2) decisions are made on two levels—the individual (or case-by-case) decision level and the policy decision level; (3) statistical methods provide an efficient means of identifying factors that are important to both the individual and the policy decision; and (4) (judicial) decisionmakers should retain the discretion to override any indicated decision, in any particular case, as well as the discretion to alter overall (court) policy.

With respect to the first tenet, most judges believe, as do the majority of decisionmakers in other fields, that they use or process all the items of information available to them in arriving at a decision. Most decisionmakers seem to feel that "more" information means "better" decisions. Unfortunately, this "more is better" attitude perpetuates a myth that is difficult to overcome. In fact, in most instances studied, the exact opposite appears to be true! A broad series of psychological decisionmaking studies, ranging over a wide spectrum of topics, has indicated that most decisions can be—and usually are—made with a limited number of information items, approximately four to ten depending on the type of decision involved. Once that limited set of items has been processed and an initial decision made, the selection and processing of additional items of information does not usually affect that decision. In fact, it seems that too much information may "overload" the decisionmaker—that is, with increasing information, the decisionmaking task may become so complex that the result is actually a less efficient use of the data. As others before us, we have found this concept of "information overload" and limited information use for the sake of true efficiency to be accurate for the sentencing decisionmaking task as well.[8]

The second tenet on which guidelines are based is that in any task involving repeated decisions, two different levels of decisionmaking can be distinguished. First, there is the *individual* level where the decisionmaker arrives at one decision at a time. The second level, the *policy* level, results from the aggregation of those individual decisions. At the policy level, it is possible to derive an equation to predict decisions on the basis of case information. This predictive ability may be interpreted as a description of latent or implicit policy that in turn provides the basis for the open articulation of that policy. Thus, for example, there does exist in each jurisdiction an implicit policy formulation that acts as an underpinning for judicial decisionmaking in sentencing. The preliminary guidelines models developed were each representations of that implicit policy, made explicit, thereby allowing each judicial body to alter immediately any mistaken policy formulation and to guide the final model toward desired policy results.

The third tenet is based on the results of numerous studies that have demonstrated that statistical methods are far more valid and reliable in predicting phenomena than are clinical methods. One reason for the superior performance of statistical methods of prediction is that human decisionmakers have difficulty in integrating information from diverse sources, while statistical methods are not bound by this limitation. Another reason for the superiority of statistical methods is that human decisionmakers tend to be inconsistent over time and across cases. Consequently, the description provided by statistical methods represents a more efficient approach for the initial identification of policy.

However, as the fourth tenet makes clear, this should in no way be read to say that the computer should replace the judge; that would be a perversion of the sentencing guidelines approach. Statistical analysis and computation can—and must—only be employed to aid human decisionmakers, thus facilitating their case and policy control. Statistical prediction methods rely only on a limited number of information items—even though these items are the factors that have been identified as usually the most critical in forecasting decisions. Nevertheless, since these items necessarily cover only a limited range of human behavior, it is necessary that the human decisionmaker retain the discretion to override the indicated decision in any particular case because of factors unique to that case.

Sentencing guidelines are designed to provide specific, articulated criteria for sentences, but they are not meant to apply in every case. There may be very sound reasons for a judge to decide that the guideline sentence does not apply in a particular case, and we expect and account for that. Judges are free to go outside the suggested guidelines, providing only that they state the reason why the guideline sentence is inappropriate for that case. These reasons, as I noted in Chapter 2, in turn provide the basis for the subsequent feedback and review sessions that are an integral feature of sentencing guidelines systems. At these meetings, the decisionmakers conduct systematic and periodic reassessments of policy, thus insuring the coincidence of practice and policy. In this way, the sentencing guidelines system provides for the individualization of justice as well as for evenhandedness of treatment.

CONTROVERSIAL VARIABLES: MITIGATING AND AGGRAVATING FACTORS INVOLVED IN ASSESSING OFFENSE AND OFFENDER CHARACTERISTICS

While the researchers themselves may thus be seen to have taken a relatively nonnormative view of these issues, the judges could not; it was the task of the research staff to analyze those variables that brought contentiousness to the early meetings of the Steering and Policy Committee, as well as to each jurisdiction considering sentencing reform. In writing about the nature and effect of mitigating and aggravating circumstances on a criminal sentence, however, one is confronted with a problem that has been largely ignored in jurisprudential writing. Instead of being examined directly, such questions have only been vaguely alluded to in discussions of responsibility, culpability, seriousness, and so forth rather than specifically being said either to ameliorate or to exacerbate a sentence.[9]

Just what is a mitigating or an aggravating factor: how are these terms defined? Mitigation, as opposed to the legal defenses of justification or excuse,[10] presupposes that someone is convicted of violating a criminal law and is therefore liable to be punished. A mitigating circumstance may be considered as one that extenuates or reduces the degree of moral culpability. Fairness and mercy are the qualities that mitigate a sentence because of circumstances special either to the offender or to the offense. H. L. A. Hart writes that justice "requires that those who have special difficulties to face in keeping the law which they have broken should be punished less":

> The special features of Mitigation are that a good reason for administering a less severe penalty is made out if the situation or mental state of the convicted criminal is such that he was exposed to an unusual or specially great temptation or his ability to control his actions is thought to have been impaired or weakened otherwise than by his own action so that conformity to the law which he has broken was a matter of special difficulty for him as compared with normal persons normally placed.[11]

Aggravating circumstances, on the other hand, are conventionally defined as those circumstances attending the commission of a crime that increase its culpability or add to its injurious consequences. Nevertheless, it is arguable that there are two distinct types of aggravating circumstances. The first is generally consistent with the above definition, and its effect is to increase a sentence from a presumptive average toward its aggravated high. In opposition to the general view of the American judicial system, however, one might also define aggravating circumstances in terms of mitigating ones—that is, relevant factors are almost never neutral in value, and therefore those factors that do not mitigate a sentence aggravate it. Sometimes, the mere consideration of information, because of its "negative" connotation, can only adversely influence the judge away from decreasing a sentence. Thus, in practical terms, by "prohibiting" such a reduction, the factor "aggravates" a sentence from its potential mitigated low to some higher level. For this definition to be applicable, however, there must be at least one mitigating factor present that would have lessened the penalty (toward its mitigated low) except for the presence of the aggravating factor(s).

While aggravating considerations are most usually associated in the public mind with events surrounding the commission of the offense (as with an excessive display of brutality accompanying robbery), they may very well relate to the offender (as, for example, an extensive and violent criminal history record). Similarly, while the public associates the concept of mitigation with offender characteristics (e.g., Hart's discussion of offenders with "special difficulties"), there may very well be mitigating factors surrounding the commission of the offense (e.g., the rendering of aid to a citizen unintentionally injured during the course of a burglary).

A combined reading of two U.S. Supreme Court decisions has been the impetus for the current judicial practice of considering virtually any and all information available about a defendant to be sentenced. In *Williams v. Oklahoma,* the Court stated: "In discharging his duty of imposing proper sentence, the sentencing judge is authorized, if not required, to consider all of the mitigating and aggravating circumstances involved in the crime."[12] Ten years earlier, in *Williams v. New York,* Justice Black wrote, "Highly relevant—if not essential—to his [the sentencing judge's] selection of an appropriate sentence is the possession of the fullest information possible concerning the defendant's life and characteristics." He added, "The belief no longer prevails that every offense in a like legal category calls for an identical punishment without regard to the past life and habits of a particular offender."[13] Although *Williams v. New York* was a 1949 decision that many thought had been eroded over the years, its continuing vitality, in this respect, was strongly affirmed in 1978 by the six to three Supreme Court decision in *United States v. Grayson.*[14]

Thus it is that, in general, a vast number of mitigating and aggravating factors may be considered by the sentencing judge with regard to both offender and offense characteristics. However, it remains for each judge to consider, in each individual case, which factors it is desirable to consider and what weight should be accorded those factors. It will be a prime task of policymaking bodies employing sentencing guidelines systems to decide the issue of desirability, or propriety (and, to a lesser extent, that of weight), with regard to the vast majority of cases. To that end, the remainder of this chapter will be devoted to detailing the issues that such bodies should consider concerning each of the most significant variables likely to result from statistical analysis.

OFFENDER VARIABLES

Preoffense Factors: Prior Record

From an analysis of the views of those judges in jurisdictions that have considered and adopted sentencing guidelines, it would appear that the offender's prior record is the paramount judicial consideration among offender characteristics, although serious ethical concerns remain in the definition of prior record. It might very well be argued (and is, by many) that only prior adult convictions should be considered. It is said that a juvenile record must be held confidential and considered closed upon the offender's achieving majority; similarly, arrests are arguably invalid considerations, invading as they do a constitutionally protected domain of presumed innocence and reflecting (as they are said to do) more upon police procedure than upon offender behavior. On the other hand, it is said, realistic considerations involving knowledge of arrest, charging, and plea bargaining practices in each state may arguably necessitate greater input than mere knowledge of the title of a reduced plea. Other issues calling for resolution: Should all prior offenses be considered or only those deemed "serious"? Should only offenses "similar" in nature to the instant offense be considered? Should an "old" record be excluded from consideration after a certain number of years have elapsed? Should the type of prior sentence affect current sentencing practice? (For example, was the offender previously placed on probation? Have lesser penalties "failed"?)

Convictions versus Charges. Some courts take the position that it is proper to use almost any material relating to the defendant's prior record.[15] Several state courts, however, have ruled otherwise or have limited its consideration. The Supreme Court of New Jersey noted: "[Unproved] allegations of criminal conduct should not be considered by a sentencing judge."[16] A Michigan Court of Appeals wrote: "A sentencing judge may not take into consideration offenses denied by the defendant without proof that they had in fact been committed."[17] A Pennsylvania Superior Court said that arrest records could be misleading and that to use them ignored the presumption of innocence.[18]

Obviously, the Supreme Court decisions in *Williams v. Oklahoma* and *Williams v. New York* have not resolved the questions surrounding the use of material relating to preoffense behavior of the offender. In 1965, the Second Circuit of the Federal Court of Appeals approved a sentencing court's consideration of charges that had been dismissed without an adjudication on the merits.[19] Seven years later, it was also established that a sentencing judge could properly consider evidence with respect to crimes of which the defendant had even been acquitted![20] The third circuit has held that pending indictments for other criminal activity were of sufficient reliability to warrant consideration by a sentencing judge.[21]

Baker v. United States, a fourth circuit case, appears to be the only federal case that in some manner has limited the consideration of prior criminal activity at sentencing. It concluded: "No conviction or criminal charge should be included in the [presentence] report, or considered by the Court, unless referable to an official record."[22]

The American Bar Association has taken the position that a presentence report should include only those charges that have resulted in a conviction:

> Arrests, juvenile dispositions short of an adjudication, and the like, can be extremely misleading and damaging if presented to the court as part of a section of the report which deals with past convictions. If such items should be included at all—and the Advisory Committee would not provide for their inclusion—at the very least a detailed effort should be undertaken to assure that the reader of the report cannot possibly mistake an arrest for a conviction.[23]

Juvenile Record. The issue of whether an adult offender's prior juvenile record should be considered has generally been resolved in favor of such disclosure. In 1973, the Michigan Supreme Court, in approving that practice, wrote:

> A judge needs complete information to set a proper individualized sentence. A defendant's juvenile court history may reveal a pattern of law breaking and his response to previous rehabilitative efforts. This, together with information concerning underlying social or family difficulties, and a host of other facts are essential to an informed sentencing decision, especially if the offender is a young adult.[24]

The majority of the problems involved with the consideration of a juvenile record appear to center around an unstated lack of faith in the ability of a juvenile to get a fair trial with due process rights protected (even with *Gault* protections)[25] and the belief that a youth frequently will not contest a charge because of the relatively minor punishment he or she is offered in return for a plea of guilty. Finally, and no less important, is the *parens patriae* philosophy of the court. It is probable that, on occasion, juvenile court judges "lean" toward adjudicating a youth delinquent so that they are able to force the youth to participate in a rehabilitative program. If the crime is so serious that one would be doing an "injustice" to society by subsequently not being able to consider that information when sentencing the same person as an adult (if the youth later is convicted of another offense as an adult), then perhaps juvenile courts should be encouraged to "waive" the youth to adult court as permitted by the United States Supreme Court in *Kent v. United States*.[26]

Seriousness, Similarity, and "Decay" of Record. Another of the major subissues within this area concerns limits on the aggravating effects of prior convictions based on the type of previous convictions and the effect of "decay" in (or age of) an offender's criminal record. Should all prior offenses be considered or only those deemed "serious"? Should relatively minor or trivial convictions be taken away from a judge's consideration as not being relevant and as only intruding potentially prejudicial factors? Should the number or frequency of prior convictions be regarded as a significant demonstration of antisocial conduct, even though the offenses were trivial in and of themselves?

It would seem fair, for example, for a sentence to be influenced more by the seriousness of previous offenses than by the frequency of prior convictions. Nevertheless, difficulties abound in assessing the seriousness of offenses. One method would be to make a subjective, judicial ranking of offenses; this is a method that we have indeed used, for a slightly different purpose, but with good effect. The maximum and/or actual penalties imposed perhaps offer another means of assessment. Finally, a more objectively derived measure (one like the Sellin-Wolfgang seriousness scale, for example) might be employed.[27]

Whether prior offenses are similar in nature to the present offenses would also seem relevant. Should we allow consideration only of prior offenses alike in nature to the instant offense on the theory that even a series of prior rapes, say, could have no relevant, nonprejudicial bearing on the sentencing of an offender for, say, the crime of shoplifting?

Should a "forgiveness" factor be built into any review of prior convictions, with some mitigating allowance made for the amount of time, or "decay" of record, since last conviction or release from prison.[28] These allowances would themselves constitute a mitigation of the aggravating influence of prior record. Long intervals between arrests might also be similarly treated.

Finally, should prior record be considered at all? If an ex-convict has truly "paid for his crime," as is so often said, upon his release from custody or supervision, then it would arguably be morally invalid to exact any further payment from him in later years by giving him a greater sentence than a first offender otherwise similarly situated. While this last point is interesting, no court of which I am aware goes this far.[29]

Preoffense Factors: Socioeconomic Variables

While I label this a preoffense factor, anyone engaging in guidelines research should consider the coding of this variable very carefully. Several jurisdictions have used employment as a mitigating variable (with a point being deducted if there was employment present), but have split on whether to code employment as of the date of the offense or as of the time of sentencing. One school of thought contends that using the latter time may be demonstrative of the offenders' desires to rehabilitate themselves. Others, however, argue that if coded at the time of sentencing, employment might be a sham designed to "con" the judge.

There has been a sharp split of authority on the propriety of considering various indicators of social stability. As the attacks on the rehabilitation philosophy have grown more numerous,[30] the arguments against validly including any social stability indicators have grown. Andrew von Hirsch, for example, espousing a "just deserts" model of sentencing, flatly opposes the inclusion of any socioeconomic variables as factors in the sentencing decision.[31] Nevertheless, a majority of the judges considering sentencing guidelines so far have voted to include at least one measure of the offender's social stability.

In any event, the factors comprising this dimension were problematical. Would information as to marital status unfairly penalize the single or divorced? Even if information concerning a broken home should prove to have predictive value, what would be its moral worth? Should a poor school record be forever held against an offender? Is it appropriate for a sentencing judge to consider whether the incarceration of particular offenders will place their dependents on the county welfare rolls? Are the past "good works" of offenders or their future plans for "community service" validly mitigating considerations?

Troublesome as these questions were, a practical problem further intruded. The factors that nessecessily comprised this disputable dimension were the very items most often found "missing" in an analysis of presentence reports. This is not surprising, as the information desired is often subjective, usually outdated, and is never the normal object of criminal investigation—as are the components of the offense seriousness or prior criminal record dimensions. Thus, in previous research, we have sometimes found ourselves forced to "substitute" one item of information relating to a defendant's social stability for another.

For several reasons, we eventually relied most heavily on length of employment information to tap the social stability dimension (or length of school attendance, for younger offenders). First, it was the factor most often available. Second, it was one of the least subjective of these factors and, hence, potentially the most accurate. Third, previous studies have shown it to be the least class linked of those data items comprising the social stability dimension.[32]

Finally, just to confuse this issue still further, even when judges agree to consider this dimension, I have found that they place opposite values on its components! The majority school of thought views a steady job, stable home life, and advanced education as positive indicators of the future likelihood of the success of the defendant on probation. But a significant minority of judges with whom I have worked reach a conclusion 180 degrees away. They say that these steadily employed and married defendants have no excuse for their crimes, whereas the poor, unemployed youth from the ghetto, who has never had a real chance before, deserves more of a break today than the defendant who has consistently been so privileged.

Postoffense Conduct

Method of Conviction. The most significant postoffense factor is whether or not the defendant was found guilty by plea or by conviction after trial. One leading case, *United States v. Wiley,* held that a person could not be punished because in good faith he exercised his right to stand trial. Therefore, even if the effort proves unsuccessful, it is improper to increase the severity of sentence because the defendant chose to defend himself.[33] Nevertheless, courts have taken the position that they are not increasing or aggravating a sentence because a defendant stands trial, but instead are only lowering or mitigating the sentence of a defendant who pleads guilty. Indeed, while frequently stated in theory, the *Wiley* prohibition has in practice been narrowly construed. For example, in *United States v. Lehman,* the same seventh circuit court that decided *Wiley* chose to disregard lower court remarks in sentencing that seem to fall within the prohibition. Pertinent comments of the trial court judge included:

[He] had the opportunity to come in here and offer a plea .... But he chose a different course. He chose to come in, and, ... tried to convince the jury through trial tactics ... that perhaps he didn't commit this offense ....

[I] don't think that he is entitled to as much consideration as the person who comes in, admits that he is wrong, and says, "I made a mistake" and that's it.

"On that basis I am going to sentence. ..."

Despite this language, the appellate court felt that:

[The] sentencing court merely employed unfortunate phraseology and was not, in fact, imposing an unlawful penalty. In so interpreting the remarks, we give much weight to earlier comments of the court that reveal it fully appreciated the importance of Lehman's challenge to the voluntariness of his confession and of his submission of his records. We think that the court was explaining albeit somewhat ineptly, that he considered a policy of leniency following a plea of guilty to be proper but that sentence concessions flowing from such a plea are inapplicable to the full trial situation. This philosophy is not the same as the view that a defendant should receive an "extra severe" sentence if he chooses to go to trial.[34]

The Supreme Court of Wisconsin in *Lange v. State* ruled that a trial judge's remarks to the effect that it defeated the American system of justice for the court and jury to sit through a two and one-half day trial and that the jury had deliberated for only one hour did not render a lengthy sentence invalid on the basis that the defendant had requested and received a jury trial. It was deemed proper for a judge to consider a frivolous defense (lacking the *Wiley* requirement of "good faith") when imposing sentence.[35]

Significantly, the National Advisory Commission on Criminal Justice Standards and Goals felt that to permit sentencing concessions in return for a plea of guilty provides too great an incentive for innocent defendants to waive their opportunity to avoid conviction at trial. Standard 3.8 of the *Courts* volume stated: "The fact that a defendant has entered a plea of guilty to the charge or to a lesser offense than that initially charged should not be considered in determining sentence."[36]

Cooperation of Defendant. Another significant, postoffense offender variable that policy decisionmakers should consider relates to issues of propriety and questions the role and relationship of the judge to the law enforcement agencies of the jurisdiction. Often, defendants are "asked" to cooperate with law enforcement officials or to face the possibility of a more severe punishment. In *United States v. Sweig,* a sentence was affirmed over an objection to the sentencing judge's reference to the defendant's failure to cooperate with law enforcement officials. Believing that the trial judge had made it clear that he was merely leaving the door open for a reduction of sentence if Sweig should subsequently be able to show mitigating circumstances, the Second Circuit Court of Appeals was not swayed by a Fifth Amendment argument. The court remarked: "The judge stated expressly the 'universally known possibility' that cooperation with law enforcement officials would be entitled to consideration."[37]

Sweig supported the earlier case of *United States v. Vermeulen,* in which a trial court judge had commented before imposing sentence that if Vermeulen were to find some way of cooperating, then he might be able to get some help in the reduction of any term for which he might be sent up. It was decided that those remarks did not constitute a "price tag" on the constitutional privilege to remain silent, but were simply "an inquiry as to whether appellant wished to cooperate with the public authorities by giving information apparently regarding *others* involved in illegal international narcotics traffic."[38]

The District of Columbia Court of Appeals has, however, taken a contrary position. That court vacated a sentence after ruling that a trial judge failed to exercise discretion when he improperly considered the defendant's refusal to disclose the source of his narcotics. The court commented:

> Of course, every thinking person would choose to have discovered, isolated and destroyed the source of the illicit drug traffic, but to this end Fifth Amendment rights may not be subordinated to the misplaced zeal of the trial judge. The framers of the Constitution, in their wisdom, saw fit to confine the judiciary to judicial functions and to leave to the executive responsibility for the enforcement of the criminal laws.[39]

In *People v. Anderson,* the Michigan Supreme Court held that a sentencing judge could not consider his personal impression that the defendant was protecting a co-defendant. The consideration of such information was improper, as a defendant could not be punished for exercising his right to remain silent.[40]

It must be acknowledged that the potential for abuse in this area is great. The controversy surrounding Judge John J. Sirica's sentencing of the seven original Watergate burglary defendants is apposite here. The reader may recall that Judge Sirica imposed provisional maximum term sentences pending the completion of a further social history study. It has been argued that this was in fact a sham and that sentence was pending only the degree of cooperation of the seven with agencies investigating the Watergate affair. Not surprisingly, those defendants who "talked" were given relatively light sentences. G. Gordon Liddy, who refused to "cooperate," was given a substantially harsher sentence.[41] Was this proper? It did completely "break open" the Watergate affair, but at what cost? In one sense, however, this issue may not be susceptible to resolution here, for it really is a variant of the hoary philosophical question of whether and when the ends justify the means.

OFFENSE VARIABLES

Plea Bargaining

The "Real Offense." While the inclusion of a dimension of offense seriousness is easily agreed upon, the component factors to consider within that dimension raised the sort of mixed moral-pragmatic questions that I have discussed. Should we concern ourselves primarily with the statutory offense at conviction or with some assessment of the criminal behavior involved? If the former, then pleading considerations are to be ignored. Yet we saw from the start that plea bargaining was regularly found in our study sites, just as it is virtually everywhere else in America.[42]

The judges involved in the national study were obviously aware of this and spoke of their concern for information regarding the "real offense"—namely, their perception of the actual criminal behavior underlying the arrest and conviction. They felt that the sentencing decision required more information concerning the underlying physical harm and/or property loss suffered by the victim than the mere statutory label of a plea bargained conviction would provide to them. While the U.S. Supreme Court has approved the consideration of such factors, it does raise questions as to whether or not a part of the plea "bargain" is being taken away from the defendant without the defendant's knowledge. The data sources available for establishing the "real offense" also gave us pause, for they often consisted of the least verified information contained in any presentence investigative report.[43] Nevertheless, the judges in every sentencing guidelines jurisdiction have been unanimous in their support of the legitimacy of this practice and its inclusion in guidelines. They believed that making explicit what to date had been their implicit policy was the only honest approach to this issue.

This description of the judicial practice of sentencing on the basis of the judge's individual interpretation or conceptualization of the actual criminal behavior of the offender has been seen by many as one of the valuable products of the national sentencing guidelines research project. Analysis of the data, simulation research, and discussions at our Steering and Policy Committee meetings all made it clear that when judges weigh the seriousness of the offense in determining sentence, they are weighing the harm or loss suffered by the crime victim in what they perceive to be the "real offense." This finding was not announced with any claims of novelty or as a revolutionary breakthrough in the theory of sentencing. Others have alluded to this fact, including several appellate courts which have upheld lower court statements that clearly indicated that the actual offense committed—and not merely the offense of conviction—was being considered in setting sentence.[44] It is, however, significant to note it here because the implementation of guidelines will necessitate that "real offense" sentencing be made far more explicit than it has been in the past. With the implementation of such guidelines, appellate courts will no longer be able to ignore the importance of this practice by distinguishing away its actual, specifically weighted effect on the sentence to be imposed.

Is There a "Bargain"? There has also been serious concern expressed regarding this practice because, potentially, it enables prosecutors to avoid having to prove all elements of an offense beyond a reasonable doubt. In the future, when there is some doubt as to the state's ability to obtain a conviction for the "real offense," prosecutors may perhaps settle for a plea to a lesser offense, realizing that the offender still will actually be sentenced on the basis of having committed the more serious offense—within statutory and pleading confines, of course.

This moreover has important ramifications for any evaluation of the true effects of plea bargaining. By sentencing an offender—to some extent—on the basis of the "real offense," judges appear to have devised, in effect, a method for retracting much of the present benefit a defendant supposedly gets in return for a plea of guilty. Most defendants who plead guilty do so primarily in the hope of receiving a more lenient sentence than they would be likely to receive had they stood trial and been convicted. Yet the results of our national study indicate that judges are sentencing on the basis of their perception of the "real offense" irrespective of the specific offense of conviction and regardless of the means by which such an adjudication was obtained.

This is not at all to say, however, that all defendants are being deceived or that they receive nothing in exchange for their plea; indeed, there are many defendants who receive immediate sentencing leniency for having saved the state the time and expense of a trial. The most obvious example of defendants who will receive a lighter sentence are those who plead guilty to a lower class of offense and who otherwise would have received a more severe sentence than is now statutorily permissible. Perhaps the easiest and most understandable way to explain this is through an example. Let us assume that a person has committed a robbery, a Felony 4 offense in Colorado. Based on the description of the offense behavior in the presentence report and the relevant characteristics of this particular offender, let us further assume that the judge would have imposed a prison sentence of indeterminate minimum length to five years maximum—that is, a sentence five years *less* than the permissible maximum of ten years. This then would be the judge's perception of an appropriate sentence regardless of whether the defendant pleaded guilty or was convicted after a trial. Let us suppose now that this same defendant pleads guilty to the lesser offense of theft from the person, a Felony 5 in Colorado. If the judge actually sentences, as I assert, on the basis of what the offender is perceived to have done and not on the basis of what the defendant was convicted of committing, the defendant would receive the identical indeterminate to five year sentence—that is, a sentence equivalent to the statutorily permitted maximum for Felony 5 offenses. Thus, the offender receives no sentence reduction benefit by pleading guilty.

Suppose, however, that under the given circumstances, the judge would have imposed a *seven* year sentence on the defendant upon conviction for committing the robbery. As there is a five year statutory maximum permissible for a Felony 5 in Colorado, the defendant has prevented the judge from imposing a seven year sentence by pleading guilty to the theft offense. Therefore, the offender, by hypothetically crossing this real penalty line, receives a five year sentence—two years less than he or she would have received if found guilty of committing a robbery.

All of this does not imply that only a few defendants will gain from pleading guilty. First of all, we have noticed a clustering of sentences at the upper ends of statutorily prescribed sentencing ranges: my hypothetical example, therefore, may provide a more common benefit than has hitherto been acknowledged. Second, in the long run many offenders actually stand to gain substantially. The most significant deferred benefit will occur if the offender is later convicted of another offense. Because there was an earlier plea of guilty to a less heinous crime than that which was actually committed, the offender's prior record may not appear to be as serious to the later judge, and in some circumstances, this may result in a more lenient sentence for the later offense. This is especially true if the jurisdiction prohibits the consideration of prior arrest records in sentencing. Moreover, through "lateral" charge bargaining, an offender may be able to avoid the stigma generally attached to convictions for, say, sex offenses, by pleading guilty to, say, a simple assaultive crime; or, by pleading to a misdemeanor rather than a felony, an offender may successfully evade the provisions of an habitual offender type of statute.[45]

Recapturing Sentencing Authority. In jurisdictions where large-scale sentence bargaining predominates, the judge is not the effective sentencing authority; the judge is merely the ratifier of agreements worked out between prosecuting and defense attorneys.[46] Even in charge bargaining jurisdictions, as Professor Albert Alschuler has perceptively suggested,[47] as sentencing "reform" moves toward greater determinacy, so the power of the prosecutor increases and charge bargaining becomes sentence bargaining, since, in a completely determinate system, establishing the charge establishes the sentence. Furthermore, as I pointed out above, even under a sentencing guidelines system, there is a danger that prosecutors will take lesser pleas knowing that judges will actually sentence the "real offense."

Does all this mean that the judge is impotent and that the prosecutor will totally dominate sentencing? Already, many feel that local district attorneys have inordinate power. Former Supreme Court Justice Robert Jackson once wrote: "The prosecutor has more control over life, liberty, and reputation than any other person in America."[48] Part of the reason for the prosecutor's awesome power is that that power is unchecked, unreviewed, and—indeed—largely unreviewable since it is so hidden. Although I urge the reform of sentencing guidelines primarily as a means to open up sentencing, in the long run it may perhaps prove even more important as a means to begin to open up the exercise of prosecutorial discretion to significant structural controls and review procedures.

At the moment, hidden discretion prevails throughout the criminal justice system, from the police power to arrest, to prosecutorial charging and plea bargaining, to judicial sentencing, to parole release decisionmaking. It is my view, expressed at length in Chapter 2, that only by opening up this discretion to public scrutiny can we hope to control its potential abuse and assure its proper application. It is for this reason that I favor giving more power to the judge at sentencing. Sentencing is that one point in the criminal justice system already open to greatest scrutiny, the point where the public is willing to acknowledge the propriety of exercising discretionary authority—so long as that authority is structured, equitable, and accountable.

Some have written of the "hydraulic" theory of criminal justice discretion,[49] arguing that as you push in or control the discretionary powers of one actor in the system, you necessarily enlarge the powers of another. Thus, one argument against mandatory sentencing is that it shifts necessary discretion away from the open portion of the system and into the more invisible domains of the prosecutor or the parole board. I favor a reverse flow—increasing judicial discretion and therefore necessarily curbing some of the discretionary powers of both prosecutors and parole boards.

As to prosecutors,[50] it is possible for judges to recapture sentencing authority through the vehicle of sentencing guidelines, and some jurisdictions are presently planning to do just that. Through the sentencing guidelines method, the judges of a jurisdiction can establish judicial policy and thus set their own specific benchmarks against which to measure proferred pleas. Moreover, one jurisdiction is planning explicitly to recognize the plea as a factor in the guidelines. When publicly promulgated, this will have the effect of opening up the pleading process as well as the sentencing process.[51] Instead of the danger I alluded to earlier (of the prosecutor taking lesser pleas knowing the judge would sentence on the "real offense"), public promulgation of the guidelines will ensure that the defendant will have all of this information as well. The "going rates" would be known specifically, and this knowledge would provide defendants with a measure of protection against undue pressures. Plea negotiations will then be more open, and bargains will be struck on far more realistic and rational grounds than they have been in the past.

Other Offense Variables

The remaining offense seriousness variables may be dealt with briefly. The "real offense" base will appear operationally as a series of harm-loss modifiers revealed through the initial statistical analysis.

"Physical injury" is likely to appear as a significant variable. If it does, then the major problem that would arise is determining the cutoff point for assessing points for the degree of the injury—requiring emergency room treatment or hospitalization are typical examples.

"Weapons" may appear, although the judges in each guidelines jurisdiction might prefer to add distinguishing attributes that may not appear as statistically significant. For example, the data may reveal that possession, threat, and use are not weighted differently. Almost intuitively, judges will want to change this, but they must be alert to the possibility that the fact situation they really mean to cover is already covered by some other variable. For instance, one may logically want to add a point for use resulting in harm, but if the guidelines already add a point for injury, then one may be in danger of overweighting this factor. I raise this rather common example simply to illustrate that statistical results that seem intuitively peculiar may not prove so upon closer analysis.

"Victim" may or may not appear. In some jurisdictions, the type of victim (e.g., a person as against a business) has shown up as significant; in others, the relationship of the victim has proven important (e.g., a stranger, a relative, an acquaintance, etc.). A danger with using this variable is that, unless very carefully phrased, the coding may become subjective.

"Drugs" and/or alcohol involved in the offense may or may not show up. Also, the amount of monetary loss may appear. Researchers should not be surprised if they do not appear, however. As logically related as they are, they may be significant only in a statistically insignificant number of cases. The frequency of occurrence of particular offenses in each jurisdiction will sharply affect the appearance of these various harm-loss modifiers.

MULTICOLLINEARITY

Some of our data have offered the intriguing hope that the apparent conflict between our moral and pragmatic values may in fact be nonexistent. This may in part be due to what has been referred to as multicollinearity, which statisticians define as the phenomenon of a higher degree of interrelationship between independent variables that in turn are closely related to a dependent variable. According to Wilkins:

> It is possible to examine a large body of data and find one piece of information which on its own is the most useful in predicting a particular criterion. This would be that item which was most highly correlated with the criterion. Clearly we can select only one criterion at a time because the item which is most highly correlated with one criterion may not be that which is most highly correlated with another criterion. When we have identified the most powerful item of information, we can search the field of information, for another item which, *given the first item,* is *then* most highly correlated with the criterion. It is, of course, necessary, to find a means for taking out of the reckoning the power of the first item before we add the second or even attempt to assess its contribution to the prediction of the criterion. This is usually termed the problem of "overlap." If two items of information are highly

correlated with each other, then, when we have taken the first into consideration, the second will have lost almost all of its power.[52]

An example in lay language may clarify the significance of "overlap" or multicollinearity. Among the adult criminal history variables we have studied have been the total number of prior arrests and the total number of prior convictions. Most observers concede the latter to be appropriate for judicial consideration, but many grow vehement as to the arguable impropriety of considering the former. As I noted earlier, they declare it a denial of the presumption of innocence, a violation of due process, and a factor that speaks more to police practice and prejudice than to an offender's background. Many judges, however, argue the propriety, and indeed necessity, of seeing prior arrest records; they argue that it reveals the defendant's pattern of behavior and is far more likely to reveal the nature of past offenses than the title of a plea bargained conviction.

What multicollinearity means is that the argument may be resolved pragmatically. In this instance, our data do appear to reveal that, in most jurisdictions and in most instances, the total number of convictions and arrests are so closely related that the addition of the putatively "immoral" factor (i.e., number of arrests) to the number of convictions will simply make no significant difference. This is because each of these variables taps into the same underlying dimension; granted, we could choose either of them, but why not choose the one over which there is the least debate?

Before I leave this subject, however, I should point out that the overlap effect of multicollinearity can cut two ways. It is, indeed, the reason why critics oppose the inclusion of employment or education variables. These variables are said to mask race, since blacks suffer higher unemployment rates, as well as a higher school dropout rate, than whites; therefore, "penalizing" unemployment—or "rewarding" employment—effectively discriminates against blacks. Those who advocate the inclusion of these variables usually acknowledge that there is some merit to the argument, but contend that employment-education variables possess an intrinsic value in assessing the potential of an offender for rehabilitation. Moreover, they assert that judicial sentencing cannot and should not be used as a vehicle for social reform; offenders must be judged on their records as they stand before the court. Perhaps the greatest difficulty with the argument of the critics is that virtually every offender variable—even prior adult felony convictions—is race related to some degree. And there are few who would wish to go so far as to totally exclude prior criminal records from the consideration of a sentencing judge.

VARIABLES LEFT OUT: MISSING INFORMATION

Much of this chapter has been devoted to an assessment of the relative merits of employing the factors we did use. But sometimes what one did *not* do is as important as what one did, and some final discussion is in order concerning variables that appeared too infrequently in presentence reports for us to make adequate use of them. What we referred to as "missing information" was present in some cases, absent in some, and only confusingly available in others. The trouble with using some variables—such as alcohol use, dependents, relationship of victim and offender, similarity of prior convictions, type of defense counsel, and so on—is their inherent vagueness. All of these variables were difficult to ascertain from the statements made in our source documents; they caused our coders inordinate difficulties and forced us frequently to redraft coding instructions for them. Moreover, the difficulties found, or partial solutions devised, were different in each of the jurisdictions in which we worked.

While we worked out methods for coping with the missing information problem in our statistical analysis,[53] other methods may very well have been employed to better effect. More significantly, however, others should look at our limitations with an eye toward reform. For our purposes, we could perhaps assume that unavailable information was information that did not enter the sentencing decision; that may have been a sensible descriptive conclusion, but it was not necessarily a desirable one. If our goal is to improve the sentencing decision, then should we perhaps insist that presently missing information items be collected in subsequent cases? This is a logical question that deserves further analysis by future researchers.

Extrapolated to other courts considering guidelines, the results obtained by us should prove useful in improving local criminal sentencing practices, at least inasmuch as they should force a closer analysis within each court of its actual sentencing practices, thus affecting those practices in an extremely positive manner. Our field work should be seen as a guide for future court reformers to suggest and note problem areas that they might encounter within their own courts. Presently missing information need not be subsequently missing information. Future court researchers should look at the court documents in their community and suggest improvements to clarify these potentially significant items.

If the judges of a particular jurisdiction decide that these reforms are indeed important, then better instructions to probation officers preparing presentence reports would be in order. In advancing toward normative sentencing guidelines, it becomes imperative to review those items early discarded because of their frequent absence. If those data had been significantly present, it is possible that the sentencing decision—in the overall sense—would have been improved, and that, after all, is the purpose of the entire enterprise.[54]

NOTES

1. J. Rawls, *A Theory of Justice* (Cambridge, Mass.: Harvard University Press, 1971) at 238-39.

2. A. M. Gelman, J. M. Kress, and J. C. Calpin, *Establishing Sentencing Guidelines Systems: A Methods Manual* (Washington, D. C.: University Research Corp., 1978); see also J. C. Calpin, J. M. Kress, and A. M. Gelman, *The Analytical Basis for the Formation of Sentencing Policy* (Washington, D.C.: USGPO, 1980).

3. Computer programmers often refer to the dangers alluded to here as the GIGO method—Garbage In, Garbage Out.

4. See Williams v. New York, 337 U.S. 241 (1949), Williams v. Oklahoma, 385 U.S. 576 (1959), and the discussion concerning these cases, *infra*.

5. *Supra,* Chapter 2.

6. This is one aspect of the problem I discussed *supra,* in Chapter 1, concerning those who see guidelines solely as a disparity reduction device.

7. See L. Tribe, "Foreword: Toward a Model of Roles in the Due Process of Life and Law," 87 *Harvard Law Review* 1 (1973); L. Tribe, "Trial by Mathematics: Precision and Ritual in the Legal Process," 84 *Harvard Law Review* 1329 (1971); as well as the recent analysis offered in B. D. Underwood, "Law and the Crystal Ball: Predicting Behavior with Statistical Inference and Individualized Judgement," 88 *Yale Law Journal* 1408 (June 1979).

Much of this soft (relatively unquantifiable) data comes to the attention of the sentencing judge during the trial of contested cases, or at plea-bargaining conferences, or during sentencing hearings with regard to the vast majority of offenses. See A. Alschuler, "Sentencing Reform and Prosecutorial Power: A Critique of Recent Proposals for 'Fixed' and 'Presumptive' Sentencing," 126 *University of Pennsylvania Law Review* 550 (1978); A. Alschuler, "The Trial Judge's Role in Plea Bargaining, Part I," 76 *Columbia Law Review* 1059 (1976); A. M. Gelman, "The Sentencing Hearing: Forgotten Phase of Sentencing Reform," in M. Evans, ed., *Discretion and Control* (Beverly Hills: Sage Publications, 1978); J. Q. Wilson, *Thinking About Crime* (New York: Basic Books, 1975); and H. L. Packer, *The Limits of the Criminal Sanction* (Stanford: Stanford University Press, 1968).

On the negative side, many critics of judicial discretion have suggested that one unmeasurable input item is bias formed through social conditioning. See, for example, W. Gaylin, *Partial Justice: A Study of Bias in Sentencing* (New York:, 1974); E. Green, *Judicial Attitudes in Sentencing* (New York: Macmillan and Co., 1961); and J. Hogarth, *Sentencing as a Human Process* (Toronto: University of Toronto Press, 1971).

8. My attack on the "more is better" myth is far from novel: "What men need is, as much knowledge as they can assimilate and organise into a basis for action; give them more and it may become injurious," T. H. Huxley, "Technical Education" [An 1877 Essay], in T.H. Huxley, *Science and Education; Essays* (New York: D. Appleton and Company, 1898) at 422. Nevertheless, the prevalence of the myth requires a forceful reiteration of its fallaciousness. See also L. T. Wilkins, *Information Overload: War or Peace with the Computer* (Davis, Calif.: National Council on Crime and Delinquency, 1973); R. W. Burnham, "A Theoretical Basis for a Rational Case Decision System in Corrections," (Ph.D. dissertation, University of California at Berkeley, 1969); L. T. Wilkins, *Evaluation of Penal Measures* (New York: Random House, 1969); and especially G. A. Miller, "The Magical Number Seven, Plus or Minus Two: Some Limits on Our Capacity for Processing Information, 63 *Psychological Review* 81 (March 1956); and R. M. Dawes, *Fundamentals of Attitude Measurement* (New York: John Wiley and Sons, 1972).

Recognition of this fact is, of course, what makes the sentencing guidelines reform so valuable to probation departments, *supra* Chapter 1. Over the years, presentence investigative reports have indeed become more and more abbreviated. "This tendency toward shorter presentence reports marks the decline of the theory that the sentencing judge can never be provided with too much information." R. O. Dawson, "Sentencing Reform: The Current Round," 88 *Yale Law Journal* 440, 442 n.10 (1978).

9. The principal exceptions have been in the various death penalty cases, which the Court has so far steadfastly declared to be sui generis. See Furman v. Georgia, 408 U.S. 238 (1972); Gregg v. Georgia, 428 U.S. 153 (1976); Proffitt v. Florida, 428 U.S. 242 (1976); Jurek v. Texas, 428 U.S. 262 (1976); Woodson v. North Carolina, 428 U.S.280 (1976); Roberts v. Louisiana, 428 U.S. 325 (1976); Gardner v. Florida, 430 U.S. 349 (1977); and Coker v. Georgia, 433 U.S. 584 (1977).

In the Georgia statute approved by the Court in *Gregg,* at least one of ten specified aggravating circumstances had to be found by a jury to exist beyond a reasonable doubt—although the jury could consider any additional aggravating or mitigating circumstances. The statute does not require the jury to find any particular mitigating circumstance to exist in order to recommend mercy in a given case, but the jury must find one of the ten statutory aggravating circumstances to be present in order to return a recommendation or death.

The Florida statute approved in *Proffitt* specified eight aggravating and seven mitigating factors. Before imposing a sentence of death, the trial court must state in writing its findings, specifically setting forth the factual aggravating circumstances found to exist, as well as its findings that these are not outweighed by any mitigating circumstances that may be present.

In its 1976 series of decisions, the United States Supreme Court did not approve the North Carolina or the Louisiana capital punishment provisions. In *Woodson*, the Court held that North Carolina's mandatory death sentence for first degree murder was unconstitutional in that it failed to curb arbitrary and wanton discretion (of the jury) with any objective standards that could guide, regularize, and make rationally reviewable the process for imposing a sentence of death. Moreover, the Court found that the imposition of a mandatory death sentence, without consideration of the character or record of the individual offender or the circumstances of the particular offense, was inconsistent with the fundamental respect for humanity which underlies the Eighth Amendment.

More recently still, in Lockett v. Ohio, 438 U.S. 586 (1978), the Supreme Court held the Ohio death penalty statute unconstitutional in that it too narrowly circumscribed the range of mitigating factors that the sentencer could consider. According to the *Lockett* plurality, "the Eighth and Fourteenth Amendments require that the sentencer, in all but the rarest kind of capital case, not be precluded from considering *as a mitigating factor*, any aspect of a defendant's character or record and any of the circumstances of the offense that the defendant proffers as a basis for a sentence less than death" (Chief Justice Burger at 604) (emphasis in original).

Probably the best academic treatment of these issues is still to be found in the classic, H. Wechsler and J. Michael, "A Rationale of the Law of Homicide," 37 *Columbia Law Review* 701, 1261 (1937).

10. See S. H. Kadish and M. G. Paulsen, *Criminal Law and Its Processes,* 3rd ed., ch. 6 (Boston: Little, Brown, 1975); and W. R. LaFave and A. W. Scott, Jr., *Handbook on Criminal Law,* Ch. 5 (St. Paul: West Publishing, Co., 1972).

11. H. L. A. Hart, *Punishment and Responsibility* 14, 15, 25 (Oxford: Oxford University Press, 1968).

12. Williams v. Oklahoma, 385 U.S. 576, 585 (1959).

13. Williams v. New York, 337 U.S. 241, 247 (1949). See also Mc-Gee v. United States, 462 F.2d 243, 254 (2d Cir. 1972), which distinguished *Williams*. In *McGee*, the judge relied on erroneous information; in the *Williams* cases, the correctness of the evidence was not contested. United States v. Metz, 470 F.2d 1140, 1141 (3d Cir. 1972), *cert denied* 411 U.S. 919 (1973): "18 U.S.C. §3577 (1971) states: 'No limitation shall be placed on the information concerning the background, character, and conduct of a person convicted of an offense which a court of the United States may receive and consider for the purpose of imposing an appropriate sentence.' This section reflects the policy . . . expressed by the Supreme Court in Williams v. New York." United States v. Green, 483 F.2d 469, 470 (10th Cir. 1973), *cert. denied* 414 U.S. 1071 (1973): "The judge has an interest in encouraging a broad scope of knowledge so as to insure intelligent and effective sentencing."

This practice has also been called into question with regard to the controversy surrounding the exclusionary rule of evidence. See J. D. Hirschel, *Fourth Amendment Rights* (Lexington, Mass.: Lexington Books, 1979). See also United States v. Vandemark, 522 F.2d 1019, 1021 (9th Cir. 1975): "The detrimental effect of the exclusionary rule upon sentencing is apparent. It deprives the district judge of information necessary to effectuate the federal policy of individualized sentencing." Ketchum v. United States, 327 F. Supp. 768, 772 (U.S. Dist. Ct. Md. 1971): "Futhermore, under the standards of *Williams v. New York* . . ., it may well be that the defendant has no right to object to the sentencing judge being given information unconstitutionally obtained." United States v. Masthers, 539 F.2d 721, 729 (D.C. Cir. 1976): "But we believe that the interests of the appellant and the administration of criminal justice would best be served by a hearing to properly examine and assess the nature and extent of appellant's disabilities. Such information is essential whether the issue is competency to stand trial, withdrawal of a plea, criminal responsibility, or sentencing." In United States v. Schipani, 435 F.2d 27 (2d Cir. 1970), the court flatly stated that the exclusionary rule does not apply to sentencing.

Hearsay evidence may also be considered. In United States v. Seijo, 537 F.2d 694 (2d Cir. 1976), the court stated that the sentencing judge can consider hearsay: "Torre's testimony that Seijo had a major role in the drug operation can be considered an aggravating factor" (at 700). In a footnote to the above statement, what the judge can consider is specified as follows: crimes on which there has been no conviction, U.S. v Cifarelli, 401 F.2d 512, 514 (2d Cir), *cert. denied*, 393 U.S. 987 (1968); counts of an indictment dismissed by the government, U.S. v. Needles, 472 F.2d 652, 655 (2d Cir. 1973); U.S.

v. Rosner, 485 F.2d 1213 (2d Cir 1973); *cert. denied* 417 U. S. 950, 94 S. Ct. 3080, 41 L. Ed. 2d 672 (1974) evidence obtained in violation of the fourth Amendment, U.S. v. Schipani, 435 F.2d 26 (2d Cir. 1970), *cert. denied* 401 U.S. 983 (1971); U.S. v. Tucker 404 U.S. 443, 446, 92 S. Ct. 589, 591, 30 L.Ed. 2d 592 (1972); U.S. v. Cardi 519 F.2d 309 (7th Cir. 1975); U.S. v. Tortora 464 F.2d 1202, 1208 n.4 (2d Cir.), *cert. denied,* 409 U.S. 1063 (1972).

14. United States v. Grayson, 438 U.S. 41 (1978). With respect to other aspects of the 1949 *Williams* decision, however, see the recent case of Gardner v. Florida, 430 U.S. 349 (1977), in which the Supreme Court reversed a death sentence on the grounds that the sentencing judge relied on the confidential portion of the presentence investigation that was not disclosed to the defendant. The Court held "that petitioner was denied due process of law when the death sentence was imposed, at least in part, on the basis of information which he had no opportunity to deny or explain" (at 1207). The Court distinguished this case from *Williams,* on which the state placed its primary reliance. In the *Williams* case, the information contained in the presentence investigation was described by the judge in open court, and the defendant did not challenge its accuracy. In this case, there was no disclosure by the judge. The record on appeal did not even include the confidential portion of the presentence investigation. In this case, the jury recommended a sentence of life imprisonment, but the judge imposed the death penalty. His finding was that the felony "was especially heinous, atrocious or cruel; and that such aggravating circumstance outweighs the mitiagating circumstance, to wit: none" (Id. at 138). He stated that the conclusion was based on, among other factors, "the factual information contained in said presentence investigation" (Id).

See also United States v. Espinoza, 481 F.2d 553 (5th Cir. 1973) The court held that where a sentencing judge explicitly relies on certain information in assessing a sentence, fundamental fairness requires that a defendant be given at least some opportunity to rebut the information. In reference to the discretion of the trial judge at sentencing, the court stated: "This discretion is not, and has never been absolute, and while the appellate courts have little if any power to review substantively the length of sentences, . . . it is our duty to insure that rudimentary notions of fairness are observed in the process at which the sentence is determined" (at 558). "Despite the broad discretion left to the trial judge in assessing background information for sentencing purposes, see *Williams v. N.Y.* 337 U.S. 241 (69 S.Ct. 1079, 93 L.Ed. 1337,(1947) a defendant retains the right not to be sentenced on the basis of invalid premises. See Russo v. United States, 470 F.2d 1357 (5th Cir. 1972); Clay v. Wainwright, 470 F.2d

478 (5th Cir. 1972); Franchi v. United States, 464 F.2d 1035 (5th Cir. 1972); Lipscomp v. Clark, 468 F.2d 1321 (5th Cir. 1972); Davis v. Wainwright, 462 F.2d 1354 (5th Cir. 1972); Thomas v. United States, 460 F.2d 1222 (5th Cir. 1972); Craig v. Beto, 458 F.2d 1131 (5th Cir. 1972); Wheeler v. United States, 468 F. 2d 244 (9th Cir. 1972); Garnet v. Swensen, 459 F. 2d 464 (8th Cir. 1972); United States v. Bishop, 457 F.2d 260 (7th Cir. 1972)" (Id. at 555).

15. See People v. Lichtenwalter, 520 P. 2d 583 (Col. 1974); People v. Carter, 527 P. 2d 875 (Col. 1974); State v. Morrill, 129 Vt. 460, 282 A. 2d 811 (1971); State v. Cabrera, 127 Vt. 193, 243 A. 2d 784 (1968) *cert. denied*, 393 U.S. 968, 89 S. Ct. 404, 21 L.Ed. 2d 379 (1968).

16. State v. Farrell, 61 N.J. 99, 293 A. 2d 176, 180 (1972). See also Smith v. State, 531 P.2d 1273, 1277 (Alaska Sup. Ct. 1975): "There were hints in the record that she might have been responsible for starting other fires but reference to accusations or arrests which did not lead to convictions are not proper considerations in sentencing."

17. People v. Davis, 41 Mich. App. 683, 200 N.W. 2d 779, 783 (1972). See also People v. Hildabridle, 45 Mich. App. 93, 206 N.W. 2d 216, 217 (Mich. Ct. App. 1973): "The sentencing judge may not be presented, in the presentence report or otherwise, with information of other criminal conduct by defendant unless such allegations are amplified by information persuasive of their validity." But see People v. McFadden, 73 Mich. App. 232, 251 N.W. 2d 297, 300 (Mich. Ct. App. 1977): "Since at the sentencing hearing defendant was presented with information concerning his prior drug offenses, was given an opportunity to allocute, and the accuracy of such information was confirmed, we find no violation of due process."

18. Commonwealth v. Shoemaker, 226 P. Super. 203, 313 A. 2d 342, 347 (1973). Despite those conclusions, the court was unable to find a due process violation and affirmed the sentence. People v. Lotze, 47 Mich. App. 460, 209, N.W. 2d 497 (1973): Where there was no showing as to the sentencing judge's opinion about defendant's guilt or innocence of other charges, the fact that the judge was aware of other pending charges and referred to them in discussion prior to sentence did not invalidate the sentence.

19. United States v. Doyle, 348 F.2d 715, 720–721 (2d. Cir. 1965), *cert. denied*, 382 U.S. 843, 86 S. Ct. 89, 15 L.Ed. 2d 84 (1965). See also United States v. Majors, 490 F.2d 1321, 1324 (10th Cir. 1974): "The dismissed indictment and charge contained in it are within the kind of information which a sentencing judge may properly consider in passing sentence. The plea bargain and the indictment dismissed resulting from it did not and indeed, could not, deprive the judge of the right and probably the duty of giving consideration to it. While a constitutionally invalid conviction cannot be considered by a sentenc-

ing judge, it does not follow that there must be a constitutionally valid conviction in order that criminal conduct may be considered." Houle v. United States, 493 F.2d 915 (5th Cir. 1974) (court could consider the fact that the defendant was arrested while on bail awaiting trial, even though the arrest did not result in an indictment).

20. United States v. Sweig, 454 F.2d 181, 184 (2d Cir. 1972). United States v. Atkins, 480 F.2d 1223 (7th Cir. 1975): "A sentencing court may consider evidence of other crimes committed by the defendant even though he was never brought to trial,.... or was brought to trial and acquitted" (at 1224). Henry v. State, 315 A.2d 797 (Court of Special Appeals, Md. 1970), 20 Md. App. 296: "The clear lesson of *Scott v. State,* 238 Md. 265, 208 A.2d 575, is that a judge, for his proper purposes, may determine that certain conduct did occur, even when the jury has determined, for its distinct purposes, that such conduct was not proved beyond a reasonable doubt " (at 803). In this case, the defendant was found not guilty by jury of murder and assault, committed by his companions while the defendant drove them in a stolen car. The court felt that the judge did not err in considering its conviction that defendant "masterminded" his companions' activities as grounds for imposing maximum consecutive sentences for larceny, unauthorized use of automobile, and receipt of money stolen during the robbery in which the murder and assault occurred.

21. United States v. Metz, 470 F.2d 1140, 1142 (3rd Cir. 1972), *cert. denied,* 441 U.S. 919 (1973). See also, United States v. Cifarelli, 401 F.2d 512, 514 (2d Cir. 1968), *cert. denied,* 393 U.S. 987 (1968): "It was proper for the trial judge to consider evidence of other crimes for which appellant was neither tried nor convicted in determining sentence." United States v. Weston, 448 F.2d 626, 633 (9th Cir. 1971): "We believe that other criminal conduct may properly be considered, even though the defendant was never charged with it or convicted of it." However, the court did require that when a defendant protests his innocence of the other offenses, the fact that he committed the other offense must be established with some reliability. *United States v. Haygood,* 502 F.2d 166, 169 n. 7 (7th Cir. 1974).

Government of Virgin Islands v. Richardson, 408 F.2d 892 (3d Cir. 1974), follows *Metz* in allowing pending indictments to be considered, but allows the defendant to offer some explanation. Collins v. Buckhoe, 493 F.2d 343, 345 (6th Cir. 1974), stated that defendant should be given "the opportunity of rebutting derogatory information demonstrably relied upon by the sentencing judge, when such information can in fact be shown to have been materially false." Handel v. State, 74 Wis. 2d 699 (1976), stated that the sentencing judge's consideration of a pending charge against the defendant for carrying a concealed weapon, for which the defendant had not been convicted, did not constitute denial of due process. But see Commonwealth v. LeBlanc, 356 N.E. 2d 874 (Mass. Sup. Ct. 1976): "There is no constitutional objection to a sentencing judge knowing of the existance of other pending charges against an offender" (at 876). (However, the judge should not consider unrelated pending criminal charges.)

The reader should note the significance of the issue of current pending charges—in some jurisdictions this has been coded as equivalent to being on probation/parole, and this therefore usually increases an individual's offender score. See J. M. Kress and J. C. Calpin, "Research Problems Encountered in Moving Towards Equity in Judicial Decisionmaking." 4 *The Justice System Journal* 71 (Fall 1978).

22. *Baker v. United States*, 388 F.2d 931, 934 (4th Cir. 1968). This is not to ignore Townsend v. Burke, 334 U.S. 736, 68 S. Ct. 1252, 92 L.Ed. 1960 (1948), where the Supreme Court granted habeas corpus relief when the defendant challenged the fairness of the sentencing procedure where the trial judge had relied on apparently erroneous information (concerning defendant's criminal record) in assessing the sentence; nor to ignore United States v. Tucker, 404 U.S. 443, 92 S. Ct. 589, 30 L.Ed. 2d 592 (1972), where the Supreme Court remanded for resentencing when the sentencing judge had considered the defendant's prior convictions in which he had not been represented by counsel. See also, United States v. Weston, 448 F.2d 626 (9th Cir. 1971), United States v. Latimer, 415 F.2d 1288, 1290 (6th Cir. 1969).

23. ABA Project on Minimum Standards for Criminal Justice, *Standards Relating to Probation,* Commentary §2.3, p. 37 (New York, 1970; approved draft).

24. People v. McFarlin, 389 (Mich, 557, 208 N.W. 2d 504, 510, 513–14 (1973). The opinion thoroughly reviews the issues here discussed as well as the policy of other states. See also State v. Nobriga, 527 P. 2d 1369 (Hawaii 1974).

25. See J. Weiss, "The Poor Kid," 9 *Duquesne Law Review* 590–612 (1971); and generally on these questions the thorough and incisive commentaries contained in F. L. Faust and P. J. Brantingham, *Juvenile Justice Philosophy* (St. Paul: West Publishing, Co., 1974).

26. Kent v. United States, 383 U.S. 541 (1966).

27. T. Sellin and M. E. Wolfgang, *The Measurement of Delinquency* (New York: John Wiley and Sons, 1964).

28. D. A. Thomas, *Principles of Sentencing* 176, 179 (London: Heinemann, 1970).

29. A. von Hirsch, *Doing Justice* 103 (New York: Hill and Wang, 1976). For a reasoned argument in support of this position, however, see M. K. Harris, "Disquisition on the Need for a New Model for

Criminal Sanctioning Systems," 77 *West Virginia Law Review* 263, 324 (1975).

30. Von Hirsch, *supra* note 29. See also D. Fogel, *We Are the Living Proof* (Cincinnati: W. W. Anderson, 1975);N. Morris, *The Future of Imprisonment* (Chicago: University of Chicago Press, 1975);J. Q. Wilson, *supra* note 7;G. R. Newman, *The Punishment Response* (Philadelphia: Lippincott, 1978); and E. van den Haag, *Punishing Criminals* (New York: Basic Books, 1975).

31. Von Hirsch, *supra* note 29 at 87–88.

32. F. H. Simon, *Prediction Methods in Criminology* 67–71, 145–47 (London: HMSO, 1971).

33. United States v. Wiley, 278 F.2d 500, 505 (7th Cir. 1960); United States v. Floyd, 477 F.2d 225 (19th Cir. 1973); United States v. Stockwell, 472 F.2d 1186 (9th Cir. 1973); *cert. denied*, 411 U.S. 948, 93 S. Ct. 1924, 36 L.Ed. 2d 409 (1973); United States v. Lehman, 468 F.2d 93 (7th Cir. 1972), *cert. denied*, 409 U.S. 967, S. Ct. 273, 34 L.Ed. 2d 232 (1972); Baker v. United States, 412 F.2d 1069 (5th Cir. 1969), *cert. denied*, 396 U.S. 1018, 90 S. Ct. 583, 24 L.Ed. 2d 509 (1970); Thomas v. United States, 368 F.2d 941 (5th Cir. 1966); Lange v. State, 54 Wis. 2d 569, 196 N.W. 2d 680 (1972). Johnson v. State, 336 A.2d 113, 117, 274 Md. 536, (1975), found that when the trial court judge said: "if you had come in here with a plea of guilty . . . you would probably have gotten a modest sentence," he had, at least to a degree, punished the defendant more severely because that defendant failed to plead guilty and instead stood trial. The Maryland Court of Appeals stated that "a price may not be exacted nor a penalty imposed for exercising the fundamental and constitutional right of requiring the State to prove, at trial, the guilt of the petitioner as charged. This is as unallowable a circumstance as would be the imposition of a more severe penalty because a defendant asserted his right to counsel or insisted on a jury rather than a court trial." United States v. Tateo, 214 F. Supp. 560, 567 (SDNY 1963); "No matter how heinous the offense charged, how overwhelming the proof of guilt may appear, or how hopeless the defense, a defendant's right to continue with his trial may not be violated." In reference to imposing a harsher sentence because the defendant went to trial, the court stated: "To impose upon a defendant such alternatives amounts to coercion as a matter of law."

Similar cases include State v. Nichols, 247 N.W.2d 249 (Iowa Sup. Ct. 1976); United States v. Capriola, 537 F.2d 319 (9th Cir. 1976); Drinkwater v. State, 73 Wis.2d 674 (1976); United States v. Araujo, 539 F.2d 287 (2d Cir. 1976); United States v. Mantell, 335 F.2d 764 (4th Cir. 1964); People v. Moriarty, 185 N.E.2d 688 (Ill. Sup. Ct. 1962). Letters v. Commonwealth, 346 Mass. 403, 193 N. E. 578 (Sup.

Jud. Ct. Mass. 1963); People v. Snow, 182 N.W.2d 820 (Mich. Ct. App. 1970); Hanneman v. State, 184 N.W.2d 896 (Wis. Sup. Ct. 1971); United States v. Carty, 447 F.2d 964 (5th Cir. 1971); United States v. Levine, 372 F.2d 70 (7th Cir. 1967); Griggs v. Swenson, 352 F. Supp 743 (W.D. Mo. 1973); United States v. Duffy, 479 F.2d 1038 (2d Cir. 1973); North Carolina v. Pearce, 395 U.S. 711 (1969); People v. Earegood, 162 N.W.2d 802 (Mich. Ct. App. 1968); Gillespie v. State, 355 P.2d 451 (Okla. Ct. App. 1960); and United States v. Jansen, 475 F.2d 312 (7th Cir. 1973).

In State v. Rollins, 359 A.2d 315 (RI Sup. Ct. 1976), the Rhode Island Supreme Court found that *Stockwell* was not applicable where the attorney general stated that he would recommend an eight year sentence if the defendant were to plead guilty, and at trial, the trial justice sentenced the defendant to twenty years solely on the basis of the nature of the charges. In this case, the sentencing justice did not take part in the negotiations, nor did the trial justice threaten the defendant with a longer sentence if he went to trial. There was nothing to show that the trial justice had predetermined a sentence to be imposed in the event the defendant would enter a plea of guilty or that she had increased this sentence upon an unsuccessful defense at trial.

In Jung v. State, 145 N.W.2d 684, 689 (Wis. Sup. Ct. 1967), the Wisconsin Supreme Court stated: "Unless it can be shown in each case that a guilty plea is in fact evidence of repentance and demonstrates a readiness to accept responsibility for criminal acts, it is difficult to see how a plea of guilty should be a factor in giving a lenient sentence." People v. Morales, 252 Cal. App. 2d 537, 60 Cal. Rptr. 671, 677 (1967): "A trial court cannot impose a more severe punishment on the basis of its conclusion that a defendant who has not pleaded guilty presented a frivolous defense or one which the court concludes was presented in bad faith. Any such implications in the *Wiley* cases are rejected by this court." I will be discussing the matter of plea bargaining further, later in this chapter.

34. United States v. Lehman, 468 F.2d 93, 109–110 (7th Cir. 1972), *cert. denied*, 409 U.S. 967, 93 S. Ct. 273, 34 L.Ed. 2d 232 (1972), *cf.* Hess v. United States, 496 F.2d 936, 938 (8th Cir. 1974): [W]hether a defendant exercises his constitutional right to trial by jury to determine his guilt or innocence must have no bearing on the sentence imposed." People v. Jones, 350 N.E.2d 913, 915 (N.Y. Ct. App. 1976), 39 N.Y. 2d 694: "Here, it cannot be inferred that appellant was punished or further penalized by the sentencing justice because she pleaded not guilty and insisted upon her right to trial. She received the minimum punishment prescribed by law for the crime of which she was found guilty which crime was different from the ones to

which the others chose to plead." (The defendant was given an indeterminate sentence of fifteen years to life, as opposed to the three year sentence she was offered in return to a guilty plea to a lesser offense.) In State v. Mollberg, 246 N.W.2d 463, 471 (Minn. Sup. Ct. 1976), the trial court did not commit a reversible error in discussing with defense counsel, out of the presence of the jury, the subject of a plea bargain, in suggesting that maximum sentence would probably be imposed if defendant was convicted, and in suggesting that defendant would likely be convicted by the jury, in view of the fact that the record affirmatively demonstrated that the trial judge, who did not impose the maximum sentence, did not use the sentencing power to punish the defendant for exercising his right to stand trial, but based the sentence upon proper factors. Drinkwater v. State, 245 N.W.2d 664 (Sup. Ct. Wis. 1976), holding: "A mere disparity between the sentences of a defendant and his accomplice fails to establish that he was punished for exercising his right to a jury trial" (at 670); and United States v. Wilson, 506 F.2d 1252, 1259 (7th Cir. 1974): "Although a heavier sentence for one who has been convicted after trial and a lighter sentence for one who pleads guilty are in a sense two sides of the same coin, it is within proper bounds for the court to preserve some leniency in consideration of the co-operation and at least superficial penitence evidenced by one who pleads guilty." See also United States v. Hayward, 471 F.2d 388, 391 (7th Cir. 1976).

35. Lange v. State, 54 Wis. 2d 569, 196 N.W. 2d 680, 684 (1972); But see United States v. Stockwell, 472 F.2d 1186 (9th Cir. 1973), *cert. denied,* 411 U.S. 948, 93 S. Ct. 1924, 36 L.Ed. 2d 490 (1973), wherein the federal district judge had told the defendant before trial that if he pled guilty he would receive a three year sentence, but if he chose to stand trial and was convicted, he would receive a sentence of from five to seven years. After a trial and conviction on several counts, concurrent sentences of seven years were imposed. The ninth circuit, in remanding for resentencing, held: "[Once] it appears in the record that the court has taken a hand in plea bargaining, that a tentative sentence has been discussed, and that a harsher sentence has followed a breakdown in negotiations, the record must show that no improper weight was given the failure to plead guilty. In such a case, the record must affirmatively show that the court sentenced the defendant solely upon the facts of his case and his personal history, and not as punishment for his refusal to plead guilty." United States v. Stockwell, 472 F.2d at 1187.

36. National Advisory Commission on Criminal Justice Standards and Goals, *Report on Courts* 64 (Washington, D.C.: USGPO, 1973).

37. United States v. Sweig, 454 F.2d 181, 184 (2d Cir. 1972). G. Gordon Liddy, who received a harsher sentence than the other

Watergate defendants, appealed on the grounds that his sentence was based upon his refusal to cooperate. The motion for reduction of sentence was denied in United States v. Liddy, 397 F. Supp. 947 (USDC 1975). The court equated cooperation with remorse and stated: "In short, the defendant has not shown the Court the slightest remorse or regret for his actions, and has not even given the Court even a hint of contrition or sorrow, nor has he made any attempt to compensate for his illegal actions by trying to aid our system of justice in its search for the truth" (at 949). "In conclusion, the mitigating factors inherent in those cases in which a defendant has displayed some personal remorse or regret for his actions and has demonstrated a desire to reform his conduct to conform to the simple standards of a lawful society are absent in this case" (at 950).

In Jung v. State, 145 N.W.2d 684, 689 (Wis. Sup. Ct. 1966), the court found a co-defendant's plea to reflect remorse when co-defendant said "I'm sorry." State v. Tew, 54 Wis. 2d 361, 195 N.W.2d 615 (Wis. Sup. Ct. 1972), and McCleary v. State, 49 Wis. 2d 263, 182 N.W.2d 512 (Wis. Sup. Ct. 1971): the expression of remorse may be considered a mitigating factor at sentencing. In People v. Yennier 248 N.W.2d 680 (Mich. Ct. of App. 1977), the court stated: "We think there is more than semantics involved in distinguishing between properly giving consideration to remorse or its absence at sentencing and improperly penalizing an assertion of innocence at sentencing" (at 683). In this case the court saw no benefit in making the distinction between using an expression of remorse in mitigation of a sentence and considering a lack of remorse in sentencing. "[T]he court merely informed defendant that the factor of remorse or contriteness was not available to the court as it considered the defendant's request for probation. It was not improper for the court to note that defendant had not accepted responsibility for his crime" (at 684). United States v. Thompson, 476 F.2d 1196 (7th Cir. 1973): "[A] show of lenience to those who exhibit contribution by admitting guilt does not carry a corollary that the judge indulges in a policy of penalizing those who elect to stand trial" (at 1201).

38. United States v. Vermeulen, 436 F.2d 72, 76 (2d Cir. 1970), *cert. denied,* 402 U.S. 911 (1971). In United States v. Rogers, 504 F.2d 1079 (5th Cir. 1974), the court held that, in view of Fifth Amendment considerations, the trial court could not impose a greater sentence on the defendant because of his refusal to "sing" about others involved in the narcotics conspiracy. Even though the trial court did not directly ask the defendant to confess his guilt, the defendant would have admitted his guilt in his implication of the others involved. The court determined that the defendant could not be penalized for refusing to confess. However, in Holmes v. State, 251

N.W.2d 56, 73 (Wis. Sup. Ct. 1977), the Wisconsin Supreme Court held that "it was entirely proper for the trial court to consider on sentencing the defendant's cooperativeness as manifested by his refusal to name his accomplices. The consideration of that factor did not constitute an abuse of discretion." The court felt that no Fifth Amendment rights were involved since the defendant had pleaded guilty.

In a related matter, the U.S. Supreme Court recently upheld the right of a trial court judge to enhance a defendant's sentence on the ground that, at trial, the defendant had testified and perjured himself. United States v. Grayson, 438 U.S. 41 (1978). Interestingly, this controversial opinion was premised primarily on a rehabilitative rationale. Chief Justice Burger, speaking for a six justice majority, declared that the Court was "reaffirming the authority of a sentencing judge to evaluate carefully a defendant's testimony on the stand, determine—with a consciousness of the frailty of human judgment—whether that testimony contained willful and material falsehoods, and, if so, assess in light of all the other knowledge gained about the defendant the meaning of that conduct with respect to his prospects for rehabilitation and restoration to a useful place in society" (at 55).

39. Williams v. United States, 293 A.2d 484, 487 (D.C. App. 1972); see also Bertrand v. United States, 467 F.2d 901 (5th Cir. 1972); United States v. Acosta, 501 F.2d 1330 (5th Cir. 1974); Mitchell v. Sirica, 502 F.2d 375, 384 n. 17 (D. C. Cir. 1974), *cert. denied,* 418 U.S. 955 (1974).

40. People v. Anderson, 391 Mich. 419, 216 N.W. 2d 780, 781 (1974).

41. See also the discussion *supra* note 37.

42. *See generally,* J. M. Kress, "Progress and Prosecution," 423 *The Annals of the American Academy of Political and Social Science* 99 (January 1976); D. Newman, *Conviction: The Determination of Guilt or Innocence Without Trial* (Boston: Little, Brown, 1966); A. Alschuler, "The Trial Judge's Role in Plea Bargaining," *supra* note 7; J. Bond, *Plea-Bargaining and Guilty Pleas* (New York: Clark Boardman, 1977); and Georgetown University Law Center, *Plea Bargaining in the United States–Phase I Report* (Washingon, D.C.: Georgetown University Law Center, 1977).

43. See J. C. Coffee, "The Future of Sentencing Reform: Emerging Legal Issues in the Individualization of Justice," 73 *Michigan Law Review* 1425-27 (1975). See also United States v. Weston, 448 F.2d 6261 (9th Cir. 1971), *cert. denied,* 404 U.S. 1060 (1972).

44. See for example, Henry v. State 173 Md. 131, 328 A.2d 293 (Ct. App. 1974); and State v. Shlarp, 25 Ariz. App. 85, 541 P. 2d 41 (1975). United States v. Marines, 535 F.2d 552, 554 (10th Cir. 1976):

"It is perfectly acceptable for the district court to consider the fact that a felony indictment, based upon the same set of facts, was dismissed pursuant to a plea bargain by which Marines pleaded guilty to a misdemeanor."

45. It is surprising that previous writers have failed to emphasize the significant fact that plea bargaining most often aids recidivist, career criminals and provides far fewer rewards to the one time offender. See generally the authorities referred to *supra* note 42. See particularly the views of Professor Alschuler.

46. R. H. Kuh, "Plea Bargaining Guidelines for the Manhattan District Attorney's Office," 11 *Criminal Law Bulletin* 48 (January-February 1975).

47. A. Alschuler, "Sentencing Reform," *supra* note 7.

48. R. H. Jackson, "The Federal Prosecutor," 24 *Journal of the American Judicature Society* 18–20 (1940); See also, A. Alschuler, "The Prosecutor's Role in Plea Bargaining," 36 *University of Chicago Law Review* 50 (1968); and authorities cited *supra* note 42.

49. D. J. Newman, *Introduction to Criminal Justice,* 2nd ed. (Philadelphia: J. B. Lippincott, 1978); see also R. O. Dawson, *Sentencing: The Decision as to Type, Length and Conditions of Sentence* 188–92 (Boston: Little, Brown, 1969); and Alschuler, "Sentencing Reform," *supra* note 7 at 557–61. Professor Dawson has phrased the problem as follows: "To some extent, one could predict that discretion denied to the trial judge will be exercised at another stage of the process, in more plea bargaining, more charge selection, more police discretion." Dawson, *supra* note 8 at 449.

50. I have discussed parole boards, *supra* Chapter 2, but I will also discuss them further *infra* Chapter 9.

51. See Kuh, *supra* note 46.

52. L. T. Wilkins, *The Problem of Overlap in Experience Table Construction* 6–7 (Davis, Calif.: National Council on Crime and Delinquency, 1973); See also H. M. Blalock, Jr., "Correlated Independent Variables: The Problem of Multicollinearity," 42 *Social Forces* 233 (1963).

53. See particularly L. T. Wilkins, J. M. Kress, D. M. Gottfredson, J. C. Calpin, and A. M. Gelman, *Sentencing Guidelines: Structuring Judicial Discretion–Report on the Feasibility Study* (Washington, D.C.: USGPO, 1978); and the sources cited *supra* note 2.

54. I should note, however, that although we did express these concerns to the judges on our Steering and Policy Committee, they were unanimous in viewing the problem as minor; they felt certain that the information items we *were* able to collect and evaluate provided a perfectly adequate base for the sentencing decision in the overwhelming majority of cases.

Establishing Sentencing Guidelines: A Strategy for Reform

The general objectives of sentence review are ... to promote the development and application of criteria for sentencing which are both rational and just.—American Bar Association[1]

A PROPOSED PLAN

In this chapter, I offer a proposal to sentencing authorities that incorporates both normative and descriptive perspectives and aims at achieving a rational and just sentencing system. It is a general research plan applicable to states considering the adoption of sentencing guidelines, whether through court rule, legislative enactment, or administrative promulgation by a sentencing commission—although I will shortly state my preference for the latter approach. First and foremost, this program is practical and realistic, taking full cognizance of the democratic process through which this prescription for justice reform will be filled.

The overall goal of an appropriate sentencing research effort should be to provide a relevant body of information so that sentencing authorities will be able to build upon a conceptual and factual base of knowledge. A fundamental premise of any useful empirical research is that baseline data only have meaning in the context of a conceptual framework for comprehending that data. The alternative sentencing guidelines systems to be discussed here may therefore be seen as the essential frames of reference for organizing and analyzing data derived from a study of any judicial system.

Figure 9–1 outlines the research approach I suggest. According to the charge given the Federal Sentencing Commission in S.1437, for example, the commission staff will have to consider both the "Is" and the "Ought" of federal sentencing[2]—that is, presently existing practices with regard to sentencing federal offenders, as well as the efficacy and desirability of those practices and ways of improving

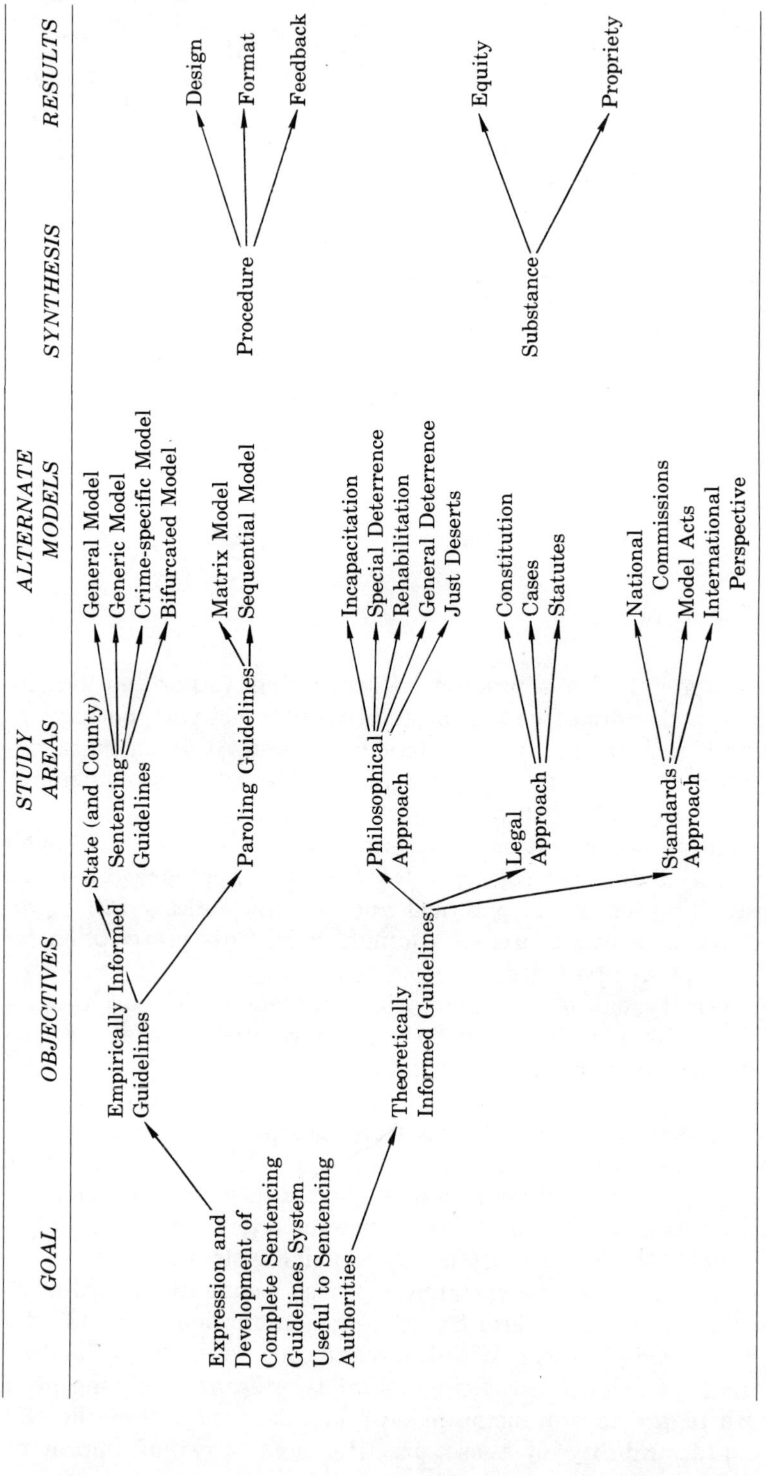

Figure 9–1. Establishing Sentencing Guidelines: Outlines

upon them. Because of the emphasis we placed in our own early research on objective description, many commentators have missed the point that such empirical research only forms the necessary base upon which intelligent and useful prescriptive programs may be built. Thus, a primary research objective must be to provide background information for sentencers regarding both empirical and theoretical approaches to developing sentencing guidelines.

DETERMINING THE APPROPRIATE SENTENCING AUTHORITY

Jurisdictional Breadth

Assuming the desirability of constructing a sentencing guidelines system, our first question becomes the mixed practical, political, and constitutional one of what level of government should be encompassed by a sentencing guidelines system. There are five possible jurisdictional levels at which to establish sentencing guidelines: the individual judge, the county, a region, the state, or the nation. The first is too narrow a base to be worth the effort, while the fifth is unrealistic to expect in our federal system—save for the federal courts themselves, of course. That leaves countywide, regional, and statewide possibilities.

Most sentencing guidelines work to date has been at the county level, and there is thus a proven methodology upon which to build.[3] The county is a compact and comprehensible criminal justice unit and relatively simple to analyze. On the other hand, the need for guidelines is likely to be less pressing on the county level, as the communication between judges, which guidelines valuably facilitate, already likely exists to some degree. Moreover, some might view separate countywide guidelines systems as actually institutionalizing disparity within the overall statewide system and hence an unattractive alternative.

The next possible approach to establishing sentencing guidelines would entail regionalized development. The state could be broken down into different regions with separate guidelines developed for each region. But would this violate the equal protection guarantee of the Constitution?[4] Politically, would the agency or branch of government with which researchers would primarily work wish frankly to acknowledge regional differentiation? If it would, then the researchers would be faced with the herculean task of carefully delineating those regional boundaries. One might, for example, have city guidelines in one part of the state; while suburban areas might possess another set of guidelines, and rural areas might apply yet a third set.

On the other hand, there may be a sharp distinction only between urban and rural areas or, perhaps, between farm and industrial areas; or, some other demographic distinction might prove significant. In addition, highly state-specific regional differences would have to be taken into account. New York State, for example, has the largest of all urban areas, in New York City; then, there are the New York City suburbs; there are also a number of other large cities in the state, such as Buffalo and Syracuse; and, finally, New York State has many rural areas that are very divergent in their outlooks, such as those with French-speaking populations on the Quebec border and those adjacent to Pennsylvanian Indian reservations. How would all of these differences be taken into account? What about states such as Missouri or California that have two major metropolices at different points in the state and even two apparently different philosophies in different halves of the state? As the reader may see, these issues intrigued me as a researcher, and they have similarly interested a number of other researchers since I first raised them several years ago. Frankly, however, they have failed to elicit much more than theoretical discussion.[5] Judges across the country have almost always preferred the countywide or statewide approach, with the latter becoming more and more the guidelines vehicle of choice.

Thus, the statewide (or, for the federal courts, the nationwide) sentencing guidelines system is the final possibility. This has the advantage of uniformity and avoids the lack of equal protection concerns that the other systems raise. On the other hand, such a system presents numerous data collection and analysis difficulties. First, there will be a great problem in reconciling the data bases since different sources of information exist throughout the state and there is little uniformity as to the type of data presently collected, the places in which they are kept, or the uses to which they are put.[6] Second, there are often different sentencing alternatives available about the state; work release or drug rehabilitation programs, for example, may be an available option only for sentenced offenders in the state's largest city.[7] Third, there may be sharp philosophical differences between judges in different parts of the state; this, together with a history of strong judicial independence, provides judges with either a reluctance to face up to and deal with the facts of sentence variation across the state or a conscious decision to maintain "home rule" in the setting of criminal penalties and thus take differing community standards into account.

Nevertheless, I should point out that most judges with whom I have spoken see insurmountable equal protection problems with any county-by-county or regionalized approach to guidelines. Even given the historically local orientation of criminal justice, there is a view I have heard voiced repeatedly: the state has one penal code and one correctional system and must have one sentencing policy uniformly established across the state.

Under our federal system, it would be impossible to establish uniform national standards to be applied across the states; in addition to principles of state sovereignty, individual state penal codes, sentencing alternatives, resources, and so forth simply vary too much. This does not necessarily mean, however, that the federal courts should lack uniform standards. One of the principal issues to confront the sentencing commission proposed in S.1437 would be whether or not the sentencing guidelines it promulgates should be nationally applicable. While no consensus has yet been achieved on this matter, I believe that the commission will eventually opt for a uniform system, primarily on equal protection grounds.

The Sentencing Commission

Whatever level of government is covered by a sentencing guidelines system, whatever jurisdictional scope is encompassed, a pragmatic question must be answered: How will the guidelines actually be developed, implemented, administered, and monitored? Further, what agency will perform these tasks? While perhaps not as difficult to resolve as the one of jurisdictional breadth, the issue I deal with now is far more fundamental—the proper placement of a sentencing guidelines structure within the constitutional framework of each state. The issue involves the basic separation of powers constitutionally established between the three branches of government. Because criminal law is so locally oriented, I am not dealing with the question of federal-state relations; rather, the issue here manifests itself in every state constitution in America: What is the proper allocation of sentencing powers between the three branches of government as we move to further implementation of sentencing guidelines systems across the United States?

On the county level, the issues are simpler. Rarely do county executives or county legislatures intrude on the county judiciary, who have a freer hand to run their courts: the comparable concern at the county level has been the relationship to the local court administrator and the probation department, although we were offered total cooperation by those agencies in our endeavors reported earlier. Future countywide guidelines systems should similarly find no difficulty in answering this question. On a county level, all of the local judges should be involved, perhaps with the assistance of the local trial court administrator; in the larger cities, a representative committee might be appointed.

At the regional or statewide levels, however, such a system could work only in the smallest states. In the larger states, the state supreme court—through its administrative rule-making powers—or the state court administrator might be the logical vehicle for sentencing guidelines development. At the meetings of our Steering and Policy Committee, this question was raised, and many judges expressed sharp reservations about involving any branch of government other than the judiciary. The supreme courts of many states have sufficient administrative rule-making powers to establish guidelines on a statewide basis, but, in the past, supreme courts have proven most reluctant to exercise such powers. In some states, such as New Jersey, court administrators have had a good deal of leeway in aiding local courts, and guidelines were seen there as a logical court improvement mechanism.

The most popular and practical suggestion, however, appears to be the sentencing commission. Judge Frankel first proposed this body in 1971 and referred to it as his book's "most important single suggestion":

> The proposed Commission would be a permanent agency responsible for (1) the study of sentencing, corrections, and parole; (2) the formulation of laws and rules to which the studies pointed; and (3) the *actual enactment of rules,* subject to traditional checks by Congress and the courts.[8]

In most of its present incarnations, the sentencing commission is offered as a quasi-administrative agency empowered to promulgate sentencing guidelines ranges within the outer statutory bounds set by a legislature. Already established in Minnesota and Pennsylvania, S.1437, the Criminal Justice Reform Act of 1978, provides for a sentencing commission for the federal system,[9] and the draft Uniform Corrections Act calls for one in every state.[10] Indeed, each of the above call for the sentencing commission to incorporate a sentencing guidelines system modeled after the early, empirically informed efforts described in earlier chapters of this book.[11] We are apparently living in what one commentator has referred to as "The Era of the Sentencing Commission."[12] Left to legislation alone, the guidelines would not be sufficiently flexible or able to adapt to changed conditions (such as overcrowded prisons) on relatively short notice.[13] Left to judges, alone and unaided, there exists a reasonable fear that present practices might be accepted as desirable without sufficient scrutiny.[14] Moreover, there is a compelling necessity for the establishment of an overall statewide sentencing policy in most jurisdictions. Even with the best of intentions, judges who meet only once a year at a judicial conference cannot hope to achieve any valid policy consensus; they require a research staff to collect and analyze data and provide them with guidance, a staff that also serves as a means of communication to the legislative and executive branches of governments. Furthermore, judges are engaged in too many other endeavors to monitor such a system. In some states, this role could be performed by a court administrator,[15] but the sentencing commission concept appears useful as a check against the development of too much rigidity in the sentencing guidelines system. As one analyst has noted: "No *a priori* system can answer all the problems of sentencing for all time. The Commission with its power to devise guidelines and policy statements, provides the necessary flexibility."[16]

As I have consistently declared reasons for supporting the local trial court judge in sentencing, it may appear strange to find me also supporting the sentencing commission concept. The point is, however, that I see the two as essential partners in effective sentencing reform—working together, indeed, with the appellate courts to develop a common law of sentencing.

One valuable aspect of the commission approach is that it represents an acknowledgment of the importance of sentencing and a recognition that sentencing reform is law reform. The very creation of a separate body charged with enunciating the purposes and reviewing the practices of sentencing does much to assure that this vital function is both open and accountable, yet removed from partisan politics.

This is perhaps the most important reason for supporting the establishment of a Sentencing Commission. Divorced from the daily pressures of the courts and the legislative process, the Commission can objectively, over a period of time and after public hearings, propose a system of proportionate sentences that would reflect society's general view of the seriousness of specific offenses.[17]

Thus, while sentencing guidelines systems may continue to be developed on a county level and may continue to be totally controlled by local judges, I conclude that, in most jurisdictions, the future of sentencing reform lies in the establishment of a separate state agency, a sentencing commission, that will not take away judicial discretion but will actually enhance it by promulgating sentencing guidelines, all the while taking judicial views and practices into account.

Abolish Parole?

The question arises as to whether the sentencing commission should exist in place of a parole board or in conjunction with one. I feel that the answer to this is simple and certainly not as radical as it sounds: abolish the parole board! While many today advocate determinate sentencing, they flinch from the natural consequences of their views with regard to parole. There are three principal reasons for this: (1) the parole concept consists of two distinct components (release and supervision), and there is a legitimate fear that the move to abolish one will destroy the other; (2) misunderstandings and fears abound concerning both the current practices of parole boards and the future practices of sentencing commissions; and finally (3) a combination of inertia and emotion serve to hinder efforts at reform.

As to the first reason, parole release decisionmaking and the supervision of released parolees bear neither a theoretical nor a practical relationship one to the other. Parole board members tend to be executive appointees from diverse backgrounds—often officials from other agencies entirely—who perform their primary tasks at prisons where they review inmate files, interview prisoners, and decide whether (and when) to release them. Parole supervisors, on the other hand, work closely with the now released parolee, often facing a dilemma as to whether that task is more to assist parolees or more to "watchdog" their activities. It is not my purpose here to resolve that dilemma, but simply to note that it is the same dilemma faced by probation officers. Indeed, many states already join probation officers and parole officers into one state agency since their supervisory functions are so alike.

Therefore, abolishing parole boards will not mean the end of parole supervision.[18] Instead, the provision of clear and unified direction to parole officers should prove valuable as an administrative reform in streamlining the parole agency to cope with its proper functions rather than the quasi-judicial one it has lately assumed.

While on this subject, I should point out that recent research indicates that the function of parole and/or probation supervision is most effective during the first year of release (or sentence, if probation). After that, there is a sharp dropoff in value to the probationer (or the parolee) or to society at large; a point of diminishing returns, if you will, tends to set in. These findings suggest, on the one hand, that more intensive supervision during the first year holds promise for perhaps improving the "effectiveness" of sentencing[19] and, on the other hand, that such concepts as "lifetime parole" (which has achieved some popularity in state legislatures)[20] will prove counterproductive.

Thus, the abolition of parole release decisionmaking will not lead to any deleterious effects upon parole supervision and may even improve its management. Still, why adopt a drastic change from present practice and abolish parole release decisionmaking? The most important reason for abolishing parole is that the historical raison d'être for the parole board has disappeared. Its existence was predicated on the indeterminate sentence and the rehabilitative ideal; but in the last decade, the evils and failings of both, in theory and in practice, have became manifest.[21] Parole release decisionmaking was supposed to be something performed by rehabilitative experts who could tell us when inmates were "ready" for release and could "safe-ly" return to the community; but study after study indicates that this is not the basis upon which the release decision is actually being made.[22]

However, those who would salvage the institution from destruc-tion urge upon it a new purpose, one more in line with its actual present practice.[23] Its main function now would be to remedy judicial sentencing disparities![24] Acknowledging that—contrary to all theo-ry—postsentencing institutional behavior has very little effect upon the parole release decision, the would-be saviors of the parole board urge the reform of parole guidelines—admittedly a valuable reform, but only in the context of the present, non-sentencing commis-sion/judicial sentencing guidelines system. Moreover, these parole guidelines would be based almost exclusively upon factors that were already known to the sentencing judge.

Surely it would be an even more drastic (and perhaps not totally honest) step to alter completely the purpose and function of an ex-isting institution than to abolish it frankly and replace it with one whose stated functions coincide with its actual ones. Moreover, if we do accept this new mission for parole boards, then the best that can be said for them will be that they are merely superfluous rather than injurious. If we reform sentencing decisionmaking through the medi-um of a sentencing commission/judicial sentencing guidelines ap-proach, then there is no reason to *re*-reform sentencing through parole guidelines!

Nevertheless, the parole board advocates point out that we our-selves have recognized the sentencing decision to be a bifurcated one[25] and therefore that separate decisions are made as to whether to incarcerate and how long to incarcerate. These parole board retainers argue that at least that latter decision should be reserved to a sepa-rate agency. But why should that be so? We are aiming for one con-sistent sentencing policy that may merely take effect in two stages, not two policies enunciated by and effectuated through two different administrative agencies. Not only would fracturing sentencing policy decisionmaking in this manner make it more difficult to assign ac-countability, but even more importantly, policy disparity would be assured of continuation with two separate administrative agencies competing for legitimacy. (In fact, limiting the sentencing commis-sion to the in/out decision alone would logically suggest yet a third body—one created to choose among the various nonincarcerative pen-alties—and the mind boggles at the policy disparities that such a sys-tem would create!)

Real sentencing reform requires one responsible and accountable sentencing agency, open to public criticism and scrutiny and able to assess present practice and promote reform both as to incarcerative alternatives and to the vast range of nonincarcerative options (such as drug and alcohol rehabilitation programs, work release projects, etc.) that should be reviewed by the sentencing commission.

Finally, supporting the continuation of the parole board, we find a certain nostalgic sentiment combined with the normal opposition one encounters to any reform. That normal opposition consists of an inertial unwillingness to change old habits, as well as self-serving declarations of dismay from those whose positions would be eliminated. Moreover, we were all raised on the notion that rehabilitation was doing "good," and it is hard to come to grips emotionally with the negative results that one can perhaps accept rationally. Therefore, we find it a difficult chore to eliminate the seemingly benevolent administrator of the indeterminate sentence, particularly when parole board members do in fact tend to be truly decent people with noble motivations. My attacks on the parole decisionmaking process should not be read, therefore, as attacks on the people who make those decisions. Uniformly, in fact, the many parole board heads and members I have met have been honest, dedicated, hard working, and frequently misunderstood public servants performing their thankless tasks to the best of their abilities; but the imperfect tools at their disposal could not measure up to the moral worth of these people.

Partly for this reason, but also for one extremely important other one, I urge a further reform upon any sentencing commission to be established. I believe it to be crucial that the initial membership of the sentencing commission have a substantial number of commissioners, perhaps even a majority, chosen from among actively serving parole board members. The major reason for this is the concept of "real time" that I discussed in Chapter 2. Present parole board members deal constantly in real time and thus have a sense of the actual time served by prisoners today, rather than the "stated" time announced by the judge at sentencing. There would be a natural but unfortunate tendency to push up actual time to meet stated time if future sentencing commissioners were only used to dealing with the latter.

Some have suggested meeting this danger by sharply increasing the amount of "good time" granted prisoners ("day for day" is one proposal, thus halving the stated sentence),[26] but I regard that as a somewhat dishonest approach—even though proposed with the best of intentions. It is said that the public would simply be unwilling to accept that actual time spent in prison is much less than the time stated at sentencing. But I perhaps naïvely believe that the public could accept some honesty from its public officials. In fact, my view is that a major part of the current disrespect for the courts may be found in the laughter that greets newspaper headlines declaring a murderer to be sentenced to twenty-five, fifty, ninety-nine, or even two hundred years. The inevitable first question: "Yeah, but when will they *really* let him out?"

It is time to abandon both the concept and the practice of the "noble" lie. The only way to gain the respect of the public is for government to tell the truth, continually and completely. In my view, a signal advantage of the sentencing commission/judicial sentencing guidelines approach is this very "truth–in–packaging" aspect of it. The sentence handed down by the judge would be the sentence served, for incarcerative and nonincarcerative sanctions. At the time of sentencing, uncertainty would end for the inmate as to when to expect release and for the victim and the public as to whether justice means what it says.

> [T]he inmate would know when he would be released at the time he entered the institution, assuming he or the government does not appeal the sentence. He would not be required to feign rehabilitation or religious conversion in order to win release. Sentencing uniformity would be enhanced by the Commission guidelines and by appellate review. The fiction that release from prison is a function of institutional rehabilitation would be abandoned in favor of a notion that the individualized sentence set at the beginning of the correctional process will be the sentence served, absent extraordinary circumstances.[27]

The reader will recall that sentencing guidelines may continue to operate on a county level and continue to be wholly controlled by judges. But whether that administrative route is chosen or whether a statewide sentencing commission is established as I suggest, it still remains to explain just how a sentencing authority should operate and how it should go about producing a reformed sentencing system fusing together both empirical and theoretical components.

EMPIRICALLY INFORMED GUIDELINES

To recapitulate briefly the research described in Part Two of this book, the logic behind empirically informed sentencing guidelines systems has been one of utilizing judicial experience to focus on the equity dimension within the larger concept of justice. An assumption has been the desirability of ensuring that similar offenders, in similar circumstances, be accorded similar sentences. This may readily be seen as implying a statistical classification scheme, as opposed to a more contentiously philosophical one. As decisions become more consistent (less variable) with respect to a given classification scheme, then the resultant decisions may be considered more equitable or "fair."

By carefully distinguishing this equity (or evenhandedness) dimension of justice, preliminary guideline constructs initially ignore the propriety (or individualization) dimension of the whole justice concept—that is, whether or not presently existing implicit policy is "wrong" in a more fundamental, moral sense. Nevertheless, the careful and explicit articulation of present policy serves to open it up for clear discussion and cogent review. Moreover, it has always been the stated position of those of us who have developed empirically informed guidelines systems that the delineation of equity considerations will only be a starting point toward the evolution of a system of whole justice involving a synthesis with the propriety dimension as well.

Sentencing authorities should study both theoretical and empirical systems with a view toward incorporating the best features of each into an eventually synthesized sentencing guidelines system. The first value of an empirical approach is a moral-legal one. It is not by accident, for example, that S.1437 instructs the sentencing commission to consider present practices;[28] a similar proposal was recently advanced by New York State's Executive Advisory Committee on Sentencing.[29] Evenhandedness of justice is universally viewed as desirable; the principal public dissatisfaction with existing practices has been a perception of disparities and inequities.

The second value of the empirical approach is a pragmatic-systemic one. In order for improvements in the administration of justice best to take hold in our legal system, they should be incremental ones, building upon precedent and our present body of knowledge. A priori legislative or executive establishment of the "right" sentence, with little or no factual support, would be met with justifiable opposition by any agency, but especially by a judiciary accustomed to a history of independence.[30] Moreover, one must account for the necessary and expectable consequences that a proposed decrease in discretion at one decision point will bring. If theoretical guidelines are too much at variance with actual practice, then discretion will assuredly flow to less visible components of the criminal justice system, and the entire reform effort will be rendered nugatory, merely serving to enhance the remaining discretionary powers of police, prosecutors, and parole boards. My years working together with sentencing judges leads me furthermore to the conclusion that improvements will be far more acceptable to the judiciary when placed in the self-regulating context of an empirically informed system.

So far, five conceptually distinct methods of developing such guidelines systems have been employed, two in the paroling and three in the sentencing field. While even more methods may be uncovered with regard to sentencing decisions, prior efforts do offer a useful methodological history from which to proceed in developing a sentencing guidelines system uniquely designed for the use of each state's own trial court judges.

The five empirical models are ones that have been tested by me and my colleagues in the field in terms of federal parole guidelines and state parole guidelines, as well as countywide and statewide sentencing guidelines systems. All five of the present empirically informed models have at the core of their philosophy the desire, initially, to replicate the ongoing decisionmaking practices of the present policy body, whether paroling or sentencing; the various statistical tests that we have employed have been directed toward that end. While a main purpose of these empirical approaches has been to achieve consistency over time, they each seek to avoid static reinforcement of the status quo through the construct of a dynamic feedback loop.

Parole Guidelines

As related in Chapter 4, the sentencing guidelines research project itself grew out of the successful completion of a study that developed operating guidelines for the United States Parole Commission. That three year study resulted in the adoption and official administrative promulgation of guidelines in the watershed year of 1972. They have been revised and publically disseminated every year since.[31] That early study provided the initial conceptual and methodological analogies for subsequent sentencing research.

Federal Parole Guidelines. The United States Parole Commission's decisionmaking guidelines are characterized by a two dimensional model that links the intersection of the dimension of offense seriousness and the dimension of parole prognosis with a time (in months) to be served prior to release on parole. In actual use, a parole hearing examiner scores an individual case for offense seriousness and parole prognosis and then locates their cell of intersection; this provides an expected range of months to be served by the offender. A range in time is provided to allow for some variation in the broad categories of risk and severity, but hearing examiners must usually set the exact length of incarceration within that range. If the examiner decides to depart from the range called for in a particular case, written reasons must be provided for doing so. These are later reviewed, first by a panel of three decisionmakers and then by the full commission, both on a case-by-case basis and in terms of their overall policy implications.

The reader should be aware that even though the decisionmaking task at the parole level is far less complex than that at the sentencing level, only 80 to 85 percent of paroling decisions in the federal system are accounted for by the published guidelines. The results achieved at the countywide sentencing guidelines level thus compare quite favorably.

State Parole Guidelines The federal parole guidelines have proven so popular, indeed, that a number of states have adopted variants of them. In the eight states that have so far adopted parole guidelines (a number of other states are working toward such adoption), two types of guidelines models have emerged.[32] One type, referred to as the "matrix" model, is based on the identification of two or more general dimensions of concern, as in the United States Parole Commission's guidelines. The range of expected decisions is then displayed in a grid format. Matrix models have been adopted by the California Youth Authority, as well as by the adult paroling authorities in Minnesota, New Jersey, and the state of Washington.

The other type of parole guidelines model is called the "sequential" model and has been employed by the adult paroling authorities of Louisiana, Missouri, North Carolina, and Virginia. In the sequential model, a series of decision rules is defined as if the decision process followed a sorting procedure, according to significant aspects of the inmate's situation. Different factors appear to affect inputs differentially at each step of this more complicated decisionmaking process. A number of sequentially ordered decision points have to be individually overcome, or "hurdled," before the decisionmaker will effectively process further information regarding the offender.[33]

Sentencing Guidelines in State Courts

As described earlier, America's first sentencing guidelines were implemented in the Denver County District Court in November 1976. Since sentencing guidelines had to account for the large number of convicted offenders not sent to prison (as well as those who were so incarcerated), they were necessarily different from parole guidelines. In the event, the sentencing guidelines systems established in Denver and Chicago were of the type that I have referred to as the "general" or "class" model. The reader is reminded that, in this approach, the decisionmaking grids are developed parallel to, and coordinate with, the statutory classification system established by the state's penal code. Since many types of offenses are found in any one statutory class, the grids necessarily relate to a broad range of offenses, encompassing a wide range of criminal activity and behavioral patterns.

The sentencing guidelines developed for Newark, Phoenix, and Philadelphia, on the other hand, employed the "generic" model of sentencing guidelines, wherein typological crime classification systems (so far of violent, property, drugs, and miscellaneous) have been created as information sorting mechanisms. This system relies on the theoretical assumption that information items will make a differential impact upon the sentencing decisionmaker depending upon the type of crime committed.[34]

We have preliminarily tested another empirical model, the "crime-specific" approach, but data bases have so far been insufficient to allow for the development of crime-specific guidelines beyond the two or three most frequently occurring offenses in the jurisdiction. The logic underlying this approach is an extrapolation of the logic of the generic model—that is, the information items and weightings affecting sentencing decisions may vary from crime to crime.[35]

THEORETICALLY INFORMED GUIDELINES

As they have been developed, parole guidelines to some extent, and sentencing guidelines to a great extent, have consistently incorporated a normative component in addition to initially descriptive modeling. The data collection and statistical analysis performed have been intended to achieve only a clearly articulated descriptive base from which the policymakers could then consciously and explicitly depart. Each of the guidelines systems has attempted to distinguish case-by-case decisionmaking from the overall policy decisions made by the judges (or parole board members) in each jurisdiction. Upon completion of the preliminary statistical analyses, we have always offered the policymaking body a choice of models. In fact, the judges would often request that we further develop a model of presently lower predictive accuracy as that model incorporated more prescriptive norms to which the group preferred to adhere in the long run.

We may conveniently divide our theoretically informed guidelines objective into three major study areas, each of which may in turn be subdivided into a number of lines of inquiry. The philosophical approach incorporates an analysis of the logics that the various theories of punishment provide to the sentencing judge. The legal approach offers a comparative survey of how various jurisdictions have dealt with the controversial issues surrounding the factors potentially includable in sentencing guidelines systems. The standards approach outlines and compares the diverse normative stands that have been taken by prominent study commissions and reform groups.

The Philosophical Approach

Sentencing serves many, frequently contradictory, purposes. The principal theories of punishment are often spoken of as "guides" for the sentencing judge, but not in any specifically useful sense. While a vast body of literature exists with regard to these theories,[36] few have even considered the possibility of providing for any systematic codification or categorization of the criteria (or their weights) that any theory suggests and that should thus be considered by the judge at the time of sentencing.[37]

Incapacitation, for example, refers to a concern for isolating a given offender for a period during which the offender is rendered incapable of committing crimes. As the perceptively straightforward James Q. Wilson has observed: "The purpose of isolating—or, more accurately, closely supervising—offenders is obvious: Whatever they may do when they are released, they cannot harm society while confined or closely supervised."[38] This theory is usually offered to justify an incarcerative sentence[39] and involves a prediction that, if released, the offender is likely to commit a "dangerous" act. If such a justification were to form the core of theoretically derived sentencing guidelines, then a more delineated scaling of the seriousness of offenses would be required,[40] as well as better predictive instruments[41] and a way of coping with the "false positive" problem.[42] Our procedural concerns would be with more secure (and internally safer) institutions, reduced charge bargaining, and increased psychological evaluation and testing.

Special deterrence has been said by Zimring and Hawkins to be merely a more intense version of general deterrence;[43] others see it as a rephrasing of rehabilitation.[44] Nevertheless, we may conceptually distinguish it as implying a present punishment sufficient to induce in the present offender a fear of future punishment following the criminal act, so as to reduce significantly the possibility of that offender repeating his or her offense for some period of time; by some definitions, a reduction in the relative gravity of subsequent offenses would be viewed as sufficient.[45] This theory is offered to justify all forms of punishment and also involves a prediction, although arguably a more objective one. It assumes a rational offender applying a utilitarian calculus to criminal acts and suggests the applicability of cost-benefit analysis and similar econometric techniques,[46] as well as the psychometric calculation of a "threat" threshold sufficient to reduce the antisocial behavior of specific offenders.[47]

There is currently a sharp debate in the criminal justice literature as to the best method to assess the relative effectiveness of concepts relating to the philosophy of sentencing.[48] The most recent review of the literature in this area, for example, was conducted by the Panel on Research on Deterrent and Incapacitative Affects, convened by the National Research Council, operating arm of the National Academy of Sciences, and it concluded: "In summary, then, we cannot yet assert that the evidence warrants an affirmative conclusion regarding deterrence."[49] Similar inconclusive results were described after a review of the literature on incapacitation.[50]

Rehabilitation is similar in goal to special deterrence in that it seeks to reduce the propensity of the individual offender to recidivate. It is different, however, in its focus on attempting to change the underlying motivational patterns of the offender so as to induce prosocial conduct. This theory is usually offered to justify a sentence of probation[51] with an emphasis on the ability of the probation officer to assist the offender in better coping with the social environment. Advocates of this approach often apply differing models of criminality,[52] but may usually be said to seek more social work facilities, psychiatric counseling, employment training, and education—sometimes in the context of a prison setting. It is argued that the offender's prior vocational and educational achievements may legitimately serve to reduce the potential sanction imposed upon that offender, whereas the gravity of the instant offense is considered of less significance under a rehabilitation rationale. As noted earlier, however, the rehabilitative ideal has recently come under sharp attack in terms of both its efficacy[53] and its morality.[54]

General deterrence refers to punishing this offender at a level sufficient to convince other potential offenders in the population not to engage in crime.[55] This category has been urged by some as an overall explanation for the penal code and by many as the justification for particular penalties attached to specific crimes. It has been most studied, for example—with equivocal results—on the question of the death penalty as a deterrent to murder.[56] It has a strong education component, and public perceptions are significant under a general deterrence theory. Tittle and Logan[57] remind us of how little we empirically know, even today, concerning Jeremy Bentham's utilitarian touchstones of celerity, severity, and certainty.[58] General deterrence is the major theory that looks beyond the results affecting one individual offender to those affecting others. It would appear most applicable to crimes that are most calculated[59]—such as traffic offenses,[60] embezzlement, or income tax evasion—and judges may legitimately "set examples" of individual offenders under this rationale. The study of effectiveness measures, improved information systems, and the public dissemination of sentencing information is called for, while the changing incidence of crime in the community—and public and press commentary concerning it—are legitimate concerns for the sentencing judge under a general deterrence rationale.[61]

Just deserts, or retribution, is intended as a reinforcement of the community's commitment to legal norms and looks exclusively to the gravity of the single past offense for which the offender has just been convicted,[62] whereas each of the other theories seeks to curb the offender and others from committing antisocial acts in the future.[63] The perceptions of the general public appear relevant to any attempt at scaling the seriousness of given offenses,[64] since this theory requires a proportionality between the gravity of the offense and the severity of the punishment meted out to the offender. Most recent literature on the philosophy of punishment has generally supported a just deserts theory.[65]

These various purposes have each often been urged as the basis for a system of sanctions, but usually in the context of some confusing "combination"; rarely has the individual significance of each theory been considered.[66] Moreover, the very categorization of theories proferred here is not exhaustive; rather, it is suggestive of the philosophical currents that a sentencing commission should explore in greater depth.[67] Future research is needed in this area, and it should consist of three main components: (1) a review of the literature with an eye toward discerning and categorizing the specific criteria (and weighting systems) suggested by the various theories; (2) an assessment of the relevance of each of these theories (and their principal criteria) to pertinent offense categories; and (3) the development and testing of alternative guidelines models specifically derived from such assessments.

The Legal Approach

In constructing empirically derived sentencing guidelines systems, we have found that analogies and precedents for our work have been strongly welcomed by the judicial consumers of our research. Thus, the statistical concept of "mean terms-decisions," for example, has seemed less foreign to judges when explained in terms of making the presently implicit "going rate" or tariff system more explicit.[68] Similarly, while the canvas of a broadly philosophical body of literature is essential to provide a conceptual framework for the endeavors of researchers working for a sentencing commission, we must remember the judicial audience to which the guidelines will eventually be addressed. The examination and summary of a relevant body of case law, statutory compilations, administrative regulations, and law review commentary will provide this audience with the desired precedents upon which to base a useful sentencing guidelines system. Analogies from other states and nations will be useful and appreciated.

As surveyed in Chapter 8, at both the Supreme Court level and in the other federal and state courts, there is a present body of case law concerning sentencing. The 1949 *Williams v. New York*[69] and 1959 *Williams v. Oklahoma*[70] decisions by the U.S. Supreme Court, in particular, gave trial court judges an extremely wide latitude to consider any items they deemed relevant to sentencing given offenders. Indeed, the Eighth Circuit Court of Appeals has referred to these two decisions as providing "sentencing guidelines" to trial court judges.[71] In the Supreme Court, the various death penalty cases provided us with express Supreme Court language concerning the relevance of the various theories of punishment to the infliction of a particular sanction.[72] Moreover, in terms likely to be applied in the future to less grave penalties than capital punishment, the Supreme Court insisted that mandatory sanctions will not be permitted when they fail to provide an opportunity for reflection upon specific aggravating and mitigating circumstances concerning the offense and the offender.[73]

At the federal circuit court and district court levels, specific factors of apparent relevance have been dealt with on a constitutional basis. There is a developing body of case law, touched upon in Chapter 8, concerning the propriety of considering arrest records and other unproven charges as against convictions only, the effect of pleading guilty as opposed to being convicted after a jury trial, and many other specific variables such as whether the sex or age of an offender is as illegitimate a sentencing consideration as the race or the religion of that offender. Nowhere have these decisions been collected or analyzed, however, with regard to developing a coherent body of useful information for sentencing judges. An operational sentencing guidelines system must assemble and organize this body of precedent if we expect that system to be actually utilized in practice. This is a logical task for a sentencing commission to undertake.

In addition, I would note that the concept of sentencing guidelines—in a much different context—is not unknown to the justice system. Various statutes and administrative orders have often spelled out factors that should or must be considered and that should also be collected and analyzed. As one example, on February 24, 1977, Assistant Attorney General Donald I. Baker issued an internal memorandum entitled "Guidelines for Sentencing Recommendations in Felony Cases Under the Sherman Act." In that document, Mr. Baker began: "A primary purpose of these guidelines is to provide a means by which sentencing recommendations will be more rationale and equitable."[74] This is, of course, the same purpose that a sentencing commission's sentencing guidelines are intended to serve with regard to sentencing itself. One significant difference is that Mr. Baker's guidelines related to a narrow category of antitrust offenses and failed therefore to incorporate any context of proportionality with regard to other federal offenses.[75] Nevertheless, this and other relevant documents must be thoroughly reviewed, summarized, and categorized in terms of their ultimate utility for any sentencing commission.

Each jurisdiction's statutory structure must also be analyzed; useful comparisons could furthermore be drawn to the statutes in other states. Many states place, in their penal codes, listings of aggravating and mitigating factors—such as were described in Chapter 8, but in a different format. As crime-specific guidelines are developed these comparisons should prove especially valuable. During the national study, we prepared such comparisons for our internal use. C example may help explain their usefulness. Suppose we are constructing guidelines for assaultive offenses in a hypothetical jurisdiction and are considering whether or not particular victims of the assault should be looked upon differently. Would it not be helpful to know, as we found out, that twenty-six states enhance the penalty for an assault if it is upon a police officer or correctional employee? Or that thirteen states aggravate penalty if the attack is upon a child? Or that five raise the penalty if the assault is upon a teacher? Such statutory aggravating or mitigating factors—especially if they are not found in the instant jurisdiction's penal code—provide useful discussion points for the consideration of those establishing sentencing policy.

The Standards Approach

While the precise way of looking at the problem that I suggest here has not been attempted before, analogous efforts have been made, and they need to be carefully scrutinized, reviewed, and assessed with regard to their relevance for a sentencing commission. A number of prominent national commissions and reform groups have studied sentencing and suggested standards, many of which should be incorporated in an operational sentencing guidelines system. Recent government efforts must also be evaluated for the theoretical and practical contributions they can make to guidelines development.

As a demonstration of how often we seem to "reinvent the wheel" in our perceptions of research needs, we could turn to the 1931 Report of the National Commission on Law Observance and Enforcement (the Wickersham Commission). In their "Summary of Major Subjects or Topics Requiring Further Study or Research," the commission proposed: "Development, in some detail, of the procedure which should govern the ascertainment of facts and hearings on the 'isposition of the offender, such as types of evidence ... and other 'ated problems; indeed an intensive and comprehensive search into, lysis of and statement concerning the principles, techniques and dures to be applied to the disposition of the offender."[76] The ent's Commission on Law Enforcement and Administration of (1967)[77] and the National Advisory Commission on Criminal tandards and Goals (1973)[78] in many ways echoed these con-ll three commissions, however, did make detailed studies endations that must be taken into account.[79]

of prominent law reform groups have also addressed same issues and come up with model acts or suggest-he American Law Institute, as part of its monumen-reating the Model Penal Code, studied sentencing distinguishing "persistent," "professional," and ly abnormal" offenders for extended terms of incarceration, because their patterns of behavior were felt to be significant.[80] The National Council on Crime and Delinquency has promulgated a Model Sentencing Act that stresses the concept of "dangerousness" and the value of distinguishing "racketeers" for special treatment.[81]

The American Bar Association Project on Standards for Criminal Justice several years ago completed an eighteen volume series reporting its conclusions relating to the desirable standards that should obtain in the administration of the criminal justice system.[82] At least five of those volumes impinge directly on our concerns, while others do so peripherally. The commentary to these standards provides some of the sharpest legal analysis available on these important issues. The ABA is presently updating these standards, and the views of the organized bar must of course be considered.

The National Conference of Commissioners on Uniform State Laws is about to adopt a *Uniform Corrections Act* that comes nearest of all to our concerns. The recent draft of the sentencing article proposes a sentencing commission model for the nation, and the commentators urge our own earlier empirical efforts as the basis for an operational sentencing guidelines system: "Since the U. S. Board of Parole's experience proved successful, work has begun on the development of sentencing matrices for the front end of the sentencing system—Sentencing Guidelines: Structuring Judicial Discretion, a project funded by L. E. A. A. . . . Sentencing Commissions established under the act will have a base of methodology from which to proceed.[83]

Other recent governmental efforts must also be assessed and incorporated. First, the predecessor legislation to S. 1437 elicited voluminous commentary and congressional reports, as well as a Library of Congress impact statement, all of which will have to be digested. Second, the National Institute of Corrections recently funded an ongoing effort to study some of these very same issues; as the results of that effort become available, additional insights may be offered. Third, the Department of Justice recently awarded a contract to survey public opinion, as well as the opinions of federal justice system personnel, concerning their perceptions of the efficacy of a sentencin guidelines system. Fourth, the sentencing guidelines research eff that I directed has produced a number of internal reports on man the issues discussed in this book. Fifth, a number of states—inc ing New York, Massachusetts, Minnesota, Florida, Michigan, consin, New Jersey, and Pennsylvania—have engaged in voluminous sentencing commission/judicial sentencing gui studies that are well worth reviewing.

Finally, although international comparisons are alwa they are often extremely worthwhile. England's prestigious fice Advisory Council on the Penal System, for example, had been charged with surveying that nation's sentencing procedures and found it very useful to compare present English practice with that prevailing in other countries; indeed, I testified by invitation before that body. In its final report, the Council summarized its findings:

> We looked at the various penalty systems current in the different juris-
> dictions of the United States, and noted in particular the recent legisla-
> tive moves away from indeterminacy in sentencing towards a more
> fixed and rigid penalty structure. The system of sentencing guidelines,
> now making headway in the United States as a compromise between
> indeterminate sentencing and a system of more or less fixed penalties,
> was of special interest to us, both because the philosophy of steering a
> middle course between a wide and a narrow discretion in sentencing
> was the one which most appealed to us, and because the practical solu-
> tion of adopting a penalty system based on the existing practice of the
> courts was that which we ourselves ultimately decided to recommend.[84]

Education by comparative example is not a one way street; it should prove very helpful to our own work to add the insights of those not constrained by our assumptions as to what is the usual or normal practice. It is often noted, for example, that American sentences are longer than those prevailing elsewhere in the world.[85] Verified and crime-specific information of this nature would be an interesting component of any sentencing commission's efforts to sug-gest equitable sentence lengths, as well as providing assistance to judicial resolution of the crucial "in/out" decision.

'MUTATIONS

our earlier empirical work, we realized that a multifaceted
was essential in order to deal with the complex phenomena
behaviors and societal response mechanisms. During our
earch, for example, the branching network, or bifurcat-
cisionmaking (See Figure 9-2) evolved.[86] This view of
bifurcated decision allowed us to contemplate differ-
l combinations. On the one hand, the most signifi-
involved the "in/out" decision, and this could be
d indeed, this is the approach that Justice
k in developing a sentencing guidelines sys-
ington. In Chicago, Newark, Denver, and
elines accounted for both the "in/out" de-
g decision in terms of incarcerative
ate doing so in the future, we have not
es for the "out" decision—that is, a model

that would suggest which among a range of nonincarcerative sentences would be most equitable and/or effective. (This would be a major and innovative reform that should be evaluated by a sentencing commission.) The significance of the bifurcated model is that different factors (and different weightings) may very well be involved in the distinct stages of the decisionmaking process, and this model allows us to account for these differences.

Figure 9–2. Sentencing as a Bifurcated Decisionmaking Process.

"In"	Decision as to Length of Incarceration Probation
"Out"	
	Fine
	Other (nonincarcerative)

Over time, the general model for Denver has become a mixed general-generic model. It is possible that crime-specific guidelines and branching network systems will be combined in the future. Indeed a host of empirically derived permutations are conceivable. We have a cautionary lesson from the history of parole guidelines. In "transferring" the guidelines concept from the federal to the state systems, qualitative differences emerged that had important content (not merely stylistic) consequences. In the actual case, the federal matrix approach had to be abandoned for a sequential model in the Southern states. The lesson is that if we treat concept "transfer" as we do technology transfer, then the likelihood is that the situational facts in each state will be forced out of shape to conform to a model developed earlier for a different set of facts. This creates a false reality—an artificial construct—that can only damage the viability of the guidelines concept. Instead, an open and basic approach is essential in order to ensure that any models developed will be designed to conform to reality rather than vice versa.

Taking the philosophical approach by itself, we may find value as well in separating the five principles, then associating them with specific crimes, and then relating each one of them to the others. As Lejins has noted, we have too often in the past ignored the *interactive* effects of the aims of punishment. "Current practice is to consider each of these goals one at a time. . . . Research should be undertaken to determine the effects of achieving each of these objectives separately and in combination."[87]

The various models falling under the "legal approach" and "standards approach" study areas could similarly be compared and combined. Indeed, they already have been in many jurisdictions, as witness the various state commissions set up to perform comparative analyses of existing statutes with the ABA standards and/or the National Advisory Commission's standards and goals.

SYNTHESIS

Once we have adequately studied both the "is" and the "ought" of sentencing guidelines, we may combine them in a manner to assure that both eventually coincide in the final products promulgated by a sentencing commission. While some might argue the value of the "ought" concept alone, we must measure the dangers inherent in such potentially artificial constructs; one trap, for example, that constantly bedevils researchers—particularly those of an academic bent with few "real world" policy concerns—is the extreme position that one may be forced to take to maintain a consistent model. Pushed to their extremes, for example, each of the philosophical theories addressed above fails to take account of two significant realities—the pragmatic compromises necessary to achieve constructive reform in a democratic society and, even more important, the incredible richness and diversity of human behavior, desire, and philosophy.

As to the first of these, no one even remotely familiar with the debates surrounding the passage of S. 1437 can fail to be impressed with the legislative compromise that it represents on so many controversial issues. While dogmatic theorists are angered and dismayed, the results are usually to the public's benefit, since all segments of society will have had a felt input in this important aspect of our justice system. Further compromises may be expected in the selection of commissioners, the appointment of staff, and—much to the point here—the actual construction and implementation of sentencing guidelines systems.

The second reality is even more significant, for it makes us realize that the minor "inconsistencies" in philosophy inherent in this particular compromise are not only pragmatically necessary, but philosophically desirable. Over the past few years, I have had occasion to discuss these issues with literally hundreds of trial court judges, as well as with other system officials and members of the general public. I have often heard stories about the consistently "tough" or "soft" or "right-wing" or "left-wing" judge, parole board member, and so on. I have just as often been struck by the reality that the criminal justice system is comprised of complicated human beings, who are usually striving to do good in their own view and who, in their own way, achieve pragmatic behavioral philosophies that avoid extremes and reflect the varied human experience. Even the stern retributionist judge, for example, will often slip into rehabilitationist jargon and thought to deal with a youthful first offender; judges who scoff at psychological explanations of criminal behavior will still "take a chance" on alcohol detoxification and drug treatment programs. Conversely, even the most treatment-oriented judge will "let the public know" (general deterrence) that white collar criminals cannot get away with their crimes or that "enough is enough" (specific deterrence) with regard to an incorrigible petty offender.

If the guidelines promulgated by a commission are to have meaning, they must account for this fact by identifying and weighting factors not simply according to abstract philosophy or even present practice, but in a synthesis geared to suit the infinite variety of criminal behavior situations encompassed by the realities facing the local trial court judge—that judge must receive concrete and useful guidance from the sentencing commission. Long-range philosophical goals must consider short-term realities; case law must be summarized to a useful end; statutory compilations must provide practical guidance; suggested standards must be made to conform to useful classifications.

The synthesis must involve both procedure and substance. The procedural synthesis will involve the design of a guidelines system uniquely constructed to suit the requirements of local sentencing judges, taking account of their needs and their wishes so as to establish a working system that these judges will want to use. The format of the system may take the grid, or grid alternate, approach often used in the past, but not necessarily; we have indeed previously considered at least two percentile approaches. One of these involves calculating scores as fractions of the maximum possible sentence based on identified criteria; the other involves a scaling procedure analogous to that often employed in judging government contracts (i.e., a certain number of points or percentage based on just deserts criteria, legal criteria, consistency criteria, etc.).[88]

The procedures of the sentencing commission should involve a commitment to research that will study much more than present practice; a major research area must be an assessment of the *effectiveness* of alternative sentencing measures. The procedural realities of each jurisdiction will have to be taken into account. Where, how, and under what circumstances, for example, does the choice of incarcerative institution or nonincarcerative program become a consideration? We may hope that the staff of the sentencing commission will conduct its research into sentencing in a scientific, investigatory rulemaking environment rather than an adversary or adjudicatory one; this is one of the benefits of the commission approach. Therefore, it may be expected that principled reform suggestions, based on practice and policy, are likely to emerge.[89]

A major procedural component, however, must be the dynamic feedback loop built into the system, which acts as an internal-external cybernetic review mechanism. As Judge Frankel emphasized: "There must be a commitment to change, to application of the learning as it is acquired. There must be a recognition that the subject will never be definitively 'closed,' that the process is a continuous cycle of exploration and experimental change."[90] While judges may sentence outside the suggested range, they must offer reasons for doing so. This takes advantage of the distinction between individual case-by-case decisionmaking and overall policy decisionmaking, providing an enabling mechanism for policy control and continuous modification. This is an evolutionary procedure aimed at improving justice and provides four protections against abuse of the system— self-review, peer review, commission review, and appellate review. The guideline sentence is a check, first of all, against the judge's own conscience, for—in the cases where the judge would go outside the guidelines—clearly articulable reasons must be offered, and unconscious bias should thus be averted. Peer review will take place at judicial conferences and also in the law review literature, as formerly hidden reasoning becomes open, acknowledged, and subject to critical commentary. Commission review and appellate review (each provided for in S. 1437) should provide a welcome start to finally developing a common law of sentencing.

The prescription offered in this book is not a panacea for the many ills of the criminal justice system. Obviously, for example, it does not address at all such issues as the root causes of crime, but it does deal with, and tries to relieve, the very real problems faced daily in the administration of justice.[91] The substantive synthesis that I propose will mean an integration of the "is" and the "ought," the present and the future, the practical and the hoped for, the empirical and the theoretical. We should aim at achieving no less than a system of whole justice, one that is sufficiently humane and individualized as to account for the unique circumstances of each offender, yet one that is also evenhanded enough to provide for an end to disparities and for the actual achievement of a system that openly and honestly provides equal justice under law.

NOTES

1. American Bar Association, Project on Minimum Standards for Criminal Justice, *Standards Relating to Appellate Review of Sentences,* Standard 1.2 (iv) (New York, 1968; approved draft); see

also J. J. Kilpatrick, "Study Fixes Guidelines for Equal Justice" (syndicated column), *Washington Star,* February, 12, 1977: "For the first time, some rational guidelines have been developed to assist judges in the agonizing task of fixing sentences on guilty defendants" (describing the federal project).

2. See S. 1437, The Criminal Justice Reform Act of 1978, Chapter 58, 95th Cong., 2d sess. (1978); *see* S. Rep. No. 605, 95th Cong., 1st sess., pt. I (1977).

3. As indicated *supra* Chapter 4, however, there is also a good deal of statewide guidelines activity by now.

4. See *supra* Chapter 3.

5. The National Institute of Law Enforcement and Criminal Justice has, however, recently funded research in Maryland and Florida that is intended to explore aspects of this regionalized approach and I have served as a consultant for this "Multijurisdictional Sentencing Guidelines Field Test."

6. On the other hand, the very concrete recognition of these differences would be a useful preliminary step to improving the state's data system.

7. This has been a particular problem for Minnesota's research team as the "outstate" area (i.e., those portions of the state outside the Minneapolis-St. Paul area) lacks many of the options available in the Twin Cities. Again, however, the clear recognition of this problem becomes suggestive of the necessary reforms *other* than guidelines that a sentencing commission will be uniquely capable of recommending.

8. M. E. Frankel, *Criminal Sentences: Law Without Order* 119 (New York: Hill and Wang, 1972) (emphasis in original). Note the much expanded charge given the Federal Sentencing Commission in S. 1437 at § §994–995. See also the charges given the Pennsylvania and Minnesota Sentencing Commissions, as well as the recent proposals of the New York State Executive Advisory Committee on Sentencing (The Morgenthau Committee), in its report, *Crime and Punishment in New York: An Inquiry Into Sentencing and the Criminal Justice System* (New York: Executive Advisory Committee on Sentencing, 1979).

9. *Supra* note 2; see also 1978 Minn. Laws, Ch. 723; and Pa. Act 319, November 1978.

10. National Conference of Commissioners on Uniform State Laws, *Uniform Corrections Act* §3-109 (Chicago: National Conference of Commissioners on Uniform State Laws, 1978 draft).

11. *Id.*, Comments to §3-112.

12. J. C. Coffee, Jr., "The Repressed Issues of Sentencing: Accountability, Predictability, and Equality in the Era of the Sentencing Commission," 66 *Georgetown Law Journal* 975 (1978). See also

the thoughts of the originator, M. E. Frankel, *supra* note 8 at 118–24. Two other extremely useful and thoughtful appraisals of the sentencing commission/judicial sentencing guidelines approach may be found in M. Zalman, "A Commission Model of Sentencing," 53 *Notre Dame Lawyer* 266 (1977); and P. O'Donnell, M. Churgin, and D. Curtis, *Toward a Just and Effective Sentencing System* (New York: Praeger, 1977). The most recent body to exhaustively review the various alternatives for sentencing reform, New York State's Executive Advisory Committee on Sentencing, *supra* note 8, recommended the guidelines approach and declared:

> The role of the Sentencing Commission is a key element of the guidelines model—and in our view a cardinal virtue. Unlike the legislature, such a Commission would have the time, the expertise and the flexibility to establish guidelines on the basis of careful and exhaustive study of existing sentencing practices, and to prescribe sentences designed to make informed use—when appropriate—of incapacitation and deterrence. The Commission would also monitor the operation of its guidelines, and periodically alter them on the basis of on-going research regarding their effectiveness and impact on other components of the criminal justice system (at 224–26).

13. *Supra*, Chapter 2.

14. R. Singer, "In Favor of 'Presumptive Sentences' Set by a Sentencing Commission," 24 *Crime and Delinquency* 401, 418–19 (October 1978).

15. This is in fact what happened in the states of New Jersey and Washington.

16. See Zalman, *supra* note 12.

17. Singer, *supra* note 14 at 419. The primary author and sponsor of S. 1437 is Massachusetts Senator Edward M. Kennedy, and he—certainly no novice in comprehending the realities of the legislative process—sees the very detachment of the commission as a major benefit:

> One of the strengths of the bill is that the commission, not the Congress, would determine the guidelines. The Congress does not have time to establish sentencing ranges for all the criminal situations which could develop. Nor is there much chance that it could avoid politicizing the entire issue of sentencing with vocal debate centering around harsher versus more lenient punishment. If the subjects of capital punishment, gun control, and criminal code reform offer any indication of how Congress would deal with the sensitive area of sentencing, the commission approach is much to be preferred.

E. M. Kennedy, "Criminal Sentencing: A Game of Chance," 60 *Judicature* 208, 213 (December 1976).

18. Here, I am in disagreement with some other sentencing commission advocates, notably O'Donnell, Churgin, and Curtis, *supra* note 12, who advocate, I think unnecessarily and undesirably, the abolition of both functions of parole. But see the reasoned analysis offered by D. T. Stanley, *Prisoners Among Us: The Problem of Parole* (Washington, D.C.: The Brookings Institute, 1976). See also the statement of R. Martinson and J. Wilks on saving the parole supervision function, prepared for delivery before the Senate Judiciary Committee and reprinted in *Reform of the Federal Criminal Laws: Hearings on S. 1437 and S. 31, S. 45, S. 181, S. 204, S. 260, S. 888, S. 979, and S. 1221, Part XIII*, 95th Cong., 1st sess., 9257–62 (1977). But see, however, I. Waller, *Men Released from Prison* (Toronto: Butterworths, 1974).

19. See the provisions to this effect in California. Cal. Penal Code §300 (West, 1977).

20. New York's "Rockefeller Drug Laws" provided lifetime parole for many drug offenders. (The harshest features of these laws were repealed as of September 1, 1979.)

21. *Supra* Chapter 2.

22. *Id.* Especially sources cited at note 28.

23. See the statement of Cecil C. McCall, Chair of the United States Parole Commission, prepared for delivery to the House Judiciary Subcommittee on Criminal Justice on April 18, 1978; see also J. J. Maffucci, "The New York State Board of Parole: Scapegoats of the Criminal Justice System," 50 *New York State Bar Journal* 640 (1978).

24. "It is significant to note that one of the most important problems within prison walls is that of coping with the often wide disparity of sentences. ... The Parole Board provides a safety valve to relieve inmate tensions by equalizing sentences and giving hope to those who live in despair." Maffucci, *supra* note 23 at 642. See also M. H. Sigler, "Abolish Parole?" 39 *Federal Probation* 42 (June 1975). In fact, the future functions of sentencing commissions in this regard are little understood, and I hope that this book will go a long way to explain of what those functions may be expected to consist.

25. L. T. Wilkins, J. M. Kress, D. M. Gottfredson, J. C. Calpin, and A. M. Gelman, *Sentencing Guidelines: Structuring Judicial Discretion–Report on the Feasibility Study* 1–3 (Washington, D.C.: USGPO, 1978).

26. See *The Uniform Corrections Act, supra* note 10.

27. R. O. Dawson, "Sentencing Reform: The Current Round," 88 *Yale Law Jounal* 440, 447 (1978), reviewing the book by O'Donnell, Churgin, and Curtis, *supra* note 12. The only exceptions proposed are

a small (10 percent) amount of good time to be used as an internal prison disciplinary sanction and, of course, executive clemency powers in extraordinary and compelling circumstances. With regard to this latter situation, the history of the special clemency board set up to review the cases of Viet Nam war draft evaders is instructive; see W. Strauss and L. Bashir, "Controlling Discretion in Sentencing," 51 *Notre Dame Lawyer* 919 (July 1976).

It is a sad commentary on our times that supporters of the guidelines approach have to defend its declaration of true time served from those who fear such statements will foster a public demand for longer sentences:

> It is important to point out that the fixed sentencing range agreed upon by the commission and imposed by the court would be very close to the *actual sentence now served by the offender*. It is likely that the guidelines would mandate sentences substantially less than the maximums now authorized by law. But in terms of actual time served, I do not see a radical change. Nor do I perceive the possibility of the guidelines approach increasing prison populations.

E. M. Kennedy, *supra* note 17 at 214 (emphasis in original).

28. See S. 1437 §994 (1).

29. *Supra* note 8.

30. "The guideline approach suggested by Kennedy and McClellan recognizes the intellectual difficulty of prescribing by statute precise penalties for scores of crimes and many kinds of offenders and defers to the political objections, raised most strongly by judges, to any sentencing system that denies them discretionary power." J. Q. Wilson, "Changing Criminal Sentences," *Harpers* 16, 17 (November 1977).

31. 28 C.F.R. §2.20 (revised 1978); see also 18 U.S.C. §4206.

32. D. M. Gottfredson, C. A. Cosgrove, L. T. Wilkins, J. Wallersten, and C. Rauh, *Classification for Parole Decision Policy* (Washington, D.C.: USGPO, 1978).

33. *Id.*

34. Interestingly enough, in developing sentencing guidelines for the use of the Washington state judiciary, we found that a general model fit the needs of the judges of the courts of general jurisdiction, whereas a generic model appeared more appropriate for use by the judges of the courts of limited jurisdiction (see Appendix D to this book); contact Justice Analysis Center, 301 Parkview Drive, Schenectady, New York 12303 for further information.

35. The large statewide data base available in New Jersey has already permitted the application of crime-specific models there.

36. As suggested *supra* Chapter 3, this discussion may actually be seen as an aspect of substantive due process. See M. Angel, "Substan-

tive Due Process and the Criminal Law," 9 *Loyola University of Chicago Law Journal* 61 (1977); and H. Packer, "The Aims of the Criminal Law Revisited: A Plea for a New Look at 'Substantive Due Process,' " 44 *Southern California Law Review* 490 (1971). Some of the literature on this subject will be touched upon in the present discussion.

37. One modern and useful exception is O'Donnell, Churgin and Curtis, *supra* note 12, who advocate just such judicial consideration, although in the context of an unfortunately mechanistic "lockstep" approach.

38. J. Q. Wilson, *Thinking About Crime* 173 (New York: Basic Books, 1975). Some antagonists of incapacitation point out that it ignores in-prison crime, particularly the homosexual rape that appears to be incident to long-term incarceration. Moreover, the societal gains of incapacitation are "necessarily limited. Almost all inmates are eventually released, and if the ex-offender leaves prison embittered, abandoned by family and friends, and without employable skills, he or she is likely to return to crime." R. McKay, "It's Time to Rehabilitate the Sentencing Process," 60 *Judicature* 223, 226 (December 1976). The public, however is fairly in tune with the short-term, outside of prison, crime-reduction goals of incapacitation. See also A. Blumstein, ed., *Deterrence and Incapacitation: Estimating the Effects of Criminal Sanctions on Crime Rates* (Washington, D.C.: National Academy of Sciences, 1978).

39. Ernest van den Haag does point out, however: "The only total, permanent, and irrevocable incapacitation is execution. Other punishments, such as imprisonment, produce partial, revocable, and usually temporary incapacitation." Professor van den Haag further notes that some "punishments, such as fines, are not incapacitating at all; others, such as denying a license to practice a profession or to engage in an activity (e.g., driving) are partially incapacitating." E. van den Haag, *Punishing Criminals: Concerning a Very Old and Painful Question*, ch. 5 (New York: Basic Books, 1975).

40. See T. Sellin and M. E. Wolfgang, *The Measurement of Delinquency* (New York: John Wiley and Sons, 1964); C. F. Wellford and M. Wiatrowski, "On the Measurement of Delinquency," 66 *Journal of Criminal Law and Criminology* 175 (1975); G. S. Bridges and L. S. Lisagor, "Scaling Seriousness: An Evaluation of Magnitude and Category Scaling Techniques," 66 *Journal of Criminal Law and Criminology* 215 (1975); and R. Figlio, "The Seriousness of Offenses: An Evaluation by Offenders and Non-Offenders," 66 *Journal of Criminal Law and Criminology* 189 (1975).

41. See H. Mannheim and L. T. Wilkins, *Prediction Methods in Relation to Borstal Training* (London: HMSO, 1955); L. T. Wilkins,

"Statistical Methods of Parole Prediction: Their Effectiveness and Limitations" (Paper presented at the Annual Meeting of the American Academy of Psychiatry and the Law, Boston, Massachusetts, October 1975); and F. H. Simon, *Prediction Methods in Criminology* (London: HMSO, 1971).

42. The "false positive" problem has spurred much discussion of late; it is complex but important to understand. Assume, for the purposes of this explanation, that incapacitation is the exclusive purpose of sentencing and that probation and prison are the exclusive options available to the sentencing judge. The judge's sole function then becomes predicting the offender's dangerousness (which, for the sake of simplicity, I will here equate with recidivism). If the judge predicts that the offender will recidivate, then the judge sentences the offender to prison; if the judge predicts the offender will *not* recidivate, then the judge sentences the offender to probation.

Now, using this incapacitative model, what outcomes are possible? The following table may clarify the concept, as well as explain the literal significance of the term "false positive":

Table 9–1. Hypothetical Sentencing Example Illustrating the False Positive Problem.

Initial Prediction of Recidivism (Sentence)			Actual Outcome of Prediction	
			True	False
	Positive (incarceration)	40%	T+ 25%	F+ 15%
	Negative (probation)	60%	T− 50%	F− 10%
			75%	25%

Judges in this hypothetical example have made a *positive* prediction (i.e., that the defendant *will* recidivate) 40 percent of the time and a *negative* prediction (i.e., that the defendant will *not* recidivate) 60 percent of the time; thus, 40 percent of this sample population was incarcerated and 60 percent placed on nonincarcerative probation.

Now, what results *occur*, and what results do we *perceive*? In this hypothetical example, the predictions of the local judiciary have actually been correct 75 percent of the time. As Dean Norval Morris reminds us, however, the judicial failure rate will only be *recognized* as 10 percent rather than 25 percent. This is because of what he refers to as "the mask of over-prediction." The 10 percent of false negative predictions have been found out; they will violate probation and be returned to court. Those falsely incarcerated, however, will not be known to us, for their "success" on probation will never be ascertained. Dean Morris poses the dilemma this way: "How many false positives can be justified for the sake of preventing crimes by the true positives?" Dean Morris's perceptive elaboration of this point may be found in *The Future of Imprisonment*, ch. 3 (Chicago: University of Chicago Press, 1974); see also B. D. Underwood, "Law and the Crystal Ball: Predicting Behavior with Statistical Inference and Individualized Judgment," 88 *Yale Law Journal* 1408 (June 1979); and A. J. Reiss, Jr., "The Accuracy, Efficiency and Validity of a Prediction Instrument," 61 *American Journal of Sociology* 552 (1951).

The reader will note that the problem is not limited to a theory of incapacitation; it applies to any theory involving some element of prediction, specifically including deterrence and rehabilitation. For an explanation of how this problem affected the national sentencing guidelines research project and how we coped with it, see J. M. Kress and J. C. Calpin, "Research Problems Encountered in Moving Towards Equity in Judicial Decisionmaking," 4 *Justice System Journal* 71 (Fall 1978).

43. F. Zimring and G. Hawkins, *Deterrence: The Legal Threat in Crime Control* (Chicago: University of Chicago Press, 1973). See also F. Zimring, *Perspectives on Deterrence* (Washington, D.C.: USGPO, 1971); G. Antunes and A. L. Hunt, "The Deterrent Impact of Criminal Sanctions: Some Implications for Criminal Justice Policy," 51 *Journal of Urban Law* 145 (1973); Blumstein, *supra* note 38; and N. Morris and F. Zimring, "Deterrence and Correction," 381 *The Annals of the American Academy of Political and Social Science* 137 (1969).

44. E. van den Haag, *supra* note 39 at ch. 13.

45. Thus, not all repeat offenses would be seen as signs of "failure" or count as recidivism. A rapist later arrested for shoplifting, for example, might be viewed as a relatively "successful" case.

46. G. S. Becker, "Crime and Punishment: An Economic Approach," 78 *Journal of Political Economy* 169 (1968); R. A. Carr-Hill and N. H. Stern, "An Econometric Model of the Supply and Control of Recorded Offenses in England and Wales," 2 *Journal of Public Economics* 289 (November 1973); G. J. Stigler, "The Optimum Enforcement of Laws," 78 *Journal of Political Economy* 526 (1970); and S. S. Brier and S. E. Fienberg, *Recent Econometric Modelling of Crime and Punishment: Support for the Deterrence Hypothesis?* (St. Paul: University of Minnesota, Department of Applied Statistics, Technical Report No. TR-307, 1978).

47. See R. M. Dawes, *Fundamentals of Attitude Measurement* (New York: John Wiley and Sons, 1972).

48. Compare, for example, T. Chiricos and G. P. Waldo, "Punishment and Crime: An Examination of Some Empirical Evidence," 18 *Social Problems* 200 (1970); to Zimring and Hawkins, *supra* note 43.

49. Blumstein, *supra* note 38.

50. *Id.*

51. Much of the criticism of rehabilitative theory, however, has been directed at the attempt to achieve *prisoner* reform. As Senator Kennedy put it:

> I am not, of course, advocating the abolition of prison rehabilitation programs. Indeed, I believe they should be encouraged and expanded. What I am advocating is an end to the comforting but totally unrealistic notion that rehabilitation of the convicted criminal can serve as a justification for imposing a prison sentence. Not only is such a sentence unfair to the individual, it doesn't seem to do much good in "curing" the offender.

Kennedy, *supra* note 17 at 212. The attack may sound novel, but as long ago as 1861, Fyodor Dostoevsky wrote: "Of course, prisons and penal servitude do not reform the criminal; they only punish him and protect society from further attacks on its security." *The House of the Dead* (prison life in Siberia) (New York: Macmillan, 1915) at 13.

52. See, for example, C. S. Lewis, "The Humanitarian Theory of Punishment," 144 *Twentieth Century* 1 (Autumn 1948); S. Glueck and E. Glueck, *Unravelling Juvenile Delinquency* (Cambridge, Mass.: Harvard University Press, 1951); M. Fry, *Aims of the Law* (London: Victor Gollancz, 1951); B. Wootton, *Crime and the Criminal Law* (London: Stevens and Sons, 1963); F. A. Allen, "Legal Values and the Rehabilitative Ideal," in *The Borderland of Criminal Justice* 25 (Chicago: University of Chicago Press, 1964); K. Menninger, *The Crime of Punishment* (New York: Viking Press, 1966); and D. J. Rothman, *The Discovery of the Asylum* (Boston: Little, Brown and Co., 1971).

53. See R. Martinson, "What Works? Questions and Answers About Prison Reform," 35 *The Public Interest* 22 (Spring 1974); F. Cole and S. M. Talarico, "Second Thoughts on Parole," 63 *American Bar Association Journal* 972 (July 1977); W. C. Bailey, "Correctional Outcome: An Evaluation of 100 Reports," 57 *Journal of Criminal Law and Criminology* 153 (1966); R. Hood and R. Sparks, *Key Issues in Criminology* (New York: Macmillan, 1970); and L. T. Wilkins, *Evaluation of Penal Measures* (New York: Random House, 1969).

54. See, for example, American Friends Service Committee, *Struggle for Justice* (New York: Hill and Wang, 1971); D. Fogel, *We*

Are the Living Proof: The Justice Model for Corrections (Cincinnati: W. H. Anderson Co., 1975); Morris, *supra* note 42; G. R. Newman, *The Punishment Response* (Philadelphia: J. B. Lippincott, 1978); Twentieth Century Fund Task Force on Criminal Sentencing, *Fair and Certain Punishment* (New York: McGraw-Hill, 1976); van den Haag, *supra* note 39; A. von Hirsch, *Doing Justice: The Choice of Punishments* (New York: Hill and Wang, 1976); and Wilson, *supra* note 38.

55. J. Andenaes, *Punishment and Deterrence* (Ann Arbor: University of Michigan Press, 1974); and Zimring and Hawkins, *supra* note 43.

56. M. E. Wolfgang and M. Reidel, "Race, Judicial Discretion, and the Death Penalty," 407 *The Annals of the American Academy of Political and Social Science* 119 (1973); I. Ehrlich, "The Deterrent Effect of Capital Punishment: A Question of Life and Death," 65 *American Economic Review* 397 (1975); T. Sellin, *Capital Punishment* (New York: Harper and Row, 1967); van den Haag, *supra* note 39; Newman, *supra* note 54; and H. Bedau, ed., *The Death Penalty in America* (Chicago: Aldine Publishing Co., 1967).

57. C. R. Tittle and C. H. Logan, "Sanctions and Deviance: Evidence and Remaining Questions," 7 *Law and Society Review* 371 (1973). See also C. F. Wellford, "Deterrence: Issues and Methodologies in the Analysis of the Impact of Legal Threat in Crime Control," 65 *Journal of Criminal Law and Criminology* 117 (1974).

58. J. Bentham, *An Introduction to the Principles of Morals and Legislation*, in *Collected Works*, ed. H. J. Burns and H. L. A. Hart (London: Athcone Press, 1970). For a valuable summary of Bentham's views, see G. Geis, "Pioneers in Criminology: Jeremy Bentham," *Journal of Criminal Law and Criminology* 159 (1955). See also C. Beccaria, *On Crimes and Punishments*, tr. H. Paolucci (New York: Bobbs-Merrill, 1963); G. Newman, *supra* note 54; and L. Radzinowicz, *A History of English Criminal Law and Its Administration from 1750* (London: Stevens, 1948). Although most modern writers on deterrence refer back to the works of Jeremy Bentham and Cesare Beccaria, the theory of deterrence is at least as old as Aristotle. In his *Nicomachean Ethics*, Aristotle proclaimed: "[I]t is the nature of the many to be ruled by fear rather then shame, and to refrain from evil not because of the disgrace but because of the punishments." *Ethics of Aristotle* (tr. J. A. K. Thomson) (Middlesex: Penguin, 1976) at 336. Probably the most ardent advocate of the general deterrent principle today is Professor van den Haag, *supra* note 39.

59. Morris, *supra* note 42; I. Ehrlich, "The Deterrent Effect of Criminal Law Enforcement," 1 *Journal of Legal Studies* 259 (1972); and J. Andenaes, "Deterrence and Specific Offenses," 38 *University of Chicago Law Review* 537 (1971).

60. See William J. Chambliss's classic study of parking law violators, "The Deterrent Influence of Punishment," 12 *Crime and Delinquency* 70 (January, 1966); as well as H. L. Ross, "The Scandinavian Myth: The Effectiveness of Drinking-and-Driving Legislation in Sweden and Norway," 4 *Journal of Legal Studies* 19 (1975).

61. J. Feinberg, *Doing and Deserving* (Princeton, N.J.: Princeton University Press, 1970); H. L. A. Hart, *Punishment and Responsibility* (New York: Oxford University Press, 1968); and H. M. Hart, "The Aims of the Criminal Law," 23 *Law and Contemporary Problems* 401 (1958).

62. See M. K. Harris, "Disquisition on the Need for a New Model for Criminal Sanctioning Systems," 77 *West Virginia Law Review* 263 (1975). I should add, however, that most present-day advocates of a just deserts theory would also include the offender's past criminal record as a legitimate judicial consideration. See von Hirsch, *supra* note 54; and Twentieth Century Fund, *supra* note 54.

63. It is for this reason that Baroness Wootton, *supra* note 52, has declared retribution a backward approach not worthy of consideration. On the other hand, the absence of predictions under a strict just deserts theory avoids the false positive problem (*supra* note 42) and thus provides just deserts with its moral justification, according to its advocates.

64. See the sources cited *supra* notes 40 and 47.

65. See American Friends Service Committee, *supra* note 54; Morris, *supra* note 42; Newman, *supra* note 54; Twentieth Century Fund, *supra* note 54; von Hirsch, *supra* note 54; and O'Donnell, Churgin, and Curtis, *supra* note 12.

66. See the typical penal code provision, and the quotation from State v. Ivan, 33 N.J. 197 (1960), found *supra* Chapter 3 at notes 29 and 30.

67. Much fuller discussions of the philosophies of punishment may be found in Newman, *supra* note 54; N. Walker, *Sentencing in a Rational Society* (Middlesex: Penguin, 1969); G. O. W. Mueller, *Sentencing–Process and Purpose* (Springfield, Ill.: Charles C. Thomas, 1977); van den Haag, *supra* note 39; A. Neier, *Criminal Punishment: A Radical Solution* (New York: Stein and Day, 1976); von Hirsch, *supra* note 54; H. M. Hart, *supra* note 60; and H. L. A. Hart, *supra* note 60. This list is not exhaustive as there has been a recent resurgence in the popularity of these issues. An illustrative (and again not exhaustive) list of purposes of punishment *other* than the five I listed—and ones that do not necessarily fall neatly into my divisions—that have been suggested by the foregoing authors includes atonement, denunciation, education, expiation, humanitarianism, moral reinforcement, neutralization, penitence, reform, reintegration, replacement, resocialization, restraint, retali-

ation, separation, social cohesion, social defense, social protection, vengeance, and vindication.

68. I should mention the particular forthrightness displayed by the British Home Office with regard to this recognition of a tariff. See Advisory Council on the Penal System, *Sentences of Imprisonment–A Review of Maximum Penalties* (London: HMSO, 1978). See also R. Hood, *Sentencing the Motoring Offender* (London: Heinemann, 1972); and D. R. Cressey, "Law, Order and the Motorist," in R. Hood, ed., *Crime, Criminology, and Public Policy* (New York: Free Press, 1974). But see L. Radzinowicz and R. Hood, "An English Attempt to Reshape the Sentencing Structure," 78 *Columbia Law Review* 1145 (June 1978).

69. Williams v. New York, 337 U.S. 241 (1949).

70. Williams v. Oklahoma, 385 U.S. 576 (1959).

71. Woosley v. United States, 478 F.2d 139, 143 (8th Cir. 1973).

72. See Furman v. Georgia, 408 U.S. 238 (1972); Gregg v. Georgia, 428 U.S. 153 (1976); Proffitt v. Florida, 428 U.S. 242 (1976); Jurek v. Texas, 428 U.S. 262 (1976); Woodson v. North Carolina, 428 U.S. 280 (1976); Roberts v. Louisiana, 428 U.S. 325 (1976); Gardner v. Florida, 430 U.S. 349 (1977); and Coker v. Georgia, 433 U.S. 584 (1977).

73. See cases cited *supra* note 72.

74. Unpublished Memorandum. See, however, Mr. Baker's published views in D. I. Baker and B. A. Reeves, "The Paper Label Sentences: Critiques," 86 *Yale Law Journal 619*–25 (1977).

75. *Supra,* Chapter 3.

76. National Commission on Law Observance and Enforcement ("Wickersham Commission"), *Report on Penal Institutions, Probation and Parole* (Washington, D.C.: USGPO, 1931) at 48.

77. President's Commission on Law Enforcement and the Administration of Justice, *The Challenge of Crime in a Free Society* (Washington, D.C.: USGPO, 1967).

78. National Advisory Commission on Criminal Justice Standards and Goals, *A National Strategy to Reduce Crime*(Washington, D.C.: USGPO, 1973).

79. See specific references to the relevance of the work the National Advisory Commission on Criminal Justice Standards and Goals in Wilkins et al., *supra* note 25 at 77–79.

80. American Law Institute, *Model Penal Code*, Proposed Official Draft (Philadelphia; American Law Institute, 1962) (especially article 7.); P. W. Tappan, "Sentencing Under the Model Penal Code," 23 *Law and Contemporary Problems* 528 (1958); and H. Wechsler, "Sentencing, Correction, and the Model Penal Code," 109. *University of Pennsylvania Law Review* 465 (1961).

81. Advisory Council of Judges, National Council on Crime and Delinquency, "Model Sentencing Act," see also Advisory Council

Judges, National Council on Crime and Delinquency, "Guide to the Judge in Sentencing in Racketeering Cases," 14 *Crime and Delinquency* 97 (1968); and H. L. Kozol, R. J. Boucher, and R. F. Garofalo, "The Diagnosis and Treatment of Dangerousness," 18 *Crime and Delinquency* 371 (October 1972).

82. See, for example, American Bar Association, Project on Minimum Standards for Criminal Justice, *Standards Relating to Sentencing Alternatives and Procedures* (approved draft) (New York: American Bar Association, 1968).

83. National Conference on Commissioners on Uniform State Laws, *supra* note 10 at Comments to §3-112.

84. Advisory Council on the Penal System, *supra* note 68 at 8.

85. Id., see also I. Waller, *Men Released from Prison* (Toronto: University of Toronto Press, 1974).

86. Wilkins, et al., *supra* note 25 at 1–2.

87. P. Lejins in Hearings, *supra* note 18.

88. See O'Donnell, Churgin, and Curtis, *supra* note 12.

89. Dawson, *supra* note 27 at 449.

90. Frankel, *supra* note 8 at 118–19.

91. Kilpatrick *supra* note 1:

> If the guidelines catch on—and there is every reason to believe they will—the system will provide the greatest advance in criminal justice since the development of probation and parole systems many years ago. Equal justice under law, as every court observer knows, is an unattainable ideal. We will never get there. But it remains the great goal—and these guidelines constitute a big step in the right direction.

Appendixes

Introduction

These appendixes are included as a demonstration of the range and variety of sentencing guidelines systems; they also further elaborate upon the explanations offered in Part Two of the main text. Each appendix consists of a different instructional booklet for the calculation of guideline sentences. Such booklets are prepared for the use of each jurisdiction's judiciary and are applicable only in that jurisdiction.

Appendix A reprints a booklet prepared in October 1977, for the Denver District Court, by the staff of the sentencing guidelines research project described earlier in this book. It is included in full as an example of a general model even though it is actually somewhat "mixed," as presented here, including as it does some generic components in the Felony 4 and Felony 5 classes of crime.

Appendix B reprints one of three booklets prepared in December 1977, for the Maricopa County Superior Court, also by the staff of the sentencing guidelines research project. Only the booklet used in sentencing drug offenders has been included since this should be sufficient to give the reader a sense of how a generic model may more specifically describe a type of criminal behavior; the booklets relating to violent and property offenses have not been included.

Appendix C reprints one of two manuals prepared by the staff of the Philadelphia Court of Common Pleas in March 1979; the other manual is applicable to crimes not against a person. This manual is included as one example of how guidelines were developed by a research team not directed by this author.

Appendix D reprints one of two booklets prepared by Justice Analysis Center, Inc., under contract to the State of Washington Administrator for the Courts; the other was prepared for use by the judges of the courts of general jurisdiction and covered a wider range of offenses. The sentencing guidelines system for the courts of limited jurisdiction was approved and went into effect in April 1979. This booklet is included not only as an example of a statewide system, but also because it demonstrates that guidelines are applicable to a range of less serious offenses as well as to those included in most of the earlier sentencing guidelines systems.

While every effort has been made to provide accurate and timely examples, the reader should be aware of certain limitations in reviewing these appendixes. (1) Sentencing guidelines systems are intended to be flexible representations of present operational court policy and thus change over time; the systems described here may therefore not represent the contemporary system observed by the reader. For example, it is already known that, by the time of this book's publication, the Maricopa system will have been drastically revised to reflect changes made in the Arizona penal code. (2) None of the booklets reprinted here reflect the complete package of materials received by the judge prior to sentencing a given offender or, indeed, even the complete sentencing guidelines system available to the judge; that would have been prohibitively voluminous to reprint as well as too individualized to each case. Nevertheless, Appendix A contains a relatively complete general model, and Appendix B does reprint in full the Maricopa generic model's booklet for drug offenses. (3) Minor stylistic changes have been made in the versions reprinted here so as not to confuse the reader. For example, the pagination of the booklets has been revised and booklet appendixes have been incorporated. (4) Finally, none of these systems are offered as exemplary models for other jurisdictions to apply. Each was uniquely constructed to fulfill the needs and desires of the local judiciary in each of the given jurisdictions.

Appendix A

Denver District Court Instructional Booklet for the Calculation of Guideline Sentences (General Model)

COMPUTATION OF GUIDELINE SENTENCES

The guideline sentence is computed by adding weights assigned to items of information relating to pertinent characteristics of both the crime and the criminal. The weights are then totaled into a separate score for the offense (Offense Score) and the offender (Offender Score). Those scores are then located on a two-dimensional sentencing grid. There is a different grid for each statutory class of offense. The Offense Score is located on the Y, or vertical, axis and the Offender Score on the X, or horizontal, axis. By plotting the two scores against each other (much as one plots mileage figures on a road map), one is directed to the cell in the grid which indicates the suggested length and/or type of sentence.

Three items of information comprise the Offense Score. First, is the intra-class rank which will either be a "1," "2," or "3" for all classes except Felony Four in which a rank of "4" is possible. Second, is the seriousness modifier. As will be noted later (see seriousness modifier), the three factors which make up this item (injury, weapon usage, drug sale) are not additive and only the highest score of the three is to be included in the computations. Therefore, it is impossible to add a "3" or "4" for this factor and the only way a "2" can be added is if a death occurred. Third, is the victim modifier. Although it is being added in a purely mathematical sense, note that it can only be a zero or a negative one and thus the overall score will either not change or will be reduced by one. Add the three coded values to obtain an Offense Score which will range from one to five for a Felony Three, Felony Five and Misdemeanor One, Two, or Three and from one to six for a Felony Four.

GUIDELINE SENTENCE WORKSHEET

Offender ——————————————————Docket Number ——————————
Judge ——————————————————————Date ———————————
Offense(s) Convicted Of: ——————————————————————
——————————————————————
——————————————————————

OFFENSE CLASS (MOST SERIOUS OFFENSE)
  A.   Intra-Class Rank   ———+
  B.   Seriousness Modifier   ———+

       0 = No injury 0 = No weapon 0 = No sale of drugs
       1 = Injury   1 = Weapon   1 = Sale of drugs   OFFENSE CLASS
       2 = Death
  C.   Victim Modifier (Crime Against Person)   ———=

       0 = Unknown victim
       −1 = Known victim
OFFENDER SCORE
  A.   Current Legal Status   ———+

       0 = Not on probation/parole, escape   OFFENSE SCORE
       1 = On probation/parole, escape
  B.   Prior Juvenile Convictions   ———+

       0 = No convictions
       1 = 1–3 convictions
       2 = 4 or more convictions
  C.   Prior Adult Misdemeanor Convictions   ———+

       0 = No convictions
       1 = 1–3 convictions
       2 = 4 or more convictions
  D.   Prior Adult Felony Convictions   ———+

       0 = No convictions
       1 = 1 conviction
       3 = 2 or more convictions
  E.   Prior Adult Probation/Parole Revocations   ———+

       0 = None
       2 = One or more revocations
  F.   Prior Adult Incarcerations (Over 30 Days)   ———=

       0 = None   OFFENDER
       1 = 1 incarceration   SCORE
       3 = 2 or more incarcerations
Guideline Sentence ——————————————————————

Actual Sentence   ——————————————————————

Reasons (if actual sentence does not fall within guideline range):

Six items of information comprise the Offender Score: current legal status, prior juvenile convictions, prior adult misdemeanor con victions, prior adult felony convictions, prior adult probation/parole revocations, and prior adult incarcerations (over 30 days). Add the six coded values to get an Offender Score which will range from zero to 13.

GUIDELINE SENTENCE WORKSHEET

DATE

Code the date of sentencing, deferred prosecution, or deferred judgment.

OFFENSE(S) CONVICTED OF (TITLE AND STATUTE NUMBER)

In those cases involving an attempt (18-2-101) or conspiracy (18-2-201) conviction, please do not list the title or statute number of those general sections but rather that of the specific offense for which the offender was convicted of attempting or conspiring to commit.

For example, a conviction for an attempt to commit second degree burglary should be written as "18-4-203—attempt to commit second degree burglary."

OFFENSE CLASS (MOST SERIOUS OFFENSE)

When coding the Offense Class, use an "F"' to abbreviate Felony and an "M" to abbreviate Misdemeanor. For example a conviction for a Misdemeanor Two offense would be coded as "M2."

Use the statutory class as the criterion to decide seriousness, e.g., a Felony Three would be the more serious offense when a defendant was convicted of a Felony Three and a Felony Four. Drug offenses have been placed in the closest appropriate Felony/Misdemeanor class based on the maximum sentence possible. For example, possession of narcotic drugs which carries a maximum sentence of fourteen years incarceration is classified with the Felony Four's whose maximum period of incarceration is ten years. Dispensing of dangerous drugs carries a five year maximum sentence and accordingly is classified with Felony Five's.

OFFENSE SCORE

Intra-Class Rank

Refer to the appropriate category *infra* for the intra-class rank. When an offender has been convicted of more than one offense, code the intra-class rank of the most serious offense (see instructions for offense class). If the offender has been convicted of two offenses of the same intra-class rank, select the offense whihc is against the person. Robbery (18-4-301), aggravated robbery (18-4-302) and theft from the person (18-4-401 (5)) are considered offenses against the person for purposes of this item. If neither offense of the same class and rank is against the person or if they both are against the person, it does not matter which offense you focus on.

Seriousness Modifier

0=No injury	0=No weapon	0=No sale of drugs
1=Injury	1=Weapon	1=Sale of drugs
2=Death		

The three factors that comprise this item are not additive and only the highest score of the three is to be coded. Therefore, it is impossible to code a "3" or "4" and the only way a "2" can be coded is if a death occurred. Base your assessment of seriousness on the "official version of the offense" section of the presentence investigation report. The first modifier is that of physical injury. Value "1" includes both minor and serious injury.

The second modifier concerns weapon usage. "Weapon" refers to any article or device which is capable of causing injury. It does not include parts of the body, e.g., hand or foot, unless the offender is a professional in some form of self-defense. Value "1" includes the presence and/or use of a weapon. When unclear as to whether a weapon was present, e.g., hand in the pocket, score "0."

The third modifier concerns the distribution and/or manufacture of drugs. If the offender was the seller, dispenser, or manufacturer of drugs, score as "1." If the offender had in his possession a drug with the intent to dispense that drug (see e.g., 12-22-412(3)), score as "1." If the offender was in possession of a drug, or if his role in a drug offense is unclear, code as "0."

Victim Modifier

0=Unknown victim or crime not against person
−1=Known victim

Since this item is only concerned with victims of a crime against the person, automatically code a "0" when the crime is not one against the person.

Robbery (18-4-301), aggravated robbery (18-4-302) and theft from the person (18-4-401 (5)) are considered offenses against the person for purposes of this variable. A victim known to the offender would be a person with whom the offender had contact prior to the occasion of the offense, such as family, friends, acquaintances, or professional associates (e.g., employer/employee). Consider a bar fight victim as being known to the offender unless circumstances to the contrary are indicated. Where there is no information concerning the victim, code as "0."

OFFENDER SCORE

Current Legal Status

0=Not on probation/parole, escape
1=On probation/parole, escape
Code "1" if, at the time the current offense was committed, the offender was on escape status, or on adult probation or parole as a result of an earlier adjudication. Consider supervision under a deferred prosecution or deferred judgment agreement as probation. All other situations, including pending charges, bail, ROR, are not probation or parole and therefore should be coded "0."

Prior Juvenile Convictions

0=No convictions
1=1-3 convictions
2=4 or more convictions
Count only juvenile convictions or juvenile court equivalents which are for offenses which would be criminal if the offender was processed as an adult. Exclude juvenile "status" offenses, (e.g., PINS, Wayward Youth, Truancy, Neglected Youth), and traffic convictions. Do not count a probation or parole revocation as a "conviction" unless an actual conviction for a new criminal offense took place. Convictions which cannot be clearly identified as being "criminal" in nature should not be counted. Convictions for multiple offenses at one adjudication are to be counted as one conviction.

Prior Adult Misdemeanor Convictions

0=No convictions
1=1-3 convictions
2=4 or more convictions
Exclude present conviction. Prior deferred prosecution and deferred judgments which still appear in the offender's prior criminal history record are to be considered convictions for this variable. Ex-

clude all traffic offenses except the two which are considered criminal—vehicular homicide (18-3-106) and vehicular assault (18-3-205). However, note that both those are felonies and therefore would not be included in a misdemeanor count. Exclude military offenses for which there is no criminal counterpart, e.g., AWOL. Convictions which are not clearly identified by a statute number but which appear to be comparable to either a felony or misdemeanor under Colorado statutes are to be counted as misdemeanors. If the prior conviction was for an offense which is not clearly identified but appears to be comparable to either a misdemeanor or a petty offense under the Colorado statutes, do not count it. Offenses for which no information is given, just that a conviction was obtained, are also not to be counted. If convicted of multiple offenses at one adjudication count as one conviction and use the most serious offense (see Offense Class) for determining whether it was a misdemeanor or a felony.

Prior Adult Felony Convictions

0=No convictions
1=1 conviction
3=2 or more convictions

Exclude present conviction. Prior deferred prosecution and deferred judgments which still appear in the offender's prior criminal history record are to be considered convictions for this variable. Exclude all traffic offenses except the two which are considered criminal—vehicular homicide (18-3-106) and vehicular assault (18-3-205). Exclude military offenses for which there is no criminal counterpart, e.g., AWOL. Convictions which are not clearly identified by a statute number but which appear to be comparable to either a felony or misdemeanor under Colorado statutes are to be counted as misdemeanors. Offenses for which no information is given (i.e., beyond the fact that a conviction was obtained) are also not to be counted. If convicted of multiple offenses at one adjudication count as one conviction and use the most serious offense (see Offense Class) for determining whether it was a misdemeanor or felony.

Prior Adult Probation/Parole Revocations

0=None
2=One or more revocations

This is a dichotomous yes/no item which refers to any *adult* probation or parole revocation up to the time the presentence investigation report was written. Assume that the offender successfully completed any prior probation/parole unless it was specifically noted that he/she was revoked. Do not presume that a conviction for a new offense, while the offender was on probation/parole, to have resulted in a revocation unless it was so stated.

Prior Adult Incarcerations (over 30 days)

0=None
1=1 incarceration
3=2 or more incarcerations

This item refers to actual incarcerations resulting from *adult* criminal convictions. Do not count pre-trial or presentence detentions. Do not count incarcerations of 30 days or less or one month or less. Confinement after an escape or parole violation is not a new incarceration; revocation of probation resulting in incarceration is a new incarceration for this item.

INTRA-CLASS RANKS

Felony 3

Intra-Class Rank 1
18-4-202	First Degree Burglary
18-4-203(2)	Second Degree Burglary (if burglary is of a dwelling)

Intra-Class Rank 2
18-3-202	Assault in the First Degree
18-8-208(2)	Escapes (if escapee convicted of a felony other than a class one or two felony)

Intra-Class Rank 3
18-3-402	Sexual Assault in the First Degree
18-4-302	Aggravated Robbery

Felony 4

Intra-Class Rank 1
18-4-401(2)	Theft (if amount taken is $200 or more)
18-4-402(4)	Theft of Rental Property (if value is $200 or more)
18-4-410(2)	Theft by Receiving ($200 or more)
18-4-501	Criminal Mischief (if damage amounts to $100 or more)
18-5-102	First Degree Forgery
18-5-103	Second Degree Forgery

Intra-Class Rank 2

18-3-106	Vehicular Homicide
18-3-203	Assault in the Second Degree
18-4-103(2)	Second Degree Arson (if damage amounts to $100 or more)
18-4-202	Conspiracy to Commit First Degree Burglary
18-4-203(2)	Attempt to Commit Second Degree Burglary (if burglary is of a dwelling)
18-4-203(2)	Second Degree Burglary

Intra-Class Rank 3

18-3-207	Criminal Extortion
18-3-403	Attempt to Commit Sexual Assault in the Second Degree (use of force, intimidation, or threat)
18-3-403	Sexual Assault in the Second Degree
18-3-404	Sexual Assault in the Third Degree (use of force, intimidation, or threat)
18-4-301	Robbery
18-4-302	Attempt to Commit Aggravated Robbery
18-4-302	Conspiracy to Commit Aggravated Robbery
18-8-502	Perjury in the First Degree
18-12-109(3)	Unlawful Possession or Use of Explosives or Incendiary Devices

Intra-Class Rank 4

18-3-104	Manslaughter
18-3-405	Sexual Assault on a Child

Felony 4 Drugs

Intra-Class Rank 1

12-22-302	Unlawful to Possess (narcotic drugs) (possess, sell, receive, buy, dispense)
12-22-412(1)	Unlawful Acts (dangerous drugs) (dispense)
12-22-412(3)	Unlawful Acts (dangerous drugs) (possession with intent to dispense)
12-22-412(12D)	Cannabis (possession of more than one ounce) (second offense)

Intra-Class Rank 2

12-22-322(4)	Narcotic Drugs (theft from person authorized to administer)
12-22-412(12G)	Cannabis (transfer or dispense to person under 18)

Felony 5

Intra-Class Rank 1

14-6-101	Non-Support of Spouse and Children—Penalty—Bond
18-4-203(2)	Attempt to Commit Second Degree Burglary
18-4-204	Third Degree Burglary
18-4-205	Possession of Burglary Tools
18-4-401(2)	Attempt to Commit Theft (if amount taken is $200 or more)
18-4-401(2)	Conspiracy to Commit Theft (if amount taken is $200 or more)
18-4-402(4)	Attempt to Commit Theft of Rental Property (if value is $200 or more)
18-4-501	Attempt to Commit Criminal Mischief (if damage amounts to $100 or more)
18-4-502	Attempt to Commit First Degree Criminal Trespass
18-4-502	Conspiracy to Commit First Degree Criminal Trespass
18-4-502	First Degree Criminal Trespass
18-5-102	Attempt to Commit First Degree Forgery
18-5-103	Attempt to Commit Second Degree Forgery
18-5-205(3C)	Fraud by Check ($200 or more)
18-7-206	Pimping
18-8-105(5)	Accessory to Crime (if person so helped committed a class 3, 4, or 5 felony)
26-2-130(1)	Fraudulent Acts ($500 or more)

Intra-Class Rank 2

18-3-203	Attempt to Commit Assault in the Second Degree
18-3-205	Vehicular Assault
18-3-206	Menacing (if deadly weapon employed)
18-4-203(2)	Conspiracy to Commit Second Degree Burglary
18-4-301	Attempt to Commit Robbery
18-4-401(5)	Attempt to Commit Theft From the Person of Another (if no force, threat or intimidation used, no matter what the value unlawfully appropriated)
18-4-401(5)	Conspiracy to Commit Theft From the Person of Another (if no force, threat or intimidation used, no matter what the value unlawfully appropriated)

18-4-409(4)	Joyriding (if person is in possession of car for over 72 hours)
18-5-113	Criminal Impersonation
42-2-206	Driving After Judgment Prohibited

Intra-Class Rank 3

18-3-405	Attempt to Commit Sexual Assault on a Child
18-4-301	Conspiracy to Commit Robbery
18-4-401(5)	Theft From the Person of Another (if no force, threat or intimidation used, no matter what the value unlawfully appropriated)
18-12-108	Possession of Weapon by Previous Offender

Felony 5 Drugs

Intra-Class Rank 1

| 12-22-302 | Attempt to Possess Narcotic Drugs |
| 12-22-412(1) | Attempt to Commit Unlawful Acts (dangerous drugs) (dispense) |

Intra-Class Rank 2

| 12-22-319 | Fraud or Deceit (narcotic drugs) (1st offense) |
| 12-22-412(1) | Conspiracy to Commit Unlawful Acts (dangerous drugs) (dispense) |

Misdemeanor 1

Intra-Class Rank 1

18-4-505	First Degree Criminal Tampering
18-5-104	Third Degree Forgery
18-5-106	Criminal Possession of a Second Degree Forged Instrument

Intra-Class Rank 2

| 18-3-204 | Assault in the Third Degree |

Intra-Class Rank 3

| 18-3-105 | Criminally Negligent Homicide |
| 18-3-404 | Sexual Assault in the Third Degree |

Misdemeanor 2

Intra-Class Rank 1

| 12-22-412(6) | Unlawful Acts (dangerous drugs—except cannabis) |
| 12-22-412(12D) | Cannabis (possession of more than one ounce) (first offense) |

18-3-204	Attempt to Commit Assault in the Third Degree
18-4-402(3)	Theft of Rental Property (if value is $50 or more and less than $200)
18-4-409(2)	Joyriding
18-4-410(3)	Theft by Receiving ($50-199)
18-4-501	Criminal Mischief (if the damage amounts to less than $100)
18-4-506	Second Degree Criminal Tampering
18-5-107	Criminal Possession of Third Degree Forged Instrument
18-5-202	Fraudulent Use of a Credit Device (if value amounts to less than $100)
18-5-204	Criminal Possession of Credit Device
18-12-105	Unlawfully Carrying a Concealed Weapon

Intra-Class Rank 2

18-3-303	False Imprisonment
18-4-401(3)	Theft (if value is $50 or more and less than $200)
18-5-205(3B)	Fraud by Check ($50-199)
18-8-103	Resisting Arrest

Intra-Class Rank 3

18-4-103(3)	Second Degree Arson (if damage amounts to less than $100)
18-6-401	Child Abuse
18-12-106	Prohibited Use of Weapons

Misdemeanor 3

Intra-Class Rank 1

26-2-130(1)	Fraudulent Acts (less than $500)
26-2-130(2A)	Fraudulent Acts (aid to dependent children)

Intra-Class Rank 2

18-3-208	Reckless Endangerment
18-4-401(3)	Attempt to Commit Theft (if value is $50 or more and less than $200)
18-4-503	Second Degree Criminal Trespass

Intra-Class Rank 3

18-3-206	Menacing (if no deadly weapon involved)

SENTENCING GRIDS

FELONY 3

Offender Score

Offense Score	0-1	2	3	4	5-8	9-10	11-13
4-5	5-7 yrs. minimum 8-10 yrs. maximum	7-9 yrs. minimum 12-15 yrs. maximum	10-12 yrs. minimum 15-20 yrs. maximum	12-15 yrs. minimum 15-20 yrs. maximum	12-15 yrs. minimum 15-20 yrs. maximum	17-22 yrs. minimum 35-40 yrs. maximum	17-22 yrs. minimum 35-40 yrs. maximum
3	OUT	7-9 yrs. minimum 12-15 yrs. maximum	7-9 yrs. minimum 12-15 yrs. maximum	7-9 yrs. minimum 12-15 yrs. maximum	8-10 yrs. minimum 15-20 yrs. maximum	17-22 yrs. minimum 35-40 yrs. maximum	17-22 yrs. minimum 35-40 yrs. maximum
2	OUT	5-7 yrs. minimum 12-15 yrs. maximum	5-7 yrs. minimum 12-15 yrs. maximum	5-7 yrs. minimum 12-15 yrs. maximum	8-10 yrs. minimum 12-15 yrs. maximum	17-22 yrs. minimum 35-40 yrs. maximum	17-22 yrs. minimum 35-40 yrs. maximum
1	OUT	OUT	OUT	5-7 yrs. minimum 12-15 yrs. maximum	5-7 yrs. minimum 12-15 yrs. maximum	8-10 yrs. minimum 12-15 yrs. maximum	8-10 yrs. minimum 15-20 yrs. maximum

FELONY 4
Offender Score

Offense Score	0-1	2	3	4-5	6-7	8	9-10	11-13
4-6	Indeterm minimum 8-10 yrs. maximum	Indeterm. minimum 8-10 yrs. maximum	Indeterm. minimum 8-10 yrs. maximum	Indeterm. minimum 8-10 yrs. maximum	Indeterm. minimum 8-10 yrs. maximum	Indeterm. minimum 8-10 yrs. maximum	Indeterm. minimum 8-10 yrs. maximum	Indeterm. minimum 8-10 yrs. maximum
3	OUT*	Indeterm. minimum 3-5 yrs. maximum	Indeterm. minimum 3-5 yrs. maximum	Indeterm. minimum 3-5 yrs. maximum	Indeterm. minimum 5-7 yrs. maximum	Indeterm. minimum 8-10 trs. maximum	Indeterm. minimum 8-10 yrs. maximum	Indeterm. minimum 8-10 yrs. maximum
2	OUT	OUT*	Indeterm. minimum 3-5 yrs. maximum	Indeterm. minimum 3-5 yrs. maximum	Indeterm. minimum 5-7 yrs. maximum	Indeterm. minimum 8-18 yrs. maximum	Indeterm. minimum 8-10 yrs. maximum	Indeterm. minimum 8-10 yrs. maximum
1	OUT	OUT	OUT*	Indeterm. minimum 3-5 yrs. maximum	Indeterm. minimum 3-5 yrs. maximum	Indeterm. minimum 3-5 yrs. maximum	Indeterm. minimum 5-7 yrs. maximum	Indeterm. minimum 8-10 yrs. maximum

*Potential candidate for work project, split sentence, or community corrections.

FELONY 4
Drug Offenses

Offense Score	Offender Score						
	0	1	2–4	5–6	7–9	10–13	
3	OUT	2–3 yr. minimum 5–7 yr. maximum	2–3 yr. minimum 5–7 yr. maximum	2–3 yr. minimum 5–7 yr. maximum	2–3 yr. minimum 5–7 yr. maximum	2–3 yr. minimum 5–7 yr. maximum	
2	OUT	OUT	2–3 yr.* minimum 5–7 yr. maximum	2–3 yr. minimum 5–7 yr. maximum	2–3 yr. minimum 5–7 yr. maximum	2–3 yr. maximum 5–7 yr. maximum	
1	OUT	OUT	OUT	OUT	2–3 yr. minimum 2½–4 yr. maximum	2–3 yr. minimum 2½–4 yr. maximum	

*Potential candidate for work project, split sentence, or community corrections.

FELONY 5
Offender Score

Offense Score	0–1	2	3	4–5	6–8	9–13
4–5	Indeterm. minimum 4–5 yrs. maximum	Indeterm. minimum 4–5 yrs. maximum	Indeterm. minimum 4–5 yrs. maximum	Indeterm. minimum 4–5 yrs. maximum	Indeterm. minimum 4–5 yrs. maximum	Indeterm. minimum 4–5 yrs. maximum
3	OUT	OUT*	Indeterm. minimum 4–5 yrs. maximum	Indeterm. minimum 4–5 yrs. maximum	Indeterm. minimum 4–5 yrs. maximum	Indeterm. minimum 4–5 yrs. maximum
2	OUT	OUT	OUT	Indeterm. minimum 4–5 yrs. maximum	Indeterm. minimum 4–5 yrs. maximum	Indeterm. minimum 4–5 yrs. maximum
1	OUT	OUT	OUT	Indeterm. minimum* 3–4 yrs. maximum	Indeterm. minimum 3–4 yrs. maximum	Indeterm. minimum 3–4 yrs. maximum

*Potential candidate for work project, split sentence, or community corrections.

FELONY 5
Drug Offenses

Offender Score

Offense Score	1	2	3–4	5–8	9–10	11–13
3	OUT	OUT	1½–2 yrs. minimum 3–4 yrs. maximum	2–3 yrs. minimum 4–5 yrs. maximum	3–4 yrs. minimum 4–5 yrs. maximum	3–4 yrs. minimum 4–5 yrs. maximum
1–2	OUT	OUT	OUT	1–1½ yrs. minimum 2½–4 yrs. maximum	1–1½ yrs. minimum 3–4 yrs. maximum	2–2½ yrs. minimum 4–5 yrs. maximum

MISDEMEANOR 1

Offender Score

Offense Score	0–1	2–3	4–5	6–7	8–11	12–13
4–5	20–24 mo.	20–24 mo.	20–24 mo.	20–24 mo.	20–24 mo.	20–24 mo.
3	OUT*	9–12 mo.	14–18 mo.	20–24 mo.	20–24 mo.	20–24 mo.
2	OUT	OUT	14–18 mo.	14–18 mo.	14–18 mo.	20–24 mo.
1	OUT	OUT	OUT	9–12 mo.	14–18 mo.	14–18 mo.

Potential candidate for work project or community corrections.

MISDEMEANOR 2

		Offender Score					
Offense Score		0	1	2	3-4	5-7	8-13
	4-5	9-12 mo.	9-12 mo.	9-12 mo.	9-12 mo	9-12 mo.	9-12 mo.
	3	OUT*	9-12 mo.	9-12 mo.	9-12 mo.	9-12 mo.	9-12 mo.
	2	OUT	OUT	OUT	4-7 mo.	5-8 mo.	9-12 mo.
	1	OUT	OUT	OUT	OUT	3-5 mo.	7-10 mo.

*Potential candidate for work project or community corrections.

MISDEMEANOR 3

Offender Score

	0–1	2–3	4–5	6–8	9–13
4–5	4–6 mo.	4–6 mo.	4–6 mo.	4–6 mo.	4–6 mo.
3	OUT	2–4 mo.	2–4 mo.	2–4 mo.	4–6 mo.
2	OUT	OUT	2–4 mo.	2–4 mo.	2–4 mo.
1	OUT	OUT	OUT	2–4 mo.	2–4 mo.

Offense Score

Appendix B

Maricopa County Instructional Booklet for the Calculation of Guideline Sentences—Drugs (Generic Model)

This is one of three different manuals that will be used in providing additional information for the sentencing judge when imposing criminal sentences in Maricopa County. These manuals have been divided into the following offense types: Violent, Property, Drugs. The Sentence Data Analysis Program herein outlined is a result of a sentencing study project conducted with the assistance of staff from the Federally Funded Sentencing Guidelines Research Project.

The project studied actual case histories in Maricopa County and sentences imposed by the judges sitting there for the purpose of determining and analyzing the essential factors involved in the sentencing decision. A statistical analysis of this information was made. The end-product produces in graph form the projected median sentences in the cases analyzed. The purpose of these graphs is to supply the judge with statistical information not previously available to him/her. They are intended as tools to aid the judge in the exercise of his/her sentencing discretion. The information supplied herein is not binding on the sentencing judge in any sense.

In determining which offense and offense type is to be used in calculating the Data Sentencing Range, the following rules will apply:

(1) ONE OFFENSE AT CONVICTION

When there is one offense at conviction, use the manual whose type is the same as the offense at conviction.

Before coding, check to see that the offense is listed in the particular manual being used. If the offense is *not* listed, check each of the other manuals. If the offense is not listed in any, use the manual whose offense type is the same as the offense at conviction.

(2) MULTIPLE OFFENSES AT CONVICTION— SAME OFFENSE TYPE

(a) When there are two or more offenses at conviction, all of which are of the same offense type, the crime with the highest inter-class rank is to be considered the most serious.
(b) When there are two or more offenses at conviction, all of which are of the same offense type and have the same inter-class ranks, any of the offenses can be considered the most serious.
(c) When there are two or more offenses at conviction, all of which are of the same offense type, and one or more of the offenses has not been listed, determine the inter-class ranks of those offenses. The offense with the highest inter-class rank is to be considered the most serious.

(3) MULTIPLE OFFENSES AT CONVICTION— DIFFERENT OFFENSE TYPES

(a) When there are two or more offenses at conviction, of different offense types, the offense which would receive the more severe Data Sentencing Range is to be considered the most serious offense. Refer to the section on Preparation of the Sentencing Data Analysis Sheet for instructions on how to determine the Data Sentencing Range.
(b) When there are two or more offenses at conviction, and one or more of the offenses has not been listed, determine the inter-class ranks and type of that offense. The offense whose Data Sentencing Range is the most severe is to be considered the most serious.

OFFENSE SCORE

A. Inter-Class Rank

Refer to the listing of inter-class ranks. When there are two or more offenses at conviction of the same offense type, code the highest inter-class rank. If one or more of the offenses at conviction has not been ranked here, then apply the following rules to determine the offense's inter-class rank:

Inter 1: This category contains those crimes that by statutory definition can receive a maximum sentence of up to and including ten years.

Inter 2: Within this category you will find those crimes as defined by statute which can receive a possible maximum sentence of up to and including thirty years.

Inter 3: Within this category are crimes that may receive a maximum sentence of up to and including life.

B. Description of Drug Involved

−1 =Cannabis or drugs listed in Dangerous Drug Act (§632-1901 and seq.)

1=Drugs listed in Uniform Narcotic Drug Act (§36-1001 and seq.) This item is concerned with the actual criminal behavior of the offender as delineated in the official description of the offense in the presentence report. If both of the above categories of drugs are involved in the real offense behavior, code "1." For example, if the official description of the offense shows that the offender was found in possession of both heroin and marijuana, code "1."

C. Number of Criminal Events

0=One

1=Two or more

The focus of this item is on the actual criminal behavior of the offender as detailed in the official description of the offense contained in the presentence investigation report. Criminal events are distinct crimes, separated either by time or distance and are to be distinguished from multiple charges or counts that may emerge from one criminal event, and from prior criminal behavior that has previously been disposed of by the criminal justice system. For example, if the official description of the offense indicates that the offender has burglarized three homes before his apprehension, the number of events would be coded "1," even though the three burglaries may have been joined in a single indictment/information. Count only incidents of criminal behavior that can clearly be distinguished as separate events.

OFFENDER SCORE

Legal Status at Time of Offense

0=Not under State control

1=Under State control

Code "0" if at the time of the commission of the offense, the offender was not under State control as a result of civil or criminal action. Voluntary hospitalization (as opposed to court-ordered hospitalization) and military service (absent disciplinary actions) should not be considered forms of social control for the purposes of this item.

Code "1" if, at the time of the commission of the offense, the offender was subject to criminal justice control—such as the following: other criminal actions pending; outstanding bench, arrest or extradition warrants; pre-trial release (bail, bond, ROR); pre-trial or post-conviction incarceration; escape; deferred prosecution; adult or juvenile probation, parole or temporary release. Also include such forms of State control as mandatory hospitalization for treatment, observation, diagnosis, diagnostic and treatment center commitments, AWOL, escape from military confinement, or pending military disciplinary action.

Prior Juvenile Convictions

0=None or one
1=Two or more

Consider only prior juvenile convictions for offenses that would be criminal had the offender been convicted as an adult. Exclude juvenile status offenses such as PINS, Wayward Youth, Truancy, Neglected Youth, etc., and traffic and military convictions for which there is no civilian counterpart. Do not regard a probation or parole revocation as a prior juvenile conviction unless an actual conviction for a new crime has occurred in conjunction with it. If an offender has been convicted of multiple offenses at one adjudication, count as one prior conviction. Prior juvenile convictions for offenses that are not clearly identified by statutory title or code are to be counted, but if there is no way to discern whether or not the multiple offenses mentioned stem from the same adjudication, count as one prior conviction. For example, if the record shows that the offender has been previously convicted as a juvenile, with no further elaboration, code "0."

Prior Juvenile Incarcerations (Over 30 Days)

0=None
1=One or more

Consider only prior juvenile incarcerations resulting from convictions for offenses that would be criminal had the offender been convicted as an adult. Do not count pre-trial or presentence detentions. Exclude prior juvenile incarcerations after convictions for juvenile status offenses such as PINS, Wayward Youth, Truancy, Neglected Youth, etc., and for traffic and military offenses for which there is no civilian counterpart. Do not count incarcerations of one month or less. Reconfinement after an escape or parole violation is *not* a new incarceration for the purposes of this item; revocation of probation resulting in incarceration *is* a new incarceration.

Prior Adult Convictions

0=None or one
1 =Two or more

Exclude present offense(s), juvenile adjudications and traffic and military offenses for which there is no civilian counterpart. A conditional release is *not* a conviction for this item. A probation or parole revocation should not be counted as a prior adult conviction unless it occurs in conjunction with an actual conviction for a new crime. If an offender has been convicted of multiple offenses at one adjudication, count as one prior conviction. Prior adult convictions for offenses that are not clearly identified by statutory title or code are to be counted, but if there is no way to discern whether or not the multiple offenses mentioned stem from the same adjudication, count as one prior conviction. For example, if the record indicates that the offender has prior adult convictions, with no additional information provided, code as "0."

Prior Adult Convictions Against-the-Person

0=None
1=One or more

This item refers to prior adult convictions for offenses listed in the Violent manual and also to prior adult convictions for offenses not included therein that can be characterized as personal (e.g., Rape, Second Degree). Exclude present offense(s) and juvenile adjudications. Do not count prior adult convictions for crimes belonging to Property and Drug crime groupings, or traffic and military convictions for which there is no civilian counterpart. A conditional release is *not* a conviction for this item. A probation or parole revocation should not be counted as a prior adult conviction against-the-person unless it occurs in conjunction with a new conviction for a crime against-the-person. If an offender has been convicted of multiple crimes against-the-person at one adjudication, count as one prior adult conviction against-the-person. Prior adult convictions for offenses that cannot be clearly identified as violent should not be considered for the purposes of this item. For instance, if the record shows that an offender has been previously convicted as an adult, with no further elaboration, code "0."

Prior Adult Incarcerations (over 30 days)

0=None
1=One
2=Two or More

This item refers to incarcerations of over 30 days, resulting from prior adult convictions. Do not count pre-trial or presentence detentions. Exclude prior adult incarcerations for traffic and military offenses for which there is no civilian counterpart. Reconfinement after an escape or parole violation is *not* a new incarceration; revocation of probation resulting in incarceration *is* a new incarceration for this item.

Employment Status

−1=Employed full or part-time
0=Unemployed

This variable is to be coded for those offenders who were free at the time of the presentence investigation report and for those who were detained (e.g., no bail).

If detained at any time prior to sentencing for the present offense, code the offender's status immediately prior to the initial detention. If the offender was not detained, code work status at time of presentence investigation. Detention refers to pre- or post-trial confinement (e.g., not bailed). If more than one period of detention as a result of the present offense, consider the first substantial detention only in coding this item. Detention does *not* refer to detention upon arrest while awaiting initial appearance for bail setting. As a rule-of-thumb in coding this item, consider detentions only if longer than 48 hours.

Code "−1" if the offender was employed full or part-time. Include here those in the military service.

Code "0" for those offenders who were unemployed or incarcerated for a prior offense (regardless of any prison employment).

INTER-CLASS RANKS DRUGS

Inter 1: Maximum Sentence Up to and Including Ten Years (Least Serious)

32-1969(A)	Attempt to Commit Illegal Sales, Disposition or Possession of Prescription Only Drugs (No Intent to Defraud)
36-1017(A)	Attempt to Obtain Narcotics by Fraud or Deceit
36-1002.05(A)	Conspiracy to Grow, Process, and Possess Marijuana

36-1002(A)	Conspiracy to Possess Narcotic Drugs
13-379	Drug Incapacitation, Toxic Vapors, Poisons
36-1002.05(A)	Growing, Processing and Possession of Marijuana
32-1969(A)	Illegal Sales, Disposition and Possession of Prescription Only Drugs (No Intent to Defraud)
32-1970(C)	Manufacture, Equipment Disposition, and Possession of Dangerous Drugs (No Intent to Sell)
32-1970(C)	Manufacture, Equipment Disposition, and Possession of Dangerous Drugs (No Intent to Sell—First Offense)
36-1017(A)	Obtaining Narcotics by Fraud or Deceit
36-1002.06(A)	Possessing Marijuana for Sale
36-1002(A)	Possession of Narcotic Drugs

Inter 2: Maximum Sentence Up to and Including Thirty Years

36-1002.07(A)	Conspiracy to Import and Transport Marijuana
36-1002.02(A)	Conspiracy to Import and Transport Narcotic Drugs, Sales and Traffic
36-1002.05(B)	Growing, Processing and Possessing Marijuana (Prior Felony Drug Offense)
36-1002.06(B)	Possessing Marijuana for Sale (Prior Felony Drug Offense)
36-1002(B)	Possession of Narcotic Drugs (Prior Felony Drug Offense)
36-1002.01(A)	Possession of Narcotic Drugs for Sale

Inter 3: Maximum Sentence Up to and Including Life (Most Serious)

36-1002.07(A)	Attempt to Import and Transport Marijuana
36-1002.07(A)	Import and Transport of Marijuana
36-1002.07(C)	Import and Transport of Marijuana (Two or More Prior Felony Drug Offenses)
36-1002.02(A)	Import and Transport of Narcotic Drugs, Sales and Traffic
36-1002.02(A)	Import and Transport of Narcotic Drugs, Sales and Traffic—Enhancement
36-1002.02(B)	Import and Transport of Narcotic Drugs, Sales and Traffic (Prior Felony Drug Conviction)
32-1970(C)	Manufacture, Equipment Disposition, Possession of Dangerous Drugs (Intent to Sell)
36-1002.01(B)	Possession of Narcotic Drugs for Sale (Prior Felony Drug Offense)

36-1002.01(A)   Possession of Narcotic Drugs for Sale—Enhancement

PREPARATION OF THE SENTENCING DATA ANALYSIS SHEET

The Data Sentencing Range is computed by adding weights assigned to items of information relating to pertinent characteristics of both the crime and the criminal. The weights are then totaled into a separate score for the offense (Offense Score) and the offender (Offender Score). Those scores are then located on a two-dimensional sentencing grid. There is a different grid for each offense type. The Offense Score is located on the Y, or vertical, axis and the Offender Score is on the X, or horizontal, axis. By plotting the two scores against each other (just as one plots mileage figures on a road map), one is directed to the cell in the grid which indicates the range length and/or type of sentence.

The Offense Score for drug offenses has three items of information: the Inter-Class Rank, the Type of Drug Involved, and the Number of Criminal Events, and ranges from "0" to "5."

Seven items of information comprise the Offender Score: Legal Status at Time of Offense, Prior Juvenile Convictions, Prior Juvenile Incarcerations, Prior Adult Convictions, Prior Adult Convictions Against-the-Person, Prior Adult Incarcerations, and Employment Status. Add the seven coded values to obtain an Offender Score that will range from "−1" to "7."

SENTENCING DATA ANALYSIS SHEET—DRUGS

OFFENSE TYPE (MOST SERIOUS OFFENSE)

|DRUGS|

OFFENSE TYPE

OFFENSE SCORE
A. Inter-Class Rank   ____ +
B. Description of Drug Involved   ____ +
  −1 = Cannabis or drugs listed in
      Dangerous Drug Act 632-1901 and
      seq.)
   1 = Drugs listed in Uniform
      Narcotic Drug Act (36-1001 and
      seq.)
C. Number of Criminal Events   ____ =
  0 = One
  1 = Two or more

OFFENSE SCORE

OFFENDER SCORE
A   Legal Status at Time of Offense   ____ +
  0 = Not under State control
  1 = Under State control
B. Prior Juvenile Convictions   ____ +
  0 = None or one
  1 = Two or more
C. Prior Juvenile Incarcerations (Over 30   ____
      Days)
  0 = None
  1 = One or more
D. Prior Adult Convictions   ____ +
  0 = None or one
  1 = Two or more
E. Prior Adult Convictions Against-the-   ____ +
      Person
  0 = None
  1 = One or more
F. Prior Adult Incarcerations (Over 30 Days) ____ +
  0 = None
  1 = one
  2 = Two or more
G. Employment Status   ____ =
  −1 = Full or part-time employment   **OFFENDER**
   0 = Unemployed   **SCORE**

Sentencing Data Analysis Report

Superior Court of Arizona, Maricopa County

CR_____   State vs._____

Offense(s) Convicted of: _____

(title and statute   _____
number)

   I. Data Sentencing Range:

_____

_____

   II. Sentence Imposed:

_____

_____

_____

_____

   III. Reasons for Difference in Sentence Imposed:

_____

_____

_____

Date:_____   Judge:_____

SENTENCING GRID: DRUGS

Offender Score

Offense Score	−1	0	1	2	3	4	5	6	7
5	6–8	6–8	6–8	10–12	60 60–72	60 60–72	60–72 120–144	60–72 120–144	60–72 120–144
4	6–8	6–8	6–8	10–12	48–60 60–72	48–60 60–72	60–72 120–144	60–72 120–144	60–72 120–144
3	1–3	2–4	4–6	6–9	48–60 60–72	48–60 60–72	48–60 60–72	48–60 60–72	48–60 60–72
2	OUT	OUT	OUT	6–9	24 48	24 48	48–60 60–72	48–60 60–72	48–60 60–72
1	OUT	OUT	OUT	OUT	OUT	OUT	4–6	4–	4–6
0	OUT	OUT	OUT	OUT	OUT	OUT*	4–6	4–	4–6

*Weekends

Appendix C

Philadelphia Court of Common Pleas Manual for the Use of the Sentencing Grid—Crimes Against a Person (Locally Developed Model)

IMPORTANT NOTE

As you know, effective January 1, 1979 and until the Sentencing Commission establishes statewide guidelines, Senate Bill 195 set forth an interim minimum guideline of four (4) years imprisonment for certain target crimes (see Bulletin No. 78-265). The four (4) year minimum guideline sentence applies to offenders who have been convicted of the following crimes or attempts to commit the following crimes: third degree murder, voluntary manslaughter, rape, robbery, involuntary deviate sexual intercourse, arson, kidnapping, felony aggravated assault as defined in 18 Pa. C.S. 2702(a) (1) involving the use of a firearm, and who have been previously convicted of any of those offenses. While the interim statutory guidelines are not mandatory, the Bill does require that you consider them and that you provide a contemporaneous written statement when you sentence an offender to a term of less than four (4) years imprisonment. You should, of course, consider the statutory guidelines where appropriate.

INSTRUCTIONS

This is one of the two manuals that will be used in the calculation of the guideline sentence in Philadelphia. These manuals describe four offense types, Felonies against a person, Misdemeanors against a person, Felonies not against a person and Misdemeanors not against a person. This manual is to be used for both Felonies and Misdemeanors *against a person*. A crime against a person is defined as one in which there is a confrontation between the offender and the victim and in which there is bodily harm or threat of bodily harm, whether implicit or explicit. Thus a robbery is a crime against a person while a theft by unlawful taking is a crime not against a person. To determine which offense and offense category are to be used in calculating the guideline sentence, the following rules are to apply:

Most Serious Offense at Conviction—One Offense

The most serious offense at conviction determines which manual is to be used for the calculation of the guideline sentence. Use *this* manual *only* if the most serious offense at conviction was a Felony *against a person* or a Misdemeanor *against a person*.

More Than One Offense at Conviction—Different Categories

(1) When there are two or more offenses at conviction all of which are the same offense type, i.e. felony, the crime with the highest ranking is to be considered the most serious. Thus, if the offender is convicted of a robbery with a seriousness ranking of eight (8) and a burglary with a seriousness ranking of seven (7), the robbery is the most serious and should be used in the calculation of the guideline sentence.

2) When there are two or more offenses at conviction, all of which are the same offense type and rank, any of the offenses may be considered the most serious and used in the calculation of the guideline sentence.

More Than One Incident

If the case involved more than one criminal incident and the incidents were unrelated and occurred more than one (1) day apart, use a separate score sheet for each incident. Follow the scoring rules set out in the appropriate manual for each incident.

THE OFFENSE SCORE

The Offense Score is made up of items which describe what actually happened during the commission of the offense. The items are seriousness ranking, victim injury, weapon usage, property loss and number of victims.

A. Seriousness Ranking

9 = Murder (3rd degree)
8 = Felony I Against a Person
6 = Felony II Against a Person
4 = Felony III Against a Person

2=Misdemeanor Against a Person

Give eight (8) points if the most serious offense at conviction is a Felony I against a person, six (6) points if the most serious offense at conviction is a Felony II against a person, and four (4) points if it is a Felony III against a person. A Misdemeanor against a person should be given two (2) points. See the crime–specific index of offense ranking.

B. Victim Injury

0=No Injury
1=Non-permanent Injury
2=Permanent Injury and Rape
3=Death

If the victim received a non-permanent injury during the commission of the offense, add one (1) point to the score. If the victim was permanently injured or raped, add two (2) points to the score. If the victim was killed, add three (3) points.

C. Weapon Usage

0=No Weapon Used
1=Weapon Used

If the offender used a weapon in any way during the commission of the offense, add one (1) point to the score. Weapon refers to any article which, if used as a weapon, is capable of causing injury. This includes such things as firearms, explosives, incendiaries, knives, pocket knives or even a large stick if used as a weapon.

D. Amount of Property Involved

0=$500 or less
1=Over $500

If the amount of property involved in the offense exceeded $500, add one (1) point.

E. Victim Number

If there was more than one (1) victim of the offense, add one (1) point.

Total Offense Score

To obtain the total Offense Score, add the seriousness ranking (A), the victim injury score (B), the weapon usage score (C), the property amount score (D) and the victim number score (E). For example, suppose an offender is convicted of a Felony I Robbery in which there was no victim injury, weapon usage, $15.00 property involved and only one victim. The seriousness ranking is eight (8), victim injury is zero (0), weapon usage is one (1), property is zero (0) and victim number is zero (0) points. The total Offense Score is, therefore, nine (9). The maximum Offense Score an offender may receive for a crime against a person is fifteen (15), the minimum score he may receive is two (2).

THE OFFENDER SCORE

The Offender Score is made up of items relating to the offender and his prior criminal record which were found to be the most highly related to the sentencing decision. These items are prior adult incarceration, the offender's relationship to the criminal justice system at the time of his arrest, total prior adult convictions, prior felony against a person convictions, and social stability. Education and employment were found to be the best indicators of social stability. In calculating the Offender Score the following rules are to apply:

A. Total Number of Prior Adult Incarcerations

0=None
1=One
2=Two
3=Three or more

This item refers to actual incarcerations resulting from adult criminal convictions. Do *not* count incarcerations of thirty (30) days or less. *Confinement* and *escape* or *parole* violation is *not* a new incarceration. *Revocation of probation* resulting in incarceration *is* a new incarceration for purposes of this item. Count only *prior* adult incarcerations. Do not count any incarceration which may be imposed for the instant offense.

Give (0) points if the offender has never been incarcerated as a result of conviction for an adult criminal offense, give one (1) point if the offender has been incarcerated one time. Two (2) points should be given if the offender has been incarcerated two (2) times, three (3) if he has been incarcerated three (3) or *more* times. *Never* give more than three (3) points.

B. Relationship to the Criminal Justice System—Time of Arrest

0=None of Cases Pending
1=Court or Criminal Justice Supervision

No (0) points should be added to the Offender Score if the offender has had no previous connection with the adult criminal justice system, if he is free on bail with another case or cases pending or if he is on some form of deferred prosecution (ARD, DDPIP, Diversion).

One (1) point should be added to the Offender Score if the offender is on adult probation or parole, if he managed to commit the instant offense while incarcerated or if he committed the instant offense when he had escaped from incarceration.

C. Total Number of Prior Adult Convictions

0=None
1=One
2=Two
3=Three or more

This item refers to *prior* adult convictions only. The present offense(s) and juvenile adjudications should *not* be counted for this item. Exclude traffic, military and civil offenses. If the offender has no convictions prior to the conviction for the instant offense, do not add any points to the Offender Score. If the offender has one (1) prior conviction, add one (1) point, if two (2) prior convictions add two (2) points, if three (3) or *more* prior convictions add three (3) points to the Offender Score. *Never* add more than three (3) points to the Offender Score.

D. Prior Adult Felony Against a Person Convictions

0=None
1=One or more

This item was included because it was found that it was significantly related to the sentencing decision. It reflects the Philadelphia judges' serious concern with violence and personal crime. A crime against a person was defined above as one in which there is confrontation between the offender and the victim and in which there is actual bodily harm or the threat of bodily harm whether implicit or explicit. A robbery, for example, may involve neither actual bodily harm nor the explicit threat of bodily harm, but the threat is certainly implied in the act of taking valuable property from a person. For a complete list of felonies against a person, see the Crime–Specific Index of Offense Ranking.

Note that for this item only *felony* against a person convictions are to be considered. To score this item add one (1) point if the offender has one (1) or more prior convictions for a felony against a person. *Never* add more than one (1) point for this item.

E. Social Stability

0=Not Employed Time of Arrest, No High School Degree
−1=Employed Time of Arrest or High School Degree

After extensive analysis it was found that employment and education are the best indicators of social stability. Social stability factors were found to be so highly correlated that only one or two are needed as an indicator of an offender's social stability.

Note that this item is used to give the offender credit for his stability so it is *subtracted* from the Offender Score. Subtract no (0) points if the offender was not employed at the time of his offense *and* did not graduate from high school. If the offender was employed at the time of his arrest *or* has graduated from high school, subtract one (−1) point. High school graduation includes a G.E.D.

Total Offender Score

To obtain the total Offender Score add the scores for prior adult incarceration (A), relationship to the criminal justice system (B), prior adult convictions (C), prior adult felony against a person convictions (D), and *subtract* (E). The maximum Offender Score an offender may receive is eight (8), the minimum Offender Score is minus one (−1). The higher the score, the worse the offender.

For example, using the offender described above with an Offense Score of 9, to obtain the guideline sentence his Offender Score must also be calculated. Suppose he has never been incarcerated (A), was on probation at the time of his arrest (B), had three (3) prior convictions (C), no (0) prior conviction for felony against a person (D) and was a high school graduate but unemployed at the time of his arrest (E). Adding A, B, C, D and *subtracting* E gives an Offender Score of three (3).

THE GUIDELINE SENTENCE—SENTENCING GRID

To find the model sentence locate the point on the sentencing grid where the Offense and Offender Scores intersect. The Offense Score is located on the *vertical* axis, the Offender Score is located on the *horizontal* axis of the sentencing grid. The cell or point on the sentencing grid where the two scores intersect indicates the guideline sentence.

In our example, look at the sentencing grid for Felonies Against a Person, find the Offense Score of nine (9) on the vertical axis and the Offender Score of three (3) on the horizontal axis. The point at which these scores intersect is the guideline sentence. In this case it is an IN sentence with a minimum ranging from one and a half (1-1/2) years to three (3) years and a maximum ranging from four (4) years to six (6) years. The guideline or model sentence is the typical sentence given this particular type of offender for this particular type of offense in the Philadelphia jurisdiction.

SENTENCE AND REASONS

If your sentence differed from the guideline sentence, state the reasons for your sentence and why it differed from the guideline sentence. If you find it necessary to give a sentence of incarceration for more than one offense and the sentences are consecutive, please so indicate on the sentencing score sheet. Please note that your reasons for going outside the guidelines are for internal use by the court research analysts. Whether or not the sentence falls within the Philadelphia guidelines does not, of course, affect the requirements imposed by the *Riggins* decision. You should continue to record the reasons for your sentence as required by *Riggins*.

CRIME-SPECIFIC INDEX OF OFFENSE RANKING

Felony I Offenses

Offenses Against a Person (Seriousness Ranking = 8, 9)
Arson, endangering persons
Kidnapping
Murder, third degree
Rape
*Robbery
Sexual Intercourse, involuntary deviate

Offenses Not Against a Person (Seriousness Ranking = 7)
Burglary
Castastrophe, Intentional
Corrupt Organizations

Felony II Offenses

Offenses Against a Person (Seriousness Ranking 6)
*Assault, aggravated
Assault by prisoner
Manslaughter, voluntary
Rape, statutory
Robbery

Offenses Not Against a Person (Seriousness Ranking = 5)
Arson, endangering property
*Forgery
Trespass, criminal
*These offenses carry different grades depending on the circumstances of the offense and therefore, appear on more than one offense list.

Felony III Offenses

Offenses Against a Person (Seriousness Ranking = 4)
*Robbery

Offenses Not Against a Person (Seriousness Ranking = 3)
*Aiding consumation of crime
 Catastrophe, creating risk
*Credit Cards
*Default in required appearance
*Escape
*Forgery
*Mischief, criminal
*Receiving stolen property
 Riot
*Tampering with public records
*Theft by deception *Theft by extortion
*Theft by unlawful taking
*Theft of lost, etc. property
*Theft of services
*Theft of unpublished dramas
*Threats, official and political
*Witness, tampering

Misdemeanor Offenses

Offenses Against a Person (Seriousness Ranking = 2)
*Assault, aggravated
 Assault, simple
 Felonious restraint
 Manslaughter, involuntary
 Propulsion missiles into vehicle
 Recklessly endangering another person
 Suicide, causing or aiding
 Terroristic Threats
*Theft by extortion

Offenses Not Against a Person (Seriousness Ranking = 1)
*Aiding consummation of Crime
 Bad Checks
 Bookmaking, pool selling
 Breach of privacy, electronic eavesdropping
 Business practices, deceptive
 Catastrophe, failure to prevent

*These offenses carry different grades depending on the circumstances of the offense and therefore appear on more than one offense list.

Children, dealing in
Coercion, criminal
Commercial bribery
Compounding
Contraband
Copying, recording
*Credit Cards
Cruelty to animals
Custody interference with children
Custody, interference with committed person
*Default in required appearance
Destruction of objects, corpses
Disorderly conduct
Escape
Escape, implements
Explosives, carrying and shipping
Exposure, indecent
Failure to disperse
False alarms
False imprisonment
False reports
False swearing
Falsifying to authorities
Firearms, uniform act
Flag, desecration, insult
Flag, damage, destruction
*Forgery
Gambling devices, etc.
Harassment by communication
*Hindering apprehension
Injury, tampering with fire apparatus, hydrants
Impersonating a public servant
Jury, unlawful listening
Keys, master to motor vehicle
Labor disputes, use of gas
Lewdness, open
Loitering and prowling at night
Lotteries
Minors, prohibited sale
Misapplication of entrusted funds
Mischief, criminal
Nonsupport

*These offenses carry different grades depending on the circumstances of the offense and therefore appear on more than one offense list.

Obscenity
Obstructing highways
Obstructing justice, picketing
Obstructing administration of law
Official action, speculating on
Official oppression
Possessing instruments of crime
Prohibited offensive weapon
Prostitution
Receiving stolen property
Records, Tampering with
Resisting arrest
Retaliation for past action
Sexual intercourse, voluntary deviate
Simulating objects of art
Tampering with physical evidence
*Tampering with public records
Telecommunications, theft of
*Theft by deception
Theft by trade secrets
*Theft by unlawful taking
*Theft of lost property, etc.
*Theft of services
*Theft of unpublished dramas
*Threats, official, political
Trespasser, defiant
Vehicle, authorized use

---

*These offenses carry different grades depending on the circumstances of the offense and therefore, appear on more than one offense list.

MISDEMEANORS AGAINST A PERSON

OFFENSE SCORE

OFFENDER SCORE	-1	0	1	2	3	4	5	6	7	8
5+	OUT	OUT	3–6 mos / 21–25 mos	3–6 mos / 21–25 mos	3–6 mos / 21–25 mos	3–6 mos / 21–25 mos	3–6 mos / 21–25 mos	3–6 mos / 21–25 mos	3–6 mos / 21–25 mos	3–6 mos / 21–25 mos
4	OUT	OUT	OUT	OUT	OUT	OUT	OUT	3–6 mos / 21–25 mos	3–6 mos / 21–25 mos	3–6 mos / 21–25 mos
3	OUT	OUT	OUT	OUT	OUT	OUT	OUT	OUT	3–6 mos / 21–25 mos	3–6 mos / 21–25 mos
2	OUT	OUT	OUT	OUT	OUT	OUT	OUT	OUT	3–6 mos / 21–25 mos	3–6 mos / 21–25 mos
1	OUT	OUT	OUT	OUT	OUT	OUT	OUT	OUT	3–6 mos / 21–25 mos	3–6 mos / 21–25 mos
									2–4 mos / 21–25 mos	3–6 mos / 21–25 mos

FELONY AGAINST A PERSON

OFFENSE SCORE

	−1	0	1	2	3	4	5	6	7	8
12+	3–5 yrs 6–10 yrs	4–6 yrs 10–20 yrs	4–6 yrs 10–20 yrs	4–6 yrs 10–20 yrs	5–7 yrs 10–20 yrs	5–7 yrs 10–20 yrs	5–7 yrs 10–20 yrs	6–8 yrs 12–20 yrs	6–8 yrs 12–20 yrs	8–10 yrs 16–20 yrs
11	6–11½ mos 23 mo–4 yrs	18 mo–3½ yrs 3–7 yrs	2–4 yrs 4–8 yrs	2–4 yrs 4–8 yrs	2–4 yrs 4–8 yrs	2–4 yrs 4–8 yrs	3–5 yrs 6–10 yrs	6–8 yrs 12–16 yrs	6–8 yrs 12–16 yrs	6–9 yrs 12–16 yrs
10	6–11½ mos 23–4 yrs	18–3½ yrs 2–7 yrs	2–4 yrs 4–8 yrs	2–4 yrs 4–8 yrs	2–4 yrs 4–9 yrs	2–4 yrs 4–8 yrs	3–5 yrs 6–10 yrs	6–8 yrs 12–16 yrs	6–8 yrs 12–16 yrs	6–9 yrs 12–16 yrs
9	OUT	6–11½ mos 8 mo–2½ yrs	1½–3 yrs 4–6 yrs	1½–3 yrs 4–6 yrs	1½–3 yrs 4–6 yrs	1½–3 yrs 4–6 yrs	1½–3 yrs 4–6 yrs	1½–3 yrs 4–6 yrs	1½–3 yrs 4–6 yrs	1½–3 yrs 4–6 yrs
8	OUT	OUT	OUT	1–6 mos 18 mos–2½ yrs	6–11½ mos 18 mos–2½ yrs	6–11½ mos 18 mos–2½ yrs	6–11½ mos 18 mos–2½ yrs	1–2½ yrs 23 mos–5 yrs	8	OUT
6–7	OUT	OUT	OUT	OUT	OUT	OUT	TIME IN	TIME IN	6–12 mos 1½–2½ yrs	6–12 mos 1½–2½ yrs
4–5	OUT	OUT	OUT	OUT	OUT	TIME IN	TIME IN	TIME IN	TIME IN	1–6 mos 1½–2½ yrs

OFFENDER SCORE

2/14/79

Appendix D

State of Washington Instructional Booklet for the Calculation of Guideline Sentences—Courts of Limited Jurisdiction (Statewide Model for Less Serious Offenses)

TABLE OF CONTENTS

A. Coding Instructions
 1. Offense Score
  A. Property Damage and/or Personal Injury to Victim
  B. Use of Alcohol or Drugs at Time of Offense

 2. Offender Score
  A. Current Legal Status
  B. Total Number of Prior Adult and Juvenile Convictions
  C. Total Number of Prior Incarcerations
  D. Offender's Job Stability

B. Computation of Guideline Sentences

C. Guideline Sentence Worksheet—Non-Traffic

D. Sentencing Grid—Non-Traffic

I. TRAFFIC OFFENSES

A Coding Instructions

Traffic Offenses: (The traffic offenses covered by the guidelines are Driving While Intoxicated, Reckless Driving and Driving While License Suspended.)

1. Offense Score

A. Property Damage and/or Personal Injury to Victim:
0 = No damage or injury
1 = Property damage
2 = Personal injury
  Do not count property damage or personal injury suffered by the offender, such as damages to his/her own vehicle; code only for damage or injury to others. If both property damage and personal injury occurred, code for the most serious, "2."

B. Blood-Alcohol Level
0 = Blood-alcohol level under .15
1 = Blood-alcohol level .15 or over

Code this item from the breathalyzer results listed on the docket. If the blood-alcohol level is less than .15, code "0." If it is equal to or greater than .15 code "1."

2. Offender Score

A. Current Legal Status
0 = Not under court supervision or control
1 = Under some form of court supervision or control (e.g., on bail, supervised or unsupervised probation, parole, escape, deferred sentence, deferred prosecution, etc.)
Code "1" if, *at the time of the commission of the present offense,* the offender had other criminal actions pending, was on juvenile or adult probation or parole, or was an escapee from incarceration.

B. Total Number of Prior Traffic Offenses Identical to the Target Offense
0 = None
1 = One or more
The target offense is the most serious offense the offender was convicted of, using statutory class as the criterion to decide seriousness. NOTE: Physical control should be considered identical to DWI for purposes of coding and coded as such.

C. Total Number of Prior Convictions for Non-Identical Traffic Related Crimes
0 = None or one
1 = Two or more
Count those prior convictions (juvenile and adult) and bail forfeitures for traffic-related crimes which are not identical to the target offense. For this item, count *all* traffic related crimes, regardless of whether the offender is subject to a possible sentence of incarceration (i.e., jail). If the prior conviction was for multiple offenses at one adjudication, count as one conviction and code only for the most serious offense. For example, if convictions for simple assault for DWI occurred simultaneously, it would count as a conviction for assault.

D. Total Number of Prior Convictions for Non-Traffic Offenses
0 = None
1 = One or more
Count all prior adult convictions (felony and/or misdemeanor) as well as any bail forfeitures for such offenses. Do not count any traffic-related offenses. Count only those juvenile convictions (or juvenile court equivalents for offenses) which would be considered criminal if

the offender had been convicted as an adult (i.e., exclude juvenile "status" offenses).

E. Offender's Job Stability

−1 = Employed or attending school

0 = Unemployed

Code "−1" if the offender was employed, full or part-time, at the time of sentencing. If, however, the offender was detained in jail prior to sentencing, code for employment status just prior to detention. The term "employed" is used to describe the defendant's stability or productivity and would include "homemaking."

B Computation of Guideline Sentences

The guideline sentence is computed by adding weights assigned to items of information relating to pertinent characteristics of both the crime and the criminal. The weights are then totaled into a separate score for the offense (Offense Score) and for the offender (Offender Score). Those scores are then located on a two-dimensional sentencing grid. There are separate grids for Traffic Offenses and Non-Traffic Offenses. The Offense Score is located on the Y, or vertical, axis and the Offender Score on the X, or horizontal, axis. By plotting the two scores against each other (much as one plots mileage figures on a road map), one is directed to the cell in the grid which indicates the guideline type and/or length of sentence.

Two items of information comprise the Offense Score for Traffic Offenses: Property Damage and/or Personal Injury to Victim, and Blood-Alcohol Level. Add the two coded values to get an Offense Score which will range from zero to three. Five items of information comprise the Offender Score for Traffic Offenses: Current Legal Status, Total Number of Identical Prior Offenses to Target Offense, Total Number of Prior Convictions for Non-Identical Traffic-Related Crimes, Total Number of Prior Adult and Juvenile Convictions, and Offender's Stability or productivity measured in terms of productive activity. Add the five coded values to get an Offender Score which will range from negative one to four.

C. Guideline Sentencing Worksheet

OFFENDER_____ CAUSE NO._____

COURT_____

OFFENSE(S) CONVICTED OF:
Driving While Intoxicated
Reckless Driving
Driving While License Suspended   DATE OF SENTENCING

_____/_____/_____

OFFENSE SCORE:

A.   Property Damage/Personal Injury to Victim   _____+

    0 = No damage or injury
    1 = Property damage
    2 = Personal injury

B.   Blood-Alcohol Level   _____+

    0 = Blood-alcohol level below 0.15
    1 = Blood-alcohol level of 0.15 or more

OFFENDER SCORE: OFFENSE SCORE

A.   Current Legal Status
    0 = Not under state supervision or control
    1 = Under some form of state supervision or control
        (e.g. bail, probation, parole, escape)

B.   Total Number of Prior Offenses Identical to Target Offense   _____+

    0 = None
    1 = One or more

C.   Total Number of Prior Convictions for Non-Identical Traffic Related Crimes   _____+

    0 = None or one
    1 = Two or more

D.   Total Number of Prior Convictions   _____+

    0 = None
    1 = One or more

E.   Offender's Job Stability   _____+

    –1 = Employed   OFFENDER SCORE
    0 = Unemployed

GUIDELINE SENTENCE: _____ Days of Jail

ACTUAL SENTENCE:_____ Days of Jail; $_____ Fine; _____ Days Supervised Probation;

    In-Patient Treatment; ☐ Out-Patient Treatment; ☐ A.I.S.; ☐ D.I.S.;
    Other Conditions _____

REASON(S) (If Sentence outside Guidelines) _____

D. Sentencing Grid
TRAFFIC OFFENSES

OFFENDER SCORE

OFFENSE SCORE	-1	0	1	2	3-4
3	2 to 20 Days	2 to 20 Days	10 to 30 Days	30 to max Days	60 to max Days
2	2 to 10 Days	2 to 10 Days	5 to 20 Days	30 to max Days	60 to Max Days
1	No Jail	No jail	2 to 10 Days	5 to 20 Days	15 to 45 Days
0	No Jail	No Jail	No Jail	2 to 10 Days	15 to 45 Days

NOTE: The guideline sentence is only concerned with the sanction of jail and does not preclude the use of any alternatives such as restitution, fines or educational programs in conjunction with it.

Mandatory jail sentences override the guidelines.

II. Non-Traffic Offenses

A. Coding Instructions

Non-Traffic Offenses. (The non-traffic offenses covered by the guidelines are Simple Assault, Theft in the Third Degree, Shoplifting, and Unlawful Issuance of a Bank Check.)

1. Offense Score

A. Property Damage and/or Personal Injury to Victim

0 = No damage or injury
1 = Property damage or property taken (including credit)
2 = Personal Injury

"Property damage" refers to property other than the object of offense. Do not count property damage or personal injury suffered by the offender, such as injuries sustained in a brawl; code only for damage or injury to others. If both property damage and personal injury occurred, code for the most serious. "2."

B. Use of Alcohol or Drugs at Time of Offense

0 = Nothing used
1 = Alcohol and/or drugs used

Code "1" if, according to the official report, the offender was considered "under the influence" (of either alcohol or drugs).

2. Offender Score

A. Current Legal Status

0 = Not under court supervision or control
1 = Under some form of court supervision or control (e.g., on bail, supervised or unsupervised, probation, parole, escape, deferred sentence, deferred prosecution, etc.)

Code "1" if, *at the time of the commission of the present offense,* the offender had other criminal actions pending, was on juvenile or adult probation or parole, or was an escapee from incarceration.

B. Total Number of Prior Adult and Juvenile Convictions

0 = None
1 = One or more

Count all prior adult convictions (felony and misdemeanor), and any bail forfeitures. Include only those traffic-related offenses which are subject to incarceration (i.e. jail). Count only those juvenile convictions (or juvenile court equivalents for offenses) which would be considered criminal if the offender had been convicted as an adult (i.e., exclude juvenile "status" offenses).

C. Total Number of Prior Incarcerations (over two days)
0 = None
1 = One
2 = Two or more

This item refers to actual incarcerations, resulting from adult and juvenile criminal convictions. Do not count incarcerations of two days or less or pretrial detentions. Confinement after escape or parole violation is not a new incarceration, whereas revocation of probation resulting in an incarceration *is* counted as a new incarceration.

D. Offender's Job Stability
−1 = Employed or attending school
0 = Unemployed

Code"−1" if the offender was employed or attending school full or part-time, at the time of sentencing. If, however, the offender was detained in jail prior to sentencing, code for employment status just prior to detention. The term "employed" is used to describe the defendant's stability or productivity and would include "homemaking."

B Computation of Guideline Sentences

The guideline sentence is computed by adding weights assigned to items of information relating to pertinent characteristics of both the crime and the criminal. The weights are then totaled into a separate score for the offense (Offense Score) and for the offender (Offender Score). Those scores are then located on a two-dimensional sentencing grid. There are separate grids for Traffic Offenses and Non-Traffic Offenses. The Offense Score is located on the Y, or vertical, axis and the Offender Score on the X, or horizontal, axis. By plotting the two scores against each other (much as one plots mileage figures on a road map), one is directed to the cell in the grid which indicates the guideline type and/or length of sentence.

Two items of information comprise the Offense Score for Non-Traffic Offenses: Property Damage and/or Personal Injury to Victim and Use of Alcohol or Drugs at Time of Offense. Add the two coded values to get an Offense Score which will range from zero to three. Four items of information comprise the Offender Score for Non-Traffic Offenses: Current Legal Status, Total Number of Prior Adult and Juvenile Convictions, Total Number of Prior Incarcerations (over two days), and Offender's Stability or productivity measured in terms of productive activity. Add the four coded values to get an Offender Score which will range from negative one to four.

C. Guideline Sentence Worksheet — Non Traffic

OFFENDER _____ CAUSE NO. _____

COURT _____

OFFENSE(S) CONVICTED OF:
☐ Simple Assault
☐ Theft, Third Degree
☐ Shoplifting
☐ Unlawful Issuance of Bank Check   DATE OF SENTENCING ____/____/____

OFFENSE SCORE:
A.   Property Damage/Personal Injury to Victim   ____ +

    0 = No damage or injury
    1 = Property damage
    2 = Personal Injury
B.   Use of Alcohol or Drugs at Time of Offense   ____ =

    0 = Nothing Used
    1 = Alcohol and/or drugs used   OFFENSE
OFFENDER SCORE: SCORE
A.   Current Legal Status   ____ +

    0 = Not under state supervision or control
    1 = Under some form of state supervision or control
    (e.g. bail, probation, parole, escape)
B.   Total number of Prior Convictions   ____ +

    0 = None
    1 = One or more
C.   Total Number of Prior Incarcerations (over two days) ____ +

    0 = None
    1 = One
    2 = Two or more
D.   Offender's Job Stability   ____ =

    −1 = Employed   OFFENDER
    0 = Unemployed   SCORE

GUIDELINE SENTENCE: _____ Days of Jail

ACTUAL SENTENCE: _____ Days of Jail; _____ Fine;

_____ Days Supervised Probation;
    ☐ In-Patient Treatment; ☐ Out-Patient Treatment; ☐ A.I.S.;

Other Conditions _____

REASON(S) (If Sentence outside Guidelines) _____

D. Sentencing Grid
NON-TRAFFIC OFFENSES

Offender Score

		-1	0	1	2	3-4
	3	5 to 20 Days	5 to 20 Days	15 to 45 Days	30 to Max Days	Max Days
	2	2 to 10 Days	2 to 10 Days	5 to 20 Days	15 to 45 Days	60 to Max Days
Offense Score	1	No Jail	No Jail	2 to 10 Days	5 to 20 Days	15 to 45 Days
	0	No Jail	No Jail	No Jail	2 to 10 Days	15 to 45 Days

NOTE: The guideline sentence is only concerned with the sanction of jail and does not preclude the use of any alternatives such as restitution, fines or educational programs in conjunction with it.

The above recommendations are the minimum jail sentences to be served. They do not include suspended jail time.

Bibliography

Advisory Council of Judges, National Council on Crime and Delinquency. "Model Sentencing Act." 9 *Crime and Delinquency* 339–69 (October 1963).

Advisory Council on the Penal System. *Sentences of Imprisonment–A Review of Maximum Penalties.* London: HMSO, 1978.

Allen, Frederick A. *The Borderland of Criminal Justice.* Chicago: University of Chicago Press, 1964.

Allen, Harry E. "Indeterminate Sentencing in America: An Empirical Test." 19 *Proceedings of the Southern Conference on Corrections* 77–89 (February 27, 1974).

Allen, Ronald J. "Retribution in a Modern Penal Law: The Principle of Aggravated Harm." 25 *Buffalo Law Review* 1–35 (Fall 1975).

Alschuler, Albert W. "The Defense Attorney's Role in Plea Bargaining." 84 *Yale Law Journal* 1179–1314 (1975).

——. "The Prosecutor's Role in Plea Bargaining." 36 *University of Chicago Law Review* 50–112 (1968).

——. "The Trial Judge's Role in Plea Bargaining, Part I." 76 *Columbia Law Review* 1059–1154 (1976).

——. "Sentencing Reform and Prosecutorial Power: A Critique of Recent Proposals for 'Fixed' and 'Presumptive' Sentencing." 126 *University of Pennsylvania Law Review* 550–77 (1978).

American Bar Association, Commission on Standards of Judicial Administration. *Standards Relating to Court Organization.* New York: ABA, 19

American Bar Association, Project on Minimum Standards for Criminal Justice. *Standards Relating to Discovery and Procedure Before Trial.* Approved Draft. New York: American Bar Association, 1970.

——. *Standards Relating to Probation.* Approved Draft. New York: American Bar Association, 1970.

——. *Standards Relating to Sentencing Alternatives and Procedures.* Approved Draft. New York: American Bar Association, 1968.

——. *Standards Relating to Appellate Review of Sentences.* Approved Draft. New York: American Bar Association, 1968.

American Friends Service Committee. *Struggle for Justice: A Report on Crime and Punishment in America.* New York: Hill and Wang, 1971.

American Law Institute. *Model Penal Code.* Proposed Official Draft. Philadelphia, 1962.

Ancel, Marc. *Social Defense: A Modern Approach to Problems.* New York: Schocken, 1965.

Andeneas, Johannes. "Deterrence and Specific Offenses." 38 *University of Chicago Law Review* 537–53 (1971).

——. "Does Punishment Deter Crime?" 11 *Criminal Law Quarterly* 76–93 (1968).

——. "The General Preventive Effects of Punishment." 114 *University of Pennsylvania Law Review* 949–983 (1966).

——. "The Morality of Deterrence." 37 *University of Chicago Law Review* 649–664 (1970).

——. *Punishment and Deterrence.* Ann Arbor: University of Michigan Press, 1974.

Anderson, Linda S. "The Deterrent Effect of Criminal Sanctions." In Paul J. Brantingham and Jack M. Kress, eds., *Structure, Law, and Power: Essays in the Sociology of Law.* 120–34. Beverly Hills: Sage Publications, 1979.

Angel, Marina. "Substantive Due Process and the Criminal Law." 9 *Loyola University of Chicago Law Journal* 61–135 (1977).

Antunes, George, and A. Lee Hunt. "The Deterrent Impact of Criminal Sanctions: Some Implications for Criminal Justice Policy." 51 *Journal of Urban Law* 145–61 (1973).

"The Impact of Certainty and Severity of Punishment on Levels of Crime in American States: An Extended Analysis." 64 *Journal of Criminal Law and Criminology* 486–93 (1973).

Ares, Charles E.; Anne Rankin; and Herbert Sturz. "The Manhattan Bail Project: An Interim Report on the Use of Pre–Trial Parole." 38 *New York University Law Review* 67–95 (1963).

Aristotle. *The Ethics of Aristotle.* Trans. J. A. K. Thomson. Middlesex: Penguin, 1976.

Arnold, William R. "A Functional Explanation of Recidivism." 56 *Journal of Criminal Law, Criminology and Police Science* 212–20 (1965).

Ashley, Joe. "An Experiment in Fixed Sentencing: Ohio's Norwood Law." 38 *American Journal of Corrections* 39, 41 (January–February 1976).

Atkins, Burton, and Jack Pogrebin, eds. *The Invisible Justice System: Discretion and the Law.* Cincinnati: Anderson Publishing Co., 1978.

Baab, George William, and William Royal Furgeson, Jr. "Texas Sentencing Practices: A Statistical Study." 45 *Texas Law Review* 471–503 (1967).

Babst, Dean V.; Mary Koval; and M. G. Neithercutt. "Relationship of Time Served to Parole Outcome for Different Classifications of Burglars Based on Males Paroled in Fifty Jurisdictions in 1968 and 1969." 9 *Journal of Research in Crime and Delinquency* 99–116 (1972).

Bailey, Walter C. "Correctional Outcome: An Evaluation of 100 Reports." 57 *Journal of Criminal Law, Criminology and Police Science* 153–71 (1966).

Bailey, William C.; J. David Martin; and Louis N. Gray. "Crime and Deterrence: A Correlation Analysis." 11 *Journal of Research in Crime and Delinquency* 124–43 (1974).

Bailey, W. C., and Ronald W. Smith. "Punishment: Its Severity and Certainty." 63 *Journal of Criminal Law, Criminology and Police Science* 530–39 (1972).

Baker, Donald I., and Barbara A. Reeves. "The Paper Label Sentences: Critiques." 86 *Yale Law Journal* 619–25 (March 1977).

Baldus, David C., and James W. L. Cole. "A Comparison of the Work of Thorsten Sellin and Isaac Ehrlich on the Deterrent Effect of Capital Punishment." 85 *Yale Law Journal* 170–86 (1975).

Ball, John C. "The Deterrence Concept in Criminology and Law." 46 *Journal of Criminal Law, Criminology and Police Science* 347–54 (1955).

Ball, Richard A. "A Theory of Punishment: Restricted Reprobation and the Reparation of Social Reality." In Paul J. Brantingham, and Jack M. Kress, eds., *Structure, Law, and Power: Essays in the Sociology of Law* 135–49. Beverly Hills: Sage Publications, 1979.

Ballard, Kelley B., Jr., and Don M. Gottfredson. *Predictive Attribute Analysis and the Prediction of Parole Performance.* Vacaville, California: Institute for the Study of Crime and Delinquency, December 1963.

Barkin, Eugene N. "The Emergence of Correctional Law and the Awareness of the Rights of the Convicted." 45 *Nebraska Law Review* 669–89 (1966).

————. "Impact of Changing Law Upon Prison Policy." 48 *Prison Journal* 3–20 (1968).

Bastress, Robert M., Jr. "The Less Restrictive Alternative in Consitutional Adjudication: An Analysis, A Justification, and Some Criteria." 27 *Vanderbilt Law Review* 971–1041 (1974).

Beccaria, Cesare. *On Crimes and Punishments.* Translated by Henry Paolucci. New York: Bobbs–Merrill, 1963.

Becker, Gary S. "Crime and Punishment: An Economic Approach." 78 *Journal of Political Economy* 169–217 (1968).

————. *Essays in the Economics of Crime and Punishment.* New York: National Bureau of Economic Research, 1974.

Bedau, Hugo A. "Capital Punishment in Oregon, 1903–64." 45 *Oregon Law Review* 1–36 (1965).

————. *The Death Penalty in America.* Rev. ed. Chicago: Aldine Publishing Co., 1967.

————. "Felony Murder, Rape and the Mandatory Death Penalty: A Study in Discretionary Justice." 10 *Suffolk University Law Review* 493–520 (Spring 1976).

Beer, Stafford. *Decision and Control: The Meaning of Operational Research and Management Cybernetics.* New York: John Wiley and Sons, 1966.

Bell, Daniel. *The End of Ideology.* New York: The Free Press, 1965.

Bennett, James V. "The Sentence—Its Relation to Crime and Rehabilitation." *University of Illinois Law Forum 1960,* pp. 500–11.

Bentham, Jeremy. *The Works of Jeremy Bentham.* Edited by J. H. Burns and H. L. A. Hart. London: Athcone Press, 1970.

Biderman, Albert D. "Victimology and Victimization Surveys." In *Victimology: A New Focus,* vol. 3, ed. by Israel Drapkin and Emilio Viano. Lexington, Massachusetts: Lexington Books, 1975.

————. "Notes on the Significance of Measurements of Events and Conditions by Criminal Victimization Surveys." Washington, D.C.: Bureau of Social Science Research, July 1975.

Biddle, W. Craig. "A Legislative Study of the Effectiveness of Criminal Penalties." 15 *Crime and Delinquency* 354–58 (1969).

Bishop, Yvonne M.M.; S. E. Feinberg; and P. W. Holland. *Discrete Multivariate Analysis, Theory and Practice.* Cambridge, Massachusetts: MIT Press, 1975.

Bittner, Egon, and Anthony M. Platt. "The Meaning of Punishment." 2 *Issues in Criminology* 79–99 (1966).

Blake, Catherine C. "Appellate Review of Criminal Sentencing in the Federal Courts." 24 *University of Kansas Law Review* 279–305 (1976).

Blalock, Hubert M., Jr. "Correlated Independent Variables: The Problem of Multicollinearity." 42 *Social Forces* 233–37 (1963).

————. *Social Statistics.* 2nd ed. New York: McGraw–Hill, 1972.

Blalock, Hubert M., Jr., and Ann B. Blalock. *Methodology in Social Research.* New York: McGraw–Hill Book Comp., 1968.

Bloch, Herbert A., and Gilbert Geis. *Man, Crime, and Society.* New York: Random House, 1962.

Block, Michael K., and Robert C. Lind. "An Economic Analysis of Crimes Punishable by Imprisonment." 4 *Journal of Legal Studies* 479–92 (1975).

Blumberg, Abraham S. *Criminal Justice.* Chicago: Quadrangle, 1967.

Blumstein, Alfred, ed. *Deterrence and Incapacitation: Estimating the Effects of Criminal Sanctions on Crime Rates.* Washington, D.C.: National Academy of Sciences, 1978.

——. "Developing National Debate on Punishment Policy." 23 *Operations Research* 305–21 (1975).

——. "Seriousness Weights in an Index of Crime." 39 *American Sociological Review* 854–64 (1974).

Blumstein, Alfred, and Jacqueline Cohen. "A Theory of the Stability of Punishment." 64 *Journal of Criminal Law and Criminology* 198–207 (1973).

Blumstein, Alfred, and Richard Larson. "Models of a Total Criminal Justice System." 17 *Operations Research* 199–232 (March–April 1969).

Blumstein, Alfred, and Richard Larson. "Problems in Modeling and Measuring Recidivism." 8 *Journal of Research in Crime and Delinquency* 124–32 (July 1971).

Bohmer, Carol, E. "Judicial Use of Psychiatric Reports in the Sentencing of Sex Offenders." Ph.D. thesis. University of Pennsylvania, 1975.

Bohmer, Carol, and Audrey Blumberg. "Twice Traumatized: The Rape Victim and The Court." 58 *Judicature* 390–99 (1975).

Bond, James E. *Plea–Bargaining and Guilty Pleas.* New York: Clark Boardman Co., 1975.

Bowers, William J., and Glenn L. Pierce. "The Illusion of Deterrence in Isaac Ehrlich's Research on Capital Punishment." 85 *Yale Law Journal* 187–208 (1975).

Boydell, Craig L., and Carl F. Grindstaff. "Public Opinion Toward Legal Sanctions for Crimes of Violence." 65 *Journal of Criminal Law and Criminology* 113–16 (1974).

Boyle, John S. "Making A Big Court Better." 60 *Judicature* 233–38 (December 1976).

Brantingham, Paul J., and Jack M. Kress, eds. *Structure, Law, and Power: Essays in the Sociology of Law.* Beverly Hills: Sage Publications, 1979.

Breitel, Charles D. "Controls in Law Enforcement." 27 *University of Chicago Law Review* 427 (1960).

Bridges, George S., and Nancy S. Lisagor. "Scaling Seriousness: An Evaluation of Magnitude and Category Scaling Techniques." 66 *Journal of Criminal Law and Criminology* 215–21 (1975).

Brier, S. S., and S. E. Fienberg. *Recent Econometric Modelling of Crime and Punishment: Support for the Deterrence Hypothesis?* St. Paul: University of Minnesota, Department of Applied Statistics, Technical Report No. PR–307, 1978.

Brody, S. R. *The Effectiveness of Sentencing–A Review of the Literature.* London: Her Majesty's Stationary Office, 1976.

Brooker, Frank. "The Deterrent Effect of Punishment." 9 *Criminology* 469–90 (1972).

Brown, William P. "Local Policing—A Three Dimensional Task Analysis." 3 *Journal of Criminal Justice* 1–15 (1975).

Browne, Steven F.; John D. Carr; Glenn Cooper; and Thomas A Giancinti. *Adult Recidivism: Characteristics and Recidivism of Adult Felony Offenders in Denver.* Denver: High Impact Anti–Crime Program, 1974.

Bullock, Henry Allen. "Significance of the Racial Factor in the Length of Prison Sentences." 52 *Journal of Criminal Law, Criminology and Police Science* 411–17 (1961).

Burger, Warren E. "School for Judges." 33 *F.R.D.* 139 (1969).

Burnham, R. William. "A Theoretical Basis for a Rational Case Decision System in Corrections." Ph.D. dissertation, University of California at Berkeley, 1969.

Burns, James M., and Joseph S. Mattina. *Sentencing.* Reno: National Judicial College, 1978.

Cahalan, W. L. "Certainty of Punishment." 9 *Prosecutor* 476–78 (1974).

Calpin, Joseph C.; Jack M. Kress; and Arthur M. Gelman. *The Analytical Basis for the Formulation of Sentencing Policy.* Washington, D.C.: USGPO, 1980.

Caraway, William L. "Sentencing Reform in Multiple Offense Cases: Judicial and Legislative Avenues." 7 *Connecticut Law Review* 257–286 (Winter 1974–1975).

Carey, Hugh L. "The Role of a Prosecutor in a Free Society." 12 *Criminal Law Bulletin* 317–25 (1976).

Cargan, L., and M. A. Coates. "The Indeterminate Sentence and Judicial Bias." 20 *Crime and Delinquency* 144–56 (1974).

Carney, F. L. "The Indeterminate Sentence at Patuxent." 20 *Crime and Delinquency* 135–43 (1974).

Carr–Hill, R. A., and N. H. Stern. "An Econometric Model of the Supply and Control of Recorded Offenses in England and Wales." 2 *Journal of Public Economics* 289–318 (1973).

Carter, Robert M. "The Presentence Report and the Decision–Making Process." *Journal of Research in Crime and Delinquency* 128–37 (1967).

Carter, Robert M.; R. McGee; and K. Nelson. *Corrections in America.* New York: Lippincott, 1975.

Carter, Robert M., and Leslie T. Wilkins. "Some Factors in Sentencing Policy." 58 *Journal of Criminal Law, Criminology and Police Science* 503–14 (1967).

Cederbaum, J. B., and William L. Blizek. *Justice and Punishment.* Cambridge, Massachusetts: Ballinger Publishing Co., 1977.

Chambliss, William J. "The Deterrent Influence of Punishment." 12 *Crime and Delinquency* 70–75 (January 1966).

——. "Types of Deviance and the Effectiveness of Legal Sanctions." 1967 *Wisconsin Law Review* 703–19 (1967).

Chauncey, R. "Deterrence: Certainty, Severity and Skyjacking." 12 *Criminology* 447 (1975).

Chiricos, Theodore G., and Gordon P. Waldo. "Punishment and Crime: An Examination of Some Empirical Evidence." 18 *Social Problems* 200–17 (1970).

——. "Socioeconomic Status and Criminal Sentencing: An Empirical Assessment of a Conflict Proposition." 40 *American Sociological Review* 6 (1975).

Christie, Nils. S. "Utility and Social Values in Court Decisions on Punishment." In Roger Hood, ed., *Crime, Criminology and Public Policy: Essays in Honor of Sir Leon Radzinowicz.* 281–96. New York: Free Press, 1975.

Clark, Ramsey. *Crime in America.* New York: Simon and Schuster, 1970.

Clark, Ramsey, and David Rudenstine. *Prison Without Walls: Report on New York Parole.* New York: Praeger, 1974.

Clarke, Stevens H. "Who Goes to Prison? The Likelihood of Receiving an Active Sentence." 41 *Popular Government* 25–37 (Fall 1975).

Clear, Todd; John D. Hewitt; and Robert M. Regoli. "Discretion and the Determinate Sentence." Paper presented to the American Society of Criminology, November 1977.

Clinard, M. B. "An Assessment of Prisons With Recommendations for Policies." 11 *Wisconsin Sociologist* 35–39 (1974).

Coffee, John C., Jr. "The Future of Sentencing Reform: Emerging Legal Issues in the Individualization of Justice." 73 *Michigan Law Review* 1362–1462 (1975).

——. "The Repressed Issues of Sentencing: Accountability, Predictability, and Equality in the Era of the Sentencing Commission." 66 *Georgetown Law Journal* 975–1107 (1978).

Cohen, Murray; Nicholas A. Groth; and Richard Siegel. *Clinical Prediction of Sexual Dangerousness.* Boston: Boston University, 1975.

Cole, G. D. H., ed. *The Essential Samuel Butler.* New York: E. P. Dutton & Company, 1950.

Cole, George F. "Will Definite Sentences Make A Difference?" 61 *Judicature* 58–65 (1977).

Cole, George F., and Susette M. Talarico. "Second Thoughts on Parole." 63 *American Bar Association Journal* 972–76 (1977).

Commission to Investigate Prison Administration and Construction (Lewisohn Commission). *Prisoners: Their Crimes and Sentences.* New York, 1933.

Connolly, P. K. "The Possibility of a Prison Sentence is a Necessity." 21 *Crime and Delinquency* 356–59 (1975).

Conrad, John. *Crime and Its Correction: An International Survey of Attitudes and Practices.* Berkeley: University of California Press, 1965.

Corgan, L., and M. A. Coates. "The Indeterminate Sentence and Judicial Laws." 20 *Crime and Delinquency* 144–56 (1974).

Corrections Magazine. Special Report, September 1977.

Council of Judges, National Council on Crime and Delinquency. "Guides to the Judge in Sentencing Racketeering Cases." 14 *Crime and Delinquency* 97–106 (April 1968).

"Model Sentenceing Act, Second Edition." 18 *Crime and Delinquency* 335–70 (October 1972).

Council of Europe. *Collected Studies in Criminological Research.* Strasbourg, 1967.

Cousineau, D. F. "A Critique of the Ecological Approach to the Study of Deterrence." 54 *Social Science Quarterly* 152–58 (1973).

Cressey, Donald R. "The Functions and Structure of Criminal Syndicates." In President's Commission on Law Enforcement and the Administration of Justice," *Task Force Report: Organized Crime.* Washington, D.C.: USGPO, 1967.

——. "Law, Order and the Motorist." In Roger Hood, ed., *Crime, Criminology, and Public Policy* 213–34. New York: Free Press, 1974.

——. "The Nature and Effectiveness of Correctional Techniques." 23 *Law and Contemporary Problems* 754–71 (August 1958).

——. *Other People's Money.* New York: The Free Press, 1953.

—. *The Prison: Studies in Institutional Organization and Change.* New York: Holt, Rinehart & Winston, 1961.

Criminal Courts Technical Assistance Project. "Overview of State and Local Sentencing Guidelines Activity." Washington, D.C.: American University Law Institute, April 1979.

Critelli, Anthony M. Preface. In Leslie T. Wilkins; Jack M. Kress; Don M. Gottfredson; Joseph C. Calpin; and Arthur M. Gelman, *Sentencing Guidelines: Structuring Judicial Discretion–Report on the Feasibility Study* xi–xii. Washington, D.C.: USGPO, 1978.

Cross, A. R. *Paradoxes in Prison Sentences*. Oxford: Oxford University Press, 1965.

Crowther, Carol. "Crimes, Penalties and Legislatures." *Annals of the American Academy of Political and Social Sciences* 147–57 (1969).

Crystal, Daniel. "The Proposed Federal Criminal Justice Reform Act of 1975: Sentencing—Law and Order With a Vengeance." 7 *Seton Hall Law Review* 33–107 (1975).

Czajkoski, Eugene H. "Exposing the Quasi–Judicial Role of the Probation Officer." 37 *Federal Probation* 9–13 (September 1973).

Dash, Samuel. "Cracks In the Foundation of Criminal Justice." 46 *Illinois Law Review* 385–406 (1951).

Davis, Kenneth Culp. *Discretionary Justice: A Preliminary Inquiry*. Baton Rouge: Louisiana State University Press, 1969.

——. *Police Discretion*. St. Paul: West Publishing Co., 1975.

——. *Administrative Law and Government*. St. Paul: West, 1960.

Dawes, Robyn M. *Fundamentals of Attitude Measurement*. New York: John Wiley and Sons, 1972.

Dawes, Robyn M., and Bernard Corrigan. "Linear Models in Decision–Making." 81 *Psychological Bulletin* 95 (1974).

Dawson, Robert O. "The Decision To Grant or Deny Parole: A Study of Parole Criteria in Law and Practice." 1966 *Washington University Law Quarterly* 243–303 (June 1966).

——. *Sentencing: The Decision as to Type, Length and Conditions of Sentence*. Boston: Little, Brown and Co., 1969.

——. "Sentencing Reform: The Current Round." 88 *Yale Law Journal* 440–50 (December 1978).

Denning, Richard. *Freedom Under the Law*. London: Stevens and Sons, 1949.

Dershowitz, Alan M. "Criminal Sentencing in the United States: An Historical and Conceptual Overview." 423 *Annals of the Amer-ican Academy of Political and Social Science* 117–32 (January 1976).

——. "Intermediate Confinement: Letting The Therapy Fit the Harm." 123 *University of Pennsylvania Law Review* pp 297–339 (1974).

——. "Letting the Punishment Fit the Crime." *The New York Times Magazine,* December 28, 1975, pp. 7, 20, 26–27.

Devlin, Patrick. *The Enforcement of Morals*. London: Oxford University Press, 1959.

Diamond, Bernard L. "The Psychiatric Prediction of Dangerousness." 123 *University of Pennsylvania Law Review* 439–52 (1974).

Diamond, Shari Seidman, and Hans Zeisel. "Sentencing Councils: A Study of Sentence Disparity and its Reduction." 43 *University of Chicago Law Review* 109–49 (1976).

Doleschal, E. "The Deterrent Effect of Legal Punishment—A Review of the Literature." 1 *National Council on Crime and Delinquency* 1–17 (1969).

Dowling, Noel T., and Gerald Gunther. *Cases and Materials on Constitutional Law.* 8th ed. Mineola: Foundation Press, 1970.

Downie, Leonard, Jr. *Justice Denied.* New York: Praeger, 1971.

Doyle, R. F. "A Sentencing Council in Operation." 1961 *Federal Probation* 27–30 (September 1961).

Draper, N. R., and H. Smith. *Applied Regression Analysis.* New York: John Wiley and Sons, 1966.

Drapkin, Israel, and Viano, Emilio, eds. *Theoretical Issues in Victimology.* International Symposium on Victimology, 1973. Lexington, Massachusetts: Lexington Books, 1974.

——. *Exploiters and Exploited: The Dynamics of Victimization.* International Symposium on Victimology, 1973. Lexington, Massachusetts: Lexington Books, 1975.

Drew, James "Judicial Discretion and the Sentencing Process." 17 *Howard Law Journal* 858–64 (1973).

Duffee, David. *Correctional Policy and Prison Organization.* Beverly Hills: Sage Publications, 1975.

Ehrlich, Isaac. "Capital Punishment and Deterrence: Some Further Thoughts and Additional Evidence." 85 *Journal of Political Economy* 741–88 (1977).

——. "Deterrence: Evidence and Inference." 85 *Yale Law Journal,* 209–27 (1975).

——. "The Deterrent Effect of Capital Punishment: A Question of Life and Death." 65 *American Economic Review* 397–417 (1975).

——. "The Deterrent Effect of Capital Punishment: Reply." 67 *American Economic Review* 452–58 (1977).

——. "The Deterrent Effect of Criminal Law Enforcement." 1 *Journal of Legal Studies* 259–76 (1972).

——. "Participation in Illegitimate Activities: A Theoretical and Empirical Investigation." 81 *Journal of Political Economy* 521–65 (1973).

Ehrlich, Isaac, and Joel C. Gibbons. "On the Measurement of the Deterrent Effect of Capital Punishment and the Theory of Deterrence." 6 *Journal of Legal Studies* 35–50 (1977).

Eichman, Charles J. *Impact of the Gideon Decision Upon Crime and Sentencing in Florida: A Study of Recidivism and Sociocultural*

Change. Tallahassee: Florida Division of Corrections, Research and Statistics Section, 1966.

Ennis, Philip H. *Criminal Victimization in the United States: A Report of a National Survey.* Report of the President's Commission on Law Enforcement and Administration of Justice, Field Surveys. Washington, D.C.: USGPO, 1967.

Erickson, Maynard L., and Jack R. Gibbs. "The Deterrence Question: Some Alternative Methods of Analysis." 54 *Social Science Quarterly* 534–51 (1973).

———. "Specific Versus General Properties of Legal Punishments and Deterrence." 56 *Social Science Quarterly* 390–97 (December 1975).

Erickson, Maynard L.; Jack R. Gibbs; and G. F. Jensen. "The Deterrence Doctrine and the Perceived Certainty of Legal Punishments." 42 *American Sociological Review* 305–17 (1977).

Evans, Margaret, ed. *Discretion and Control.* Beverly Hills: Sage Publications, 1978.

Evans, Walter, and Frank Gilbert. "The Case For Judicial Discretion in Sentencing." 61 *Judicature* 66–69 (August 1977).

———. "The Sentencing Process: Better Methods Are Available." 39 *Federal Probation* 35–39 (December 1975).

European Committee on Crime Problems. *Short–term Treatment of Adult Offenders.* Strasbourg: Council of Europe, 1974.

Executive Advisory Committee on Sentencing. *Crime and Punishment in New York: An Inquiry Into Sentencing and the Criminal Justice System.* New York, 1979.

Fahringer, Herald Price. "Sentencing—Making the Best of a Bad Situation." 46 *New York State Bar Journal,* 279–89 (1974).

Faust, Frederick L., and Paul J. Brantingham. *Juvenile Justice Philosophy.* St. Paul: West Publishing Co., 1974.

Feinberg, Joel. *Doing and Deserving.* Princeton, New Jersey: Princeton University Press, 1970.

Ferguson, Gerard A., and Darrell W. Roberts. "Plea Bargaining: Directions for Canadian Reform." 52 *Canadian Bar Review* 497–576 (1974).

Fersch, Ellsworth. "When to Punish, When to Rehabilitate." 61 *American Bar Association Journal* 1235–37 (1975).

Figlio, Robert M. "The Seriousness of Offenses: An Evaluation by Offenders and Nonoffenders." 66 *Journal of Criminal Law and Criminology* 189–200 (1975).

Finkelstein, Michael O. "A Statistical Analysis of Guilty Plea Practices in the Federal Courts." 89 *Harvard Law Review* 293–315 (1975).

Fisher, David F. "Creative Punishment: A Study of Effective Sentencing Alternatives." 14 *Washburn Law Journal* 57–75 (1975).

Fisher, Franklin M., and Daniel Nagin. "On the Feasibility of Identifying the Crime Function in a Simultaneous Model of Crime Rates and Sanction Levels." In Alfred Blumstein, ed., *Deterrence and Incapacitation: Estimating the Effects of Criminal Sanctions on Crime Rates*. Washington, D.C.: National Academy of Sciences, 1978.

Fleming, M. *Price of Perfect Justice: The Adverse Consequences of Current Legal Doctrine on the American Courtroom*. New York: Basic Books, 1974.

Flynn, Edith E. "Turning Judges Into Robots?" 12 *Trial* 20–21 (March 1976).

Fogel, David. *"We Are the Living Proof": The Justice Model for Corrections*. Cincinnati, Ohio: W. H. Anderson Co., 1975.

Foote, Caleb. "The Coming Constitutional Crisis in Bail." 113 *University of Pennsylvania Law Review* 959–99, 1125–85 (1965).

———. "The Sentencing Function." In *A Program for Prison Reform*. New York: Roscoe Pound American Trial Lawyers Foundation, 1972.

Forst, Brian E. "The Deterrent Effect of Capital Punishment: A Cross–State Analysis of the 1960's." 61 *Minnesota Law Review* 743–67 (1977).

Foster, J. D. *Definite Sentencing: An Examination of Proposals in Four States*. Lexington, Kentucky: The Council of State Governments, 1976.

Fox, Richard G., and Bernard M. O'Brien. "Fact–Finding for Sentencers." 10 *Melbourne University Law Review* 163–206 (1975).

Fox, Vernon. *Introduction to Corrections*. Englewood Cliffs, New Jersey: Prentice–Hall, 1972.

———. *Introduction to Criminology*. Englewood Cliffs, New Jersey: Prentice–Hall, 1976.

Frankel, Marvin E. *Criminal Sentences: Law Without Order*. New York: Hill and Wang, 1972.

Friloux, C. Anthony, Jr. "Equal Justice Under The Law: A Myth, Not a Reality." 12 *American Criminal Law Review* 691–707 (1975).

Fry, Marjorie. *Aims of the Law*. London: Victor Gollancz, 1951.

Fuller, Lon L. *The Morality of Law*. New Haven: Yale University Press, 1964.

Galaway, Burt. "The Use of Restitution." 23 *Crime and Delinquency* 57–67 (January 1977).

Galaway, Burt, and Joe Hudson, eds. *Considering the Victim: Readings in Restitution and Victim Compensation*. Springfield, Illinois: Charles C. Thomas, 1975.

Gartner, Paul E., Jr. "Withdrawal of Guilty Pleas in The Federal Courts Prior to Sentencing." 27 *Baylor Law Review* 793–99 (1975).

Gaylin, Willard. *Partial Justice: A Study of Bias in Sentencing*. New York: Knopf, 1974.

Geis, Gilbert. *White Collar Criminal: The Offender in Business and the Professions.* New York: Atherton Press, 1968.

Gellhorn, Walter. *Ombudsmen and Others: Citizen Protectors in Nine Countries.* Cambridge, Massachusetts: Harvard University Press, 1966.

———. *When Americans Complain.* New York: Columbia University Press, 1966.

Gellhorn, Walter, and Charles Byse. *Administrative Law.* 5th ed. Mineola, New York: Foundation Press, 1970.

Gelman, Arthur M. "The Sentencing Hearing: Forgotten Phase of Sentencing Reform." In Margaret Evans, ed., *Discretion and Control* 124–41. Beverly Hills: Sage Publications, 1978.

Gelman, Arthur M.; Jack M. Kress; and Joseph C. Calpin. *Establishing A Sentencing Guidelines System: A Methods Manual.* Washington, D.C.: University Research Corporation, 1978.

Genego, William J.; Peter D. Goldberger; and Vicki C. Jackson. "Parole Release Decisionmaking and the Sentencing Process." 84 *Yale Law Review* 810–902 (1975).

Georgetown University Law Center. *Plea Bargaining in the United States–Phase I Report.* Washington, D.C., 1977.

Gibbs, Jack. "Crime, Punishment and Deterrence." 48 *Social Science Quarterly* 515–30 (1968).

———. *Punishment and Deterrence.* New York: Elsevier, 1975.

Gilman, David. "The Sanction of Imprisonment: For Whom, For What, and How." 21 *Crime and Delinquency* 337–47 (1975).

Glaser, Daniel. "Achieving Better Questions: A Half Century's Progress in Correctional Research." 39 *Federal Probation* 3–9 (September 1975).

———. *The Effectiveness of a Prison and Parole System.* New York: Bobbs–Merrill, 1964.

Glueck, Sheldon. "Predictive Devices and the Individualization of Justice." 23 *Law and Contemporary Problems* 461–76 (1958).

Glueck, Sheldon, and Eleanor Glueck. *Unravelling Juvenile Delinquency.* Cambridge, Massachusetts: Harvard University Press, 1951.

Goffman, Erving. *Asylums: Essays On the Social Situation of Mental Patients and Other Inmates.* Chicago: Aldine, 1961.

Goldfarb, Ronald L. "American Prisons: Self–Defeating Concrete." 7 *Psychology Today* 20 (1974).

———. *Jails.* New York: Anchor, 1975.

———. *Ransom: A Critique of the American Bail System.* New York: Harper and Row, 1965.

Goldfarb, Ronald L., and Linda R. Singer. *After Conviction.* New York: Simon & Schuster, 1973.

Goldstein, Herman. *Policing A Free Society.* Cambridge, Massachusetts: Ballinger Publishing Co., 1976.

Goldstein, Joseph. "Police Discretion Not To Invoke the Criminal Process: Low–Visibility Decisions in the Administration of Justice." 69 *Yale Law Journal* 543–94 (1960).

Gottfredson, Don M. "Assessment and Prediction Methods in Crime and Delinquency." In President's Commission on Law Enforcement and Criminal Justice, *Task Force Report: Juvenile Delinquency,* Appendix K. Washington, D.C.: USGPO, 1967.

———. "The Base Expectancy Approach." In Norman Johnston, Leonard Savitz, and Marvin Wolfgang, eds., *The Sociology of Punishment and Correction.* New York: John Wiley and Sons, Inc., 1970.

Gottfredson, Don M., and Kelley Ballard. *The Validity of Two Parole Prediction Scales: An Eight Year Follow–Up Study.* Sacramento: Institute for the Study of Crime and Delinquency, 1965.

Gottfredson, Don M.; Colleen A. Cosgrove; Leslie T. Wilkins; Jane Wallerstein; and Carol Rauh. *Classification for Parole Decision Policy.* Washington, D.C.: USGPO, 1978.

Gottfredson, Don M.; Peter B. Hoffman; Maurice H. Sigler; and Leslie T. Wilkins. "Making Parole Policy Explicit." 21 *Crime and Delinquency* 34 (January 1975).

Gottfredson, Don M.; Leslie T. Wilkins; and Peter B. Hoffman. *Guidelines for Parole and Sentencing.* Lexington, Massachusetts: Lexington Books, 1978.

Goulden, Joseph C. *The Benchwarmers.* New York: Ballantine Books, 1976.

Gray, L. N., and J. D. Martin. "Punishment and Deterrence: Another Analysis of Gibbs' Data." 50 *Social Science Quarterly* 189 (1969).

Green, Edward. "Inter– and Intra–Racial Crime Relative to Sentencing." 55 *Journal of Criminal Law, Criminology and Police Science* 58 (1964).

———. *Judicial Attitudes in Sentencing.* London: Macmillan and Co., Ltd., 1961.

———. "Research on Disparities." In Leon Radzinowicz and Marvin Wolfgang, eds., *Crime and Justice Volume II: The Criminal in the Arms of the Law.* New York: Basic Books, 1971.

Greenberg, David F. "The Incapacitative Effect of Imprisonment: Some Estimates." 9 *Law and Society Review* 541–80 (1975).

Greenwood, Peter W., and S. Wildhorn. *Prosecution of Adult Felony Defendants in Los Angeles County: A Policy Perspective.* Santa Monica: Rand, 1973.

Grindstaff, Carl F. "Public Attitudes and Court Dispositions: A Comparative Analysis." 58 *Sociology and Social Research* 417–26 (July 1974).

Grosman, Brian A. *New Directions in Sentencing.* Toronto: Butterworths, 1980.

——. *The Prosecutor: An Inquiry Into the Exercise of Discretion.* Toronto: University of Toronto Press, 1969.

Hagan, John. "Extra–Legal Attributes and Criminal Sentencing." 8 *Law and Society Review* 357–83 (1974).

——. "Law, Order and Sentencing: Study of Attitude in Action." 38 *Sociometry* 374–84 (1975).

——. "Parameters of Criminal Prosecution: An Application of Path Analysis to a Problem of Criminal Justice." 65 *Journal of Criminal Law and Criminology* 536–44 (1974).

Hall, Albert H. "Indeterminate Sentence and Release on Parole." 2 *Journal of Criminal Law, Criminology and Police Science* 832–42 (1912).

Hall, Donald J. "The Role of the Victim in the Prosecution and Disposition of a Criminal Case." 28 *Vanderbilt Law Review* 931–85 (1975).

Hall, Edwin L., and Albert A. Simkus. "Inequality in the Types of Sentences Received by Native Americans and Whites." 13 *Criminology* 199–222 (1975).

Hall, Williams. "Sentencing in Transition." In Tadeusz Grygier et. al., eds., *Criminology in Transition.* London: Tavistock, 1965.

Hand, Richard C., and Richard G. Singer. *Sentencing Computation Laws and Practice–A Preliminary Survey.* Washington, D.C.: Correctional Law Center, 1974.

Harkness, Robert Andrew. "Due Process in Sentencing: A Right to Rebut the Presentence Report?" 2 *Hastings Constitutional Law Quarterly* 1065–89 (1975).

Harries, Keith D., and Russell P. Lura. "The Geography of Justice: Sentencing Variations in U.S. Judicial Districts." 57 *Judicature* 392–401 (1974).

Harris, M. Kay. "Disquisition on the Need for a New Model for Criminal Sanctioning Systems." 77 *West Virginia Law Review* 263 (1975).

Harris, Robert Jennings. *The Quest for Equality: The Constitution, Congress, and the Supreme Court.* Baton Rouge: Louisiana State University Press, 1960.

Hart, H. L. A. *Law, Liberty and Morality.* Oxford: Oxford University Press, 1963.

——. *Punishment and Responsibility.* Oxford: Oxford University Press, 1968.

Hart, Henry M., Jr. "The Aims of the Criminal Law." 23 *Law and Contemporary Problems* 401–41 (Summer 1958).

Hawkins, Gordon. "Punishment and Deterrence: The Educative Moralizing and Habituative Effects." 2 *Wisconsin Law Review* 550–65 (1969).

Hayner, Norman S. "Sentencing by an Administrative Board." 23 *Law and Contemporary Problems* 477–94 (1958).

Heinz, Anne M.; John P. Heinz; Stephen J. Senderowitz; and Mary Anne Vance. "Sentencing by Parole Board: An Evaluation." 67 *Journal of Criminal Law and Criminology* 1–31 (1976).

Henderson, Charles R., ed. *Prison Reform.* New York: Charities Publication Committee of The Russell Sage Foundation, 1910.

Heumann, Milton. "A Note on Plea Bargaining and Case Pressure." 9 *Law and Society Review* 515–28 (1975).

Hirschel, J. David. *Fourth Amendment Rights.* Lexington, Massachusetts: Lexington Books, 1979.

Hodges, E. F. "Crime Prevention by the Indeterminate Sentence Law." 128 *American Journal of Psychiatry* 291–95 (1971).

Hogan, William T., Jr. "Sentencing and Supervision of Organized Crime Figures." 40 *Federal Probation* 21–24 (March 1976).

Hogarth, John. *Sentencing as a Human Process.* Toronto: University of Toronto Press, 1971.

Home Office Advisory Council on the Penal System. *Sentences of Imprisonment: A Review of Maximum Penalties.* London: HMSO, 1978.

Honderich, Ted. *Punishment: The Supposed Justifications.* New York: Harcourt, Brace, World, 1969.

Hood, Roger, ed. *Crime, Criminology, and Public Policy.* New York: Free Press, 1974.

———. "Research on the Effectiveness of Punishments and Treatments." In Council of Europe, *Collected Studies in Criminological Research* 74. Strasbourg, 1967.

———. *Sentencing in Magistrates Court.* London: Stevens and Sons, Ltd., 1962.

———. *Sentencing the Motoring Offender—A Study of Magistrates' Views and Practices.* London: Heinemann, 1972.

Hood, Roger, and Richard Sparks. *Key Issues in Criminology.* New York: World Univeristy Library, 1970.

Hopkins, A. "Imprisonment and Recidivism: A Quasi–Experimental Study." 13 *Journal of Research in Crime and Delinquency* 13–32 (1976).

Hopkins, James D. "Reviewing Sentencing Discretion: A Method of Swift Appellate Action." 23 *University of California at Los Angeles Law Review* 491–500 (1976).

Hotis, John B. "A Law Enforcement Officer Looks At Sentencing." 36 *Federal Probation* 23–26 (March 1972).

Howard, Joseph C. "Racial Discrimination in Sentencing." 59 *Judicature* 120–25 (1975).

Hussey, Fred; John Kramer; Daniel Katkin; and Stephen Lagoy. "The Anatomy of Law Reform: The Effect of Criminal Code Revision on Sentencing—The Maine Experience." Paper presented to the American Society of Criminology, November 1976.

Huxley, Thomas Henry. *Science and Education: Essays.* New York: O. Appleton and Company, 1899.

Imlay, Carl H., and Elsie L. Reid. "The Probation Officer, Sentencing, and The Winds of Change." 39 *Federal Probation* 9–17 (December 1975).

Inciardi, James A.; D. V. Babst; and M. Koval. "Computing Mean Cost Ratings (MCR)." 10 *Journal of Research in Crime and Delinquency* 22–28 (1973).

Jackson, D. P. *Judges.* New York: Atheneum, 1974.

Jackson, Robert H. "The Federal Prosecutor." 24 *Journal of the American Judicature Society* 18–20 (June 1940).

Jacob, Bruce R. "Reparation or Restitution by the Criminal Offender to His Victim." 61 *Journal of Criminal Law, Criminology and Police Science* 152–67 (1970).

Jacob, Herbert, and James Eisenstein. "Sentences and Other Sanctions in the Criminal Courts of Baltimore, Chicago and Detroit." 90 *Political Science Quarterly* 617–35 (Winter 1975–1976).

James, Howard. *Crisis in the Courts.* New York: David McKay Company, Inc., 1967.

Johnston, Barbara L.; Nicholas P. Miller; Ronald Schoenberg; and Laurence Ross Weatherly. "Discretion in Felony Sentencing—A Study of Influencing Factors," 48 *Washington Law Review* 857–89 (August 1973).

Joint Committee on New York Drug Law Evaluation. *The Nation's Toughest Drug Law: Evaluating the New York Experience.* Washington, D.C.: Drug Abuse Council, 1977.

Judson, Charles J.; James J. Pandell; Jack B Owens; James L. McIntosh; and Dale S. Matschullat. "A Study of the California Penalty Jury in First Degree Murder Cases." 21 *Stanford Law Review* 1297–1336 (1969).

Kadish, Sanford H. "Legal Norm and Discretion in the Police and Sentencing Processes." 75 *Harvard Law Review* 904–31 (1962).

Kadish, Sanford H., and Monrad G. Paulsen. *Criminal Law and Its Processes.* 3rd ed. Boston: Little, Brown, 1975.

Kalven, Harry, and Hans Zeisel. *The American Jury.* Boston: Little, Brown, 1966.

Kamisar, Yale; Wayne R. LaFave; and Jerold H. Israel. *Modern Criminal Procedure.* 4th ed. St. Paul: West, 1975.

Kaplan, John. "The Prosecutorial Discretion—A Comment." 60 *Northwestern University Law Review* 174–93 (1965).

Kassebaum, G.; D. Ward; and D. Wilner. *Prison Treatment and Parole Survival: An Empirical Assessment.* New York: Wiley, 1971.

Kellogg, F. "From Retribution to 'Desert': The Evolution of Criminal Punishment." 15 *Criminology* 179 (1977).

Kennedy, Edward M. "Criminal Sentencing: A Game of Chance." 60 *Judicature* 208–15 (1976).

——. "Making Time Fit the Crime." 12 *Trial* 14–15, 23 (March 1976).

Kerlinger, Fred. *Foundations of Behavioral Research,* 2nd ed. New York: Holt, Rinehart and Winston, 1973.

Kerlinger, Fred, and Elazar J. Pedhuzur. *Multiple Regression in Behavioral Research.* New York: Holt, Rinehart and Winston, 1973.

Kilpatrick, James J. "Study Fixes Guidelines for Equal Justice." *Washington Star,* February 12, 1977. (Syndicated column.)

Kittrie, Nicholas N. *The Right To Be Different: Deviance and Enforced Therapy.* Baltimore: Johns Hopkins Press, 1971.

Knowles, Marjorie Fine. "Lawlessness in Our Criminal Law: Criminal Sentences and the Need for Appellate Review." 35 *Alabama Lawyer* 450–69 (1974).

Korbakes, Chris A. "Criminal Sentencing: Is the Judge's Sound Discretion Subject to Review; Should . . . (it) . . . be explained?" 59 *Judicature* 112–19 (1975); 184–91 (1975).

Kozol, Harry L.; Richard J. Boucher; and Ralph F. Garofalo. "The Diagnosis and Treatment of Dangerousness." 18 *Crime and Delinquency* 371–92 (October 1972).

Krantz, Sheldon. *Law Of Corrections and Prisoners' Rights: Cases and Materials.* St. Paul: West, 1973.

Kress, Jack M. "Progress and Prosecution." 423 *The Annals of the American Academy of Political and Social Science* 99 (January 1976).

——. "Sentencing: The Search for Rational Criteria." Paper presented at the Annual Meeting of the American Society of Criminology, Toronto, Canada, 1975.

——. *Sentencing in Four Courts.* Washington, D.C.: USGPO, 1980.

——. "Who Should Sentence?" 17 *The Judge's Journal* 12–15, 44–45 (Winter 1978).

Kress, Jack M., and Joseph C. Calpin. "Research Problems Encountered in Moving Towards Equity in Judicial Decisionmaking." 4 *Justice System Journal* 71–87 (Fall 1978).

Kress, Jack M., and Saundra L. Dillio. "Sentencing Guidelines: Judicial Reform in the Philadelphia Court of Common Pleas." In Margaret Evans, ed., *Discretion and Control* 142–57. Beverly Hills: Sage Publications, 1978.

Kress, Jack M.; Leslie Wilkins and Don M. Gottfredson. "Is the End of Judicial Sentencing in Sight?" 60 *Judicature* 216 (1976).

Kuh, Richard H. "How To Make Plea Bargaining Work." 57 *The New Leader* 10–12 (January 7, 1974).

——. "Plea Bargaining: Guidelines for the Manhattan District Attorney's Office." 11 *Criminal Law Bulletin* 48–61 (1975).

——. "Sentencing: Guidelines for the Manhattan District Attorney's Office." 11 *Criminal Law Bulletin* 62–66 (1975).

Kulig, Frank H. "Plea Bargaining, Probation, and Other Aspects of Conviction and Sentencing." 8 *Creighton Law Review* 938–78 (1975).

Kutak, Robert J., and J. Michael Gottschalk. "In Search of a Rational Sentence: A Return to the Concept of Appellate Review." 53 *Nebraska Law Review* 463–520 (1974).

Lacy, James L., and Judith S. Dammann. *Targeted Prosecution: The Career Criminal.* 4 vols. Washington, D.C.: The MITRE Corporation, 1977.

LaFave, Wayne R. "Alternatives To The Present Bail System." 1965 *University of Illinois Law Forum* 8–19 (Spring 1965).

——. *Arrest: The Decision To Take A Suspect Into Custody.* Boston: Little, Brown, 1965.

LaFave, Wayne R., and Frank J. Remington. "Controlling the Police: The Judge's Role In Making and Reviewing Law Enforcement Decisions." 63 *Michigan Law Review* 987–1012 (April 1965).

LaFave, Wayne R., And Austin W. Scott, Jr. *Handbook on Criminal Law.* St. Paul: West Publishing Co., 1972.

La Font, H. M. "Assessment of Punishment—A Judge or Jury Function?" 38 *Texas Law Review* 835–48 (1960).

Landes, William M. "Legality and Reality: Some Evidence on Criminal Procedure." 3 *Journal of Legal Studies* 287–37 (1974).

Laster, Richard E. "Criminal Restitution: A Survey of Its Past History and an Analysis of Its Present Usefulness." 5 *University of Richmond Law Review* 71–98 (1970).

Law Reform Commission of Canada. *Studies on Sentencing.* Ottawa: Information Canada, 1974.

Lejins, Peter. "The Systematic and the Composite Models for Planning and Evaluation of the Criminal Justice System." In Ronald L. Akers and Edward Sagarin, eds., *Crime Prevention and Social Control,* 155–65 New York: Praeger Publishers, 1974.

Lerner, M. "The Effectiveness of a Definite Sentencing Parole Program." 15 *Criminology* 211 (1977).

Levi, Edward H. "U.S. Department of Justice Materials Relating to Prosecutorial Discretion." 24 *Criminal Law Reporter* 3001–3008 (November 22, 1978).

Levin, Martin A. "Crime and Punishment and Social Science." 27 *Public Interest* 96–103 (1972).

——. *The Impact of Criminal Court Sentencing Decisions and Structural Characteristics*. Springfield, Virginia: National Technical Information Service, 1973.

Levin, Theodore. "Toward A More Enlightened Sentencing Procedure." 45 *Nebraska Law Review* 499–512 (1966).

Lewis, C. S., "The Humanitarian Theory of Punishment." 144 *Twentieth Century* 1–10 (October 1948).

Lindsey, Edward. "Historical Sketch of the Indeterminate Sentence and Parole System." 16 *Journal of Criminal Law and Criminology* 9–126 (1925).

Lipton, Douglas; Robert Martinson; and Judith Wilks. *The Effectiveness of Correctional Treatment: A Survey of Treatment Evaluation Studies*. New York: Praeger Publishers, 1975.

Logan, Charles H. "General Deterrent Effects of Imprisonment." 51 *Social Forces* 64–73 (1972).

Lohman, J. D.; A. Wall; and R. M. Carter. "Decision–Making and the Probation Officer." *San Francisco Project Research Report Seven*. Berkeley: School of Criminology, University of California, June 1966.

MacNaughton–Smith, Peter. *Some Statistical and Other Numerical Techniques for Classifying Individuals*. London: Her Majesty's Stationery Office, 1965.

Maffucci, John J. "The New York State Board of Parole: Scapegoats of the Criminal Justice System." 50 *New York State Bar Journal* 640–43, 669–70 (December 1978).

Mannheim, Herman, and Leslie T. Wilkins. *Prediction Methods in Relation to Borstal Training*. London: Her Majesty's Stationery Office, 1955.

Martinson, Robert. "What Works?—Questions and Answers About Prison Reform." 35 *Public Interest* 22 (Spring 1974).

Mattina, Joseph S. "Sentencing: A Judge's Inherent Responsibility." 57 *Judicature* 105–110 (October 1973).

McAnany, Patrick D.; Frank S. Merritt; and Edward Tromanhauser. "Illinois Reconsiders 'Flat–Time': An Analysis of the Impact of the Justice Model." 52 *Chicago–Kent Law Review* 621–62 (1976).

McCaldon, R. J. "Reflections on Sentencing." 16 *Canadian Journal of Criminology and Corrections* 291–97 (1974).

McGee, Richard A. "A New Look at Sentencing: Part I." 38 *Federal Probation* 3–8 (June 1974); and "Part II", 38 3–11 (September 1974).

——. "What's Past is Prologue." 381 *Annals of the American Academy of Political and Social Science* 1–10 (1969).

McIntyre, Jennie. "Public Attitudes Toward Crime and Law Enforcement." 34 *The Annals of the American Academy of Political and Social Science* 34–46 (1967).

McKay, Robert. "It's Time to Rehabilitate the Sentencing Process." 60 *Judicature* 223–28 (1976).

McKelvey, Blake. *American Prisons.* Montclair, New Jersey: Patterson Smith, 1972.

Megargee, Edwin I. "Prediction of Dangerous Behavior." 3 *Criminal Justice Bulletin* 3–22 (1976).

Meier, R., and W. T. Johnson. "Deterrence as Social Control." 42(2) *American Sociological Review* 292–304 (1977).

Menninger,Karl. *The Crime of Punishment.* New York: Viking, 1966.

Menninger, Karl A., II, and Karl A. Menninger. "The Senselessness of Sentencing." 14 *Washburn Law Journal* 241–51 (1975).

Miller, C. H. "The Fine: Price Tag or Rehabilitative Force?" 2 *National Probation and Parole Association Journal* 377–84 (1956).

Miller, Frank W. *Prosecution–The Decision to Charge A Suspect With A Crime.* Boston: Little, Brown, and Co., 1969.

Miller, George A. "The Magical Number Seven, Plus or Minus Two: Some Limits on Our Capacity for Processing Information." 63 *Psychological Review 81 (March 1956).*

Miller, Lowell B. "Judicial Discretion to Reject Negotiated Pleas." 63 *Georgetown Law Journal* 241–55 (1974).

Miller, M. B. "The Indeterminate Sentence Paradigm: Resocialization or Social Control." 7 *Issues in Criminology* 101–24 (1972).

Mitford, Jessica. *Kind and Usual Punishment: The Prison Business.* New York: Knopf, 1973.

Monahan, J., and L. Cummings. "Prediction of Dangerousness as a Function of Its Perceived Consequences." 2 *Journal of Criminal Justice* 239–42 (1974).

Morris, Norval. "Conceptual Overview and Commentary on the Movement Towards Determinancy." In Proceedings of the Special Conference on Determinate Sentencing, *Determinate Sentencing: Reform or Regression?* Washington, D.C.: USGPO, 1978.

——. *The Future of Imprisonment.* Chicago: University of Chicago Press, 1974.

——. *The Habitual Criminal.* Cambridge, Massachusetts: Harvard University Press, 1951.

——. "Impediments to Penal Reform." 33 *University of Chicago Law Review* 627–56 (1966).

——. "The Sentencing Disease." 18 *The Judges' Journal* 8–13, 50 (Summer 1979).

Morris, Norval, and Gordon Hawkins. *The Honest Politician's Guide to Crime Control.* Chicago: University of Chicago Press, 1970.

Morris, Norval, and Frank Zimring. "Deterrence and Correction." 381 *Annals of the American Academy of Political and Social Science* 137–46 (1969).

Mueller, Gerhard O. W. "Penology on Appeal: Appellate Review of Legal but Excessive Sentences." 15 *Vanderbilt Law Review* 671–97 (June 1962).

———. *Sentencing–Process and Purpose.* Springfield, Illinois: Charles C. Thomas, 1977.

Murphy, J. G. *Punishment and Rehabilitation.* Belmont, California: Wadsworth Publishing Co., 1973.

Murrah, Alfred P., and Sol Rubin. "Penal Reform and The Model Sentencing Act." 65 *Columbia Law Review* 1167–83 (1965).

Nagel, Stuart. "Disparities in Criminal Procedure." 14 *U.C.L.A. Law Review* 1272–1305 (1967).

———. *The Legal Process From A Behavioral Perspective.* Homewood, Illinois: The Dorsey Press, 1969.

Nagin, Daniel. "General Deterrence: A Review of the Empirical Evidence." Carnegie–Mellon University, School of Urban and Public Affairs, Pittsburgh, Pennsylvania, August 1975.

National Advisory Commission on Criminal Justice Standards and Goals. *Criminal Justice System.* Washington, D.C.: USGPO, 1973.

———. *A National Strategy to Reduce Crime.* Washington, D.C.: USGPO, 1973.

———. *Report on Corrections.* Washington, D.C.: USGPO, 1973.

———. *Report on Courts.* Washington, D.C.: USGPO, 1973.

———. *Report on Police.* Washington, D.C.: USGPO, 1973.

National Commission on Law Observance and Enforcement (Wickersham Commission). *Report on Penal Institutions, Probation and Parole.* Washington, D.C.: USGPO, 1931.

National Conference of Commissioners on Uniform State Laws. *Uniform Corrections Act.* Draft. Chicago; March 1978.

National Council on Crime and Delinquency. *Model Sentencing Act.* 2nd ed. Reprinted in 18 *Crime and Delinquency* 335 (1972).

National Probation and Parole Association. *Guides for Sentencing.* New York: Carnegie Press, 1957.

Nedilsky, Sofron B. "How Can A New Judge Know What To Do?" 18 *The Judges Journal* 34–39 (Summer 1969).

Neier, Aryeh. *Criminal Punishment: A Radical Solution.* New York: Stein and Day, 1976.

Nettler, Gwynn. "Cruelty, Dignity, and Determinism." 24 *American Sociological Review* 375–84 (1959).

Newman, Donald J. *Conviction: The Determination of Guilt or Innocence Without Trial.* Boston: Little, Brown, and Co. 1966.

——. *Introduction to Criminal Justice.* 2nd ed. Philadelphia: J. B. Lippincott, 1978.

Newman, Graeme R. *Comparative Deviance.* New York: Elsevier, 1976.

——. *The Punishment Response.* Philadelphia: J. B. Lippincott, 1978.

——. "Theories of Punishment Reconsidered: Rationalizations for Removal." 3 *International Journal of Criminology and Penology* 163–82 (May 1975).

Newman, Graeme R., and Carol Trilling. "Public Perceptions of Criminal Behavior." 2 *Criminal Justice and Behavior* 217–36 (September 1975).

Newman, Jon O. "A Better Way To Sentence Criminals." 63 *American Bar Association Journal* 1562–66 (November 1977).

New York State Special Commission on Attica. *Attica: The Official Report of the New York State Speical Commission on Attica.* New York: Bantam Books, 1972.

Note. "Fines and Fining—An Evaluation." 101 *University of Pennsylvania Law Review* 1013–30 (1953).

——. "Jury Sentencing in Virginia." 53 *Virginia Law Review* 968–1001 (1967).

——. "The Presentence Report: An Empirical Study of Its Use in the Federal Criminal Process." 58 *Georgetown Law Journal* 451–86 (1970).

——. "Statutory Structures for Sentencing Felons to Prison." 60 *Columbia Law Review* 1134–72 (December 1960).

Nozick, Robert. *Anarchy, State and Utopia.* New York: Basic Books, 1974.

O'Connell, Kenneth J. "Continuing Legal Education for the Judiciary." 16 *Journal of Legal Education* 405–15 (1964).

O'Donnell, Pierce; Michael J. Churgin; and Dennis E. Curtis. *Toward A Just and Effective Sentencing System: Agenda for Legislative Reform.* New York: Praeger, 1977.

Ohlin, Lloyd E., ed. *Prisoners in America.* Englewood Cliffs, New Jersey: Prentice–Hall, 1973.

Ohlin, Lloyd E., and Frank Remington. "Sentencing Structure: Its Effects Upon Systems for the Administration of Justice." 23 *Law and Contemporary Problems* 495–503 (1958).

O'Leary, Vincent; Michael Gottfredson; and Arthur Gelman. "Contemporary Sentencing Proposals." 11 *Criminal Law Bulletin* 555–86 (1975).

Orland, Leonard. *Justice, Punishment, Treatment.* New York: Free Press, 1973.

Orland, Leonard, and Harold R. Tyler, Jr. *Justice in Sentencing: Papers and Proceedings of the Sentencing Institute for the First and*

Second U.S. Judicial Circuits. Mineola, New York: Foundation Press, 1974.

Osborn, H. "On Crime, Punishment, and Deterrence." 49 *Social Science Quarterly* 157–60 (1969).

Packer, Herbert L. "The Aims of the Criminal Law Revisited: A Plea for a New Look at 'Substantive Due Process.' " 44 *Southern California Law Review* 490–98 (1971).

———. *The Limits of the Criminal Sanction.* Stanford: Stanford University Press, 1968.

Palmer, Ted. "Martinson Revisited." 12(2) *Journal of Research in Crime and Delinquency* 133–52 (July 1975).

Parisi, Nicolette. "The Effects of Pretrial Status on Adjudication and Sentencing." In *Proceedings of the 21st Annual Meeting of the Southern Conference on Corrections* 372–92. Tallahassee: Florida State University, 1976.

Partridge, Anthony, and William B. Eldridge. *Second Circuit Sentencing Study: A Report to the Judges of the Second Circuit.* Washington, D.C.: Federal Judicial Center, 1974.

Pepinsky, Harold E. "Generation of Discretion by Specification of Criminal Law." 3 *International Journal of Criminology and Penology* 111–21 (1975).

Petersilia, Joan, and Peter W. Greenwood. "Mandatory Prison Sentences: Their Projected Effects on Crime and Prison Populations." An abstract. Santa Monica, California: RAND, 1977.

Phillips, L., and H. Votey. "An Economic Analysis of the Deterrent Effect of Law Enforcement on Criminal Activity." 63 *Journal of Criminal Law, Criminology and Police Science* 330–43 (1972).

Pierce, Lawrence W. "Rehabilitation in Corrections: A Reassessment." 38 *Federal Probation* 14–19 (June 1974).

Pierson, H. "Fair and Equitable Punishment." 42 *Police Chief* 10 (1975).

Pound, Roscoe. *Criminal Justice in America.* New York: Holt & Co., 1930.

President's Commission on Law Enforcement and Administration of Justice. *The Challenge of Crime in a Free Society.* Washington, D.C.: United States Government Printing Office, 1967.

———. *Task Force Report: The Courts.* Washington, D.C.: United States Government Printing Office, 1967.

"President's Message to Congress on Crime." 17 *Criminal Law Reporter* 3089 (June 25, 1975).

Proceedings of the Special Conference on Determinate Sentencing. *Determinate Sentencing: Reform or Regression?* Washington, D.C.: USGPO, 1978.

Quinney, Richard. *Crime and Justice in Society.* Boston: Little, Brown, and Co., 1969.

Rabinowitz, Mark Phillip. "Criminal Sentencing: An Overview of Procedures and Alternatives." 45 *Mississippi Law Journal* 782–99 (1974).

Radzinowicz, Leon. *A History of English Criminal Law and Its Administration from 1750.* London: Stevens and Co., 1948.

——. *Ideology and Crime.* New York: Columbia University Press, 1966.

Radzinowicz, Sir Leon, and Roger Hood. "An English Attempt to Reshape the Sentencing Structure." 78 *Columbia Law Review* 1145–58 (June 1978).

Rankin, Anne. "The Effect of Pretrial Detention." 39 *New York University Law Review* 641–55 (1964).

Rawls, John. *A Theory of Justice.* Cambridge, Massachusetts: Harvard University Press, 1971.

Raymond, S. D. "Standardized Presentence Report: One State's Response." 41 *Federal Probation* 40 (June 1977).

Reasons, C. E., and R. L. Kaplan. "Tear Down the Walls: Some Functions of Prisons." 21 *Crime and Delinquency* 360–72 (1975).

Rector, Milton G. "The Extravagance of Imprisonment." 21 *Crime and Delinquency* 323–30 (1975).

Reich, M. "Therapeutic Implications of the Indeterminate Sentence." 2 *Issues in Criminology* 7–28 (1966).

Reiss, Albert J., Jr. "The Accuracy, Efficiency and Validity of a Prediction Instrument." 61 *American Journal of Sociology* 552–61 (May 1951).

——. "Discretionary Justice in the United States." 2 *International Journal of Criminology and Penology* 181–205 (1974).

——. *Studies in Crime and Law Enforcement in Major Metropolitan Areas, Vol. 1.* Report of the President's Commission of Law Enforcement and Administration of Justice, Field Surveys III. Washington, D.C.: U.S. Government Printing Office, 1967.

Remington, Frank J., and Donald J. Newman. "The Highland Park Institute on Sentence Disparity." 26 *Federal Probation* 3–9 (March 1962).

Remington, Frank J.; Donald J. Newman; Edward L. Kimball; Marygold Melli; and Herman Goldstein. *Criminal Justice Administration: Materials and Cases.* Indianapolis: Bobbs–Merrill, 1969.

Riedel, Marc. "Perceived Circumstances, Inferences of Intent and Judgments of Offense Seriousness." 66 *Journal of Criminal Law and Criminology* 201–208 (1975).

——. "The Perception of Crime: A Study of the Sellin–Wolfgang Seriousness Index." Paper presented at the Annual Meetings of the Inter–American association of Criminology and the American Society of Criminology, Caracas, Venezuela, November 1972.

Roben, Gerald C. "Judicial Resistance to Sentencing Accountability." 21 *Crime and Delinquency* 201–12 (1975).

Robison, James O., and Gerald Smith. "The Effectiveness of Correctional Programs." 17 *Crime and Delinquency* 67 (1971).

Roethlisberger, F. J., and W. J. Dickson. *Management and the Worker*. Cambridge, Massachusetts: Harvard University Press, 1939.

Rosett, Arthur. "Discretion, Severity and Legality in Criminal Justice." 46 *Southern California Law Review* 12–50 (December 1972).

Rosett, Arthur, and Donald R. Cressey. *Justice by Consent: Plea Bargaining in the American Courthouse*. Philadelphia: Lippincott, 1976.

Ross, H. Laurence. "Law, Science and Accidents: The British Road Safety Act of 1967." 2 *Journal of Legal Studies* 1–78 (1973).

——. "The Scandinavian Myth: The Effectiveness of Drinking–and–Driving Legislation in Sweden and Norway." 4 *Journal of Legal Studies* 285–310 (1975).

Ross, John, and Perry Smith. "Orthodox Experimental Designs." In Hubert M. Blalock, Jr., and Ann B. Blalock, *Methodology in Social Research*. New York: McGraw–Hill Book Comp., 1968.

Rothman, David J. *Discovery of the Aylum: Social Order and Disorder in the New Republic*. Boston: Little, Brown and Co., 1971.

Rubin, Sol. "Allocation of Authority in Sentencing—Correction Decision." 45 *Texas Law Review* 455–69 (1967).

——. "Disparity and Equality of Sentences—A Constitutional Challenge." 40 *Federal Rules Decisions* 55–78 (1966).

——. "The Indeterminate Sentence—Success or Failure." 28 *Focus* 47–52 (1949).

——. *The Law of Criminal Correction*. 2nd ed. St. Paul: West, 1973.

——. "The Model Sentencing Act." 39 *New York University Law Review* 251–62 (1964).

——. "Probation or Prison: Applying the Principle of the Last Restrictive Alternative." 21 *Crime and Delinquency* 331—36 (1975).

Ruth, Henry S., Jr. *Research Priorities for Crime Reduction Efforts*. Washington, D.C.: The Urban Institute, 1977.

Salem, R. G., and W. J. Bowers. "Severity of Formal Sanctions As A Deterrent to Deviant Behavior." 5 *Law and Society Review* 21–40 (1970).

Sandhu, H. S. "The Impact of Short–Term Institutionalization on Prison Inmates." 4 *British Journal of Criminology* 461–74 (1964).

Schafer, Stephen. "Restitution to Victims of Crime—An Old Correctional Aim Modernized." 50 *Minnesota Law Review* 243–54 (1965).

Schmidt, F. K. "The Jail as a Treatment Center." 16 *Police* 19–22 (1971).

Schrag, Clarence. *Crime and Justice: American Style.* Washington, D.C.: USGPO, 1971.

Schuessler, Karl F. "The Deterrent Influence of the Death Penalty." 284 *The Annals of the American Academy of Political and Social Science* 54–62 (November 1952).

Schulhofer, Stephen J. "Harm and Punishment: A Critique of Emphasis on the Results of Conduct in the Criminal Law." 122 *University of Pennsylvania Law Review* 1497–1607 (1974).

Schur, Edwin M. *Labeling Deviant Behavior.* New York: Harper and Row, 1971.

Schur, Edwin M., and Hugo Bedau. *Victimless Crimes: Two Sides of a Controversy.* Englewood Cliffs, New Jersey: Prentice–Hall, 1974.

Scott, Joseph E. "The Use of Discretion in Determining the Severity of Punishment for Incarcerated Offenders." 65 *Journal of Criminal Law and Criminology 214*–24 (1974).

Seagraves, Roy W. "Is Punishment an Adequate Deterrent to Crime?" 55 *Judicature* 236–38 (1972).

Sebba, Leslie. "Minimum Sentences: Courts v. Knesset." 6 *Israel Law Review* 227–39 (1971).

Sellin, Thorsten. *Capital Punishment.* New York: Harper and Row, 1967.

———. *Slavery and the Penal System.* New York: Elsevier, 1976.

Sellin, Thorsten, and Marvin E. Wolfgang. *The Measurement of Delinquency.* New York: John Wiley and Sons, Inc., 1964.

Selltiz, Claire; Marie Johoda; Morton Deutsch; and Stuart Cook. *Research Methods in Social Relations.* 2nd ed. New York: Holt, Rinehart and Winston, 1959.

Serrill, Michael S. "Critics of Corrections Speak Out." *Corrections Magazine,* March 1976, p. 3.

Shapiro, Barbara A., and Catherine Clement. "Presentence Information in Felony Cases in the Massachusetts Superior Court." 10 *Suffolk University Law Review* 49–75 (1975).

Sherman, Richard C., and Michael D. Dawdle. "The Perception of Crime and Punishment: A Multidimensional Scaling Analysis." 3 *Social Research* 109–26 (June 1974).

Siegal, Sidney. *Nonparametric Statistics for the Behavioral Sciences.* New York: McGraw–Hill Book Co., 1956.

Sigler, Maurice H. "Abolish Parole?" 39 *Federal Probation* 42–48 (June 1975).

Silberman, Charles E. *Criminal Violence, Criminal Justice.* New York: Random House, 1978.

———. *National Law Journal* (February 12, 1979) at 19.

Simon, Caroline K. "Needed: A New Look at Punishments." 62 *American Bar Association Journal* 1296–1300 (1976).

Simon, Frances H. *Prediction Methods in Criminology*. London: Her Majesty's Stationery Office, 1971.

Simon, Julian L. *Basic Research Methods in the Social Sciences*. New York: Random House, 1969.

Singer, Richard G. "In Favor of 'Presumptive Sentences' Set by a Sentencing Commission." 5 *Criminal Justice Quarterly* 88–105 (Fall–Winter 1977).

——. *Just Deserts: Sentencing Based on Equality and Desert*. Cambridge, Massachusetts: Ballinger Publishing Company, 1979.

Singer, Richard G., and Richard C. Hand. "Sentencing Computation: Laws and Practices." 10 *Criminal Law Bulletin* 318–47 (1974).

Skogan, Wesley G. "The Use of Victimization Surveys in Criminal Justice Planning." In *Quantiative Tools for Criminal Justice Planning*, Leonard Oberlander, ed. Washington, D.C.: USGPO, 1975.

Skolnik, Jerome. *Justice Without Trial: Law Enforcement in Democratic Society*. New York: John Wiley and Sons, Inc., 1966.

Smith, R. *Who Returns? A Study of Recidivism for Adult Offenders in the State of Washington*. Olympia, Washington: Department of Social and Health Services, 1976.

Sophocles. *The Trachiniae*. Trans. Sir Richard C. Jebb. Amsterdam: Adolf M. Hakkert, 1962.

Stanley, David T. *Prisoners Among Us: The Problem of Parole*. Washington, D.C.: The Brookings Institute, 1976.

Stigler, George J. "The Optimum Enforcement of Laws." 78 *Journal of Political Economy* 526–36 (1970).

Strand, Roger G. "Sentencing Disparity: How One Jurisdiction Reduced It." 17 *The Judges' Journal* 33–34 (Spring 1978).

Strauss, William A., and Lawrence M. Baskir. "Controlling Discretion in Sentencing: The Clemency Board as a Working Model." 51 *Notre Dame Lawyer* 919–45 (July 1976).

Stricker, George, and George L. Jurow. "The Relationship Between Attitudes Toward Capital Punishment and Assignment of the Death Penalty." 2 *Journal of Psychiatry and Law* 415–22 (1974).

Sturz, Herbert. "Experiments in the Criminal Justice System." 25 *Legal Aid Briefcase* 111–15 (1967).

Sutherland, Edwin H., and Donald R. Cressey. *Criminology*. 10th ed. Philadelphia: J. B. Lippincott Co., 1979.

Szasz, Thomas. *Ideology and Insanity*. Garden City, New York: Doubleday Anchor, 1970.

——. *Law, Liberty and Psychiatry*. New York: MacMillan and Company, 1963.

——. *Psychiatric Justice*. New York: MacMillan, 1965.

Tappan, Paul W. "Sentencing Under the Model Penal Code." 23 *Law and Contemporary Problems* 528–43 (1958).

Taylor, Victor. "The Correctional Institution as a Rehabilitation Center—A Former Inmate's View." 16 *Villanova Law Review* 1077–81 (1971).

Thomas, David A. "Equity in Sentencing." Sixth Annual Pinkerton Lecture, presented at Albany State University, April 1977.

———. *Principles of Sentencing.* London: Heinemann, 1970.

Tiffany, Lawrence P.; Yakov Avichai; and Geoffrey W. Peters. "A Statistical Analysis of Sentencing in Federal Courts: Defendants Convicted After Trial, 1967–1968." 4 *Journal of Legal Studies* 369 (1975).

Tittle, Charles R. "Crime Rates and Legal Sanctions." 16 *Social Problems* 109 (1969).

———. "Punishment and Deterrence of Deviance." In *The Economics of Crime and Punishment,* Simon Rottenberg, ed., p. 85. Washington, D.C.: American Enterprise Institute, 1973.

Tittle, Charles R., and Charles H. Logan. "Sanctions and Deviance: Evidence and Remaining Questions." 7 *Law and Society Review* 371 (1973).

Tittle, Charles R., and A. R. Rowe. "Certainty of Arrest and Crime Rates: A Further Test of the Deterrence Hypothesis." 52 *Social Forces* 455–62 (1974).

Toch, Hans. *Living in Prison: The Ecology of Survival.* New York: Free Press, 1977.

———. *Men in Crisis.* Chicago: Aldine, 1976.

———. *Violent Men: An Inquiry Into the Psychology of Violence.* Chicago: Aldine, 1969.

Tribe, Laurence H. "Foreword: Toward A Model of Roles in the Due Process of Life and Law." 87 *Harvard Law Review* 1–53 (1973).

———. "Trial By Mathematics: Precision and Ritual in the Legal Process." 84 *Harvard Law Review* 1329–62 (1971).

Tullock, Gordon. "Does Punishment Deter Crime?" 35 *The Public Interest* 103–19 (Summer 1974).

Tussman, Joseph, and Jacobus tenBroek. "The Equal Protection of the Laws." 37 *California Law Review* 341–81 (1949).

The Twentieth Century Fund. Task Force on Criminal Sentencing. *Fair and Certain Punishment.* New York: McGraw–Hill, 1976.

Underwood, Barbara D. "Law and the Crystal Ball: Predicting Behavior With Statistical Inference and Individualized Judgment." 88 *Yale Law Journal* 1408–48 (June 1979).

van den Haag, Ernest. "Deterrence, Deterrability, and Effective Sanctions." In Ernest van den Haag and Robert Martinson, *Crime*

Deterrence and Offender Career, 1–99. New York: City College of the City University of New York, 1975.

———. *Punishing Criminals: Concerning a Very Old and Painful Question.* New York: Basic Books, 1975.

von Hirsch, Andrew. "Prediction of Criminal Conduct and Preventive Confinement of Convicted Persons." 21 *Buffalo Law Review* 717–58 (1972).

———. *Doing Justice: The Choice of Punishments.* New York: Hill and Wang, 1976.

Wainer, Howard. "Estimating Coefficients in Linear Models: It Don't Make No Nevermind." 83 *Psychological Bulletin* 213–17 (1976).

Wainwright, L. L. *A Comparison of Flat–Time Sentencing With Existing Sentencing Practice in Florida.* Tallahassee: Research and Statistics Section, Bureau of Planning, Research and Staff Development, 1975.

Wald, Patricia, "Pretrial Detention And Ultimate Freedom: A Statistical Study." 39 *New York University Law Review* 631–40 (1964).

Waldo, Gordon P., and Theodore G. Chiricos. "Perceived Penal Sanction and Self–Reported Criminality: A Neglected Approach to Deterrence Research." 19 *Social Problems* 522–40 (1972).

———. "Work Release and Recidivism: An Empirical Evaluation of a Social Policy." 1 *Evaluation Quarterly* 87–108 (1977).

Walker, Nigel. *The Aims of the Penal System.* Edinburgh: Edinburgh University Press, 1966.

———. *Sentencing In A Rational Society.* Middlesex: Penguin, 1969.

Waller, Irvin. *Men Released From Prison.* Toronto: University of Toronto Press, 1974.

Waller, Irvin, and Norman Okihiro. *Burglary: The Victim and the Public.* Toronto: University of Toronto Press, 1978.

Wechsler, Herbert. "The Challenge of a Model Penal Code." 65 *Harvard Law Review* 1097–1133 (May 1952).

———. "The Model Penal Code and the Codification of American Criminal Law." In Roger Hood, ed., *Crime, Criminology, and Public Policy: Essays in Honor of Sir Leon Radzinowicz 419*–68. New York: Free Press, 1975.

———. "Sentencing, Correction, and the Model Penal Code." 109 *University of Pennsylvania Law Review* 465–93 (1961).

Wechsler, Herbert, and Jerome Michael. "A Rationale of the Law of Homicide." 37 *Columbia Law Review* 701–49; 1261–1309 (1937).

Weiss, Jonathan. "The Poor Kid." 9 *Duquesne Law Review* 590–612 (1971).

Wellford, Charles F. "Deterrence: Issues and Methodologies in the Analysis of the Impact of Legal Threat in Crime Control." 65 *Journal of Criminal Law and Criminology* 117–22 (1974).

Wellford, Charles F., and Michael Wiatrowski. "On the Measurement of Delinquency." 66 *Journal of Criminal Law and Criminology* 175–88 (1975).

Wells, H. G. *The Work, Wealth and Happiness of Mankind.* Garden City, N.Y.: Doubleday, Doran and Company, 1931.

Wheeler, Malcolm E. "Toward A Theory of Limited Punishment II: The Eighth Amendment After *Furman v Georgia.*" 25 *Stanford Law Review* 62–83 (1972).

White, G. F. "Public Responses to Hypothetical Crimes: Effects of Offender and Victim Status and Seriousness of Offense on Punitive Reactions." 53 *Social Forces* pp. 411–19 (1975).

Wilkins, Leslie T. *Evaluation of Penal Measures.* New York: Random House, 1969.

———. "Information Overload: War or Peace With the Computer." Davis, Calif.: National Council on Crime and Delinquency, 1973.

———. "The Problem of Overlap in Experience Table Construction." Davis, California: National Council on Crime and Delinquency, 1973.

———. "Problems in Prediction Methods: The Unique Individual." In M. E. Wolfgang, L. Savitz, and N. Johnston, The Sociology of Crime and Delinquency. New York: John Wiley and Sons, 1962.

———. *Social Deviance: Social Action, Policy, and Research.* London: Tavistock, 1964.

———. "Statistical Methods of Parole Prediction: Their Effectiveness and Limitations." Paper presented at the Annual Meeting of the American Academy of Psychiatry and the Law, Boston, Massachusetts, October 1975.

Wilkins, Leslie T., and Ann Chandler. "Confidence and Competence in Decision Making." 5 *British Journal of Criminology* 1 (January 1965).

Wilkins, Leslie T.; Jack M. Kress; and Don M. Gottfredson. "Guidelines for Sentencers: Strategy of the Research and Management of the Feasibility Study." Unpublished staff working paper, 1977.

Wilkins, Leslie T.; Jack M. Kress; Don M. Gottfredson; Joseph C. Calpin; and Arthur M. Gelman. *Sentencing Guidelines: Structuring Judicial Discretion–Report on the Feasibility Study.* Washington, D.C.: USGPO, 1978.

Wilks, Judith and Robert Martinson. "Is the Treatment of Criminal Offenders Really Necessary?" 40 *Federal Probation* 3–9 (1976).

Wilson, James Q. "Changing Criminal Sentences." *Harpers* 16–20 (November 1977).

———. *Thinking About Crime.* New York: Basic Books, 1975.

———. *Varieties of Police Behavior.* Cambridge, Massachusetts: Harvard University Press, 1968.

Wolfgang, Marvin E. *Patterns in Criminal Homicide.* Philadelphia: University of Pennsylvania Press, 1958.

Wolfgang, Marvin E.; Robert Figlio; and Thorsten Sellin. *Delinquency in a Birth Cohort.* Chicago: The University of Chicago Press, 1972.

Wolfgang, Marvin E., and Marc Riedel. "Race, Judicial Discretion, and the Death Penalty." 407 *Annals of the American Academy of Political and Social Science* 119–33 (May 1973).

Wootton, Barbara. *Crime and the Criminal Law.* London: Stevens and Sons, 1963.

Zalman, Marvin. "A Commission Model of Sentencing." 53 *Notre Dame Lawyer* 266–90 (1977).

——. "The Rise and Fall of the Indeterminate Sentence." 24 *Wayne Law Review* 45–94 (November 1977).

Zander, Michael. "A Study of Bail/Custody Decisions in London Magistrates' Court." (1971) *Criminal Law Review* 196–205 (1971).

Zeisel, Hans, and Shari S. Diamond. "Search for Sentencing Equity: Sentence Review in Massachusetts and Connecticut." 4 *American Bar Foundation Research Journal* 881 (1977).

Zimring, Franklin. "Making the Punishment Fit the Crime: A Consumer's Guide to Sentencing Reform." 6 *Hastings Center Report* 1 (1976).

——. *Perspectives on Deterrence.* Washington, D. C.: USGPO, 1971.

Zimring, Franklin, and Gordon Hawkins. "Deterrence and Marginal Groups." 5 *Journal of Research on Crime and Delinquency* 100–14 (1968).

——. *Deterrence: The Legal Threat in Crime Control.* Chicago: University of Chicago Press, 1973.

——. "The Legal Threat as an Instrument of Social Change." 27 *Journal of Social Issues* 33–48 (1971).

Index

About the author

Jack M. Kress presently teaches at Russell Sage, produces a television series for WRGB-TV, and directs research for Justice Analysis Center, Inc. A graduate of Columbia College, Columbia Law School and Cambridge University, Professor Kress previously served as Assistant District Attorney to the late Frank S. Hogan in New York City and also taught law at the Graduate School of Criminal Justice, SUNYA. The author of nine books and monographs, as well as numerous articles on the law, and the courts and correctional systems, Professor Kress is an internationally recognized criminal justice authority, particularly on the subjects of sentencing and crime prevention. Professor Kress frequently serves as a consultant, and has assisted such organizations as the National Judicial College, the Vera Institute of Justice, the United Nations Association of Canada, the League of Women Voters, the Police Foundation, and the National Science Foundation.

Recently elected to the American Law Institute, Professor Kress is best known for directing the implementation of America's first sentencing guidelines systems in Denver, Newark, Chicago, Phoenix, and the State of Washington. This book represents his fullest statement on the subject of sentencing guidelines.